Also by Thomas P. Slaughter

Exploring Lewis and Clark: Reflections on Men and Wilderness

The Natures of John and William Bartram

*Bloody Dawn: The Christiana Riot
and Racial Violence in the Antebellum North*

The Whiskey Rebellion: Frontier Epilogue to the American Revolution

The Beautiful Soul
of John Woolman,
Apostle of Abolition

The Beautiful Soul
of John Woolman,
Apostle of Abolition

Thomas P. Slaughter

ĺbŋ Hill and Wang

A division of Farrar, Straus and Giroux

New York

Hill and Wang
A division of Farrar, Straus and Giroux
18 West 18th Street, New York 10011

Library of Congress Cataloging-in-Publication Data
Slaughter, Thomas P. (Thomas Paul)
    The beautiful soul of John Woolman, apostle of abolition / Thomas P.
Slaughter. — 1st ed.
        p.   cm.
    Includes bibliographical references (p.   ) and index.
    ISBN-13: 978-0-8090-9514-8 (hardcover : alk. paper)
    ISBN-10: 0-8090-9514-9 (hardcover : alk. paper)
    1. Woolman, John, 1720–1772.   2. Quakers—United States—
Biography.   3. Abolitionists—United States—Biography.   I. Title.

BX7795.W7S53 2008
289.6092—dc22
[B]
                                                              2008022765

Designed by Jonathan D. Lippincott

www.fsgbooks.com

1   3   5   7   9   10   8   6   4   2

To Dennee,
This book and what's left of my heart

The great events of world history are, at bottom, profoundly un-important. In the last analysis, the essential thing is the life of the individual. This alone makes history; here alone do the great trans-formations take place . . . In our most private and most subjective lives we are not only the passive witnesses of our age, and its suffer-ers, but also its makers.

—Carl Jung, *Civilization in Transition*

Contents

The Beautiful Soul

of John Woolman,

Apostle of Abolition

Prologue: How to Begin?

SOCIAL activists and members of his faith celebrate John Woolman (1720–72) as a founding father of the international movement to abolish slavery and one of its most effective advocates. He was also an advocate for the poor and for the humane treatment of animals, and he endorsed a frugal lifestyle balancing moderate work habits, meditation, devotional reading, and abstemious consumption of plain foods. He was an educational theorist and a pacifist. He was a deeply spiritual man, steeped in the Bible, and had a saintly demeanor. He remains an inspiring writer, a model of Christian charity, and an exemplary figure in the history of social reform.

Woolman was the grandson of English Quaker immigrants to the New World, and he grew up on his family's farm in central New Jersey. Outwardly his was an unremarkable childhood. As a young man he left the farm for the nearby town of Mount Holly, where he worked as a shopkeeper; notary; tailor; surveyor; executor of wills, estates, and deeds; minister; church leader; and schoolteacher. More important from the historical perspective, he traveled widely to share what he believed was revealed Truth. As Woolman understood his ministry, he was abiding God's call to work for social justice and the ascendance of spirituality over humanity's fallen nature.

His ascetic temperament led Woolman to purify extravagantly, denying himself food, clothing, and methods of travel that he believed were corrupted by sin. He left farming, then shopkeeping, then tailoring; each move was a step in his quest for greater personal simplicity and for a more contemplative life. During a market revolution that swept the Atlantic world, Woolman was an outspoken critic of consumption and the accumulation of wealth.

Woolman did not believe that self-abnegation freed him from complicity in the violence that others committed against slaves. Like the psalmist who begged God not to judge him because "no one living is righteous before you," Woolman blamed himself for any act that sanctioned slavery, even indirectly. Like the Old Testament prophets upon whom he modeled his ministry, Woolman identified with the moral failings of his people. He addressed Quaker slaveholders compassionately, believing that their sin was also his. The Sermon on the Mount inspired his humanitarianism; he worshiped Christ as Redeemer and took the parable of the Good Samaritan to heart.[1]

Woolman chose to walk great distances rather than accept rides on animals groomed by slaves or in commercial coaches whose teamsters drove the horses too hard. When he sailed to England in the last year of his life, he bunked in steerage to bear witness to the sailors' dismal living conditions. He renounced earthly attachments; filled with compassion for all living creatures, he wept for masters and slaves, for the greedy and the impoverished, for predators and prey.

For more than 250 years admirers have revered John Woolman for many reasons, all of them based in historical events but some exaggerated to mythic proportions: as saint, labor reformer, champion of the poor, tax resister, war protester, pacifist, prophet, mystic, inspirational writer, and a founder of the abolitionist movement in America who brought the reignited cause back to England, where such activists as Thomas Clarkson, Olaudah Equiano, and William Wilberforce carried it forward. Woolman's spiritual autobiography, or *Journal*, is a devotional tract that has stayed in print since it was first published in 1774, a literary masterpiece that testifies to our own time as profoundly as it did to his. The English literary critic Charles Lamb said it was the only book by an American that he had ever read twice, and in 1823 he encouraged others to "get the writings of John Woolman by heart." William Ellery Channing, the nineteenth-century Unitarian minister and poet, declared Woolman's *Journal* "beyond all comparison the sweetest and purest autobiography in the language." Ralph Waldo Emerson found "more wisdom in these pages than in any book written since the days of the apostles." In 1869, Henry Crabb Robinson, an English lawyer, diarist, and one of the founders of the University of London, called Woolman's *Journal* "a perfect gem! His was a *schöne Seele*"—a beautiful soul.[2]

When the American Quaker poet John Greenleaf Whittier introduced a new edition of the *Journal* in 1871, he credited Woolman with founding the abolitionist movement. Sterling Price, a proslavery governor of Missouri, had paid Woolman a comparable compliment in 1853 by blaming him personally for the "evils" of transatlantic abolitionism. Indeed, Woolman's *Journal* influenced the abolitionist leaders Clarkson in England and Jean Pierre Brissot in France, as well as Tsar Alexander II's emancipation of Russia's serfs in 1861. The socialist Fabian Society celebrated Woolman as a founder of the labor reform movement and, beginning in the 1890s, published extracts from his writings that members distributed on the streets of London. Woolman was, according to the Fabians, "the voice in the wilderness, the John the Baptist of the Gospel of Socialism."[3]

In the twentieth century the War Resisters League looked to Woolman as a founding father of its cause. In 1930 the historians Charles and Mary Beard described Woolman as a seminal social thinker and activist: "In the writings of this simple workman born on the American soil in the reign of King George II are to be found the roots of American intellectual radicalism." Willard Sperry, the dean of the Harvard Divinity School from 1925 to 1953, said of Woolman: "If I were asked to date the birth of social conscience in its present-day form, I think I should put it on . . . the day John Woolman in a public meeting verbally denounced Negro slavery."[4]

Some have compared Woolman's ethical sensitivity with that of Francis of Assisi. In the early nineteenth century Samuel Taylor Coleridge wrote, "I should almost despair of that man who could peruse the life of John Woolman without an amelioration of heart." Charles W. Eliot, the president of Harvard from 1869 to 1926, described Woolman as one of America's great spiritual leaders: "His own words in this 'Journal,' of an extraordinary simplicity and charm, are the best expression of a personality which in its ardor, purity of motive, breadth of sympathy, and clear spiritual insight, gives Woolman a place among the uncanonized saints of America."[5]

Phillips P. Moulton, the editor of the *Journal*'s modern scholarly edition (1971), declared that Woolman "deserves to be ranked among the great spiritual leaders of mankind . . . comparable to such better known figures as Albert Schweitzer and Mahatma Gandhi." During the 1960s the literary critic Edwin H. Cady ranked the significance of the *Journal* beside that of Thoreau's *Walden*, Franklin's *Autobiography*, Whitman's *Democratic Vistas*, and *The Education of Henry Adams*. Earlier in the twentieth century, Theodore Dreiser gave the *Journal* a central role in his novel *The Bulwark*. Today mystics—aspirants to direct communication with God—from different religious traditions continue to read Woolman's *Journal* as a model of spiritual practice.[6]

Woolman is best known to historians for his abolitionism. In 1746, when he sojourned in the colonial American South for the first time and drafted his influential pamphlet *Some Considerations on the Keeping of Negroes*, slavery was critical to the economy of English North America and was growing in significance throughout the colonies. In some lowland counties of South Carolina there were three times as many African slaves as whites. Imports of slaves through the port of Charleston reached 4,000 annually in the decade prior to the American Revolution; though slavery was illegal in Georgia until mid-century, the numbers of slaves there increased rapidly after that—600 in the 1750s and 15,000 by 1770. East Florida went from 300 to 2,000 slaves during the same two decades. The growth of slavery in the upper South was even more dynamic. About 43,000 slaves were living in the Chesapeake Bay region in 1720; 172,000 in 1750; and 323,000 by 1770. In the North there were 14,000 slaves in 1720, 30,000 in 1750, and almost 48,000 in 1770; New Jersey alone had 2,385 slaves in 1720, the year of Woolman's birth, 5,354 in 1750, and more than 8,500 by the time he died.[7]

Throughout the eighteenth century slaves from Africa were the largest group of immigrants to British North America. Between 1750, when demand was running ahead of supply, and 1775, about

900,000 suffered the Middle Passage. (By comparison, about 50,000 British convicts were brought to the colonies on prison ships during the same period, and roughly 143,000 unchained immigrants arrived from the British Isles.) In the 1760s alone 365,000 slaves were shipped to Anglo-America, the highest total for any decade in the history of the British slave trade. When the American Revolution began, there were more slaves on the continent than in the British Caribbean colonies for the first time in two centuries.[8]

During the early eighteenth century Quakers generally had the same views about slavery as other colonists, and slavery also grew among them. Most American Quakers either did not think much about the subject or believed they were justified in owning slaves as long as they abstained from violence against them. The antislavery flame that flickered in Woolman's conscience during the 1740s, and that he and other Quakers kindled thereafter, illuminated a vibrant and profitable institution in the colonies of New Jersey and Pennsylvania, where the reformers had the most influence.[9]

We think of globalization as a recent phenomenon, but the eighteenth-century economy was already integrated internationally, and it raised the same sort of moral questions about exploitation, equity, and greed that we face today. And while we think of freedom, liberty, and equality as more than mere catchwords for the revolutionaries who founded the United States, who liberated Haitians, and who brought the French monarchy to its knees, fully three-quarters of humanity lived in bondage during the eighteenth century, and more people were unfree, in North America and abroad, at the century's end than at its beginning.[10]

The Christian faith of antislavery reformers like Woolman inspired them to respond critically to the growth of an international market economy. Their faith was traditional; the market relations they reacted against were new to their experience. The marketplace was the seedbed of perceptions about cause and effect, new understandings about the relationships among violence, war, labor systems, and the pursuit of profit, not to mention individual and collective responsibility. Global market relations allowed for an environment in which an expansive sense of responsibility, a universal humanitarianism, blossomed, but economic self-interest, race prejudice, and indifference closed ears to the abolitionists' message un-

til the 1760s and 1770s. By then enhanced spirituality and the rhetoric of independence and natural rights, as well as a recalculation of
slavery's profitability, had made the moral logic of emancipation
more compelling. Quakers then became the first group in North
America to take a collective public stand against slavery, and slowly
the clamor grew to a din against slavery throughout the world.[11]

When we ask where the impulse for social reform comes from in
such figures as John Woolman, it is clear that the historical context
is vital. César Chávez, Martin Luther King, Jr., Nelson Mandela,
and Lucretia Mott, for example, responded to injustices around
them just as Woolman did. But environment alone is insufficient to
explain these extraordinary figures. What reformers read also influences them, of course, as do family, friends and teachers, the witnessing or experiencing of social injustice, and the religious traditions
they practice or reject. Nonetheless, countless others read the same
books, study the same lessons, walk the same streets, attend the
same churches, and witness the same injustices, and they pass by
these immense problems without comment, or despair that they can
be addressed, let alone solved.

Idiosyncrasies of personality and random combinations of genes
also play a part, and the great reformers are often more acutely sensitive than others, leading them to take extraordinary actions that
few have the imagination even to contemplate. They are able to picture a world transformed. Part of a visionary's genius is the capacity
to lead those who cannot see the way. They are morally precocious
and become passionate. They risk their lives routinely because they
consider their cause more important than themselves.

Woolman was one of many prophets in his day—within and without the Society of Friends. He was not the only abolitionist, mystic, critic of capitalism, ascetic, pacifist, holy man, or spiritual purist
of his time. Still, he was distinctive, and he cannot be explained merely
by the qualities he shared with other Anglo-American Quakers. Woolman remains a mystery, as all of us are even to ourselves, never mind
to historians writing at a distance of three centuries, and it is this
mystery that I have explored.

The model that best illustrates Woolman's own view of his spiritually inspired social activism is that of the Old Testament prophets.

He warned rather than foretold, offered a message of hope, and held himself to uncompromising standards. Like the prophets, he called the wealthy to account for the plight of the poor, declined to debate his message, and tried to love humanity universally. He believed that masters and slaves equally shared God's love, were equally human, mortal, needful of compassion to enlighten and heal; he believed that with God's help slavery could be abolished and the world would be a better place. Like the Old Testament prophets, Woolman found his authority in the message itself.

Woolman's reputation for saintliness and his self-styling as a prophet make him an elusive biographical subject. My goal is to achieve a tone of critical empathy; I am aware that the gap between hagiography and psychological reductionism is not wide. Woolman's perspective on himself has merit, but it is not the last interpretive word. The question of whether or not he had personal experience of the divine, as he believed he had, cannot be resolved by a biographer. Neither unquestioning acceptance of Woolman's mysticism nor dismissal of it on secular grounds is useful; each is a flip side of the same unanalytical coin. To approach a subject like this from the standpoint of either belief or disbelief is equally prejudiced, although belief at least has the merit of engaging the historical figure on his own terms.

William James's helpful approach to "saints," including Woolman, thoughtfully melded faith and psychology, which generally are in tension. Unfortunately, James reduced the subjects to ideal types, which limits the utility of his perspective, but tolerably. Saints are, as he explained in *Varieties of Religious Experience* (1902), inexplicably different from the rest of us: they are special, controversial, and misfit for this world. Better put, the world is misfit for them. Their condition shows the "ripe fruits of religion in a character."[12]

For the religious genius or saint, labels that James used interchangeably, there are no inner restraints to overcome. They lack the inhibitions that keep the rest of us in line. They are free to cry when sad, display rage publicly when it is called for, scold, or embrace strangers when moved to do so. James's saints are emotional, energetic, and eccentric. "Our conventionality," he writes, "our shyness, laziness, and stinginess, our demands for precedent and permission, for guarantee and surety, our small suspicions, timidities, despairs, where are they now? Severed like cobwebs, broken like bubbles in the sun."[13]

James's saints are not universally attractive. His list of exemplary individuals includes the antislavery warrior-prophet John Brown and George Fox, the avatar of Quakerism's founding generation, along with Woolman and other eccentric religious figures. Saints in the Jamesian perspective are often, perhaps even usually, not responsible or companionable in conventional ways. Their ranks could include the likes of Marie Guyart (1599–1672), a young French widow who abandoned her son for the convent and crossed the Atlantic to work among the Huron Indians in Quebec. She was not much of a mother, but she had God's work to do. Like Guyart, Buddha, the apostles, the martyrs of the early church, Teresa of Avila, and others, Woolman left his family to seek and to spread spiritual truth as he understood it. When the saint hears God's voice, family and friends become subsidiary concerns.[14]

Woolman could be petty in the demands he made on others and annoyingly persistent. He could be confrontational, and when he seized the moral high ground, he turned even aesthetic molehills into mountains of sin. He judged harshly, declining hospitality on what seemed to his family, friends, and coreligionists to have been trivial grounds. He could be detached and distracted. He may have been an uninterested father, son, and brother and a thoughtless husband; he was possibly emotionally withdrawn from those closest to him. He seems to have subsumed all human relationships to his higher calling, and this could not have been pleasant for his wife and daughter.

John Woolman was, then, an exemplary Jamesian saint, but his saintliness never approached the perfection he aimed for. His quest for purity drove him to both harmless eccentricity and self-destructive extremes. He was simultaneously a throwback, a man of his times, and a preacher too modern for his flock. He was a mystic who lived out of time, at least in his own mind. His prophecy might be more fashionable today than it was centuries ago, yet the whole package that was John Woolman would now be even less attractive than it was then. Mentally, emotionally, and stylistically he is very remote from the twenty-first century. Few, if any, of us aspire to achieve his standards of purity. He nonetheless remains an inspiring figure, a powerful prophet, a man with a heart of gold, and a model reformer.

Woolman's story is not a chapter or even a paragraph in the history of ideas. It offers, rather, an example of spiritually motivated action of the sort that led Muhammad and Joseph Smith to found religions, Joan of Arc and John Brown to lead what they believed was God's army, John Wycliffe and Jan Hus to try to reform the church, and Augustine of Hippo and Thomas Merton to write about their personal experiences of the divine. A biography of Woolman necessarily draws on philosophy, theology, psychology, and history and works the interstices among them. None is sufficient, all are useful, and each was part of the scaffolding of theory and academic debate that surrounded this project's conception, but of which the book is, I hope, largely free.

A wide array of philosophical and immediate contextual influences worked on Woolman. The Quaker roots of his moral perspective are clear. The reciprocal influences of other Quaker reformers in the mid-eighteenth century are also evident in his writings. Less obvious are the effects of the Great Awakening, the religious revival that swept the Atlantic world in the 1740s, and the Enlightenment. The Great Awakening is variously linked to the coming of the American Revolution and the growth and spread of New World evangelicalism. The Enlightenment, an eighteenth-century philosophical movement, is generally praised and blamed for the emergence of modern liberal ideas about personal freedom and secular emancipation from dogma. The relationship between the Enlightenment and the Great Awakening can reasonably be seen as both antagonistic and synergistic; the conflict is in the eye of the modern beholder. Also, the relationship between the Great Awakening and the mid-eighteenth-century Quaker reform movement associated with Woolman is difficult to pin down. Quaker sources infrequently mention the evangelical revival, and they are invariably critical of its theatrical or "enthusiastic" expressions.

The influence of the Enlightenment on Woolman is also difficult to discern. We know only that he read the Enlightenment thinkers

John Locke and John Everard (whose theology some consider an early example of rational religion). But where Woolman's ideas intersect with the Enlightenment agenda, they generally run against the grain of its secularizing tendencies. Woolman's *Journal* does not express Enlightenment influences or sympathy for its rational worldview, though several of his pamphlets have passages consistent with Enlightenment thought and vocabulary. Woolman read some writers who were themselves influenced by Enlightenment philosophy and adopted some phrasings and logic consistent with it in several of his pamphlets. But the man as we know him drew his fundamental philosophy from the Bible, from seventeenth-century Quaker texts, and from authors who wrote in the Christian mystical and ascetic traditions.

Woolman was a prophetic Old Testament radical who read the Bible selectively, especially the Sermon on the Mount, and whose understanding of Christ as Redeemer may seem jarring to modern-day sensibilities. He was not a doomsayer, but he was a prophet, and if he was enlightened, it was to the sacredness of life. He did not celebrate the wisdom of the world or the promise of the human intellect to solve the earth's problems; he advocated surrender to the spiritual and renunciation of the material. His asceticism was sometimes more Old Church than Reformation in its forms.

I have not had to recover John Woolman from history's dustbin. He has never been lost or forgotten, but this is his first full-scale biography in more than half a century. What another biographer wrote eighty years ago is still true: "There are few men so eminent as John Woolman in social or religious literature, of whose personal life and surroundings so very little is known." In *The Beautiful Soul of John Woolman*, I have tried to address that oversight as the sources allow and as the limitations of my vision permit. John Woolman's hope for the world inspires this reconsideration of a great moral leader in America's founding era, whose universal humanitarianism can be a model for our spiritually fissured world.[15]

1

Revelations

1720–28

I have often felt a motion of love to leave some hints in writing of my experience of the goodness of God, and now, in the thirty-sixth year of my age, I begin this work.

I was born in Northampton, in Burlington county in West Jersey, A.D. 1720, and before I was seven years old I began to be acquainted with the operations of divine love [and often found a care upon me how I should please him].* Through the care of my parents, I was taught to read near as soon as I was capable of it [and it was even then of use to me]; and as I went from school one Seventh Day, I remember, while my companions went to play by the way, I went forward out of sight; and sitting down, I read the twenty-second chapter of the Revelations.[1]

On the particular Saturday, what Quakers call Seventh Day, in about 1727 with which John Woolman's spiritual autobiography begins, the weather permitted a boy to sit outdoors reading the Bible. The author states the year and his age vaguely, in keeping with his view

*Bracketed phrases are from manuscript drafts of the *Journal* that were deleted for the first published edition. West Jersey was a Quaker colony from 1676 and was united with the colony of East Jersey in 1702 as the colony of New Jersey. The Quaker association with West Jersey survived into Woolman's generation.

that time is an earthly measure of secondary significance to the spirit's immortality. He offers "hints" of his spiritual experience, because he cannot find earthly words to describe what he felt. The reader should not expect temporal precision or attention to material details in Woolman's *Journal*. The subject is not his life but his experience of God, and "hints" are the closest he can bring others to the divine.

Tolerance of dampness, heat, and cold was greater in the eighteenth century than ours is today, and Woolman is not giving us much context, which readers must infer. When he writes that he sat down to read, Woolman embraces invisibility for himself and for his surroundings. "I went forward out of sight," he writes, a simple clause that encapsulates a core message. The forward movement is a self-conscious image about traversing space and time that implies spiritual growth; it suggests that the writer has already gone beyond the spiritual horizons of his peers, beyond what they can see, in more ways than one.

The *Journal* is rich in such subtle, artful expression. Whether the choices of words were divinely inspired is an unanswerable question for us. Woolman attributed his progress to God's invitation, and he believed that the *Journal* derived from the same source. Words poured from him; his hand and quill were conduits for a message that emerged from deeper inside Woolman than he could consciously know. It is not unusual for writers to be unable to explain where their creative impulses come from, to attribute their words to a transcendent source. So we can read the *Journal* on Woolman's terms, as inspired literature, *and* as a text where he lurks, invisible only to himself, the literary equivalent of a toddler who believes that no one can see him when he covers his eyes. Whatever he thinks, Woolman does not truly disappear into the passive voice and spiritual mist. Autobiography is not a good place to hide from oneself or from readers; we might also wonder whether Woolman's schoolmates knew perfectly well where he was and what he did on the day when he went forward ahead of them.

Both the filter of memory and the formulaic structure of Quaker spiritual autobiographies and of the genre going back to Augustine affect Woolman's retrospective view of his early life. We read about an idealized fall and rebirth of the sort that Catholics had reported for a millennium, and Protestants since the Reformation, and the account undoubtedly exaggerates and may even contort the writer's memories. Events were hooks on which Woolman hung spiritual lessons that he believed transcended physical experience. Some of those lessons were distinctively his, others he borrowed; but all were fashioned of new and old, never whole, cloth that he stitched with his own thread.

We can tell from the *Journal*'s opening vignette that Woolman wanted readers to see him as a serious, spiritual boy who achieved an impressive level of literacy at a young age. Readers can infer that the weather was unremarkable and that the sights, sounds, textures, and smells of his youth were irrelevant or forgotten by the time he wrote, twenty-nine years after the fact. Growth from within is the book's plot. Woolman was all about spirit, visions others could not see, and soulful interiors.

Even if Woolman's recollection is true to his memory, that does not explain why he saw the event as a defining moment in his life or why he omitted other stories about himself as a young child. After all, it is not uncommon for an autobiographer to include information that predates his earliest memories or even his life. Benjamin Franklin and John Bunyan recount family history; Augustine "recalls" learning to talk.[2]

But to the early American Quakers, including John Woolman, entertaining stories such as those Franklin told (created and embellished too) were frivolous, the written equivalent of idle chatter and therefore sinful. Woolman husbanded his words as a farmer rations winter feed. Only incidents that bore directly on his spirituality made it into his book.

Woolman started his *Journal* with the story about reading Revelation because that was how he thought a spiritual autobiography should begin. Such introductions were formulaic in Quaker journals, of which hundreds, perhaps more than a thousand, had been written during the preceding century. The first paragraphs declare the journals a record of God's grace in the autobiographer's life. "That all may know the dealings of the Lord with me," the *Journal* of George Fox (1624–91) began. John Churchman (1705–75), a "public" Friend (that is, a formally recognized minister) from Chester County, Pennsylvania, also wrote of "the reaches of divine love ... of which I am a living witness." Elizabeth Ashbridge (1713–55), an English-born Quaker who immigrated to America from Ireland as an indentured servant in 1732, "thought proper to make some remarks on the dealings of divine goodness to me." Woolman was conforming to the model when he wrote that before the age of seven he "began to be acquainted with the operations of Divine Love." A manuscript draft shows that he added "and often found a care upon me how I should please Him" to finish the thought.[3]

With the extended phrase the passage equates "Divine Love" and "Him," which accounts for the uppercase usage in Woolman's handwritten drafts. God *was* divine love to Woolman. He wants readers to understand that he lived to please God more than he worked to satisfy his teacher, parents, classmates, or himself. When he wrote this down, he knew his intense focus on the divine was remarkable for a person of any age. That is why he wrote, and that is also why a committee of Quakers edited and then published Woolman's *Journal* in 1774, two years after his death.

The passive voice—"my mind was drawn to seek"—is revealing. Woolman sustains the passive mode throughout the *Journal.* He is not telling readers how he became great, as Franklin did in his autobiography, or even how he became good, as Augustine did in *The Confessions.* The *Journal* is about God and how he bestowed divine love on John Woolman. It is less about Woolman's struggle, although there is some strife, than about his acceptance of what God gave him.

This quality marks Woolman's *Journal* as typical of Quaker spiritual autobiographies yet also gives a clue to its uniqueness. Men's memoirs in the Western European tradition are usually marked by their triumphs. They are about quests. There is action, movement across space, battles, courage, and victories. One autobiographical form descends from heroic quest narratives—think of *The Odyssey* as a model—through first-person travelers' tales, such as Marco Polo's, and down to the logs of explorers such as Christopher Columbus. Franklin's *Autobiography* and Jean-Jacques Rousseau's *Confessions* were written within this secular tradition, and they too record triumphs over self and others. Many of the books in this genre, including Franklin's, are about fame and efforts to achieve worldly success. The rewards come after the protagonists have survived the sorts of self-inflicted wounds that might have bled them to death.

Rousseau and Franklin also show their legacy from inward-looking spiritual memoirs, and in Franklin's case the Puritan heritage contributed to a fusion of the two models. By the eighteenth century books of this kind were more introspective than in the previous century: self-absorbed, celebratory of self, and inwardly probing of the writer's distinctiveness, his special, even unique qualities. But such options were denied, at least in theory, to authors writing about their spiritual journeys who presented themselves as typical of their faith communities. A focus on self breaks from the traditional Christian goal of spiritual autobiography, which was to universalize from the author's experiences, the classic narrative presenting the protagonist as lost or fallen before the grace of God inspired a transformation. The spiritual triumph is noteworthy because it is not the result of any unique personal qualities. If the writer could be saved, so can the reader.

Franklin's autobiography is a transition in this regard, because he secularizes the approach without altering the form and because he adopts the traditional pose of the everyman author, while celebrating his extraordinary accomplishments. In his account he transforms himself into a good man, a great man, and recognizes himself as a genius, but he attributes his accomplishments to hard work and self-discipline rather than to his personal gifts or grace. The goal was still to present a model, yet to recognize in the self-analysis exactly how extraordinary the author was. His experiences were not available to all readers, although the model was instructive despite being, or even because it was, unattainable—even by Franklin. One could aim to become better by following the steps of such a man, and "better" is the key; the quest for self-improvement broke from the all-or-nothing, saved-or-damned condition of the traditional Christian memoirist.

Thus did spiritual autobiography become in the eighteenth century a tool for self-examination, for exploring the realm between collective identity and independence. The ideal was not literal representation of the writer's past—not a journal in the sense of a daily chronicling of events—but retrospective analysis. The autobiographer calls attention to his unique perspective rather than submerging his self in a collective identity, as seventeenth-century Puritan writers had tried to do. Indeed, he sometimes presents himself as alienated or in conflict with his closest social and spiritual groups, accounting for himself apart from, if not in opposition to, the world. Woolman was affected by such cultural change no less than his contemporaries Jonathan Edwards and Benjamin Franklin.[4]

Spiritual autobiographies in the Western religious traditions, Puritan and Catholic being the most instructive here, had long taken the quest inward. Jonathan Edwards's "great and violent inward struggles," recalled in his "Personal Narrative," were the genre's norm. Although from Augustine and Ignatius Loyola on, such narratives focused inwardly for reasons that had to do more with culture than with spirit, men's reflections on themselves usually dealt more with the subject's relationship to the world than women's did. Augustine "walked the streets of Babylon, and . . . wallowed myself in the mire of it." The public relationships could be localized or grand in scale, but the men were agents of their own spiritual victories, even when they reported that God's assistance was essential, and they were responsible for their defeats. They triumphed, with God's help, over their depraved natures and against worldly temptations.[5]

When Edwards was a boy, he found, like Woolman, a quiet place in the woods for reading and contemplation. Unlike Woolman but in conformance with the traditional male narrative, Edwards constructed his retreat and did so publicly, with help from his boyhood friends. "I, with some of my schoolmates, joined together and built a booth in a swamp, in a very secret and retired place, for a place of prayer," he wrote. Likewise, public events helped shape him spiritually. The flowering of the Great Awakening in his father's congregation "very much affected" him "for many months." That and his prayerful practice with friends were "remarkable seasons of awakening" that inspired spiritual growth.[6]

As a young man Edwards experienced "religious delights . . . totally of another kind" from those of his youth. He began to spend an "abundance of time in walking alone in the woods," embracing the effects of "divine love" upon him. The "former delights" of his childhood spirituality had "never reached the heart," he explains. While the Quaker Woolman gained access to grace as a child, original sin left Edwards in darkness until external forces lit his spiritual flame. The experiences of both men reflect their religious traditions; neither breaks from the genre forms typical of their faiths.[7]

Autobiographies by women and by Quaker men differ in important ways from those of Catholic and Puritan men, even though they share much ground. Scholars have suggested that the model for modern female autobiographers emerged in the eighteenth century from romances rather than from the classical quest stories that influenced men, and it is true that the romantic heroine in the Western tradition lacks the power to act on her own behalf. Women autobiographers generally do not even try to shape their own destinies. But women such as Teresa of Avila (1515–82) and Margery Kempe (ca. 1373–ca. 1440), who wrote long before the emergence of the romance, also were passive; things happened to them. Kempe "was touched by the hand of the Lord" and found it difficult "to tell of the grace that I was feeling; it seemed to come from heaven, to be well beyond the reach of my own power of reason." Teresa imagined herself a garden watered by God's grace. Her triumphs were God's gifts to her. "Whenever I have surrendered to obedience," she writes, "impossible things have become simple."[8]

Quaker men too wrote about the suppression and loss of their wills. The journals of both male and female Quakers are more about God than about the writers, or so is their intent. "In my early age I was sensible of the tender impressions of divine love," wrote Mary Hagger at about the same time that Woolman independently chose very similar words. Thomas Story (1670?–1742), of Cumberland County, England, a convert to Quakerism whose itinerant ministry eventually brought him to America, recorded "the tender mercies and judgments of the Lord; to relate my own experience of his dealings with me thro' the course of my life." And so it was with other Quaker spiritual autobiographies.[9]

Woolman might have started the story of his life with a dramatic narrative about formative experiences and triumphs over external and internal forces. Instead, he wrote about the action of divine love on him. Other events in his life were irrelevant in comparison, and to discuss them in the *Journal* would be an expression of ego or "vanity," as he saw it. In any event, the Quaker editorial committee that published his *Journal* revised and deleted passages that it considered deviations. Still, Woolman addressed his adult participation in public events and explored distinct aspects of his independent self. As a Quaker he embraced spiritual enlightenment even before his conversion experience and adopted a pose even more passive than is typical of Quaker men.

We might plausibly expect, in any case, that the rest of the *Journal* will have the same passive tone as the first paragraph and will tell only the events in Woolman's life that he can present as revelations of God's grace and will. Certainly most of the narrative tries to slant his story that way. Thus the *Journal* both is and is not distinctively John Woolman's. It is essential therefore that we look for his hand, for the editorial committee's, and for touches of his spiritual forefathers and mothers in what he wrote. That is how we can best understand who he was and what his *Journal* has meant to those who admire it. Embedded in this thicket of possibilities is a narrative of Woolman's inner life as it was formed in a public arena. He can be found in the *Journal* and his other writings; sometimes he is naked, and sometimes he is clothed in an obscurity that he could neither don nor doff at will.

T HE story begins with the English Civil War, with the founding of Quakerism during those troubled times, with William Penn and the Quaker migration to West Jersey (later New Jersey) and Pennsylvania, with the settlement of Northampton, and with the three generations of American Woolmans—his great-grandfather, grandparents, and parents—who preceded John's birth. The Society of Friends, the Quakers' chosen name, was one of the radically democratic groups that rose from the ferment of the English Revolution from 1642 to 1651, during a time when people were questioning all forms of authority. A king was executed, democracy—some feared anarchy—was in the air, and the relationship between church and state was at play. The revolution established the absolute rights of property, devolved power on the landed classes, settled sovereignty on an elected Parliament and the common law, and sanctified the Protestant ethic. Quakers were at the radical fringe of the forces opposing the crown, and they shared a fundamental anticlericalism and a common people's theology with other groups that rose and fell during these difficult times. The difference between Quakers and some of the other radical sects is that the Society of Friends survived the English Revolution and continued to resist compromise, to aim for a recovery of the apostolic church, to challenge authority, and to run afoul of the law long after the monarchy had been restored.

Before the 1650s it was difficult to distinguish Friends from the other sects boiling in the revolutionary spiritual pot: Ranters, Baptists, Fifth Monarchists, Boehmenists, Seekers, and others. But Quakers were never millenarians, foretellers of the imminence of the judgment day promised in the Bible, and their evolving theology varied among ministers of the faith, whose claims of union with God, discussions of a mysterious "Light," and assertions of "perfection and freedom from sin" were controversial enough to ensure attacks from all theological sides. The Quakers' heritage included both the Puritanism from which they dissented and Continental mysticism.[10]

"Puritan" and "Quaker" both were epithets with disputed origins. The first appeared in the late sixteenth century as an insulting term for a member of the Church of England who espoused stricter, simpler forms of worship and doctrine—close to the Christianity of Christ's apostles—than those of either Roman Catholicism or the established English church. Puritans were considered arrogant and self-serving in their certainty that their own practices were pure. But the reform-minded Puritans persisted in their criticism of the Church of England as weak-kneed, a mere shadow of the fiery Calvinism known in Switzerland, France, and Germany. They became a powerful social force, central both to the reform of church and state and to the violence that racked England in the mid-seventeenth century.

Groups of dissident Protestants began to meet together as

Friends apparently as early as 1644, but the exact year of Quakerism's birth remains a subject of dispute. The Friends' belief in an interior God may have originated with a 1646 book by a Baptist minister, and the Friends may have first spun off in 1648 from a Baptist congregation in Mansfield, Nottinghamshire, but other traditions shared the same ideas and locales. Then in 1650, an unsympathetic judge in Derby mocked the defendant George Fox for being a "quaker" during his trial on blasphemy charges, because Fox had exhorted the court to "tremble at the word of the law." Eventually Friends adopted the epithet as a badge of honor. Among other explanations for its origins, quaking was a common physical expression of the ecstatic states experienced by adherents. And Quaker ministers warned those who threatened them to quake in fear of the Lord's vengeance.[11]

By 1652, when George Fox, Richard Farnworth, Thomas Aldam, Margaret Killam, William Dewsbury, and James Nayler preached in England's northern shires, the "People of God," "Children of the Light," or Friends had become a movement that appealed to a growing number of ordinary rural people, many of them farmers. The early converts tended to be young adults, both poor and prosperous, but they were not of the landed gentry or the nobility. Within a decade there may have been as many as sixty thousand Quakers, making them as numerous as English Catholics, but they never constituted more than 1 percent of the population.[12]

The early Quakers, like other Protestant groups during the sixteenth and seventeenth centuries, never intended to establish a new religion, and to his dying day Fox did not believe that they had. Like other Protestants, they envisioned a return to the early church's pure, vivid form of apostolic Christianity. The first Quaker ministers saw their followers as "seeds" that would blossom into this recovered universal church. Friends wanted to prune the accretions that had corrupted pure spirituality over the centuries: professional clergy, imposed doctrine, institutionalized sacraments, bureaucracy, hierarchy, rote prayer, iconography, elaborate architecture and vestments, hymns, and other interventions between believers and God.[13]

Quakers also declined to bow, to curtsy, to doff their hats in respect to social betters, or to take oaths, behavior that challenged the hierarchical social order as other Dissenters also did, but they went further and offended Puritans too. In their early, most radical phase, they were "Christopresent" rather than simply "Christocentric"— that is, they believed that the physical Christ, flesh and blood, possessed them. They claimed to perform miracles, curing fevers, healing the lame, casting out demons, and raising the dead. They had visions. Fox referred to 176 separate miracles in his writing. Critics charged that Fox and Nayler could disappear at will and transport themselves invisibly to distant places, opening the two men to accusations of witchcraft; some enthralled supporters believed that both of them could fend off physical threats by the power of their spirit, that they were prophets whose coming had been foretold; shamans who connected the physical and spiritual realms; and avatars—embodiments of the deity who descended from the heavens to earth.[14]

In its challenges to the presumptions of seventeenth-century English culture, Quakerism seemed anarchical, a frightening proposition in a polity already torn asunder by religious disputes. Quakers acted strangely by contemporary standards—fasting for days and weeks, stripping away their clothes as testimony to their disdain for the flesh—and made extravagant claims about their powers. People came to fear them, and this led to hostility, which fueled conspiracy theories that their ministers were Jesuits sent by the pope to destroy the English church and state. In the mid-seventeenth century the English were popularly inclined to see every expression of radical dissent as a conspiracy orchestrated from Rome. Charges that Quakers were crypto-Catholics and that Fox, Nayler, Penn, and others were Jesuits made sense to people who saw in Quakers' rejection of predestination echoes of Catholic belief in free will.[15]

Rumors had it that Quakers ritually sacrificed children, routinely committed incest and buggery, and practiced witchcraft. Such beliefs spreading through the general populace led to mob violence and state suppression of the Society of Friends. Throughout the Civil War and, notably, after the restoration of the monarchy in 1660, Quakers advocated the disestablishment of the church, disrupted Anglican services, challenged priests in their pulpits and on the streets, and opposed tithes for support of the Church of England. They often ended up in jail for these claims, rumors, actions, and threats; courts sentenced Fox to prison upward of twenty-five times, and William Penn served four terms in four years. Judges ordered Nayler branded on the forehead, bored with a hot iron through his tongue, whipped, pilloried, and otherwise humiliated for having blasphemed.[16]

Perhaps it was the influence of family groups, persecution, or simply the passage of time, but Quakerism changed, as all religions do, from the founding generation to the next one. The concept of the Inner Light, a core Quaker belief, may have evolved from their initial claims that Christ was literally in them. By substituting "Light" for "Christ," they might have been trying to avoid prosecution for blasphemy. Since the Light shines within all people, Quakers attest, everyone has the potential for salvation; therefore all are equal in the eyes of God. This meant to Quakers that a social hierarchy, including any that discriminate because of gender or race, is contrary to God's Truth. Their understanding that this is what Christ taught is what has made Quakers, over the centuries since their founding, advocate equality, simplicity, and nonviolence. From the very beginning, their radicalism was in uncompromising devotion to those principles against the authority of church and state. And their pacifism, another core belief, evolved from initially militant and martial expressions of their faith.

The Light that Quakers believe in is not the same as a conscience, because for them it is actually God, but it functions as a conscience if believers listen to God's quiet voice within them. A Quaker primer puts it this way: "Christ is the Truth. Christ is the Light." Revelation comes from within; authority emerges from a collective sense of the truth. Quakers are thus antinomian (against the law) since they elevate experience over written texts, including the Bible. "The principal rule of Christians under the Gospel," according to the seventeenth-century Quaker theologian Robert Barclay, "is not an outward letter, nor law outwardly written and delivered, but an inward spiritual law, engraven in the heart, the law of the Spirit of life, the Word that is nigh in the heart and in the mouth." The Bible is a "dead thing," Barclay explains, unless reading it is inspired by the Spirit, which is God, and one does not merely treat it as a symbol or as his quoted words. In this view of the Bible, Quakers agreed with both John Calvin and Martin Luther that its revelatory texts, however useful, were secondary to direct, personal experience of God.[17]

The Quakers never had shrines, cathedrals, or sacred places. They never sanctified buildings or grounds, believing instead that all the earth is equally sacred as a creation of God. "The Church is in God, the Father of Christ," the Quaker primer instructs, "and not a steeple-house." Quakers thus distinguish themselves from Roman Catholics and others who do not share this radical edge of Protestant spiritualism.[18]

The Society of Friends decentralized decision making, minimized hierarchy, and repudiated any spiritual authority for rituals, ceremonies, hymns, vestments, or sacraments. Quakers distributed authority among all their congregants, any of whom—women and men—could be ministers inspired directly by God without formal study and ordination. They rejected the Calvinist belief in predestination, the idea that God has selected some people but not others for salvation, and insisted that free will and grace are active agents of redemption; in this, Friends shared the Arminian understanding that salvation is available to all believers who use their free will to accept God's grace. In theory, but not in fact, they abolished doctrine, opening beliefs and practices to reconsideration in light of continuing revelation, by which they meant direct communication from God or divinely inspired reinterpretations of the Bible.

Truth, Quakers still believe, is consistent with the Bible's revelation of the word of God. But the Bible, however true, lacks the ultimate authority it has for other Protestant sects, since it is not considered sufficient. The "Light within" remains for Quakers the source of continuing revelation, facilitated by knowledge of the Bible and other spiritual texts. Indeed, Quakers during the seventeenth and eighteenth centuries taught their children to read principally to give them access to written revelation, which would help them comprehend God's revelations during silent contemplation and when they heard words spoken by inspired ministers of their faith.

Puritanism and Quakerism shared an intense conviction of sin, a fear of divine judgment, and a belief in the purifying effects of self-denial. Just as Puritanism was a reaction from within the Church of England, radical separatist sects grew out of Puritanism, and the Quakers extended separatist principles further still. Though there is, then, a direct lineage from Puritanism to Quakerism, in the seventeenth-century context the differences were more striking than their shared theological roots. Nothing defined those differences more clearly than Quaker belief that salvation comes from within, that God inhabits our bodies, that no authority external to the individual is necessary for salvation, and acceptance or rejection of grace is our choice to make. Quaker belief in the Inner Light (or Light within) is consistent with the Puritan emphasis on the Holy Spirit's dwelling in the hearts of all believers, with the discussion of "the gifts of the Spirit" by the Anabaptist sect in Holland called the Dutch Collegiants, and with the Continental mystic Jacob Boehme's "Light of the Deity" emanating from the soul.

Quakers were not at first attentive to formal theology, although the itinerant preacher Edward Burrough, among others, offered summaries of their beliefs. But by the 1670s Quakers had begun to describe their faith consistently and in positive terms—what they believed rather than what they rejected from other religions. Barclay's *An Apology for the True Christian Divinity* (1678) was an expression of this turn toward a more carefully articulated theology.[19]

Early on, Quakers decided to conduct their church business by the same model as their Meetings for Worship, in which the congregation waits expectantly for the Light that a "sense of the Meeting" then acknowledges. This "sense" is a group acceptance of an insight as a revelation. Quakers have faith that the Light will reveal Truth to them collectively, when believers are open to receive divine inspiration; the process requires a suspension of ego and surrender to the authority of the Meeting. The decision-making process itself, rather than the particular question they are addressing, is the higher point for Quakers who accept the sense of the Meeting as authoritative; they would rather not reach a decision than invoke one that has not achieved the status of collective understanding as truth. Necessarily, then, Quakers may answer a question with a lightning bolt of collective insight or, at the other extreme, by an approach to discernment that frustrates impatient members over weeks, months, or years; the latter was the case for Quaker deliberations over slavery, which took a century to resolve.

Any group of Quakers worshiping together is called Meeting for Worship. Each group that forms itself into a church is called Preparative Meeting until it reaches a point where its numbers and stability allow formal recognition as Monthly Meeting, this formal designation coming from the next administrative levels. In the eighteenth century, Preparative or Monthly Meetings generally held Meetings for Worship twice weekly, on First Day (Sunday) and again at midweek, although any gathering of Quakers could sit in silent worship with the same spiritual authority as the recognized Meetings. The next administrative level is Quarterly Meeting, to which members of Monthly Meetings are invited four times each year for worship and the consideration of collective business. The pinnacle of Quaker organization is Yearly Meeting, which is composed of members of all Preparative, Monthly, and Quarterly Meetings within its care.

During the eighteenth century, committees from each of these administrative levels reported to the collectivity; each committee had elders, financial officers, and a "clerk"; and the office of the clerk for the Meeting itself, very like a chairperson, had both spiritual and administrative authority. John Woolman, in his small town in New Jersey, was a member of Rancocas Preparative Meeting as a child and then of Mount Holly Preparative Meeting as an adult, both of which (until Mount Holly was recognized as Monthly Meeting)* were in Burlington Monthly and Quarterly Meetings, and Philadelphia Yearly Meeting.

N O single individual was more responsible for the Quakers' migration to New Jersey and Pennsylvania than William Penn (1644–1718), the son of Adm. Sir William Penn, to whom the Stuart

---

*Mount Holly was recognized as Monthly Meeting in 1776, four years after Woolman's death, when Friends moved into a new meetinghouse, which still stands as an active place of worship. Monthly Meeting for Business was held in Burlington until then. The Burlington meetinghouse is still in use.

monarchs were indebted for his support of King Charles II's restoration to the throne in 1660. A year later the younger Penn was expelled from Oxford University, where he had been influenced by religious Nonconformists, for publicly criticizing the ceremonies of the Church of England and refusing to attend compulsory chapel services. Since with the Restoration it was illegal to worship in any other faith community, Penn's religious radicalism could have landed him in jail, so his father sent him off to France, hoping that experience would lead him to reconsider his perilous path.

Upon Penn's return to England in 1664, he seemed ready to assume the responsibilities of an admiral's son. Bedecked in the latest French fashions, he at least dressed for the role and began to study law the following year. While in Ireland attending to his father's business, though, Penn converted to Quakerism. This was a daring, some at the time said foolhardy, decision. During the mid-1670s he became a trustee of the colony of West Jersey, and he promoted Quaker settlement there, envisioning a society where his coreligionists and those of other faiths would be free from the persecution they had to endure in England. With the same goals, he founded Pennsylvania in 1681 on land granted by the monarch to repay his father.

In a persecutory environment, which continued until passage of the Toleration Act in 1689, English, Irish, Scottish, and Welsh Quakers immigrated in considerable numbers to the British North American colonies, as had Pilgrims, Puritans, and Catholics before them. These immigrants tended to be the most radical, most often persecuted Quakers. Those who presented fewer blatant challenges to British society stayed behind and eventually made their accommodations with church and state. The immigrants were also among those most concerned for their families. They went to Pennsylvania and New Jersey to save their children economically and spiritually, two concerns that were intimately connected in their eyes.

These Quakers came from all over the British Isles, but especially from the North Midlands counties of Cheshire, Lancashire, Yorkshire, Derbyshire, and Nottinghamshire. About twenty-three thousand crossed the Atlantic between 1675 and 1715; half of all the colonists in Pennsylvania were Quakers when the eighteenth century began. By the 1760s there were sixty or seventy thousand in Pennsylvania alone, a significant minority. They were the third-largest religious denomination in British North America, outnumbered only by Congregationalists and Anglicans. Their rank began to fall after that, even as their real numbers increased; theirs was the fifth-largest American religion in 1775, ninth by 1820, and sixty-sixth in the 1980s. In colonial America, though, Quakers were a formidable presence.[20]

Quaker settlers were, like the Puritans, of the "middling" classes but on average poorer than Anglicans, though they pursued landownership more ambitiously, perhaps because they saw real property as the glue that would bond the family. Families were the moral centers that molded the character of children, assured marriages within the faith group, and provided a landed legacy to keep children safe and close. On the whole, the Quaker family structure was less authoritarian and more positive about children's natures than Congregationalist or Anglican ones; many Quakers did not inflict corporal punishment on their children or believe in original sin.[21]

WOOLMAN tells readers nothing of this Quaker past or of his family history, of the ten-week winter Atlantic crossing that his grandfather and great-grandfather made in 1678 on a ship called the *Shield*, the icy Delaware River where they disembarked, or how they found, marked, cleared, and built on their land in Northampton with other early settlers of what became central New Jersey. William Wills, though, who was to be their neighbor, recollected his arrival a year before they landed.

> I remember we had a southeast storm of wind and rain for forty-eight hours, and about the middle of which came the landing. And when ashore the first thing to be done was to draw lots to find which of the ten was my father's. This being done, we took up our packages and through the woods we went, to find the third lot. When there arrived all in the rain,

we set up some forks and poled them, and covered our tents with blankets, but that did little good, for it rained through upon us all night. So betwixt the rain and the smoke of our fire and wet clothes, which never dried until they dried on our back, we was very much benumbed. Had not my father had more courage than either his son or his servants to go out into the dismal dark night to get wood to recruit the fire, we might have perished.

The Woolmans' oral traditions may have included episodes of such hardship, in addition to hard work and the blessings of God. Two years after Daniel and William Wills began clearing their land, the father wrote a letter that expresses his joy at having risked the journey and endured the rough beginnings.

> Dear Friend,
>   Let every man write according to his judgment, and this is mine concerning this country; I do really believe it to be as good a country as any man need to dwell in; and it is much better than I expected every way for a land . . . Through industry here, will be all things produced that are necessary for a family in England, and far more easy.[22]

The Quaker Willses, Woolmans, and their neighbors may have been the first Europeans to farm the land they cleared, but they were not the first white settlers in the Delaware Valley. Between 1609 and 1664 Dutch traders had inhabited it as part of the colony of New Netherlands, though beginning in 1638, settlers from Sweden competed for land there. The Dutch reasserted control in 1655. They were always more interested in trade and piracy, however, and the English took control in 1664. The duke of York, the brother of the English monarch, granted two English noblemen the land between the Hudson and Delaware rivers, which they then split into two tracts, selling East Jersey to Scottish investors and, in 1674, West Jersey to English Quakers. In 1702 the crown reunited the two Jerseys as the royal colony of New Jersey.[23]

The region east of the Delaware River, where Quakers founded

Northampton in what became central New Jersey—from Camden in the south, opposite Philadelphia, to Trenton in the north—had been home to Indians for more than twelve thousand years. The natives who lived there in the seventeenth and eighteenth centuries, the Rancocas band, spoke a Unami dialect of the Lenape language group. These Lenapes believed they once had dwelled far to the northeast, where it was colder, and had moved south and west to a great lake that abounded in fish. They had crossed this water and lived in pine and hemlock forests, fighting often with other people there; then they moved farther south and east, where they allied with the Hurons to drive out the Cherokees.[24]

The Lenapes reported that they had completed their journey not long before the Europeans arrived; now they lived peacefully on the banks of the Delaware River, hunting, gathering, and gardening. They made ceramic vessels and built houses of bark and other perishable materials, without stone foundations or chimneys. Archaeologists believe that contrary to the Indians' oral traditions, the Lenapes were in the Delaware Valley for millennia; there is evidence of civilizations that passed through multiple stages of development on some of the same sites.[25]

The Lenapes practiced a harsh physical discipline, and it toughened their youth against the elements. They dressed for the season, but never too warmly. They wore deerskin moccasins, which let in water prodigiously, or went barefoot. In the coldest months they wore layered garments of animal skins, fastened at the waist with snakeskin or leather thongs. The forest was their school, and the spirits of nature spoke to them in a quiet voice, perhaps like the one that Quakers heard inside themselves.

The high-yielding red clay soil of the inner coastal plain that the Northampton Quakers farmed was better than the English dirt they had known, and better too than the rocky New Jersey piedmont and highlands in the northwestern part of the colony or the sandy outer coastal plain to the southeast along the Atlantic shore. Soft pine and hard oak, both useful for building, predominated in the mixed forests they cleared. Indians had routinely burned off the underbrush, meaning that the habitat was good for border wildlife, such as rabbits and deer, and the tree cover was less dense. The plants that thrived there were what we now call successional vegetation, with annual herbs, such as ragweed and foxtail grass, and perennials that included aster, goldenrod, and bluestem grass, all of which had their place in settlers' pharmacopeias.[26]

Poison ivy and red cedar were invading species new to the immigrants, and the forest had panthers, black bears, wolves, lynxes, skunks, wildcats, elks, raccoons, minks, red and gray foxes, muskrats, rabbits, squirrels, and snakes, including rattlesnakes, in addition to the venison on the hoof that they so enjoyed. New Jersey's rivers and streams were home to a plenitude of fish, but also otters and beavers. The howling and yelping of wolves disrupted the sleep of the first settlers, but it was the lice, ticks, and especially the mosquitoes that ravaged them. The Swedish traveler Peter Kalm remarked in 1748, "The gnats, which are very troublesome at night here, are called mosquitoes . . . In daytime or at night they come into the houses, and when the people have gone to bed they begin their disagreeable humming, approach nearer and nearer to the bed, and at last suck up so much blood that they can hardly fly away." Settlers assured Kalm that the mosquitoes were less troublesome than they had been in the seventeenth century, but the insects remained vectors for disease, especially malaria, which the inhabitants called ague. "When they stung me here at night," Kalm reported, "my face was so disfigured by little red spots and blisters that I was almost ashamed to show myself." Tent caterpillars, which the settlers combated with torches, also plagued their apple and peach trees right from the start.[27]

The first Quaker settlers harvested native plants and animals for their own consumption and also to sell in Philadelphia; game and fish provided sustenance and barter for tools and other supplies. Subsequent generations built up a healthy commercial fishery, while farming and herding domestic animals replaced hunting and gathering as commercial enterprises and as the main sources of provisions. Sturgeon fishing predominated in the Delaware, where shad were less plentiful than they were farther upstream. Trout, bass, perch, catfish, eel, and frog legs all were consumed locally. Nets and gigs (three-pronged spears) were the principal fishing tools, but the construction of ponds where fish could be stocked and

Indian methods for driving fish became common practices. By the early nineteenth century the fish populations had so declined that legislation defined fishing seasons, limits on the size and number of fish that could be taken, and the methods that could be used.

Cranberries, blueberries, and huckleberries grew wild and were widely harvested throughout the colonial period. Settlers used cordgrass for roof thatching, and they always maintained open pastures for grazing domestic animals, which expanded greatly during the first generations of settlement. Dogs were the only domestic animals the Indians kept, and the Europeans' roaming pigs, cattle, and sheep invaded their garden plots and competed with native animals in foraging for wild ground cover. The destructiveness of free-ranging hogs and the unauthorized hunting of them caused countless strains on Indian-settler relations; laws to control pigs and sheep were passed as early as the 1680s. Early Quakers gave their horses and cattle free run of the forests, but fences, built principally of red cedar, predominated by Woolman's lifetime. In 1750 about 64 percent of Burlington County land was cleared for farming; by 1769 less than 30 percent of the county's land was forested. Settlers had harvested the wood for fuel, for their own building, and for selling to Philadelphia, and now they maintained woodlots only on rocky, swampy, and otherwise agriculturally unproductive land.

By Woolman's childhood, the wolves, otters, and wildcats had gone; the deer population was severely diminished; and beavers were rare. During his adulthood laws restricted the hunting of deer and the use of dogs and animal traps for hunting, because the game had been so depleted. Before Woolman's death it was rare that a black bear, and rarer yet that a wolf or rattlesnake, would be found outside the highlands in northwestern New Jersey. Within seventy-five years of Northampton's settlement, the populations of passenger pigeons had significantly declined, as a result of netting and overgrazing of the woodlands by hogs that competed for the acorns on which the birds lived. The settlers also made a significant dent in the crow and grackle populations, which they hunted for food and destroyed as pests that consumed their grain (principally wheat, corn, and rye). By the early nineteenth century, legislated hunting seasons restricted this human predation of wildfowl.

A prosperous farm in Burlington County in the mid-eighteenth century had four hundred to five hundred acres, including pasturelands, woodlots, and orchards, and wheat was the preeminent cash crop. In the early years farmers grew both summer and winter wheat; over time winter wheat, sown in the fall and harvested in the early summer, became more common. The farmers became adept at the use of fertilizers and the rotation of crops, which helped increase the yield. Farmers learned from the Indians how to sow corn in the spring and harvest it in the summer as food for both domestic animals and themselves. They used cornstalks and straw as fodder. Buckwheat and oats were not commercial crops but were widely grown for domestic consumption. Many different vegetables grew on New Jersey soil: turnips, cabbage, asparagus, onions, carrots, peas, beans, and cauliflower. Pumpkins and other squashes were also common. Potatoes were the most important of the noncommercial crops and were consumed by farm families and fed to animals.

Flax and hemp were common nonedible crops, used for their seeds and fibers. Settlers wove the longer flax fibers into linen and the shorter, less desirable fibers into tow, a coarser cloth. They extracted linseed oil from flax and made ropes from hemp. Orchards became ubiquitous in the region, and the grafting of fruit trees was an important skill. Farmers developed many hybrid varieties of apples, some valued for cider and others for cooking or eating raw. The quantity of hard cider produced and consumed was formidable—it was the preferred drink over beer—but impossible to gauge with any precision.

New Jerseyans experimented with foraging crops—red clover, timothy, trefoil, fowl meadow grass, alfalfa, and ryegrass—because cattle were important not only for meat but also for milk, cheese, and butter. Estimates in the early eighteenth century considered that about 1,100 gallons of milk could be expected annually from the average cow in Burlington County, from which could be made 138 pounds of butter or 275 pounds of cheese, all of which had a market in Philadelphia. Corn was the preferred feed for pigs; a neighbor of Woolman's estimated that on a corn diet his hogs gained as much as three-quarters of a pound per day and reached an average size of 150 pounds at slaughter. It was not unusual for a farmer to keep one or two hogs each year for family use. Burlington County farmers raised about 10 percent of all the sheep in New Jersey in the mid-eighteenth century; mutton was not as popular as beef, though Philadelphians bought the surplus. Some farmers specialized in egg production for commercial purposes, but ducks were not widely kept for their eggs. Beekeeping was common, honey being the principal local sweetener and beeswax essential for candlemaking.[28]

THE first American John Woolman and his wife, Elizabeth, built a house within view of the Rancocas River, near what was to become the village of Rancocas in Northampton Township. A surveyor's map of the original Northampton settlement shows that John Woolman's 130-acre plot was one of the smallest, much less substantial than that of Daniel Wills, who is described in the records as a doctor. The shape and layout of the tracts reflect initial efforts to distribute more or less equally the different types of land, from the rich but often soggy riverine soil to the higher but rockier ground. The first settlers shared the benefits and deficits of the river and creeks. The first road they built passed through most of the settlers' homesteads. Part of the tax burden would have required each settler to maintain the stretch of road that crossed his land.[29]

Friends formally established Rancocas Meeting in 1681. Initially, they met in the house of one Thomas Harding; then over the years they alternated among the homes of Harding, Woolman, and Wills, whose farms all ran along the river. Generations of Woolmans gave birth in the first Woolman house, and the John Woolman of this book was born there. It stood until 1806, when descendants tore it down and used the bricks for a larger new house, possibly built on higher ground.[30]

We know little more about the first generation of American Woolmans than that they were adventurers brave enough to have crossed the ocean and resettled in an alien land, substantial members of their new community, and respected elders in the Quaker Meeting. Once a neighbor sued John when his animals broke down a fence and damaged the man's corn; eventually arbitration settled the case, apparently amicably. Woolman was also among those who

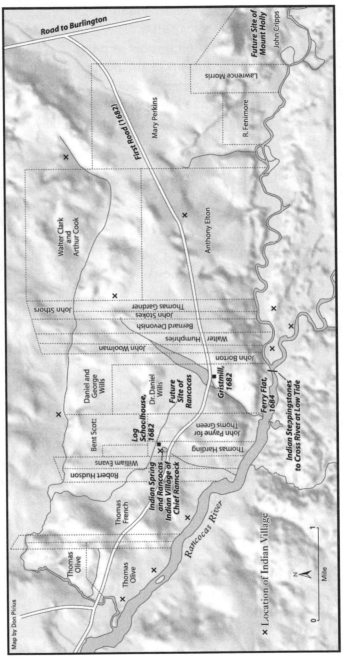

Rancocas Settlement, Northampton Township, New Jersey, ca. 1680–90. From
Charles Stokes, Survey 1872, original in collections of the Burlington County Historical Society Library

signed a complaint against rioters who broke down the Burlington jail doors in 1703 and set the prisoners free. Interestingly, John's father, William, was living in the house of a neighbor rather than with John's family when he died in 1692, and in his will he left a substantial bequest to his hosts. Had father William and son John had a falling-out? It is curious that for all they had endured together, they ended up living apart.[31]

John and Elizabeth Woolman both died in 1718, within a month of each other. Nine other people were living in the family house at that time: three unmarried daughters; their son, Samuel, Samuel's wife, Elizabeth Burr Woolman, and their three daughters; and an apprentice. Samuel inherited the farm and house, where he and his wife had already been living since 1714. Like his father, Samuel was both a weaver and a farmer. He and the apprentice practiced their trade on two looms in the house. Eventually, Samuel's three sisters left the household; one married, and the thirteen children born to Samuel and Elizabeth must have eventually squeezed out the other two. The children were, in the order of their births, Elizabeth, Sarah, Patience, John, Asher, Abner, Hannah, Uriah, Esther, Jonah, Rachel, Abraham, and Eber. All grew to adulthood in that house. The protagonist of this book, then, was the fourth child and first son in a family of seven boys and six girls. Woolman says in passing that his parents had a "large family of children," but he mentions neither parents nor siblings by name.[32]

In rural areas such as Northampton, Quaker children began their formal schooling at the age of six or seven, although occasionally as young as four, and continued for several years at most. Quakers did not farm out their children to be taught by strangers, as New England Puritans and southern planters did, so teachers were esteemed members of the community, organized around the local Meeting. The point of education was, in Quaker parents' eyes, to school their children in the ways of their faith and, by their methods, to shelter the youngsters from the outside world.[33]

Quakers were not hostile to book learning in its place, but neither did they favor development of the mind over that of the body and soul. Like John Locke, whose views on child rearing had been influenced by Quaker practices, they believed that "children's constitutions are either spoiled, or at least harmed, by *cockering* [pampering, spoiling, coddling] and *tenderness*." Locke advised against dressing children too warmly in winter or summer. "Our bodies will endure anything that from the beginning they are accustomed to," Locke wrote in *Some Thoughts Concerning Education*, a book that Woolman owned when he drafted his *Journal*. Locke directed his advice principally to the raising of boys, and acknowledged the more "tender" constitutions of girls. Boys should wash their feet in cold water daily, year-round. Going barefoot would also help toughen their constitutions. Shoes that let in water are better than those that do not, something that the Lenape Indians also believed. It is even beneficial to harden babies by degrees until they can tolerate "their feet in cold water in ice and snow," according to Locke. Teach boys to swim, expose them to the open air often, and deny them time sitting by the fire during winter months. Locke warned against hats and gloves and believed that exposure to the sun does children good. Plenty of exercise and a simple diet complemented Locke's physical regimen. Children should eat "flesh" no more than once a day and consume unbuttered bread for other meals instead of meat or fish.

> For *breakfast* and *supper, milk, milk-pottage, water-gruel, flummery,** and twenty other things that we are wont to make in England are very fit for children; only, in all these, let care be taken that they be plain and without much mixture, and very sparingly seasoned with *sugar*, or rather none at all; especially all *spice* and other things that may heat the blood are carefully to be avoided.[34]

Quaker parents who adopted such strict regimens for their children did so from love. They saw the hardening of bodies as tenderness for the soul, and they raised their children with affection rather than stern discipline. Locke's advice supported the Quakers' tender parenting, for which they were widely known and which in its

---

*Potage or pottage, synonymous with porridge, is a thick vegetable or grain soup. Gruel is a thin, watery porridge. Flummery is a gelatinous pudding made by straining boiled oatmeal. All are bland, nutritious, and easily digested.

broadest application contributed to the inculcation of self-discipline and the nurturing of warm hearts. But over the course of the eighteenth century, tender parenting lost much of its firm core among them. Woolman believed that this spiritual decline was a product of misguided love, of spoiling children rather than preparing them to make their own way in a cold world.

Quaker books of spiritual instruction set out a curriculum consistent with parents' spiritual ambitions for their children. The primer widely used in colonial America during John Woolman's youth listed vocabulary to be learned by rote ("abolished," "abomination," "absence"); consonant-vowel combinations to assist with phonetic reading (ab, abs, bab, gab, hab, habs, jab); and penmanship models for upper- and lowercase letters. It listed proper names from the Bible, divided into syllables for ease of learning. There were reading lessons—"Christ is my Life. Christ is my Saviour. Christ is my hope of Glory"—and a catechism, a summary of Christian doctrine in question-and-answer form that predated the Reformation and that students memorized and recited from prompts: "Who are true Christians? Such as believe in the Light of Christ, and are led and guided by Christ Jesus. Why are the true Christians called Quakers in this age? It is in scorn and derision that they are so called, to render them and the Truth odious to the people, that so they might not receive the Truth and be saved." The primer also included biblical proverbs, "directions to read and spell truly," "hard words used in our English tongue," Roman numerals, multiplication tables, weights and measures, an explanation of the British monetary system, guidance on keeping a record of daily expenses, and a perpetual almanac.[35]

William Penn wrote a book of maxims that Quaker schoolmasters regularly assigned to their pupils. *Some Fruits of Solitude* articulates Quaker principles and embodies the limited role that education played in Quaker thought. The truth that Penn shared with young readers came not from book learning but as "the fruit of solitude: a school few care to learn in, though none instructs us better." Listening rather than speaking, meditation rather than ceaseless action, were the paths that Penn laid out for the young scholars, who learned to read by memorizing his maxims on the right conduct of life.[36]

Eighteenth-century Quaker students did arithmetic and practiced their penmanship on paper purchased from the schoolmaster along with the books and supplies he required them to use. They read the Bible, the primer, Penn's maxims, and devotional tracts, among them Elizabeth Jacob's *An Epistle in True Love, Containing a Farewell Exhortation to Friends Families.* Jacob warned children against "the spirit of the world, pride, covetousness, [and] fleshly ease, with self-interest." She admonished them to revere their parents and to model themselves on Quaker adults, to shun the carnal world, tell the truth always, renounce vanities, and avoid "the fellowship and friendship of those who do not profess with us." Better, indeed, to retire, read, or meditate on "heavenly subjects" than to waste God's precious gift of time on frivolous games and light-hearted conviviality. John Woolman abided by this advice when he sat alone reading the Bible rather than playing with fellow students on his way home from the Quaker school.[37]

Since the revelation that Woolman recalled in his *Journal* occurred on Seventh Day, a break in the weekly routine lay ahead on the Sabbath, although not a respite from hard benches.* Quaker children began attending Meeting for Worship at about the same age they started school, and the discipline of Meeting was more challenging than the schoolmaster's. There were two First Day worship services of about two hours each and another midweek. Children sat in the silence just as adults did, waiting for the Light to inspire ministry—the quiet voice of God inside them to provide an insight, a revelation, which should then be spoken aloud. Ideally, messages delivered out of the silence were unplanned; since there was no preparation, a speaker did not know where his sermon was headed when he began. Any speaker from the congregation was a minister, although Meeting elders, the designated leaders or "weighty Friends," formally recognized some as gifted in this regard. Sermons often started slowly and quickened as ministers

---

*Quakers and Puritans used numerical references to days and months rather than what they considered "pagan" nomenclature. According to the Old Style calendar of Woolman's youth, the year began on March 25 for all the English-speaking world, and this practice continued until September 1752, when the British Empire adopted the modern Gregorian calendar, with January as the first month of the year.

spoke, eventually reaching the cadence and pitch of a song. Sometimes ministers achieved ecstatic states; trances, prophecies, and recountings of visions or dreams all were possible.[38]

In content the messages could be jeremiads—lamentations of the sort associated with the Old Testament prophet Jeremiah—on the state of the world, Quakerism, or the young. The revelations could be admonishments against worldly attachments or advice on preparing for death, but children likely welcomed these breaks in the silence nonetheless, as their lives otherwise lacked the theatricality of the spoken, chanted, or sung messages inspired by the Light. Boys and girls sat separately in the meetinghouse, often in a gallery, with adult volunteers among them to be models; children did not always behave appropriately, but the adults simply continued their silent waiting, making no comment on any ruckus around them.[39]

Woolman recalled a childhood that lacked celebration, and he did not romanticize his youth. No recollections survive from other children who attended the same Meeting for Worship or school with him, but we can surmise some things about the lives of young Friends. Children in Woolman's day bathed infrequently; their soap was not perfumed. There was less laundering and more "honest" perspiration in their lives than in those of us who exercise for our health rather than labor by the sweat of our brows. These and other features of his childhood seemed unexceptional to Woolman. In his *Journal*, the school day is there behind him, undescribed, as he sits reading the Bible, and Meeting for Worship the next day lies before him, but not out of sight. To Woolman those details are irrelevant in recounting his epiphany.

The school's immediate environs had changed between the time it was built in 1681 and when Woolman became a pupil there, almost fifty years later. Chief Ramcock, head of the Rancocas band when the first Quakers had arrived, and Thomas Harding, on whose land the school was built, both were dead; John Stokes had bought Harding's property in 1712. Cows grazed near where Woolman sat to read the Bible, though he does not mention them because he took cattle, springs, magnolias, Indians, fields, and forests for granted as part of the landscape, all of them beside the point he wanted to make in the *Journal*. The barnyard smells of chickens, manure, and sour milk dried on calves' mouths were the same then as now, and the tune of bawling bovines grows no more melodious with the passage of time, in season with caws and croaks, a daily chorus accompanying everything the students read and their teacher said. Woolman does not tell us whether students exploded from the school when their teacher dismissed them or exited decorously. They may have sounded like fireworks, but they looked plain and wore few bright colors, all cut from the same cloth. And when they careened through what was left of the forest and out into the fields and sun, Woolman sat with his Bible. Voices trailed off from his serene spot. "The place where I sat and the sweetness that attended my mind remains fresh in my memory," John Woolman wrote when he was thirty-six about himself as a boy. He told of the "sweetness" inside his head but nothing of the "place" where he sat.[40]

We do not know what the other children thought of Woolman or how he reacted to them. Were they active and he sedate? Did they find him too good to be true or was their decorum similar to his? Perhaps they shared his values and judged themselves deficient in contrast with his model. He writes nothing of his friendships in his early boyhood. We cannot tell whether he was already isolated and preaching to his classmates or the *Journal* constructs the not entirely accurate portrait of an ideal youth. There may be clues here to his later ambitions to distance himself from others, to reject intimacy on ascetic grounds, and to make harsh judgments on what he considered excessive paternal love and the spiritual pitfalls of friendship. Or he may have known, but simply did not write about, the joy of dashing through the forest with abandon.

The *Journal* describes Woolman's epiphany: "I read the twenty-second chapter of the Revelations."

Then the angel showed me the river of the water of life, bright as crystal, flowing from the throne of God and of the Lamb through the middle of the street of the city. On either side of the river is the tree of life with its twelve kinds of fruit, producing its fruit each month; and the leaves of the tree are for the healing of the nations. Nothing accursed will be found there any more. But the throne of God and of the Lamb will be in it, and his servants will worship him; they will see his face, and his name will be on their foreheads. And there will be no more night; they need no light of lamp or sun, for the Lord God will be their light, and they will reign forever and ever.

And he said to me, "These words are trustworthy and true, for the Lord, the God of the spirits of the prophets, has sent his angel to show his servants what must soon take place."

"See, I am coming soon! Blessed is the one who keeps the words of the prophecy of this book . . . ."

"And in reading it my mind was drawn to seek after [and long for] that pure habitation which I then believed God had prepared for his servants," Woolman wrote. These are images of heaven that stuck with him in the decades ahead.[41]

Revelation 22 offers a naturalistic vision of heaven. Crystalline water in abundance, the tree of life's ever-bearing fruit and healing leaves, and the comforting warmth of eternal life—these would supplant New Jersey's long, cold winter nights, ubiquitous death, and possibly even a sensitive youngster's sleep-haunting nightmares. The "pure habitation" of Revelation 22 enchanted the boy, at least as Woolman recalled the experience. As a place without artificial ornamentation, just as God created it, it also suits the Quaker aesthetic of simplicity.

Woolman did not mention the city, another vision of heaven, this one enclosed, that the angel reveals in the previous chapter of Revelation, just before the quoted passage:

The wall is built of jasper, while the city is pure gold, clear as glass. The foundations of the wall of the city are adorned with every jewel; the first was jasper, the second sapphire, the third agate, the fourth emerald, the fifth onyx, the sixth carnelian, the seventh chrysolite, the eight beryl, the ninth topaz, the tenth chrysoprase, the eleventh jacinth, the twelfth amethyst. And the twelve gates are twelve pearls, each of the gates is a single pearl, and the street of the city is pure gold, transparent as glass.

These biblical streets of gold and urban walls of precious stones were too ornate for Quaker tastes and beyond the imagination of this boy. Woolman chose a more congenial rural heaven that improved on the world he already knew.

Woolman interpreted the quiet spot he found to read scripture on that Saturday after school as an opportunity to "hear" God. "This and the like gracious visitations," he continues, "had that effect upon me, that when boys used ill language it troubled me, and through the continued mercies of God I was preserved from it." So Woolman implies that he heard God regularly, that God graciously visited him, and this kept him from "ill language." "Gracious" in this case is the adjectival form of "grace," which blessed Woolman as he welcomed the spirit within him.[42]

These concepts are not coincidentally juxtaposed in Woolman's *Journal*. Silence provided an opportunity for him to hear God. The reading of scripture did not lead him to God, but rather the voice of God led him to read Scriptures, which in turn gave him a spiritual vision and sure knowledge of the paradise that he now sought. Inspiration came directly to him, mediated by neither the book nor an adult. Ideally, this is how Quaker mysticism works. Woolman believed that God spoke to him from an internal quiet and "preserved" him from using "ill language" as he would have done without divine intercession.

All the children in Woolman's family practiced silence, as their parents required, learning not to break the quiet frivolously. On Sunday after Meeting for Worship, Woolman tells us, his mother and father "put us to read in the Holy Scriptures or some religious books, one [child] after another, the rest sitting by without much conversation, which I have since often thought was a good practice." The books are important, for they introduce language into the silence, but the relations among text, believer, quiet, and voice of God differ significantly from those of Protestants who claim the Bible as the sole source of revelation. From the very start Quakers taught their children that "carnal"—loose, frivolous, worldly—speaking corrupted them. Language could either threaten or support their faith. God was the Word to Quakers; used rightly, language was holy. They found biblical inspiration for what they called plain speech in the Gospel of Matthew 12:36–37: "I tell you, on the day of judgment you will have to give an account for every careless word you utter; for by your words you will be justified, and by your words you will be condemned."[43]

Any talking or activity that was not spiritually directed was a "corruption" of the spirit. "Ill language" is not necessarily what we would consider "bad" words—cursing, scatological references, insults, disruptive remarks, or rudeness. It might be nothing more than "loose," playful, unnecessary, what Woolman would consider "frivolous" speech. By the eighteenth century most Quakers probably did not follow such advice as strictly as the Woolmans, for whom "secular" words were "carnal." The Woolmans' practice was consistent with the perspective of the founders of the Society of Friends. What we would consider good-humored, chaste playfulness they reviled as sinful because it distracted children from God.[44]

Likewise, as adults Quakers tried to avoid spurious speech. They declined to exchange what they considered empty pleasantries, formulaic, trite, and meaningless expressions that corrupted their content. Others interpreted such behavior as rude. Quakers refused to take oaths on the ground that they were meaningless speech acts; a man who would lie in passing, they thought, was no more likely to tell the truth when he swore. It was a matter of integrity. They thought it dishonest to greet someone insincerely or to inquire about the health of another lightly; they avoided honorific and deferential titles of address—"your Excellency" and "your humble servant," for example. To call a man master when he was not your master was to lie. To describe yourself as the servant of someone to whom you were not bound in service was equally untrue. Quakers believed these conventions were sinful, and they endured the rage provoked by their lack of deference as a "cross" to bear in imitation of Christ.

The Quaker adoption of the informal "thee" and "thou" over the formal "you" also angered their social equals and betters.

"Thee" and "thou" implied familiarity and even intimacy. The English conventionally reserved the terms for close relations—parents to children, siblings to one another, husbands to wives and wives to husbands—and among good friends. But to use "thee" when addressing another man's wife, for example, was considered a provocation; to do it to a parent, teacher, or employer was grounds for a whipping, which Quakers endured often in the early years of the Society of Friends. The explanation they gave for this variant of plain speech was that "you" addressed to an individual was grammatically incorrect, since the pronoun is plural. Along with other aspects of plain speech, the Quakers' informality challenged convention and gave them a shared identity that separated them from the "carnal" world.

When young Woolman's reverie, but not his silence, broke on that Saturday after school, he walked or ran home along the dirt road that swept downhill toward the Rancocas River and transected the low ground of his family's farm. Unless he took a shortcut through forest or field, he then turned from the road to the higher ground on which the house stood. This is the entry to Woolman's life that the *Journal* provides metaphorically, allegorically, symbolically, and, in the end, literally if the reader is open to his belief that we are more our souls than our bodies, that the physical is merely a hook on which we get caught, that an author's silences are as meaningful as his words, and that our life's path is most significantly traveled inside ourselves.

2

Transition

1729–30

B ENJAMIN Franklin's *Pennsylvania Gazette* reported on Burlington (town and county), New Jersey, beginning in 1729,
when John Woolman was nine years old. Two newsworthy events
during the next decade the felling of a huge bear and a witchcraft
trial—may have occurred within several miles of Woolman's home.
Both would have warranted a prominent place in an account of his
childhood, had he written about his exterior life.

The bear was one of two sighted when Woolman was ten.

> There has lately been kill'd near Mount Holly, in the Jersies,
> the largest Bear that has been known to these Parts; his Fore-
> head measur'd two Spans wide, his Leg just above the Foot
> as big as could be well grasp'd with both Hands after the Skin
> was off, and tho' exceeding lean he weigh'd upwards of 300
> weight. There has been another of the same gigantic size
> seen about the same place.[1]

A forehead two spans wide—that is, two hands stretched wide,
thumb tip to thumb tip (the standard measure of an eighteenth-
century span is nine inches): this was indeed a large black bear. The
ankle was also monstrous, with a diameter of eight or nine inches.
Three-hundred-pound bears would have been remarkable in this

region even before the Europeans arrived. In a place where so little disrupted the daily routine, children may have gaped at the bear carcass and admired the hunter who brought it down. Since there were two sightings and only one killed, furry monsters might have chased toddlers in their dreams; adolescents, to prove themselves and to tease, could have easily startled young children with pounces and growls that evoked screams.[2]

Woolman did not see bear spirits, hear their call, or commune with them in dreams, as the neighboring Lenape Indians did. He did not wrestle with the bear part of his nature or receive the gift of bear power bestowed at the whim of the beast. Witnessing the dead animal would have been enough, though, for a spiritually sensitive child to feel the bear's mystery and perhaps its anger at the unwelcome taking of its life. No, Woolman's spiritual experiences had some parallels to those of the Indians, but they differed, since they came from within him and were, as he understood it, opposed to nature rather than emanating from it. His was not the spirit of nature, but the spirit that transcended what he came to understand were the earthbound natures of living things. Woolman took lessons from animals that instructed his spiritual growth, but he apparently did not believe that animals have souls—transcendent spirits—that made God's grace accessible to all creatures.[3]

The Philadelphia newspaper reported on other events in Burlington County. One night a farmer hunted deer in his cornfield—"venison," as the newspaper put it, leaping over the animal to get right to the meat—and mistakenly shot a horse. Franklin used the story to raise a question of law, asking whether the farmer should have to compensate the horse's owner. After all, it had been an accident and the horse a trespasser. Franklin also reported on the butchering of a hog weighing 518 pounds, the size of which made it newsworthy.[4]

A "violent" gust of wind caused something heavy, like a tree, to crush two mares in Burlington County, but the newspaper provided no details. In the same week Burlingtonians spotted a ten-foot shark in the Delaware River. A man died from unspecified injuries two days after riding a horse at high speed into a cow, right in the middle of town. Cattle rambling through the streets of Burlington were apparently no novelty, but a man running one down was news. Franklin made no mention of the cow's fate. There was also a notice of the execution of two black men for poisoning "sundry persons," and the hangings spawned another tragic death in Burlington that was even more newsworthy:

> We have received from Burlington a most melancholy Account of the Death of a Boy of 5 Years old, last Week, who hanged himself on the Stake of a Fence with a Rope he had been playing with in the Yard. He was first discover'd by means of the Crying of a younger Child, BROTHER WON'T SPEAK TO ME. 'Tis thought that the abundance of Discourse he had heard of the late Execution of Negroes for Poisoning, had fill'd his Mind, and put him on imitating what he had heard was done, not knowing the Danger. It is said, that he dreamt much of the Execution the Night before, and telling his Dream in the Morning, added, AND I SHALL DIE TO DAY; which was not then regarded.[5]

A boy from Mount Holly went hunting and shot pigeons, which he hung over his gun. The dead birds slid down the barrel after he loaded and primed it; the weight released the trigger, which discharged the gun into the boy's chest. He died "on the spot." A few months later lightning struck a man and killed him instantly too. A house burned to the ground in Burlington because fear of explosion, based on a rumor that gunpowder was stored inside, kept anyone from getting close enough to douse the flames. A ship from Philadelphia capsized in strong winds off Burlington, and four of the seven people on board drowned. Two thieves mugged a man riding from Trenton to Burlington; both sides shed blood, and the attackers escaped unidentified.[6]

Events that make headlines do not compose lives, but extraordinary occurrences affect communities as small as those in eighteenth-century Burlington County. Childhoods are more than a string of deaths—a bear shot, a hog butchered, horses felled by windblown debris, a cow ridden down by a man who tumbled from his horse, murders, executions, a suicide, a hunting accident, and lightning strikes—but these were part of John Woolman's environment, just as were his school, the Friends Meeting he attended, and his family's loving, disciplined household.

In 1731, when John Woolman was ten, smallpox "raged" in Burlington County, as well as across the Delaware River in Bucks and Delaware counties, and in Philadelphia. Northampton did not escape the wrath of this horrible disease. Even more than large bears, smallpox frightened children, who lost parents, siblings, and friends, the disease killing many more children than lightning, bears, and accidents combined. Though most survived, no community struck, no household felled, no individual afflicted by smallpox was unscarred.

> At a Petty Sessions of the Peace, held for the County of Burlington at Burlington the 16th Day of April, 1731, it was consider'd that FAIRS generally occasion great Concourse of People from the most adjacent Places, and that at present it is not meet for keeping the FAIR at Burlington as usual, by reason of the great Mortality in Philadelphia, and other Parts of Pennsylvania, where the Small Pox now violently rages. Therefore, to prevent to the utmost Power of the said Justices, the further spreading of so epidemical and dangerous a Distemper, and more especially for that the approaching Heat of Summer may render it more malignant and fatal, It is Order'd, that MAY FAIR next, be, and is hereby prohibited to be kept in the said Town of Burlington, and all Persons are hereby to take Notice accordingly, as they will answer for their Contempt at their Perils.

Such extreme measures dictated by the authority of good sense and law did not work. Smallpox came just the same. It left death and fear behind when it passed in the late fall.[7]

Yet people in Burlington County may have gathered in Mount Holly in October 1730, only months before, as if for an autumn festival. According to Franklin's newspaper, more than three hundred New Jerseyans assembled there just days before John Woolman's tenth birthday, while smallpox raged across the river. They risked contracting and spreading the vile disease, not for a celebration but for a witchcraft trial.[8]

The Woolman family would not have been in such a crowd. Quakers had stood against what they saw as superstition right from the founding years of their faith. Indeed, their disbelief in witchcraft contributed, in the persecutory environment of seventeenth-century England, to charges that they were witches. Courts in the Quaker-founded colonies of Pennsylvania and New Jersey never convicted anyone of witchcraft. A mob stoned an accused witch to death in downtown Philadelphia as late as 1787; no one was prosecuted for this murder, but such violence was not sanctioned by law.

Quakers believed in evil, but they saw magic as at best a troubling frivolity and at worst as tinkering with the universe. An event like an unauthorized witch trial invaded the province of God, distracted people from more serious business, threatened violence, and broke the peace. The Woolmans would have stayed home and prayed for the accused, the accusers, and the crowd. As an adult John Woolman was uneasy in public gatherings that were not church-related, and magic in any guise unsettled him. He also feared smallpox and judged those who followed the crowd.[9]

An untold number of neighbors had, according to the *Gazette*, accused a man and a woman of making sheep "dance in an uncommon manner," but the paper did not say what the common manner of sheep dancing was. The accused witches caused "Hogs to speak, and sing Psalms, &c. to the great Terror and Amazement of the King's good and peaceable Subjects in this Province." These were serious charges in 1730—that is, if Franklin's report was not simply a satire of rural New Jersey life—even if no statute law backed them up.[10]

How seriously did people take the charges or the tests used to identify a witch? The newspaper said that spectators expected the trials to reveal the accused as witches, suggesting that both belief in witches and faith in the time-tested folk methods of identification were widely shared. Franklin was portraying the people of Mount Holly's environs as bumpkins who lived in an outmoded mental world. Even if the witch trials were a creation of Franklin's fertile imagination, the nature of his humor, the choice of locale, and

its contrast with Philadelphia's cosmopolitan culture suggest that
Mount Holly was, at least in his mind, a backwater remarkable for ignorance and superstition, beyond the pale of the Enlightenment.[11]

The Mount Holly residents in Franklin's story were handling
the witchcraft charges extralegally but with the sanction of a local
justice. The accused and their accusers negotiated the tests without
judicial mediation, and the "mob" played a role that had no standing in law.

> The Accusers being very positive that if the Accused were
> weighed in Scales against a Bible, the Bible would prove too
> heavy for them; or that, if they were bound and put into the
> River, they would swim; the said Accused desirous to make
> their Innocence appear, voluntarily offered to undergo the
> said Trials, if 2 of the most violent of their Accusers would be
> tried with them. Accordingly the Time and Place was agreed
> upon, and advertised about the Country.[12]

The story's curious, outraged, fearful, and titillated citizens assembled at the advertised time and place, and a "grand consulta-
tion" among them ensued. Since the witnesses outnumbered the
principals in the case by about three hundred to four, the crowd
served as a jury of sorts. Whether by vote or acclamation they dictated that scales should come first. Their logic, or Franklin's, is unclear—perhaps it was traditional practice—but by selecting the
safer test first, they guaranteed that both would take place and that
the Bible would suffer no water damage. Four people were report-
edly tried that day.

> A Committee of Men were appointed to search the Men, and
> a Committee of Women to search the Women, to see if they
> had any Thing of Weight about them, particularly Pins. After
> the Scrutiny was over, a huge great Bible belonging to the
> Justice of the Place was provided, and a Lane through the
> Populace was made from the Justice's House to the Scales,
> which were fixed on a Gallows erected for that Purpose op-
> posite to the House, that the Justice's Wife and the rest of
> the Ladies might see the Trial, without coming amongst the

Mob; and after the Manner of *Moorfields*, a large Ring was also made.[13]

What a wonderful opening to the world in which the ten-year-old John Woolman lived, even if the story is not true! The scene reveals hierarchical relationships of class and gender often hidden from our view as well as both the literal and symbolic significance of gallows, witches, mobs, the Bible, and pins. The gallows demonstrates just how seriously it was understood that lives were at stake in these trials. The humorous tone in which singing and dancing animals were described was the skeptical Franklin's; the country folk took the issues more gravely.

Some people still believed (and the belief was to survive for another century or more) that witches carried pins, often invisible, to prick those they tormented. Perhaps the witches had pinpricked the animals to make the sheep dance and hogs sing, but no pins could magically lighten the "huge great" Bible. Although it did not actually outweigh the accused and their accusers, God's Word had a magic all its own that could more than balance a witch. The ceremony of carrying the sacred book to the gallows, copied from English practice, was performed at executions. It had been performed when the Burlington community hanged the two slaves for poisoning white people. Everyone got the point.

> Then came out of the House a grave tall Man carrying the Holy Writ before the supposed Wizard, &c. (as solemnly as the Sword-bearer of *London* before the Lord Mayor) the Wizard was first put in the Scale, and over him was read a Chapter out of the Books of *Moses*, and then the Bible was put in the other Scale, (which being kept down before) was immediately let go; but to the great Surprize of the Spectators, Flesh and Bones came down plump, and outweighed that great good Book by abundance.[14]

We do not know what the "grave tall" man read from the Old Testament, whether the chapter was about animals, unnatural acts, temptations of the devil, or Jehovah's retribution for sin; it was important to read the Word of God and witness the accused wizard's reaction. Did he cower, snarl, or suffer visible pain? Apparently not. It would have disappointed people who came all this way only to witness a man tip the scales against a book, hardly worth the trip. Unfortunately for those who risked smallpox and had traveled so far, the other accused witches and the two accusers also outweighed the Good Book.

The report's irreverent tone, casting the event in a festive light, suggests Franklin's lighthearted view of beliefs that Quakers judged soberly: "After the same Manner, the others were served, and their Lumps of Mortality severally were too heavy for *Moses* and all the Prophets and Apostles." A modern reader might suspect from the start that the story was a fabrication, but we have evidence of other genuine witchcraft accusations and collective violence from the period. Or perhaps the charges emanated from social stresses within the community rather than from an ongoing battle between Satan and God; the crowd at Mount Holly or newspaper readers the next week may have wondered the same thing.

On to test number two.

This being over, the Accusers and the rest of the Mob, not satisfied with this Experiment, would have the Trial by Water; accordingly a most solemn Procession was made to the Millpond; where both Accused and Accusers being stripp'd (saving only to the Women their Shifts) were bound Hand and Foot, and severally placed in the Water, lengthways, from the Side of a Barge or Flat, having for Security only a Rope about the Middle of each, which was held by some in the Flat.

Witches float; Christians sink. The catch here is that the innocent drown, leaving the witches to be executed by other means. Fortunately, the evolution of the practice since the Middle Ages added a rope by which the sinking innocent could be saved without grave risk. We now know that the world is composed of sinkers and floaters and that the difference between them has to do with relative density of fat to body type and weight. The writer for the *Pennsylvania Gazette* suspected as much, knowing that floaters considerably outnumber sinkers. (Franklin was a strong swimmer.)

The male Accuser Man being thin and spare, with some Difficulty began to sink at last; but the rest every one of them swam very light upon the Water. A Sailor in the Flat jump'd out upon the Back of the Man accused, thinking to drive him down to the Bottom; but the Person bound, without any Help, came up some time before the other. The Woman Accuser, being told that she did not sink, would be duck'd a second Time; when she swam again as light as before. Upon which she declared, That she believed the Accused had bewitched her to make her so light, and that she would be duck'd again a Hundred Times, but she would duck the Devil out of her. The accused Man, being surpriz'd at his own Swimming, was not so confident of his Innocence as before, but said, *If I am a Witch, it is more than I know*.[15]

Fascinating. Evidence did not sway the female accuser. She stubbornly insisted that her floating proved the accused had bewitched her too. Nice try. On the other hand, not sinking seemed to alarm the accused man, who evidently believed in the tests and doubted himself. The accused woman floated too, but the newspaper does not report her reaction.

The outcome was indecisive to some, and not everyone was willing to set the floaters free. The gallows were there for a purpose, and people had come a long way.

The more thinking Part of the Spectators were of Opinion, that any Person so bound and plac'd in the Water (unless they were mere Skin and Bones) would swim till their Breath was gone; and their Lungs fill'd with Water. But it being the general Belief of the Populace, that the Women's Shifts, and the Garters with which they were bound help'd to support them; it is said they are to be tried again the next warm Weather, naked.[16]

What about the floating man, who wore no shift or garters? Was he treated as a witch? The newspaper does not say, suggesting that the "more thinking Part of the Spectators" prevailed.

The "mob" of Franklin's story accepted the test as indecisive but not flawed. His spectators were reluctant to hang the women but may have been ready to string up the accused wizard. Perhaps we should also wonder whether the proposed retest with naked women had other than spiritual sources of appeal. We do not know, though, whether the Mount Holly folk dunked the women again when the weather grew warm—a thoughtful concession from a bloodthirsty crowd?—or what became of the "convicted" man. The story is intriguing even without those details, however, for its exploration of social fault lines, the enduring threat of magic and the power of folk beliefs, the delicate balance between a "mob" and those who represented the law, and the competing logics of John Woolman's community. This was the world he knew, experimental and traditional, ignorant and thoughtful—to paraphrase the *Gazette*—divided and united at the same time. Franklin got it exactly right.[17]

W OOLMAN'S concern took them all in: the hurt and the hurtful, the accusers and the accused, the judges, the witnesses, and the animals too. Perhaps it was easier for him as a moral outsider to love them all. He worried about his neighbors, mainly about their souls, but they all—black, white, and Indian—were strangers to him. He saw the hand of God in lightning strikes, killing winds, accidents, and smallpox. He saw God in nature and in humanity. He witnessed the best and testified to the worst in all of us. The question is how the boy who read the Bible became the saint and reformer that John Woolman did, why injustice moved him—to both prayer and social engagement—while others in his town, his faith community, and his family lagged behind.

Although Woolman does not tell us any specific story about Northampton during his childhood, he shares a general observation about the people around him—his parents, siblings, teachers, and fellow Quakers: "From what I had read and heard, I believed there had been in past ages people who walked in uprightness before God in a degree exceeding any that I knew, or heard of, now living; and the apprehension of there being less steadiness and firmness amongst people in this age than in past ages often troubled me while I was a child." This might be read as a harsh judgment or as a reflection of ego, but neither reading fits the *Journal* or the man who wrote it. The sentence simply expresses Woolman's regret at his lack of acquaintance with saints. This was not to say that his family and coreligionists were spiritually inadequate, for he makes clear elsewhere that he respected his parents, believed them godly people, and credited them with raising their children well. But they fell short of the saintly ideal to which the boy who became the writer of the *Journal* aspired. Nor did Woolman mean to imply that he had achieved this ideal. He would never have equated his life and spirituality with those of saints he had read about.[18]

The passage suggests that as a boy Woolman already knew *Primitive Christianity* (1672), a book by the English cleric William Cave that he owned as an adult. In the Preface, Cave explains that the "corrupt" ways of men in his time led him back to the first three or four centuries of the church in search of "true Christian Piety and Simplicity." Cave found in the early Christians what inspired young John Woolman.

Here he will find a *Piety* Active and Zealous, shining through the blackest Clouds of Malice and Cruelty; afflicted *innocence* triumphant, notwithstanding all the powerful or politick Attempts of Men or Devils; a *patience* unconquerable under the biggest Persecutions; a *charity* truly *Catholick* and unlimited; a *simplicity* and upright Carriage in all Transactions; a *sobriety* and *temperance* remarkable to the admiration of their Enemies; and in short, he will here see the Divine and Holy Precepts of the Christian Religion drawn down into Action, and the most Excellent *genius* and Spirit of the Gospel breathing in the Hearts and Lives of these good Old Christians.[19]

That was the Christian John Woolman strove to become. As a boy, though, he had a way to go. Even with the saintly model of primitive Christianity laid before him, pious parents, a sensitive nature, heaven inscribed on his mind, and God dwelling in his heart, he remained a sinner. Woolman wanted readers to know that his journey was just beginning at the age of ten and that life ahead was a thicket, cleared only in retrospect.

By composing Woolman's childhood in four stages on his way to convincement—certain knowledge of his relationship with God—the *Journal* conformed to the expectations of his church and the model of Quaker autobiography. The first stage began with his epiphany at age seven and lasted for about three years. This can be described as Woolman's age of innocence or revelations, when he was first conscious of God bestowing grace on him.

A Chester, New Jersey, Friend named John Hunt (1740–1824) experienced grace at an early age just as Woolman did.

At divers times in my very youthful days, and particularly when about eight years of age, I was favoured with the tendering visitations of Divine goodness; the effects of which were marked in my countenance and deportment, so as to attract the notice of my friends. And afterward as I grew up, and before I was of age, I used sometimes to seek places of retirement, and spend the afternoons of first-days in reading the scriptures and other religious books; refusing to go into company—and in so doing I felt the reward of peace.

John Gratton (1642–1712), an English Friend, recalled that "[I was] about ten or eleven years old, when the Lord visited me with the light of his Son, and gave me to see my vain life." William Penn did not begin this stage until the age of thirteen, when he said "the Lord first appeared unto" him, and the stage lasted for several years during which "the Lord visited" him and gave "divine impressions . . . of himself." But seven is not unusual for a birthright Quaker—one born into the faith—such as Woolman. The Irish Quaker autobiographer Joseph Pike (1657–1729) also described the origins of grace working in him: "Before I was seven years of age, the Spirit of the lord began to work in my mind, and strove with me, to bring me off from childish playfulness and vanities."[20]

The second stage of spiritual development, to which Woolman's reflections on his childhood also conformed, was marked by rejection of grace and falling away from God. Augustine entered this stage five years later than Woolman, at about the same age as William Penn did. All three believed that frivolity distracted from spirituality and thus berated themselves for compounding their sinfulness with wanton acts. For Augustine, the principal sins were sex and theft. The theft has its parallel in Woolman's *Journal*, and both writers exaggerated their sins, which of course dramatizes their redemption. Augustine reports his adolescence lasting for about fifteen years; Penn became convinced at the age of twenty-three; Woolman emerged from the darkness before he turned twenty-one.

Augustine stole pears for no good reason. He was not hungry, he did not eat the fruit, and the pears weren't as good as those that grew on his family's land: "What I stole, I already had in abundance, and of much better quality, too. I did not steal so as to enjoy the fruits of my crime, but rather to enjoy the theft itself, and the sin." Woolman also knew better yet did the same thing during the parallel stage of his spiritual life.[21]

Within the structure of Woolman's *Journal* a dream hinges the transition from graceful innocence to depraved adolescence. Again, it is an interior event that clarifies meaning. It was, as Woolman understood it, God speaking to him.

> I had a dream about the ninth year of my age as follows: I saw the moon rise near the west and run a regular course eastward, so swift that in about a quarter of an hour she reached our meridian, when there descended from her a small cloud on a direct line to the earth, which lighted on a pleasant green about twenty yards from the door of my father's house (in which I thought I stood) and was immediately turned into a beautiful green tree. The moon appeared to run on with equal swiftness and soon set in the east, at which time the sun arose at the place where it commonly does in the summer, and shining with full radiance in a serene air, it appeared as pleasant a morning as ever I saw.
>
> All this time I stood still in the door in an awful frame of mind, and I observed that as heat increased by the rising sun, it wrought so powerfully on the little green tree that the

leaves gradually withered; and before noon it appeared dry and dead. There then appeared a being, small of size, full of strength and resolution, moving swift from the north, southward, called a sun worm. Though I was a child, this dream was instructive to me.[22]

Woolman does not say what he thought he learned from the dream, but we can see that he considered it not prophetic but revelatory, which is how he understood all the dreams he reported in his *Journal*. And the sun worm dream was especially important, for it appears in all three manuscript drafts of the *Journal*. Nonetheless, the editorial committee made a large X across the passage and left the dream out of the first published edition. The dream did not make its way back into the *Journal* until the twentieth century, when editors collated the drafts to establish the author's original intent. The dream is a puzzle, but its structural significance in the *Journal* is clear. Without it the reader leaps from grace to sin with no connecting link.

Interpreting dreams is an art, never a science, informed by temporal, cultural, and personal contexts of meaning. It presented a theological problem for early modern Quakers, for they eschewed imagination in any guise that could distract them from Truth. They rejected "superstition" and disciplined members who sought advice from necromancers or who told fortunes themselves. They believed that God sometimes spoke through dreams; the problem was telling which ones were divine messages and what they meant. Any dream recorded in a spiritual autobiography was one that the dreamer understood as God's voice rather than his own or Satan's—the other two possibilities. But divine revelation through dreams was rare, and Quakers believed that most people never experienced such nocturnal visitations from the Holy Spirit and that those who did were unlikely to have it happen more than once in a lifetime. They were especially suspicious of any claims to such experiences that exceeded three times for one reporter.[23]

As was their way, Quakers saw sense in accepting the collected body of members gathered in silent waiting for the Light as the highest authority for gauging Truth. In the case of Quaker journals, a committee appointed by Yearly Meeting determined what should be published and what did not reach the dual threshold of clarity and Truth. If the committee did not have a sense of its meaning, they censored the dream even if they trusted the dreamer to be an authentic source of revelation.

The interpretive problem was compounded by the practice of editing and publishing journals after their authors died; without the assistance of the dreamer, it was difficult to ascertain the dream's symbolic landscape of meaning. The Quakers' default decision was to edit out most dreams. The published ones addressed communal concerns and collective sensibilities in stock narratives; those expunged were personal and eccentric.[24]

It was common for Quaker autobiographers to mark their transition from innocence to youthful frivolity with significant dreams. Such dreams, integrated into the structure of the journals, showed a heavenly pursuit of the soul's falling away from grace, reminding the dreamer of the need to return to the true path. It resolved conflict, and it was enlightening, often literally, making the imagery of sun, moon, and fire especially poignant; after all, Quakers called themselves Children of the Light. Numinous awe or dread in the dream inspired a near-certain fear that the message came from God. Finally, a guide often figured prominently, showing the way and explaining what the dreamer needed to know.[25]

Eighteenth-century Americans knew no such creature as a sun worm. The editorial committee crossed out the phrase "called a sun worm" from Woolman's text, perhaps believing that this would help make sense of the rest of the dream. In the end, though, they deleted the whole account. Still, worms were a symbol commonly addressed in guides to dream interpretation of the time, many of them known to readers in eighteenth-century Anglo-America. No creature was more tied to the natural world: low, legless, without wings or limbs to lift it from the surface of the earth. A sun worm would be a source of earthly, perhaps earthy, enlightenment. In those two senses, the compound symbol of sun worm might represent a guide to living with heavenly inspiration.

In Woolman's dream, the moon played a generative female role ("she") and the sun a destructive one with the tree, a feminine symbol in the eighteenth century as well as a sign for humanity. The imagery of light, so central for Quakers, could be understood as the "operations of divine love" of which Woolman wrote in the *Journal*'s Introduction. The heavenly spirit "lighted"—perhaps subconscious wordplay—on "green," the color symbolic of life, and created a "beautiful green tree." Perhaps heavenly grace created the young tree, which was beautiful, sturdy, and alive. Its destruction would then be a fall from grace or a wilting under the sun's power.[26]

The sun, a symbol of masculinity in eighteenth-century dream guides, might stand for Woolman's biological father as well as his heavenly one. Standing in the doorway of his "father's house" thus has a meaning attached to his earthly father, and it has a resonance with the New Testament in Christ's description of the temple as "my Father's house." Possibly the worm is a dream guide, moving toward the awestruck boy in the doorway to lead him with strength and resolution out into the world.[27]

Two sources with clear connections to Woolman may have contributed to the dream imagery. An unknowable number of other, now inaccessible influences may also have consciously or subconsciously affected the dream or Woolman's report of it a quarter century later. One possibility is of course the Bible, perhaps most obviously Jonah 4:6–11, in which the Lord creates a vine to shade Jonah from the sun. On God's command a worm attacks the plant, and it dies: "When the sun rose, God prepared a sultry east wind, and the sun beat down on the head of Jonah so that he was faint and asked that he might die. He said, 'It is better for me to die than to live.'" But this biblical account is not about regeneration, and Woolman's dream has a positive resolution. The boy's mind might have taken the germ of the dream from this or another Bible story and embellished, reversed, and expanded it. Since Woolman was so steeped in the Bible from an early age, it makes sense that he would communicate even with himself in biblical imagery. His recollection of the dream as an adult could likewise express itself in companionable texts or events.

The dream also parallels the first few pages of *The Threefold Life of Man*, a book we know Woolman read, by Jacob Boehme (1575–1624). Boehme's influential writings began to appear in English

Frontispiece from Erra Pater, *The Book of Knowledge*, a book of dream interpretations popular during the eighteenth century (Library Company of Philadelphia, Zinman Collection)

The EOOK of KNOWLEDGE,

I through my glafs the Planets fpy,
See them revolve the Starry Sky.

during the 1650s, and English Boehmenists and Quakers had much in common, as Woolman knew. In *The Threefold Life of Man*, like Woolman's dream concerned with spiritual rebirth, Boehme refers to the "tree of Christ" and portrays himself as "a little twig on that tree." Boehme's tree sprouts at night, under moonlight, and is remarkable for its beauty and youth.

> We are a new sprout generated out of our first mother; we were a withered dry branch on the tree, but the mother hath introduced her sap and virtue or power into us; and generated a young sprout out of her self, in which she will have joy, and through that generate her fruit; Yes, she hath generated a young son out of the old one, who shall not be blind.[28]

Boehme's view was of the ground rather than the "whole entire building of God," just as Woolman in his dream had a view of the field but not of the house he stood in. "Out of death," Boehme writes, "generated the eternal life," just as Woolman's worm emerges after the sun's heat has withered the tree, the very sort of "earthly burning" that Boehme discusses in his version of the phoenix myth. The worm in Woolman's dream has a parallel in Boehme's book too; a "sack of worms" from which emerges the "new-born or regenerate man," this "new creature" that is of nature but also transcends it embodying "the Light [that] is FREE from the nature of the fire." The boy standing in the doorway, according to such a Boehmenist (and Jungian) reading, would experience soul integration when the worm reached and united with him.[29]

Woolman's dream and Boehme's *Threefold Life* are both about spiritual rebirth. Boehme concludes this introductory passage as follows: "Therefore to be new born or generated is to generate a new son out of the old, out of itself; not a new soul but a new image out of the soul, in the virtue or power of the Holy Spirit, a twig or sprout out of its own essence springing forth in Christ's spirit; and standing in the Light of the Deity, not shining to or upon, but giving forth Light out of it SELF."[30]

Boehme's theological treatise would have been difficult reading for a nine-year-old, even a spiritually precocious eighteenth-century Quaker boy. Woolman might have struggled with it, perhaps not getting much further than the introductory passage, or an older sibling or parent might have read it aloud and offered an interpretation. Or possibly Woolman read *The Threefold Life of Man* after he had had the dream and then conflated the two, embellishing the dream (perhaps subconsciously) to conform to the book.

Jonah's worm, symbolizing the struggle between man and God, is perhaps the more likely source than the tortuously reasoned (and hamhandedly translated) tract by Boehme. But reading the dream through Boehme's imagery allows us to see it as reflecting an ambition for regeneration during a difficult adolescent transition, which fits nicely with the place of the dream in the *Journal*'s structure, while reading it through the story from Jonah lets us imagine it as illustrating the conflict itself. These two texts demonstrate a range of possibilities that fit the historical context, consistent with eighteenth-century dream interpretation, Quaker beliefs, the structural place of the dream, texts known to Woolman, and the vision realized in the *Journal*. He may have taken for granted that the dream would be comprehensible because readers of the Bible and *Threefold Life* would understand it. If so, he was mistaken; Boehme's work did not remain influential after his death and the Bible is not so familiar to readers of the *Journal* as it was in the eighteenth century.

At some point between the ages of seven and nine—a moment in the life of a tree—the heat of divine light wilted what grace had created in Woolman. This could explain why in the dream God's initial gift is not enough to save him. It was too much, too hot for him. Yet the dream told him that all would be well or at least that all was forgiven and nothing lost. More effort was before him; he had much to learn. Sin too was ahead of him.

The dream may have given Woolman confidence that he would emerge from his father's house, that he would someday become his own man, triumphing over his nature and achieving his spiritual potential. In the dream he stands in the limen, between his father's house and the outside world where he will be responsible for himself. He stands in his father's door, watching, waiting, with his own self moving toward him from the "withered" and then dead tree. The light gives him spiritual life; its warmth overwhelms him, but he will emerge stronger, like the sun worm, stronger than the "little green tree," a being "small of size" but "full of strength and resolution" moving swiftly to physical and spiritual unity with the boy in the doorway. This interpretation could explain Woolman's positive feelings about his dream, which he might have experienced, or at least recalled, as a reassuring vision of his potential for self-integration and union with the material and spiritual worlds.

The dream, then, could be understood as a comfort and a guide, revealing and reinforcing Woolman's understanding of his place in the universe. The symbols he used to communicate were on the same grid traversed by other dream reporters and interpreters of his day. And the dream's naturalistic setting artfully reminds us of Woolman's sense of heaven as a rural idyll, like the one in Revelation.[31]

WOOLMAN'S sun worm dream connects the first two distinct phases of his spiritual development as he recounts them in his *Journal*—from innocence to frivolity—and enigmatically introduces his discussion of the second stage, in which he wilts. Quakers generally claimed to pass from their awakening grace to sinful adolescence, their divided selves expressing the tension between a desire for grace and the weakness of their spiritual commitment. The last stage, of an integrated self, which Quakers often cited, was perhaps the one foretold in the dream of the sun worm approaching the boy, bringing about the union of Woolman's divided self.

But for now he remained dependent, subject to his father's will and in need of protection under his father's roof, and he continued to make the mistakes of a child even as he grew. He sinned senselessly, as writers since Augustine have reported that they have done. Woolman tells us in the *Journal* that he murdered a family of birds when he was a child, killing for the sake of killing. It is unclear whether this event came after he'd read from the Book of Revelation and had his dream or whether for other reasons he placed the story after the other two in the *Journal*. He does not say, though he specifies that the first two appear in the order of their occurrence.

This time the boy was on an errand from which he strayed. Woolman knew John Bunyan's *Grace Abounding* and *The Pilgrim's Progress*, so he understood the meaning of this image, as all eighteenth-century readers steeped in Bunyan's allegory would. Woolman's identity in his *Journal* is compatible with that of the pilgrim Christian, whose journey to salvation is fraught with peril. Distractions from the road to salvation endanger Christian's soul. During a ramble toward a neighbor's house, Woolman spots a robin sitting on her nest, and he alters his path and startles the bird. She flies off but circles, crying in fear for her young. Woolman tosses stones at the mother even though she poses no threat to him. The last of these strikes her dead.[32]

The species is significant, because in Woolman's day robins symbolized precocious rebirth, simplicity, and courage. If the birds in the story had been starlings, blue jays, pigeons, raptors, or crows, the boy's actions could even be seen as appropriate, but there is no excuse for killing a robin, a beneficial, defenseless bird that does not compete with humans for food. Robins do not destroy crops or buildings, spread disease, or harm domestic animals; they prefer worms. Robins served Woolman's intended allegorical function, which is to suggest not that the story is untrue but simply that it is ideal.

Woolman may have thought that robins, being humble, plain, peaceful, hardworking, and familial, not predaceous, malicious, frivolous, proud, or ostentatious, embodied Quaker values. In any case, he knew as he wrote that he had chosen precisely the wrong bird to kill. As with Augustine's theft of pears, Woolman's offense was inexcusable. The point of the story is that the robin alive is a pure gift to the world and of no value to anyone dead. "At first I was pleased with the exploit," he writes, "but after a few minutes was seized with horror, as having in a sportive way killed an innocent creature while she was careful for her young." Hitting the target pleased the boy emotionally; success stroked his ego. Then his conscience hit him. Sport hunting was contrary to Woolman's values. The Quaker peace testimony taught him that killing is wrong.[33]

Woolman's murder of the mother bird was not the end of the mayhem. There were the orphans to consider, only compounding Woolman's moral plight.

> I beheld her lying dead and thought those young ones for which she was so careful must now perish for want of their dam to nourish them; and after some painful considerations on the subject, I climbed up the tree, took all the young birds and killed them, supposing that better than to leave them to pine away and die miserably, and believed in this case that Scripture proverb was fulfilled, "The tender mercies of the wicked are cruel."[34]

Woolman quoted only part of Proverbs 12:10. The whole passage reads, in the New Revised Standard Version, "The righteous know the needs of their animals, but the mercy of the wicked is cruel." (The first clause in the King James Bible, the version that Woolman read, makes the same point but more obscurely to us: "A righteous man regardeth the life of his beast.") His application of the biblical aphorism to his violent act implies that the birds were his. In Genesis 1, God gives humankind "dominion over the fish of the sea and over the birds of the air and over every living thing that moves upon the earth." Dominion carries responsibilities that the righteous handle tenderly and the wicked with disregard for life. The robins were in Woolman's care, and he acted wickedly.[35]

Immediately after executing the innocent nestlings, Woolman felt remorse: "I then went on my errand, but for some hours could think of little else but the cruelties I had committed, and was much troubled." Violence had begat violence, an insight that was precisely the origin of the Quaker peace testimony, as Woolman knew. The commission of one violent act leads to more; the perpetrator becomes increasingly callous to the pain of others, making each successive cruelty easier to commit. Quakers wanted to break this chain of violence by declining to arm themselves; it was less significant whether one forswore stones, sticks, swords, or guns than that the principle applied to all facets of life.[36]

The souls of the predators were indeed of greater concern to eighteenth-century Quakers than the physical pain of their prey, whether animal or human. Cruelty endangers the souls of those who inflict violence but only the bodies of those who receive it. Pain might actually enhance the spiritual condition of physically abused humans if they bore injustice as a "cross," emulating the suffering Christ. Such ideas changed among Quakers and other Americans, and may have been evolving during Woolman's lifetime, but he applied the standard to himself and felt morally inadequate.[37]

Woolman's guilt was, he believed, a good sign. It revealed the Light within him: "Thus he whose tender mercies are over all his works hath placed a principle in the human mind which incites to exercise goodness toward every living creature." We possess knowledge of God's will, and Woolman experienced it personally. He had been inattentive, as children often are, and was deaf to God's quiet voice. In retrospect he knew the Truth, which dictated responsible care for all living things. He was remorseful, wiser, and well intentioned not to make the same mistake again. The question was whether Woolman could keep his resolve.[38]

3

Sinner and Saints

1731–35

F ROM John Woolman's early childhood, even before his epiphany at the age of seven, martyrs were the models for his spiritual ambitions. He aimed for a life of selfless dedication to God.
Saints shaped his simple tastes, and their self-denying habits became his. Like them, he expected to suffer doing God's work and
possibly to die for his faith.

Before Woolman could read, several books read *to* him forged a
link between his life and the lives of Christian saints. His parents
and older sisters read heroic Christian literature aloud to the family:
William Cave's *Primitive Christianity* and John Foxe's *Book of Martyrs*
(1563). Books such as these do not explain who John Woolman
became, of course, since he was no more the sum of what he read
or had read to him than anyone is; but they add color to the self-
portrait in the *Journal* and suggest the external influences on his
spiritual development.

Foxe divides the history of Christianity into three-hundred-year
segments leading up to the sixteenth century. The first three centuries after the death of Christ were "the suffering time," when
enemies of the faith tortured and killed his disciples and their
converts. Foxe chronicles St. Stephen's stoning and the execution
of two thousand fellow believers on the same day, the beheading of
James the Apostle, the immolation of Simon and Mark the evangel-

ist, the murder of Thomas, and the crucifixions of Andrew, Philip, and Bartholomew.[1]

The governor of Achaea warns Andrew, the apostle and brother of Peter, to stop preaching the gospel. Andrew replies, according to Foxe, that "he would not have preached the honour and glory of the cross, if he had feared the death of the cross." For his defiance, Andrew is condemed by the governor to die as Christ did.

> Andrew coming to the place, and seeing afar off the cross prepared, did change neither countenance nor colour, as the imbecility of mortal men is wont to do, neither did his blood shrink, neither did he fail in his speech; his body fainted not, neither was his mind molested; his understanding did not fail him, as it is the manner of men to do but out of the abundance of his heart his mouth did speak; and fervent charity did appear in his words as kindled sparks: he said, O cross, most welcome and long looked for; with a willing mind joyfully and desirously I come to thee, being the scholar of Him which did hang on thee; because I have been always thy lover, and have coveted to embrace thee. So being crucified, he yielded up the ghost and fell on sleep.[2]

The Woolman children imbibed a history of Christianity that dwelled on physical torment. The stories may have led to questions. Would they face danger in their ministry? Were they as spiritually strong as the primitive saints? Could they endure torture? Would they embrace martyrdom bravely and offer an example to other Christians and potential converts, thereby saving their own souls and those of others? Could they exhale forgiveness of their tormentors with their last breaths? Where did they fit in the history of persecuted Christians, especially of the seventeenth-century Quaker martyrs? Foxe encouraged such identification with the saints.

> Wherein marvelous it is to see and read the numbers incredible of Christian innocents that were slain and tormented, some one way, some another . . . some slain with sword; some burnt with fire; some with whips scourged; some stabbed

with forks of iron; some fastened to the cross or gibbet; some drowned in the sea; some their skins plucked off; some their tongues cut off; some stoned to death; some killed with cold; some starved with hunger; some their hands cut off, or otherwise dismembered, have been so left naked to the open shame of the world, etc.[3]

Likewise, from William Cave children heard that the Roman Catholic Church and its clergy suffered precipitous moral decline in the centuries leading up to the Reformation. They learned that true Christian models could be found in the primitive church that preceded the corruptions of the fourth through fifteenth centuries. Writing in the mid-seventeenth century, Cave also expressed disappointment with Protestant churches, which he believed were already in need of reform. He indicted not only the Church of Rome but the Church of England.[4]

Cave's chapter titles, which read like a list of Quaker testimonies, lay out the structure that he thought reform should take, and the chapters themselves detail the path to the past that he thought true Christians followed. What modern Christians had forgotten, according to Cave, was humility, contempt for worldly attachments, simplicity of dress, temperance, abstinence, chastity, courage, constancy in professing their religion, patience, and willingness to bear suffering bravely and joyously in God's name. All this reinforced the lessons the Woolman children learned in school from the Quaker primer and William Penn's *Fruits of Solitude*. These books placed them in the historical context of the first Christians and prepared them for lives of personal sacrifice.

Cave and Foxe are in the background of William Sewel's *The History of the Rise, Increase, and Progress of the Christian People Called Quakers* (1722), which tells the story of Quakers persecuted by Puritans in England and America. Sewel makes explicit the comparison of Reformation, Quaker, and early Christian martyrs: "It is true there have been such among the Quakers, who were exceeding bold in representing to their enemies their evil behavior and deportment; but this hath been a peculiar talent of pious men, of whom examples are extant in the books of martyrs, viz. that some of them

in very plain terms told their persecutors of their wickedness."
Sewel goes on to chronicle the history of Quaker suffering in Bristol,
England: beatings, fines, confiscations of property, imprisonments
for public testimony and private practice of their religion.

After the death of Oliver Cromwell in September 1658, the English lived through another period of acute political instability. The
army was split in its loyalties, and though within two years King
Charles II regained the throne, it was unclear how the restored
Anglican Church and the restored monarchy would deal with Dissenters. Religious uniformity was one way to consolidate royal and
ecclesiastical power and, in theory, to bring peace to the realm.
Quakers were high on the list of "fanatics" who had to be suppressed for the good of the kingdom. "Now [1658] there was great
persecution," as Sewel puts it, "both by imprisonment and breaking
up of meetings; and many died in prison."

With the rising in London of a small group of Fifth Monarchists
in 1661 and then two years later another revolt against the king
called the Northern Plot, suspicion of Quakers only increased. As
the largest of the Dissenting sects, they were by reputation the most
dangerous, and rumors abounded that they had ties to Rome. The
Corporation Act of 1661, which restricted public office to Anglicans
and required officeholders to swear an oath of allegiance, imposed a
sacramental test that Quakers could not pass. Since they refused to
take the oath of allegiance or any other oath, that was another reason
to suspect their loyalty. The Quaker Act of 1662 singled them out
for prosecution on these grounds and forced them to choose between their government and their faith. The Conventicle Acts of
1664 and 1670 then called for the prosecution of all irregular religious meetings with more than five participants beyond members of
the household where the service occurred. Sewel believed there
were more than forty-two hundred Quakers in English jails by that
time.

Many of these had been grievously beaten; and some were
put into such stinking dungeons that some great men said
they would not have put their hunting dogs there. Some prisons were crowded full both of men and women, so that there

was not sufficient room for all to sit down at once; and in Cheshire sixty-eight persons were in this manner locked up in a small room . . . By such ill-treatment many grew sick, and not a few died in such jails; for no age or sex was regarded, but even ancient people of sixty, seventy, and more years of age, were not spared.[5]

Mobs beat Quakers with stones and sticks; police used swords, pikes, and muskets, "yet all this they bore patiently, without making any resistance." Crowds dragged and stomped them, militias jailed and starved them, and gangs working at the behest of church and government officials broke up their Meetings for Worship violently, not discouraging the Quakers but only making "the most sincere amongst them . . . more zealous." Throughout decades of persecution, Sewel writes, "they continued valiant." Somewhere between fifteen and sixty thousand spent time in prison before the Toleration Act of 1689 brought the state-sanctioned violence to a close. Courts sentenced hundreds to transportation, that is, forced removal from England to one of its overseas colonies. There is no credible estimate of how many died, but those who succumbed were generally victims of prison conditions.[6]

The Woolman family's internal discipline focused the children on these heroic Quaker figures. The saints were not abstractions that achieved spiritual depth inaccessible to other mortals. The early Christian martyrs were alive for the Quakers, who aimed to restore Christianity to the conditions of the early church and anticipated suffering the same fates as saints from those first three centuries of the modern era.

Quakers suffered martyrdom not only in England but also in the New World. The Woolman children lived close in time and place to the Puritans, who from their start in New England passed laws against Quakers proclaiming their faith. The children learned from Sewel of Quaker martyrs in Massachusetts who had been branded, starved in prison, scourged, whipped, and banished. They read that the colony's law had sanctioned chopping off Quakers' ears and boring through their tongues with hot irons only sixty years before John Woolman's birth, within the memory of Quakers they knew, on the continent where they lived, and within the British Empire that still ruled over them.[7]

Sewel reported that in the mid-seventeenth century it was a crime in Massachusetts to transport, house, or feed a Quaker. American Puritans fined those who allowed Quakers in their carriages, inns, or homes and imprisoned the hosts until they paid in cash or forced labor. For a Quaker man to enter Massachusetts the penalty was the loss of one ear and hard labor until the convict worked off the costs of jailing, prosecuting, and banishing him. For a second offense, he lost his other ear and suffered imprisonment on the same terms as the first time. Women were "severely whipped" for a first or second offense and imprisoned just as the men. For a third offense, "he or she should have their tongues bored through with a hot iron, and be kept in the house of correction, close at work, till they be sent away on their own charge." These penalties were for entering Massachusetts, but Quakers presented additional challenges to Puritans' authority in church and state, meaning they suffered worse punishments yet.[8]

In Sewel's *History*, the Woolman children learned about William Brend, an elderly Quaker who refused to pay a marshal to lead him out of Massachusetts in 1658. It seemed to Brend a hard thing to bear the financial burden of his own banishment, to which he had been sentenced for proclaiming his faith and refusing to renounce it. His jailer put Brend in irons, "neck and heels so close together, that there was no more room left between each, than for the lock that fastened them. Thus he kept him from five in the morning till after nine at night." When Brend declined to work for his keep, claiming weakness after five days of forced fasting, a jailer lashed him repeatedly. The children read in Sewel's book that after such treatment, "his back and arms were bruised and black, and the blood hanging as in bags under his arms; and so into one was his flesh beaten, that the sign of a particular blow could not be seen; for all was become as a jelly." Still, Brend lived to proclaim his faith the next day, which Sewel interpreted as a miraculous healing.[9]

They read to one another about Hored Gardner, a Quaker from Newport, Rhode Island, who arrived in Weymouth, Massachusetts, in 1658 with her baby and a female servant. Gardner anticipated being imprisoned for her bold challenge to Puritan authority; she carried the baby with her in order to shame her tormentors, and brought the maid to care for her child while she was in jail. She underestimated the Puritans' ferocity, though, and miscalculated the punishment, because they whipped her and the servant in turn and made no formal allowance for the baby's needs.

> For being a Quaker, she was hurried to Boston, where both she and the [servant] girl were whipped with a three-fold knotted whip. After whipping, the woman [Gardner] kneeled down, and prayed the Lord to forgive those persecutors: which so reached a woman that stood by, that she said, surely she [Gardner] could not have done this, if it had not been by the Spirit of the Lord.

As Sewel told the story, then, Hored Gardner's courage and Christlike love for those who tormented her recruited a convert for the true church. Hers was the trial of a saint, which should inspire readers' emulation.[10]

Other Quakers who went to New England in 1658 to preach their version of the gospel refused to remove their hats when brought into court, suffered whippings, and had their tongues bored. Being asked for proof that the Lord had sent them, three Quakers "replied that it was some kind of proof the Lord had sent them, because they met with such an entertainment as Christ had told his disciples would be meted out to them, for his name's sake, viz., whippings, &c." For this insolence, the court ordered their ears cropped and had them whipped again, which, according to Sewel, only strengthened their resolve and drew more Quakers to New England. They expected to be persecuted, welcomed it even, because it ratified their apostolic mission and proved the dissolution of modern churches, Protestant and Catholic, that would torture, maim, and execute those who spread the good news of Christ's teachings.[11]

In 1659 a Massachusetts court ordered the brother and sister Daniel and Provided Southwick sold "to any of the English nation, at Virginia or Barbados." Their crime was refusal to attend Puritan church services as required by law. Their sentence was for not paying the resulting fines and refusing to work off their debt. Despite an unspecified number of attempts, the General Court could not find a county treasurer willing to sell the siblings into long-term servitude where they would perform the labor of slaves, and no ship captains would carry them as cargo.[12]

In this kind of Quaker history, New England Puritans played the biblical role of Egyptians, enslaving God's chosen people. And since the most radical Quakers and most extreme Puritans immigrated to the New World, their engagement in New England was even more violent than it had been in Great Britain. Missionary Quakers provoked ministers in their pulpits and jurists in their courtrooms. The Puritan establishment already felt beleaguered by the rising tide in their midst of Baptists, who thought the Congregationalists too liberal in their admission of children to church membership, and by the likes of the radicals Roger Williams and Anne Hutchinson, who were banished to Rhode Island. Leaders of the Massachusetts Bay Colony saw the Quaker challenge in light of the others but viewed it as perhaps even more threatening than the revolts from within. Quakers preached that salvation was accessible to all believers, assaulting the very core of Calvinist belief in predestined salvation for the chosen few.

Attempts by Massachusetts officials to make Quakers give up their religious practice were counterproductive and only brought new members to the faith. A Quaker Meeting in Salem, Massachusetts, founded in 1657, grew to more than fifty members within twenty years. In Woolman's lifetime there were thriving Meetings in Rhode Island and Long Island as well as in Salem and Plymouth, which he visited in his traveling ministry; he never made it to Meetings in such outlying areas as Maine.[13]

Thus, when Woolman wrote in his *Journal*, "From what I had read and heard, I believed there had been in the past ages people who walked in uprightness before God in a degree exceeding any that I knew, or heard of, now living," he was referring not only to early Christian martyrs but also to persecuted Quakers in England and New England. Many a time in his youth he heard Quakers rise in Meeting to lament what a fallen lot they were. He heard himself and other worshipers described as soft, self-indulgent, spiritually weak, and incapable of enduring the hardships that the early Quakers had faced on both sides of the Atlantic. Ministers reminded them that God had sent such repeated prophetic warnings to the people of Israel, yet they had continued to worship idols, defile the temple, and ridicule God's messengers: "They kept mocking the messengers of God, despising his words, and scoffing at his prophets, until the wrath of the Lord against his people became so great that there was no remedy" (2 Chronicles 36:16–21).[14]

As a boy John Woolman took such biblical passages and the elders' lamentations seriously, perhaps literally. Nowhere in his family, he believed, were to be found the likes of Gardner, Brend, and the dozens of other Quakers whom the Puritans had whipped and maimed. Neither he nor any other Quakers in his Meeting put their lives on the line for a righteous but unpopular cause. They were a fallen, vain, carnal lot compared with the four Friends who refused to abandon their apostolic ministry after passage of a 1658 law that made declarations of the Quaker faith a capital crime in Massachusetts. Mary Dyer, Marmaduke Stephenson, William Robinson, and William Leddra died bravely, having already suffered torture and maiming.

One can well imagine why Woolman, with these martyrs as models, might have thought of his adolescent self as depraved. The self-loathing reflected both his personal standard and the formulaic traditions of spiritual autobiography. From his place of grace at age seven, the Woolman of the *Journal* predictably plunged into sin by the time he killed the family of robins. From there he continued down and up on tides of spiritual loss and gain. What he had learned from killing the birds was that God "hath placed a principle in the human mind which incites to exercise goodness toward every living creature; and this being singly attended to, people become tender-hearted and sympathizing, but being frequently and totally rejected, the mind shuts itself up in a contrary disposition." We should avoid growing moral calluses, because they make us insensitive to grace's touch.[15]

In the *Journal*, Woolman may have been recalling how his boyhood years had felt to him then or how he felt about them as he wrote or how he believed the story of his salvation could best be told. But these were not mutually exclusive categories. By the time of his writing, Woolman thought he knew the path to salvation and believed he had strayed along the way. When he was twelve, he writes, his mother "reproved" him "for some misconduct," and to this reproach he "made an undutiful reply." The "misconduct" goes undescribed, and perhaps it was forgotten; it was his response to parental discipline that Woolman regretted, its being tantamount to ignoring the quiet voice of God within him. The anecdote has two meanings, then: as a personal experience of sin and as an allegory of his maturing relationship with God.[16]

Woolman's mother reported the incident to her husband when he came home, but Samuel waited for the next day, when he and his son were alone, to talk to him, and then he "advised me to be more careful in future." A gentle hand was sufficient: "Being thus awakened to a sense of my wickedness, I felt remorse in my mind, and getting home I retired and prayed to the Lord to forgive me, and do not remember that I ever after that spoke unhandsomely to either of my parents, however foolish in other things." Woolman artfully juxtaposes the metaphoric "awakened" with "retired." The alarm came from outside, in his father's advice, but the resolution came from within. What might otherwise be a dilemma about parental authority, symbolic and real, can be spiritually resolved in the Christian adolescent by total surrender to God. Woolman's reconciliation with God comes in a spiritual rebirth, also known as a conversion experience, which acknowledges personal impotence in relation to the universal father.[17]

John Locke would have taken a longer-term view of the disciplinary success of Samuel and Elizabeth Woolman with their son. "The rebukes and chiding" that he believed the natures of children make inevitable "should not only be in sober, grave, and dispassionate words, but also alone and in private; but the commendations children deserve, they should receive before others," he wrote. Locke believed that "frequent and passionate chiding" is no more effective than corporal punishment, against which he also advised: "It lessens the authority of the parents and the respect of the child . . . A look or nod only ought to correct them when they do amiss; or if words are sometimes to be used, they ought to be grave, kind, and sober, representing the ill or unbecomingness of the fault, rather than a *hasty rating* of the child for it, which makes him not sufficiently distinguish whether your dislike be not more directed to him than his fault." The sensitive, respectful adolescent who responds to his internal guide was precisely the sort of young adult whom Locke believed his methods would produce. Whether the Woolmans used *Some Thoughts Concerning Education* as a child-rearing manual or simply owned books by an author whose temperament they shared, they realized in their relationship with their son an admirable resolution to the dilemmas of adolescent rebellion.[18]

N ONETHELESS, Woolman tells us, he continued to sin. At the age of sixteen he "began to love wanton company," having within him "a plant . . . which produced much wild grapes." This kind of self-indictment might seem to the modern reader to imply drinking, parties, and sex. Woolman keeps the exact nature of his behavior vague, though, giving free rein to the reader's imagination. "I hastened toward destruction," he writes. "While I meditate on the gulf toward which I travelled . . . I weep; mine eye runneth down with water." Twenty years after the fact the recollection of his depravity brought tears to his eyes.[19]

Then, Woolman continues, he got even worse: "Advancing in age the number of my acquaintance increased, and thereby my way grew more difficult . . . I knew I was going from the flock of Christ and had no resolution to return . . . Running in this road I found many like myself, and we associated in that which is reverse to true friendship." He became more sociable, and that in itself was a distraction. "True" friends guide one another back to the path rather than enticing one another to stray. In this case it was not that the boys had wandered into depravity, but that losing their way deprived them of God. His expectations were strict, and he fell short of his ideal.[20]

From what we know about Woolman's circle of friends, it appears that he did them a disservice in writing about them in this way; they were not made from the sterner stuff of seventeenth-century Quaker martyrs, true, but neither were they a band of hooligans. Woolman spent his boyhood with other children of respected Quaker families in New Jersey. He apparently often visited the home of Richard Smith, a Burlington merchant and member of the New Jersey legislature. Smith's son Samuel was his age, and Samuel's brother John was two years younger. Biographers have described the two Smith boys as Woolman's fast friends. They were certainly among the acquaintances to which Woolman refers in the *Journal*. Along with the five Smith children, he knew teenagers from other Quaker families, and the Smiths introduced him to New Jersey's governor, Jonathan Belcher.[21]

The same problems presented by a widening social circle confronted John's younger brother Abner when he ventured beyond his childhood haunts. "And I being then an apprentice was exposed to vain company, which was a burden to me," Abner writes in his unpublished journal. The brothers felt spiritually threatened by the carnal world exterior to the familial cocoon in which their parents had wrapped them. And though it is possible that their circle grew to include non-Friends, everything we know about Woolman's youth suggests that he lived within the protective environment of his family and Meeting.[22]

It is important to stress that Woolman indicted himself and only implied criticism of unnamed others, and that his personal threshold for vanity and wantonness was not typical for a Quaker of his time. He did not mean to insult fellow Quakers when he wrote of them critically, but he did judge their lifestyles severely and possibly meant exactly what he said about the spiritual danger associated with the way his friends lived. We can learn about the social texture and style of New Jersey Quakers from the voluminous diaries that Woolman's friend John Smith kept for fourteen years, beginning in 1738, noting what he did with friends, books he read, and other information about the Quaker network that included his family and Woolman's.[23]

Woolman's family knew Elizabeth Haddon (1682–1762), the founder of Haddonfield, New Jersey, a well-to-do English Quaker of the same generation as Woolman's parents who had immigrated alone to New Jersey in 1701 at the age of nineteen to take over land her father had purchased. In 1702 she had married John Estaugh, reputedly a bookish sort, and together they had established the Haddonfield plantation while awaiting the arrival of her parents, but her father died in England before he could join them. Haddon-Estaugh became a friend and patroness of Woolman's older sister Elizabeth, who moved to Haddonfield and worked as a seamstress there. Woolman visited his sister and may have called on the Estaughs. If so, he could have taken advantage of their fine collection of books and discussed literature, among other things, with the adults.

Woolman also went as a boy to Philadelphia and spent time on the Pemberton and Logan estates. Israel Pemberton, Sr. (1684–1754), was a wealthy merchant, an influential member of the Pennsylvania Assembly, and clerk of Philadelphia Yearly Meeting. He had three sons—Israel, Jr., James, and John, whose surviving correspondence suggests close relationships with Woolman.

James Logan (1674–1751), whose wife was Mrs. Pemberton's sister, was the most important public figure in Pennsylvania at that time. Irish by birth, he had immigrated in 1699 as William Penn's secretary and had a distinguished career as an elected and appointed official: he was a judge, agent of the Penn family, land speculator, merchant, and Indian trader and negotiator. Both Mrs. Logan and Mrs. Pemberton knew Woolman's parents, for they had been members of the same Monthly Meeting when they all were growing up in New Jersey. The Logans' younger daughter Hannah, the same age as John Woolman, was by all accounts a beautiful, charming girl who was better educated than her male friends. Her father, being more liberal and more devoted to education than most Quakers, saw to it that his daughters learned Latin and Greek, and they read the classics of Western literature from his library.

Burlington was seven miles north of Woolman's home; Haddonfield was farther in the opposite direction, and Philadelphia was twenty miles southwest. At each destination John Woolman could find a formidable library (in Burlington, the Smiths' and, through them, Governor Belcher's even more impressive collection of books). And once Woolman was at the Smiths' home in Burlington, the Estaughs' in Haddonfield, or the Logans' and Pembertons' in Philadelphia, he could well have participated in the amusements enjoyed by those wealthy Quakers.

These families were practicing Quakers who lived without reproach under the discipline of their faith. Woolman's parents knew them as elders of their Monthly Meetings and respected leaders of Philadelphia Yearly Meeting. The children of their families and their friends swam together in the summer and skated when the rivers and ponds froze; Woolman may have joined them in these activities. He may even have drunk tea—the rest of them certainly did—but nothing stronger. We do not know whether Woolman read books with these friends and, if so, which ones; swam naked, as was the fashion for boys; skated with them; or rode sleighs, but if he did, these are likely among the vanities for which he later condemned himself.

None of the other members of this group left evidence that they were embarrassed by the frolics of their youthful years, as Woolman did in his *Journal*. Those who recorded their thoughts remembered the times as good ones, their friends as admirable, and their amusements as chaste. John Smith read widely in sacred and profane literature when he was young, sometimes while visiting friends, leading biographers to speculate that Woolman was part of a group that read and discussed great works of literature. If so, the practice would have expanded Woolman's literary world beyond the Bible, martyrologies, and devotional tracts with which he was already familiar. He may have considered in retrospect that reading carnal literature was idle, and discussion of it vain, the sort of "wanton" behavior for which he reproached himself and, by implication, judged his friends.

We know about John Smith's specific reading because he mentions books in his diaries. We know as well the contents of Logan's library, in which he educated his daughters and from which others borrowed. The impressive libraries of Belcher, Smith, and Estaugh also reveal their eclectic tastes. From a modern perspective but also within an eighteenth-century context, Smith's reading was morally tame. Most of his diary entries about books cited spiritual texts: the Bible; sermons, including a collection of the popular revivalist preacher George Whitefield; published journals by Quaker ministers—Edmundson, Bank, Wilson, Bancroft; devotional tracts—Drummond on internal revelation, *Piety Promoted*, which could have been one of two books by that title, but was likely the one subtitled *A Collection of Dying Sayings of Many of the People Call'd Quakers*; biblical exegesis; Quaker history—*The Suffering of the People Called Quakers*; theological disputation—Jonathan Edwards on Archbishop Tillotson (leading Smith to read Tillotson himself and decide that Edwards was unfair in his criticism); and a biography by Samuel Mather of his father, *The Life of the Very Reverend and Learned Cotton Mather*.[24]

As a young man Smith was on the editorial committee for an American edition of Thomas Chalkley's spiritual autobiography, published in 1776 by Philadelphia Yearly Meeting, an assignment that suggests the Friends' confidence in Smith's personal piety and his knowledge of the genre. He wrote "On Pure Love," a set of verses that reveal an acquaintance with the French Catholic archbishop François Fénelon's *Dissertation* on the same subject. Smith's "Meditation in Prose" displays his reflective nature. He wrote poems about suffering, prose about humility, and exegeses of the Bible. He faithfully attended Quaker Meetings for Worship, youth Meetings, Quarterly Meetings, and Yearly Meetings. One year he recorded the name of every minister who spoke in Meetings for Worship he attended: 657 messages in all, 382 delivered by forty six different men and forty-one women who spoke on 275 different occasions. John Woolman was one of those ministers.[25]

For all these reasons and in all these ways, Smith was a model Quaker youth. In addition, though (and it would be the additions that Woolman judged harshly), he read a history of Westminster Abbey, only a short step away from devotional literature. He went further afield with John Oldham's Juvenalian satires of the Jesuits; Elia Fowler Haywood's novel *The British Recluse*; Miguel de Cervantes's *Don Quixote* in English translation; John Milton's epic poem *Paradise Lost*; Daniel Defoe's *Atalantis Major*; and Thomas More's *Utopia*. Smith also noted in his diaries that he ice-skated, swam, went sleigh riding, and enjoyed sledding without a sled, which he called sliding, with his friends. And he drank tea. All this reading and revelry might have been too much for Woolman.[26]

We can plumb the difference between an exterior life of reading focused only on the Bible, theology, devotionals, and martyrologies, on the one hand, and an interior life also enriched by classic litera-ture on the other. Was Woolman put off by Cervantes, More, Milton,

or Defoe? The work of all four writers has a spiritual core in the
Christian tradition: More became a martyr for his faith, as Woolman
knew; Defoe's *Robinson Crusoe* is an allegory based on the New Testament parable of the prodigal son; Milton's *Paradise Lost* is the
work of a radical Dissenter about a heavenly battle between good
and evil; and Cervantes's *Don Quixote* engages the relationship between spirit and life. But Woolman's rejection of fiction and poetry,
whatever their spiritual content, offers a hint to the reason for his
vague criticism of his friends in the *Journal.*

There is no way to know what *Don Quixote* meant to Woolman's
friends, of course. Few works of fiction in the Western tradition can
be read at so many levels and reasonably in so many, often contradictory, ways. The reading of such great literature expands a
reader's horizons, but in which direction? Reading literary classics
enhances the lives of adolescent readers but also confuses them.
Woolman, who aimed for moral certainty, would find the ambiguity
of a novel's truth unsettling. Who is the hero of *Don Quixote*; what is
the title character's quest; is the knight a saint, a fool, neither, or
both? If Woolman participated in uproarious laughter at Cervantes's
humor, that lapse would have haunted him twice over, both for the
"frivolous" act and for why he and his friends were laughing. There
is no humor in *Don Quixote* that is not also tragic, and the sensitive
Woolman would have felt guilty about amusement at the suffering
of another, even a fictitious soul. The pain inflicted on Don Quixote
is first physical and then psychological, but the knight, like others,
suffers throughout.

Eighteenth-century readers of *Don Quixote* were in utter conflict
on how to interpret it. Then, as now, *Don Quixote* evoked passionate
disputes about the meaning of life. It is indeed about the meaning
of everything; it is as much about death as William Sherlock's *A
Practical Discourse Concerning Death* (London, 1689), a book by an
English prelate that Woolman owned; and it is as much about life as
Robert Dodaley's *The Oeconomy of Human Life* (London, 1750), another book that Woolman came to read. Cervantes does not dictate
truth, however; he artfully poses the great questions of human experience. Answers are the province of readers rather than the focus
of sermons from a voice of ministerial authority.[27]

Images of quest and crusade appealed to Woolman, and this would explain *Don Quixote*'s lure for him as for other young men. Quixotic endeavors inspired him and might have moved him even more if he had not developed his objection to fiction as a frivolous enterprise. It had the potential to broaden his view of the world and bring him back to earth from the ethereal heights where he flew, though this was all in the future. Now he was aiming to narrow rather than broaden his vision, to focus rather than to explore.

One of Woolman's early images of heaven came from Revelation, but Milton's imagery in *Paradise Lost* offers another perspective enhancing the biblically inspired view of the afterlife. The poem's heavenly war between good and evil, which Woolman believed was still palpable on earth in his lifetime, and Milton's heroic portrayal of a thoughtful, flawed, but ultimately forgiven Adam, who sins despite his deep resolve against sinning, conformed to Quaker beliefs. Indeed, Milton wrote at the time of the Quakers' rise and tapped the same Dissenters' vision of the universe that they did. The moral that Milton drew from the fall from paradise, about the need for unquestioned obedience to God, is one that Genesis also taught Quakers.

> Henceforth I learn, that to obey is best,
> And love with fear the only God, to walk
> As in his presence, ever to observe
> His providence, and on him sole depend.

Neither Milton's proselytizing impulse nor his focus on other-worldly events was alien to Woolman, as each may be to modern readers who find it difficult to identify with the poem's imagery and moral. This was literature focused on what Woolman believed essential and what he embraced spiritually. Nonetheless, it was poetry, which Woolman rejected as a literary form; it was a work of imagination, which he considered vain; and it was a distraction from the Bible and didactic spiritual tracts.[28]

Was reading *Paradise Lost* "wanton" and "depraved"? It takes the extreme standards of a saint to think so. If Woolman's friends, good people all by the judgments of their day and faith, had written about their reactions to the poem, they would more likely have re-called the experience as an impulse to spiritual growth rather than as a fall from grace. John Smith read Milton and Cervantes without fearing for his soul, and he may well have found their works aesthet-ically, morally, and spiritually uplifting.

From Woolman's perspective, his contemporaries settled too comfortably into lives of moral compromise. John Smith followed in his father's footsteps and became a merchant with interests in the West India trade. If reading novels and poetry, drinking tea, and rid-ing in sleighs were distractions, then one can readily understand why Woolman would condemn any connection, however remote, to goods produced in a slave economy. In the diary Smith kept when he sailed to the West Indies on one of his father's ships, he never mentioned slaves or meditated on the violence of slavery, and he did not write in poetry or prose about the conditions under which bound laborers lived. The diary reads like a travelogue, and Smith's engagement with what he sees is that of a vacationer visiting a trop-ical island: "Having a mind to see the Island of Barbadoes, and to know the manner of living at sea and to survey the wonders of the Lord in the deep and having my father's consent so to do, I set out from home on the 8th day of 10 mo 1741 being 3d day of the week." If he had any doubts about his father's business or his own role in the economy of slavery, he did not record them, and everything he wrote suggests that he plied his trade in good conscience.[29]

We learn from Smith's diaries how a good and successful Quaker man lived in New Jersey during the 1740s and 1750s. Smith stood at the center of socially respectable behavior in his business and faith community. Thus, when Woolman broke new moral ground, he split from some of the leading philanthropists of his faith. And when he embraced spiritual tradition, it was that of the previous century—of the Quaker martyrs—and of the more distant, idealized past.

Woolman's *Journal* suggests that he believed that engaging with secular culture on its own terms leads to a sanguine acceptance of the world. Attachment to the earth, enjoyment of simple pleasures, and distraction from the inward gaze of spirituality make the common-place acceptable and the chosen path the easy and practical one. By small steps, by a gentle slope, good people decline from reading the Bible to reading *Paradise Lost*, to swimming, to buying ice skates manufactured under harsh working conditions, to becoming attached to horses and sleighs, to owning fine clothes in great quantities, dining at expensive restaurants, living in houses larger than they need, and wasting resources that others might better use, all of which we can rationalize in terms of the acceptable moral standards of other good people around us who live in much the same way.

Where does the slope start? Where does it end? Woolman came to believe that he knew, and he may not have exaggerated the case. The human, animal, and ecological costs of practical living entail moral compromises that we, but not the saint, pay. Woolman's implied criticism of his teenage friends has always seemed harsh to his admirers, who know the lives of social commitment and faithful religious practice that such upstanding Quakers as the Logans, Smiths, and Pembertons led. Admiring readers have generally reckoned that references in Woolman's *Journal* must be to some other unknown, less respectable individuals. But that is not obviously or necessarily so. Woolman was capable of judging good people severely, albeit gently, anonymously, making his point without pointing a finger except in private, just as his father had done to him.

The fathers of Woolman's friends had bought and sold slaves. After Hannah Logan and John Smith married, they owned a slave named Menah whom she inherited from her mother in 1754. Woolman knew when he began writing the *Journal* how deeply embedded the Quaker merchants were in the slave economy. Slaves were the visible fruit of family trees with rotting limbs, if not dead roots. Where did it all start—by a too exuberant love for their children, as Woolman later argued, and by the resulting desire to leave descendants more than was necessary or good for their souls? How would it all end? Surely, Woolman believed, moral compromises and natural attachments lead to more violence and possibly war. This is what Woolman saw in the idle pleasures of teenagers from rich mercantile families. His friends were not the spiritual offspring of martyrs; they were morally compromised.

By 1756, when Woolman wrote the self-condemnatory passages in his *Journal*, he knew what kinds of adults his friends had become, but he did not know everything they would accomplish. Samuel Smith (1720–76) became a member of the New Jersey Assembly, where he served for twenty years; was the treasurer of the colony;

and was a member of the Provincial Council. He became best known for his *History of the Colony of Nova-Caesaria, or New Jersey* (1765), widely respected in his lifetime and still an essential source on the colonial origins of the state. His brother John (1722–71) became a merchant, like his father, and began his career on one of his father's ships. He was a founder of the Pennsylvania Hospital and the Philadelphia Contributorship for Insurance of Houses Lost by Fire, a member of the New Jersey Assembly, a justice of the peace, and a county judge. Israel Pemberton, Jr. (1715–99), a prominent merchant and leading Quaker, took an interest in Indian affairs. His brother James (1723–1809) was a businessman who was to succeed Benjamin Franklin as the president of the Pennsylvania Abolition Society in 1790. The third Pemberton brother, John (1727–95), a Quaker minister, was to care for John Woolman in his last illness.

Woolman neither renounced nor abandoned these friends, but he did judge others as he judged himself. As he recognized in retrospect, achieving saintliness is a process. He was not born into it. By his early teens he had passed through stages on the way to his spiritual destination, but he was far in distance, if not in time, from reaching it. Divine revelation—his epiphany while reading the Bible—preceded a period of adolescent frivolity during which he struggled to dwell in the Light. He continued to hear God's voice within him but nonetheless killed the birds, acted disrespectfully toward his mother, and, most grievously to him, indulged in light-hearted sociability with his rich friends. These were not totally bad times, and as he recalled, his "merciful father forsook [him] not utterly." Still, even with the grace of God, the good instruction of his parents, and his efforts to model himself on Quaker and early Christian saints, "the sight of my backsliding affected me with sorrow . . . vanity was added to vanity, and repentance to repentance; upon the whole my mind was more and more alienated from the Truth." This was the state of what can be termed a "divided self," which marked a period of struggle when the outcome was unclear. This was the place from which he needed a dramatic emotional breakthrough, even though he believed that he already had the seeds of grace and voice of God within him.[30]

4

Young Man Wool

1736–43

JOHN Woolman's struggle between spirit and flesh is a Christian commonplace that can be traced in the writings of the apostle Paul, Augustine, Francis of Assisi, and Thomas à Kempis, as well as Protestants such as John Bunyan, George Fox, and Jonathan Edwards. Eighteenth-century Quakers, like other Christians of their time, reduced religious belief to biblical binaries—good and evil, spiritual and profane, natural and supernatural—embodied by each individual. No wonder, then, that triumph of the good, spiritual, and supernatural over the evil, profane, and natural is a common theme in Quaker journals.[1]

Quaker and other Christian diarists often described illness as precipitating a spiritual transformation. John Churchman felt himself blessed that "in his mercy the Lord visited me with a sore fit of sickness, and by his rod of correction brought me a little more to myself." Joshua Evans (1731–98), a Quaker minister from Haddonfield, had a similar interpretation of his pleurisy as a spiritual breakthrough: "At length I thought I was willing to die, and made a covenant to amend my ways, if my life should be continued." Woolman tells readers that contracting a near-fatal illness at the age of sixteen dropped him to the bottom of an emotional pit, from which he emerged a new young man, one less attached to the world, less fearful of death, and closer than ever to God.

In this swift race it pleased God to visit me with sickness, so that I doubted of recovering. And then did darkness, horror, and amazement with full force seize me, even when my pain and distress of body was very great. I thought it would have been better for me never to have had a being than to see the day which I now saw. I was filled with confusion, and in great affliction both of mind and body I lay and bewailed myself . . . and at length that Word which is as a fire and a hammer broke and dissolved my rebellious heart. And then my cries were put up in contrition, and in the multitude of his mercies I found inward relief.

Woolman's despair led to a surrender, which he believed retrospectively was the beginning of the end of his internal trauma. He experienced further backsliding after the illness, and he recalled that it disturbed him more than ever, so he returned more quickly to the right path. In this still troubled, but less troubling, state, Woolman passed the two years leading to his eighteenth birthday, "near which time I felt the judgments of God in my soul like a consuming fire."[2]

Such an event is recognizable as a conversion experience, considered in other Protestant traditions essential to the reception of grace. Some Quakers, especially early members and converts, described a flash of spiritual rebirth, but that was not the way that eighteenth-century Friends generally experienced spiritual growth. For most, it was less traumatic and subject to setbacks along the way. Yet Woolman, consistent with his attachment to the founding generation of Quakers, experienced a flash of transformation rather than slow progress. He broke down emotionally, and then sought out "deserts and lonely places and there with tears did confess my sins to God and humbly craved help of him. And I may say with reverence he was near to me in my troubles, and in those times of humiliation opened my ear to discipline."[3]

Carl Jung calls such an experience integration (or individuation) of the self after a conflict between the conscious and subconscious mind, and he describes it as part of the human condition. William James likewise sees such a transformation as psychologically beneficial, a movement from a "sick" soul to a "healthy-minded" one. No one ever achieves complete integration, of course, but without progress soul-wrenching anxiety can be chronic. Ideally, Puritans dwelled in a state of perpetual stress; this peaceful, in many cases smooth, resolution of internal conflict is a Quaker contribution to the Protestant religious experience.[4]

Woolman registered an additional dimension to the spiritual growth brought about by his near-fatal illness: he connected mortality with empathy and reported that his encounter with death led him to a more expansive beneficence and a deeper love of the earth's beleaguered creatures. The prospect of death erased distinctions of class, race, and species. The Woolman of the *Journal* comes out the other side of his life-threatening illness with a newfound capacity for "universal love." This insight led him to love across the lines that people were wont to draw between "us," however defined, and "them," whoever they are.[5]

For two years after his illness, Woolman tells readers, he withdrew from casual social relations and devoted himself to contemplation. He retired after each Meeting for Worship to read scriptures and "other good books." In his *Journal* he attributed to this regimen several insights that helped focus his energies. He dwelled steadfastly on the inward life, "wherein the heart doth love and reverence God the Creator and learn to exercise true justice and goodness, not only toward all men but also toward the brute creatures."[6]

For Woolman, this identification with "brute creatures" is a critical juncture in his moral development. His newfound kinship with animals clarifies the significance of his story about killing the robins. As a child he had accepted an identity as a hunter, a veritable Old Testament Nimrod, who, because of his humanity, inhabits a place above and outside the rest of creation. Now Woolman understood why, when a boy, he felt so bad, why the Light within him recoiled at the violence he perpetrated on the defenseless birds. They were kin rather than prey. Familial responsibility included more than biological relations, fellow Quakers, and white Anglo-Americans; the human race and all living creatures were brothers whose keeper he was.[7]

Woolman believed that cruelty toward any being was a rejection of God, that the deity favored no particular religion and accepted all "sincere, upright-hearted people." He saw the world anew and discovered beauty, grace, and harmony where he had not noticed them before. Divine revelations moved him to tears, opened his heart to greater meekness than he had known before, and gave him access to Truth previously hidden from him.[8]

Looking back, Woolman believed that by the time he was eighteen he was on the path to his adult life. He had begun to separate emotionally from the people around him and to extend his love; he no longer felt any closer to family members than to all of creation. He craved the solitude that enhanced his saintly pursuits in the challenging environment of the carnal world. In the *Journal*, Woolman idealizes such isolation, and we have only scattered clues to how it actually changed his behavior. There are hints that his detachment and expansiveness affected people close to him, but we do not know how his friends and family perceived him.

The *Journal* alludes to an external influence on his separation from others, but as usual the reference is vague and, in the published text, easy to miss (the final draft of the manuscript is slightly more revealing): "[And now I come to a winter evening which to me is memorable.] I remember one evening I had spent some time in reading a pious author, and walking out alone I humbly prayed to the Lord for his help, that I might be delivered from all those vanities which so ensnared me [and afflicted my mind]." Woolman learned from praying that he "must not go into company as heretofore in my own will." The connection, as always for Woolman, is indirect: he read, he listened, he read and listened again, and God instructed him. We might perceive a direct link between text and enlightenment, but the intervention of direct inspiration was, for him, essential to his understanding of the process by which he discerned God's will. We could say that his reading kindled a mystical experience that might not otherwise have occurred, but that is not what he believed.[9]

It is likely that Woolman was reading Thomas à Kempis's *Imitation of Christ*, a book we know influenced his asceticism and early antislavery writings and was a likely inspiration for his self-reforms as well. Woolman's *Imitation* was an English translation from the

Latin. (It did not contain the fourth section, "On the Blessed Sacrament," for which Quakers and some other Protestant traditions had no use.) Kempis specifically instructs, in the Catholic ascetic tradition, that "unless a man is set loose from all creatures he cannot freely turn himself to divine things." This would have helped Woolman focus on the belief that "whatever is not God is nothing and ought to be recognized as nothing." Woolman echoed Kempis's ambition to separate from other humans: "If you could free yourself from all creatures Jesus would gladly dwell within you." One can see why it makes as much sense to see Woolman as a disciple of Kempis (minus the latter's celebration of the Eucharist) as to view him as an heir of the early Quaker mystics.[10]

Not that such views of God and humanity were distinctive to Kempis or Woolman. Anthony Benezet (1713–84), for example, a contemporary of Woolman's and a fellow Quaker antislavery reformer, expressed similar beliefs, though he did not practice them with the same literal devotion or draw them directly from Kempis. "I hope I am cured from any more dependence & expectation from man," Benezet wrote to a correspondent at about the same time that Woolman was drafting the early parts of his *Journal*. "May I seek comfort & establishment in God alone, by retirement, silence, and prayer." Benezet was influenced here by John Everard (1575? 1650?), the English mystic and author of *Some Gospel Treasures*, a collection of sermons that was published in an abridged American edition in 1757. Woolman also read and owned Everard's sermons, but they were not widely available in 1740, at the time of the experience he recounts in the *Journal*.[11]

Benezet, Woolman, and Everard all wrote in the same tradition, and it is likely that all read Kempis among other Christian mystics. In Everard, readers could find the same focus on Christ as Redeemer, a celebration of the cross and of "primitive Christians," a call to detachment from the material world, and a disdain for human nature. Everard drew heavily on St. Paul's two letters to the Corinthians, which preach against the "natural man," "corrupt nature," and the "wisdom of this world."[12]

Woolman surrendered his will to God's, just as Kempis advised. And he dwelled on the idea of the self-abnegating, crucified Christ the Redeemer (as opposed to God the Father, the Holy Spirit, or the New Testament alternatives of Christ as friend, teacher, or model), found not only in Kempis but in George Fox, William Dewsbury, and Robert Barclay, who believed that this self-abnegation opens oneself to God as the crucified Christ, "the True Light that enlightens every man."[13]

It is consistent with Woolman's self-portrayal as being spiritually inspired from within that he does not name Kempis as an influence and minimizes the significance of the worldly life choices he made during these crucial years. He summarizes his decision to leave home in a casual three sentences that belie the weight of an eldest son rejecting his patrimony. The Woolman farm eventually reached one thousand acres, a very sizable "plantation," and owning it would have made Woolman a man of substance. Woolman does not mention his family's financial success or the lineage that linked him, through his mother's relatives, to industrialists and slaveholders. He only hints at unnamed relatives, friends, and acquaintances who offered him business opportunities and who connected him to the wealthiest Quaker families in the New World.

Writing in the *Journal* about a later period of his life, Woolman reflects back on this transitional moment: "In my youth I was used to hard labour, and though I was middling healthy, yet my nature was not fitted to endure so much as many others, that being often weary, I was prepared to sympathize with those whose circumstance in life as free men required constant labour to answer the demands of their creditors, and with others under oppression." It is clear that he didn't want to continue with the farm's never-ending tasks. He saw a different way of doing things, but he was powerless to make changes. So he forthrightly grafted his view of the matter onto his confession that he "was not fitted to endure" farmwork.

> A belief was gradually settled in my mind that if such who had great estates generally lived in that humility and plainness which belongs to a Christian life, and laid much easier rents and interests on their lands and moneys and thus led the way to a right use of things, so great a number of people might be employed in things useful that labour both for men

and other creatures would need to be no more than an agreeable employ.[14]

Whether the break caused conflict within him or with his family, Woolman does not say. In the first and third drafts of the *Journal* but not in the published version, he makes it clear that he had been looking for a way to get away: "I had for a considerable time found my mind less given to husbandry than heretofore, having often in view some other way of living." The impression is that he wanted to find another "way of living" rather than to choose a particular alternative.

All this time I lived with my parents and wrought on the plantation, and having had schooling pretty well for a planter, I used to improve in winter evenings and other leisure times. And being now in the twenty-first year of my age, a man in much business shop-keeping and baking asked me if I would hire with him to tend shop and keep books. I acquainted my father with the proposal, and after some deliberation it was agreed for me to go.

Woolman "wrought" on the family "plantation" first cleared by his grandfather. Together the two words collaborate in a subtle judgment on the future he rejected. They imply a kind of grandeur repulsive to him.[15]

If Woolman's was a hyperbolic reading of New Testament injunctions against greed, it was the characteristic excess of an ascetic. Indeed, Christ addresses advice about renouncing possessions only to those who seek perfection on earth. His reply to his disciples who despair that camels cannot be put through the eyes of needles is that "for mortals it is impossible, but for God all things are possible" (Matthew 19:26). Humans cannot achieve perfection, and therefore pure asceticism is not essential for salvation; one must trust in God. Still, Woolman like Kempis aimed higher than the Gospels' lowest expectations. When Christ says to his disciples, "Be perfect, therefore, as your heavenly Father is perfect" (Matthew 5:48), Kempis and Woolman took him literally.

Woolman portrays himself as a passive partner in the transaction that got him off the farm—"a man . . . asked me"—and he "acquainted" his father with the "proposal," which sounds rather low-key. His unnamed future employer was likely John Ogburn, who retired five or six years later and sold Woolman some land and a small shop in 1747. "Some deliberation" could imply conflict within the family, prayerful consideration, a cautious decision-making process, or simply negotiation of terms between the man and Woolman's father. Woolman also obscures, or does not recall, whether the offer was coincident with his reaching the age of twenty-one or came after he had reached his majority, when it would have been more difficult for his father to oppose the plan.

Anxiety about the spiritual consequences of leaving home tempered the excitement of independence. Perhaps Woolman was overwrought.

> At home I had lived retired, and now having a prospect of being much in the way of company, I felt frequent and fervent cries in my heart to God, the Father of Mercies, that he would preserve me from all taint and corruption, that in this more public employ[ment] I might serve him, my gracious Redeemer, in that humility and self-denial with which I had been in a small degree exercised in a very private life.

He had only recently begun to distance himself, with much effort and backsliding, from young people who distracted him from his spiritual focus. Working in a store would open him to the "carnal temptations" from which he had been protected by the comparative isolation of the farm and the daily influence of his parents. If he was to realize the "humility and self-denial" that would enable him to join his "gracious Redeemer," he would have to work even harder on his spiritual development.[16]

The question Woolman does not ask in the *Journal* is whether taking this job was itself a vanity, a distraction, a choice that expressed worldly attachment and spiritual compromise, whether he had leaped from the frying pan of secure wealth to the fire of ambition. He may have reasoned, or even rationalized in light of his distaste for farm labor, that as a merchant he would have fewer worldly responsibilities and thus more time for prayerful withdrawal. The challenge was to avoid commercial success, and certainly riches were more accessible to a merchant than to a New Jersey planter. He might have had the ambition for an earlier retirement than a farmer could reasonably expect. He might have considered remaining single, meaning a deficit of family labor useful for farming. He may have had difficulty sorting through such subtle distinctions when he wrote in retrospect. With the benefit of hindsight, knowing how things had turned out, he may have lost touch with all the anxieties his initial decision aroused.

The shop where Woolman worked was in Mount Holly, five miles from his childhood home. His old acquaintances came to see him in the shop expecting that he would have time for them when he was not working. Perhaps they believed he would have more leisure now that he was out from under the discipline imposed by his parents and the farm's unremitting chores. Woolman writes that he prayed about this problem and God favored him with the strength to resist temptation. "And as I had now left my father's house outwardly, I found my Heavenly Father to be merciful to me beyond what I can express." He left his father for his Father, just as Francis of Assisi and many other saints had said they did. Woolman writes that he worked by day and spent the evenings alone, contributing to spiritual growth. After some time his "former acquaintance[s]" gave up on him. He then "began to be known to some whose conversation was helpful." This blessing came, as others before it, passively. "Began to be known" is an awkward construction that implies no reaching out for the unnamed people who came to him.[17]

The path Woolman took in his quest for self-improvement—isolating himself from his friends, avoiding taverns, eating abstemiously, and reading, writing, and contemplating alone—is similar to the one described by Benjamin Franklin in his *Autobiography*. Although Franklin pursued secular improvement toward material ends that Woolman rejected, both men aimed to subdue their appetites and gain self-control. Both practiced self-denial and avoided sociability on their personal roads to perfection.

Franklin, who was fourteen years Woolman's senior and outlived him by another eighteen, identified his vices and tried to eliminate them. But he was much easier on himself. He dwelled more on the appearance than the reality of virtue. And unlike Woolman, he was capable of making up a good story to illustrate an autobiographical point. Woolman continued to battle his personal flaws, but they differed from Franklin's and occurred for different reasons, among which he mentions his "feeble" nature and "timorousness." He struggled to overcome his fear of death and to become more compassionate toward fellow humans, including the acquaintances "entangled in snares like those which had entangled me."[18]

He attended Meetings for Worship with a renewed spirit that he implies was an outgrowth of his independence. Being on his own gave Woolman a sense of greater responsibility for himself, helped him separate emotionally from his family, and reinforced his commitment to love strangers as much as family and friends. He thought he was gaining greater awareness of others' perspectives and a deeper sensitivity to their plight.[19]

He reconsidered, then, the role he would play in the world. "From an inward purifying, and steadfast abiding under it," he writes, "springs a lively operative desire for the good of others." Quakers call this general concern charity, and over the course of the eighteenth century they defined it ever more expansively to reach beyond family and their faith group to slaves, Indians, the impoverished, and humanity in general. We call it empathy. Enlightenment figures called it sympathy, and the eighteenth century was a critical time in its long-term development, in which Woolman's experience was exemplary.[20]

This blossoming of Quaker charity significantly contributed to the environment in which Woolman's universal humanitarianism grew, just as his self-critical focus and interiorized faith were outgrowths of the tradition of Quaker quietism. The quietist belief that revelation comes through introspection, silence, and the overcoming of desire leads adherents to elevate inspiration above all other expressions of faith. That is why Woolman emphasizes revelation and discounts the external influences on him even where we might identify a textual source for his insights. As John Everard puts it, "we can never see the transcendent beauty and luster of the scriptures, but in the Light of God." Inspiration precedes the reading and informs it.[21]

Other influences on Woolman could have included the Great Awakening, but historians of Quakerism agree that Friends were in fact appalled by the outburst of religious enthusiasm that we associate with the revivals of the 1740s. Quakers had become collectively genteel by then, and they were sensitive to charges of excessive enthusiasm, which critics had leveled at them for a century. Now they rejected both the forms and content of enthusiastic religion, including the whole New Light movement associated with the Great Awakening, which had great appeal for people on the fringes of society, although it was not limited to the alienated and dispossessed. Perhaps the New Lights reminded them of embarrassing aspects of their own founders' behavior—preaching naked and/or loudly in town squares or interrupting church services, for example—now that they were upstanding, successful, and conservative. The open-air revivals were aesthetically unappealing, and the conflict within churches repelled them.[22]

Enlightenment ideas that favored balance, order, and rationality appealed to the same prosperous, urbane, genteel Quakers who disliked enthusiastic religion, and these were the very Quakers to whom Woolman eventually preached, whose values he rejected, and whose compromises seemed so soul-destructive to him. By any useful definition of the Enlightenment, we cannot include the Woolman of the *Journal* among its adherents. To quote the preeminent historian of the American Enlightenment, "The Enlightenment consists of all those who believe two propositions: first, that the present age is more enlightened than the past; and second, that we understand nature and man best through the use of natural faculties." Woolman rejected both propositions, and his universal humanitarianism was not based on rational calculations, an elevation of the future over the past, or a belief in the utility of our natural faculties. His writings did express both the contemporary expansion of empathy and a newly realized focus on the self, however, so there are grounds for viewing him as Enlightened in those particular ways.[23]

One can see Woolman as an Enlightenment figure in some of the same ways that William Penn was one. Penn had direct connections to the Cambridge Platonists, who highly valued human reason, and some of his work expressed a rationalist approach to religion. The Platonists emphasized the immanence of God's divine reason throughout creation and believed that through human reason one can unite with the divine mind. The Quaker beliefs in an interior God seemed compatible with this Platonic "light of God in nature" and akin to Quaker notions of divine inspiration. Woolman read at least some of Penn's writings, but curiously there is no evidence that he knew the rationalist Neoplatonic ones. From the start Quakers had drawn on the language of natural rights, which they got from the Levellers of the 1640s, a loosely grouped movement of equalitarians, rather than from later secular sources. Never slaves to consistency, they were capable of conflating quietist, Neoplatonic, and rationalist themes all in one breath. Benjamin Lay, the radical eighteenth-century Quaker social reformer, quoted widely from writers as diverse as Ovid (in Latin), the Gospels, Thomas à Kempis, and John Milton in both a prophetic voice and an occasional voice of reason with Enlightenment tones.[24]

Woolman read other writers influenced by the Enlightenment, including Alexander Arscott (1676–1737), whose *Some Considerations Relating to the Present State of the Christian Religion* was one of the few works of eighteenth-century Quaker theology reprinted in the colonies. Arscott dwelled on Christ as Redeemer, endorsed the Sermon on the Mount as a clear measure of ethical behavior, and had no use for deism, which emphasizes reason over mystical experience and the belief that God created, but is not active in, the world. Along with such companionable ideals, though, Woolman would also have gotten a dose of rationalist religion from Arscott.[25]

If the influences of the Great Awakening and the Enlightenment are difficult to discern in Woolman's *Journal*, his connections to the marketplace leap from it. His humanitarianism built on a rejection of the complacency that he thought had developed as a result of the Quakers' material success. His concern for strangers emerged from his understanding of the global network of connections woven by empire and trade, which made everyone responsible for everyone else. Woolman believed that no one is isolated from the depredations of the marketplace, all are guilty, and everyone is responsible for reform. His ability to imagine solutions to the problems that stretched beyond his ken is the same as that which enabled merchant capitalists to exploit their worldwide connections. Woolman as farmer, merchant, and, later, tailor was a creature of the marketplace he prospered in. By the time he began drafting his *Journal*, he had grasped his complicity in the moral logic of supply and demand and had realized how difficult, if not impossible, it was to extricate oneself from the chain of connections that abused slaves, wage laborers, and beasts of burden. His ministry was to address precisely these problems, and universal love was the essential step toward the reform he believed in.[26]

"All faithful people are not called to the public ministry," Woolman observes, "but whoever are, are called to minister of that which they have tasted and handled spiritually." Once it was clear to him that God intended him for public ministry, Woolman thought he had a responsibility to share his insights with those around him. "The outward modes of worship are various," he explains in the *Journal*, "but wherever men are true ministers of Jesus Christ it is from the operation of his spirit upon their hearts, first purifying them and thus giving them a feeling sense of the conditions of others." Woolman's heightened sensitivity to the needs of God's creatures led him to expansive—what practical-minded people of goodwill would see as excessive—charity. He may have empathized with strangers and people of other races as much as or more than he did with friends and relations, with non-Quakers as much as with coreligionists, with the impoverished as much as with people of his own or higher material state, domestic animals along with their human masters. He aimed not only to love all creatures equally but to love all of them more than himself. This charitable ambition was his gift and his burden; he took the parable of the Good Samaritan to heart. Jesus replied, "Go and do likewise" (Luke 10:37), and John Woolman tried to follow God.[27]

ONLY after he had left home did Woolman's gifts become clear to him. Rather than have increased contacts with the world undermine his spirituality, as he had feared, his jobs opened his heart to deeper compassion for the people he met, even those who had once tempted him. During the early 1740s he identified his public ministry and began to speak more often in Meeting for Worship: "I stood up and said some words in a meeting, but not keeping close to the divine opening, I said more than was required of me; and being soon sensible of my error, I was afflicted in mind some weeks without any light or comfort, even to that degree that I could take satisfaction in nothing."[28]

Woolman prayed to overcome these mistakes, to master his corporeal self, and for the triumph of his spirit. He continued to work to conquer his worldly ambitions, attachments, desires, intellectual impulses, and physical wants. Having feared the effects of the carnal world on his soul, he soon discovered a deeper spirituality and sense of purpose. He learned from practice and failure what it meant to speak from the heart and silence his will. Success meant dominance of his spirit over his body, which God rewarded with mercy and access to the "spring of divine love" that gave him peace of mind and heart. He learned greater humility, discipline, and patience, waiting

> in silence sometimes many weeks together, until I felt that rise which prepares the creature to stand like a trumpet through which the Lord speaks to his flock . . . This truth was early fixed in my mind, and I was taught to watch the pure opening and to take heed lest while I was standing to speak, my own will should get uppermost and cause me to utter words from worldly wisdom and depart from the channel of the true gospel ministry.[29]

Burlington Monthly Meeting formally recognized Woolman's gifts for public ministry, along with those of two others, in August 1743. This meant that it had discerned Truth in the messages delivered out of the silence of worship by the three men, and it gave them a place among its elders and ministers. At the age of twenty-two, Woolman had achieved an earthly judgment of his spiritual success; it was not God's judgment and not his own critical self-evaluation, but it was meaningful nonetheless. Only a year after he had left home, Woolman had begun his ministry, and it is significant that he did so from within the Society of Friends, not as a critic, an alienated outsider, or a disowned castaway as other reformers had done before him.[30]

The missing piece of Woolman's ministry was a focused insight into what exactly God meant him to teach the world. On this question, he saw the first glimmers of the Light shortly after he had begun living alone, and it had to do with slaves. During Woolman's childhood, slaves were at the periphery of his consciousness. Since his immediate family owned none, he had been sheltered from the larger world in which African and African American slaves were routinely bought and sold. He had witnessed social injustice and suffering when he went to Haddonfield, Burlington, and Philadelphia to visit friends, but within a year of his leaving home to work in Mount Holly, in 1742, he had a life-transforming attack of conscience. This occurred when his employer directed him to write a bill of sale for a black woman. Fifteen years later Woolman recalled in his *Journal* what happened next.

> The thing was sudden, and though the thoughts of writing an instrument of slavery for one of my fellow creatures felt uneasy, yet I remembered I was hired by the year, that it was my master who directed me to do it, and that it was an elderly man, a member of our Society, who bought her; so through weakness I gave way and wrote it, but at the executing it, I was so afflicted in my mind that I said before my master and the Friend that I believed slavekeeping to be a practice inconsistent with the Christian religion.[31]

Woolman knew that explanations for his behavior—duty to his employer, deference to the two older men, respect for the purchaser, and perhaps a belief that the new Quaker master would treat the slave better than another owner might—were rationalizations to excuse a wrongful act. Moral weakness had kept him from acting conscientiously. Woolman believed that merely voicing his concern had not been enough: "This in some degree abated my uneasiness, yet as often as I reflected seriously upon it I thought I should have been clearer if I had desired to be excused from it as a thing against my conscience, for such it was."[32]

In an earlier draft of the *Journal*, Woolman specifically linked his action to his selfishness. "I should have been clearer," the manuscript reads, "if leaving all consequences I had craved to be excused from it as a thing against my conscience." These are stronger words—"craved" rather than "desired"—and he recognizes the fear of personal "consequences" as a motive. At least by the time he wrote this, he saw himself as morally deficient rather than ethically torn, but the editorial committee reversed that judgment. They weakened the language of the published *Journal* to characterize Woolman less harshly than he judged himself.[33]

Thereafter, Woolman tells us in the *Journal*, he was able to act conscientiously, but he never overcame his guilt about the slave woman; he had lost the inner peace accessible through the discipline of the cross because of an excess of conscience, and he never recovered it. He could not have freed the slave; if he had not executed the document, his employer would have done it himself. He failed to act consistently with the argument he made after the fact to the two older men.

> And some time after this a young man of our Society spake to me to write an instrument of slavery, he having lately taken a Negro into his house. I told him I was not easy to write it, for though many kept slaves in our Society, as in others [and seemed easy in it], I still believed the practice was not right, and desired to be excused from [doing the] writing. I spoke to him in good will, and he told me that keeping slaves was not altogether agreeable to his mind, but that the slave being a gift made to his wife, he had accepted of her.

The bracketed phrase "and seemed easy in it" must have embarrassed the editorial committee; they deleted it, toning down Woolman's contention that Quakers not only owned and traded in slaves but felt no pangs of conscience.[34]

Woolman's views were contrary to widespread practice among Quakers, but he detected an opening to reform in the young man who thought that slavery was not "altogether agreeable." The rationalization that keeping a slave given to his wife was morally different from purchasing one may have worked for the man, but at least Woolman had tweaked the man's conscience. Perhaps reformation of behavior within the Society of Friends was possible in the future.

When Woolman first began to testify publicly against slavery, the views of most Quakers on the issue were no different from those of other American colonists. Some owned slaves without compunction, believed there was nothing wrong with slavery as long as they were not brutal masters, and rationalized that slavery exposed people of African descent to Christianity. Others either aspired to own slaves or did not think about slavery at all. Woolman's abolitionism, which began to clarify for him in 1742, grew from a Quaker legacy that reached back to the founding of the Society of Friends, but his approach differed from that of the Quaker reformers who had come before him.[35]

George Fox had expressed concern about the spiritual implications of slavery for Quaker masters as early as 1657. In 1671, witnessing slavery firsthand during a trip to Barbados, Fox warned American Quakers of the moral trap that endangered them. He was sensitive to the charge that Friends were aiming to stir up slave revolts in the Caribbean, so he carefully addressed himself to the spiritual welfare and humane treatment of slaves, not to their emancipation. He preached to slaves in Quaker homes, gave them rudimentary instruction on Christianity, and exhorted them to love God and behave consistently with the Ten Commandments.[36]

Asking masters to treat their slaves well, as Fox did, falls far short of opposing the institution of slavery. Indeed, exhortations on enlightened mastery could unwittingly support slavery by meliorating conditions under which rebellion was likely and by lulling critics into the false belief that the slaves were content and slavery was benign. But Fox emphasized the Quaker belief that all people are equal in the eyes of God, which was significant when applied to slavery, though unconvincing to slaveowners. He also suggested that freeing white servants created a precedent for eventually freeing African slaves too, perhaps after a given term of service—thirty years or so.[37]

Fox's logic had no effect on Quaker slaveholding or Quaker participation in the slave trade. Still, the basic contours of Quaker opposition were present in what he said, and they might have created more moral stress than they did among the Friends. Quaker testimonies on equality and integrity, and against violence and sloth, became the basis for moral incantations voiced by abolitionists in the eighteenth century.

William Edmundson (?–1712), an Irish Quaker who accompanied Fox to Barbados in 1671, is the first member of the Society of Friends known to have advocated the abolition of slavery. Initially he took the same approach as Fox, holding meetings for slaves in Quaker homes and reassuring the colony's governor that far from encouraging rebellions, he was teaching the slaves Christian principles that would make them less likely to commit violence against their masters. After he left the West Indies, though, Edmundson began to worry about the souls of slaveowners, with whom he felt a greater kinship than he did with slaves and therefore a greater responsibility. He saw the master-slave relationship as parallel to that between God and humans; he came to believe that granting physical liberty to slaves was a path to spiritual liberty for the masters.

Edmundson issued his first denunciation of slavery from Newport, Rhode Island, in 1676. Later he reached the Chesapeake colonies, where he honed his message to a moral indictment of slavery as a breach of the Golden Rule: "Which of you would have the blacks, or others, to make you their slaves without hope or expectation of freedom?" He described enslavement as "an oppression on the mind" of a slave, which bound her or his spirit to the earth. Again, as they were with George Fox, Quaker and non-Quaker masters were unmoved by what they considered impractical counsel. But the Barbados planters saw Edmundson's preaching as a threat, and laws were passed banning Quaker itinerants from holding Meetings for Worship and barring masters from taking slaves to the religious services of any faith.[38]

William Penn had no greater effect on American Quakers' participation in the slave trade than Fox or Edmundson. He never believed that slavery was part of the social design for the Quaker colony that bore his name, and his moral logic mirrored theirs. If the three of them had any influence, it came in their injunctions to treat slaves less harshly than was the norm.[39]

Other individuals during the seventeenth century, both Quaker and non-Quaker, had moral qualms about the treatment of Africans, but they too had no success in slowing the growth of slavery in Anglo-America. Roger Williams wanted Rhode Island to have a free labor system, but a 1652 law forbidding the enslavement of Indians, blacks, and whites was unenforceable, and it did not prevent the colony from becoming the center of the North American slave trade. Richard Baxter was an English Puritan who excoriated owners and traders in slaves as offenders against Christian morality. He wrote *A Christian Directory: or, A Summ of Practical Theologie and Cases of Conscience*; published in 1673, it was the earliest British antislavery tract. Baxter believed that only a criminal conviction and subsequent sentence justified enslavement and that the only just rationale for purchasing slaves was to hold them for ransom. Thomas Tryon, an English mystic, wrote several essays published in the 1680s that advocated abolition because of slavery's violence, injustice, breach of the Golden Rule, and instigation of war. Tryon was the first to represent the slaves' own perspective by composing one of his essays as a dialogue between an enslaved man and his master. The American Puritan ministers Cotton Mather and John Eliot and the English clergyman Morgan Godwyn, the last of whom spent two years in Virginia during the 1660s, cautioned masters that they were responsible for the care of slaves' souls.[40]

The only collective movement against the institution in colonial America came with the Quakers, but it was a slow and tortuous path that brought them to stand publicly against ownership of their fellow humans. Four members of a Meeting in Germantown, Pennsylvania, addressed a petition opposing slavery to Philadelphia Yearly Meeting in 1688, but Yearly Meeting tabled and thereafter ignored their plea. (Indeed, the document was forgotten until it was found more than 150 years later.) The Germantown petitioners believed slavery inconsistent with Quaker charity based on the Golden Rule. "Is there any that would be done or handled at this manner?" they asked rhetorically. Did Friends not judge Muslim pirates harshly for taking English sailors captive and enslaving them? It was hypocritical, they believed, for Christians to act more immorally than Turks, who after all freed slaves who converted to Islam, as the English never did when their slaves accepted Christianity. "And those who steal or robb men, and those who buy or purchase them, are they not all alike?" Slavery also hurt the Society of Friends, they observed, by showing others that despite their testimonies and claims to be heirs to apostolic Christianity, Quakers "handel men as they handel there ye cattle . . . Pray, what thing in the world can be done worse towards us, than if men should rob or steal us away, and sell us for slaves to strange countries; separating husbands from their wives and children. Being now this is not done in the manner we would be done at therefore we contradict and are against this traffic of men-body."[41]

Five years later George Keith (1638–1716), the controversial Scottish convert, made opposition to slavery central to his attempt to purify American Quakerism; his followers called themselves Christian Quakers to distinguish the group from the "pretended Christians," Quakers who they believed acted inconsistently with New Testament teachings. Unlike the Germantown Friends, Keith published his *Exhortation*, which gave it more influence, but its publication was unauthorized. It was a serious breach of Quaker discipline to air an internal dispute without regard to the harm it could do the Society of Friends among its detractors and to disregard the tradition of moving forward only when a sense of Yearly Meeting emerged. For his efforts, the Society of Friends disowned Keith.

Keith believed that Quakers' participation in the slave trade and ownership of slaves was a barrier to spreading the gospel and "the occasion of much War, Violence, Cruelty and Oppression, and Theft & Robery of the highest Nature." However Quakers came by the slaves they traded and owned, and however well they treated them, he held masters accountable for the violence at the institution's core. Quakers were buying stolen goods and treating other people worse than they would want themselves treated.

> Therefore, in true *Christian Love*, we earnestly recommend it to all our Friends and Brethren, Not to buy any Negroes, unless it were on purpose to set them free, and that such who

have bought any, and have them at present, after some reasonable time of moderate Service they have had of them, or may have of them, that may reasonably answer to the Charge of what they have laid out, especially in keeping Negroes Children born in their House, or taken into their House, when under Age, that after a reasonable time of service to answer that Charge, they may set them at Liberty, and during the time they have them, to teach them to read, and give them a Christian Education.[42]

Quakers could not ignore the logic of these antislavery visionaries, even as they invoked sanctions against the messengers who challenged Yearly Meeting's authority and threatened schism. They were moved by William Southeby and Cadwalader Morgan, who in 1696 advocated abolition among Quakers and a ban on members importing slaves. Philadelphia Yearly Meeting took a modest first official step that year with an "advice" to members against participation in the capture and importation of slaves. There is no evidence, though, that any Quakers took this advice and plenty of evidence that they widely ignored it.[43]

Two years later, Robert Pyle, a member of Chester, Pennsylvania, Monthly Meeting, tried to push the consensus further with a short paper questioning the morality of keeping slaves. Slaves were stolen from their homes in time of war, and Quakers opposed both theft and combat, he wrote. The slaves could also do violence to their owners, he observed: "They might rise in rebellion and doe us much mischief; except we keep a malisha [militia]," which would also be contrary to Quaker doctrine.[44]

In 1698, Richard Hill, a Maryland ship captain, a Quaker, and apparently a slaveowner himself, included a fifteen-line antislavery poem in a letter he sent to an English Quaker. Hill's rhymes are not memorable as poetry, and the unpublished poem may have influenced no one. Hill draws a parallel between "Xtian" slavery and the injustice perpetrated on Israelites by the Egyptians and alludes to the plagues God calls down on the enslavers of his people. Displaying a sympathy for the slaves that, he believes, should be universal among Christians—"objects of pity, who can but lament the inno-

110   *The Beautiful Soul of John Woolman*

cent cause of the poor ignorant"—he calls Christians to task for
excluding Africans from the message of the gospel and thus from
salvation, and protests the injustice toward those "whom God possessed with rights and liberty." His words anticipate the Enlightenment rationales that became increasingly popular during the next
century.[45]

The New England Puritan judge Samuel Sewall wrote a pamphlet titled *The Selling of Joseph* (1700), in which he denounces a fellow Puritan who held a slave in contravention of a contract that had
freed the black man. Sewall draws on both the Bible and legal logic
to indict slavery and rejects the argument that justified slavery on
the grounds that it exposed slaves to Christianity. "Evil must not be
done," Sewall reasons, "that good may come of it." Theft is theft,
he maintains, and more sinful when humans are the stolen goods.[46]

When Chester Monthly Meeting formally petitioned Philadelphia Yearly Meeting in 1711 to issue a ban on members' participation in the slave trade, it was the first indictment of the trade made
collectively by a Meeting of the Society of Friends. (The four Germantown petitioners in 1688 had acted as individuals.) Yearly Meeting deflected it on the ground that it lacked authority to go beyond
its "advice" on the subject issued in 1696. Instead it referred the
question to London Yearly Meeting in 1712, which claimed that it
too lacked authority, although three years later it advised Friends, as
Philadelphia Yearly Meeting had in 1696, to stop participating in the
international slave trade.[47]

Conservative Friends rejected the petitioners' argument and
feared the threat to the Quakers' internal harmony; they were also
offended by the public airing of what they thought of as a question
of internal discipline. Powerful elders of Yearly Meeting, among
the wealthiest and most deeply invested in slaves, tried to silence
the petitioners and end the dispute. Their response to another
petition from Chester Monthly Meeting in 1715 asked "that all
[Friends] do forbear judging or reflecting on one another either in
public or private concerning the detaining or keeping them [Ne-
groes] servants."[48]

In 1715, John Hepburn, a Quaker tailor in New Jersey, published
The American Defence of the Christian Golden Rule, which, as its title

suggests, argues against slavery from the same fundamental teachings of Christ that inspired the Germantown Quakers and George Keith. Hepburn contends that slavery not only contradicts the Golden Rule but prevents slaves from exercising their God-given free will. Since Quakers believe that salvation is available to all souls by their free choice to follow the Light within them, they were prohibiting slaves from developing the very gift that gives all humanity access to free grace. By forcibly separating man from wife and children from their parents, Quakers were responsible for their slaves committing adultery, which broke the Seventh Commandment. Arguments that slavery benefited the slaves by exposing them to Christianity were, to Hepburn, self-serving rationalizations. Masters of slaves broke the very heart of Christian teachings.

> It is not singularity or Ostentation that I appear in Print, but my Christian Duty, in Honour to God, and the Salvation and well being of the souls of men, in the Detection of the Antichristian Practice in *making slaves* of them who bear the Image of God, viz. their fellow, Creature, Man; A Practice so *cruel* and *inhumane*, that the more it is thought upon by judicious men, the more they do abhor it; It being so vile a contradiction to the Gospel of the blessed Messiah.

No record of the Quakers' response to Hepburn's pamphlet survives, but since Quaker censors did not authorize its publication, it is likely that his words were no more welcome than Keith's before him.[49]

In 1716, Chester Monthly Meeting came back to Philadelphia Yearly Meeting with a more strongly worded condemnation. This third challenge in six years did not advocate abolition but focused only on the slave trade. Again, Philadelphia Yearly Meeting dismissed the idea, this time without discussion. This enraged radicals such as William Southeby, who had agitated against slavery at least since 1696. He was one of those who had demanded abolition at Yearly Meeting in 1712 and was frustrated by the continued equivocation. He published a paper airing the dispute publicly in 1713, for which the Meeting disciplined him; in 1716 he did it again and was notified of Yearly Meeting's intent to disown him. Yearly Meeting shortly thereafter also disciplined John Farmer, a visiting Quaker minister from England, for the same cause.[50]

Even though unity mattered more than slavery to most Quakers, in 1719 Philadelphia Yearly Meeting agreed with London Yearly Meeting that as a matter of discipline, a sanction rather than advice, its members could not import slaves. For a decade thereafter the question dropped from public view. Most Quakers were content with the policy on the slave trade and with the advocacy of kindness to slaves and attention to their spiritual and moral welfare. Disownment was more for the radical abolitionists' methods than their message. The offense was refusal to accept the group's discipline. Sensitivity on this issue was both a doctrinal matter and a consequence of having survived decades of persecution, which had taught Quakers to face the world defensively.

In 1729, Chester Quarterly Meeting came back to Yearly Meeting with a petition to go a step further by prohibiting members from buying and selling slaves already imported or born in the colonies. The petition repeated the argument that since the slave trade destroyed families and encouraged adultery, it was a sin in itself and promoted sin among slaves. The logic, the respectfulness of the protest, and the incremental approach slowly influenced Philadelphia Yearly Meeting to accommodate the reformers' vision of slavery's immorality, even while disowning the most vehement advocates of abolition; it advised against buying and selling slaves with increasing conviction in 1730, 1735, 1736, and 1737. Still, Yearly Meeting's injunctions fell short of *prohibiting* the ownership of slaves or of indicting the acquisition of slaves received as gifts, inherited, or used as currency in the payment of debts.[51]

Individual Quakers continued to find the pace of reform excruciatingly slow and were not hopeful that Yearly Meeting would move forward. Some of them protested stridently within the group and publicly embarrassed Friends by unauthorized publication of their views. Ralph Sandiford, the next public antislavery voice, was, like Keith, disowned. Benjamin Franklin's publication of Sandiford's *Brief Examination of the Practice of the Times* in 1729 brought ostracism by the group and threats against Sandiford from enraged individuals whose pacifism is questionable. He decided to leave Philadelphia, and the controversy may have strained his health and contributed to his death at the age of forty.

Like the reformers before him, Sandiford believed that theft was the core of slavery and that the forced separation of husbands from wives and children from parents was irrefutable evidence of slavery's breaches of several commandments. The Quakers' complicity in slavery was undermining the Society's claims to spiritual purity, he thought.

> Had Friends stood clear of this Practice, that it might have been answered to the Traders in Slaves, That there is a People call'd *Quakers* in *Pensilvania*, that will not own this Practice in Word or Deed, then would they have been a burning and a shining Light to these poor Heathen, and a Precedent to the Nations throughout the Universe, which might have brought them to have seen the Evil of it in themselves, and glorified the Lord on our Behalf, and like the Queen of the *East* to have admired the Glory and Beauty of the Church of God.

There is no surviving evidence that Woolman read Sandiford, though Sandiford was probably the Quaker antislavery writer most influential on others in Woolman's generation, and his softly persuasive style suggests an affinity. If Woolman did read Sandiford's *Brief Examination*, its tone may have influenced him, or at least he could have identified a kindred spirit.[52]

Quakers in London, New England, and Philadelphia continued to work to achieve a new sense of their Yearly Meetings on the question of slavery and the slave trade. A small but dedicated number of Friends in Virginia and North Carolina were also active, albeit less effective, given that their coreligionists were so heavily invested in slaves. Because of these moderate internal efforts, the Society did not discipline all the Quakers who wrote antislavery tracts before John Woolman.

In 1733, Elihu Coleman, a Quaker in Nantucket, Massachusetts, published the first antislavery text approved by the Society of

Friends. Coleman's arguments against slavery had precedent, given the Quakers' belief that the operation of unfettered free will is essential for securing grace and thus salvation. He also observed that the biblical punishments for murder and theft of humans equated these capital crimes. He quoted Exodus 21:12–16: "Whoever strikes a person mortally shall be put to death . . . Whoever kidnaps a person, whether that person has been sold or is still held in possession, shall be put to death."[53]

An attempt by non-Quakers to bar slavery in Georgia in the years before Woolman's ministry also failed. Reformers had imagined the colony could thrive without slaves, but their social power was as nothing before the economic tidal waves that flooded North American shores with slaves. Slavery was not forbidden by the Charter of 1732, and Georgia's founder, James Oglethorpe, owned slaves. Others associated with Georgia's founding thought slavery would undermine their economic ambitions; instead, by extending charity to English debtors, attracting them to Georgia as a labor force, they hoped they could extend a humanitarian hand to England's poor while making a profit for themselves—all according to mercantilist principles. A law of 1735 barred slavery on the grounds that Georgia could be better defended without slaves, the logic being that their presence would induce the Spanish in St. Augustine to promote rebellion.

But soon the proslavery colonists got their way, even though some German settlers in Georgia argued against slavery on the ground that slaves would rob their houses and gardens, and eighteen Scots at Darien also claimed to the trustees in 1739 that slaves would threaten security, create an additional debt burden on planters, and require an escalation in the demands of militia duty. They found it "shocking to human Nature, that any Race of Mankind, and their Posterity, should be sentenced to perpetual Slavery."[54]

Then, in 1742, a South Carolinian by the name of Hugh Bryan predicted violence if slavery continued in that colony, but he recanted in the face of an investigation into rumors that he was fomenting a slave rebellion there. So in addition to the half dozen isolated voices from England and New England raised against slavery, Hugh Bryan and the Darien Scots were notable examples of non-Quakers who publicly—and vainly—opposed the institution before John Woolman did.[55]

Benjamin Lay, the last in the line of Quaker radicals preceding John Woolman, wrote only a few years before Woolman began his crusade. Lay was an eccentric Englishman who had been disowned by London Yearly Meeting before he emigrated. He had owned slaves in Barbados, which apparently created the guilt that inspired his radical campaign against slavery when he reached the mainland colonies, and Sandiford also influenced him. Lay adopted tactics that angered Quakers but that they could not ignore. Among other provocative acts, he splattered pokeberry juice on worshipers as a symbolic reminder of the slaves' blood that stained their hands, and he kidnapped a slaveowner's son to show the father how the families of abducted Africans must have felt when they lost their children. Eventually Quakers banned him from Meetings in an attempt to stop his theatrics, at which point Lay left Philadelphia to live several miles away, where he raised vegetables for food and flax to make cloth and lived in a cave. He also wrote a furious attack on Quakers and slavery that Benjamin Franklin published in 1737. The next year Philadelphia Yearly Meeting confirmed London Yearly Meeting's disownment of the hunchbacked, dwarf, vegetarian abolitionist.

At 278 pages, Lay's *All Slave-keepers That Keep the Innocent in Bondage: Apostates* (1737) is by far the longest, most rambling of the early abolitionist tracts. He discusses Sandiford (whom he defended in public) and reiterates the arguments made by Robert Pyle, the Germantown Friends, Keith, Hepburn, and Coleman. But for all his words, Lay broke no new philosophical ground. His contributions were rage and a complete absence of Quaker gentility, which he considered an expression of the sect's hypocrisy. He focused, as others had before him, on violence, the Golden Rule, and theft as the foundation for his opposition to slavery. Sloth was a soul-destroying inevitability for slaveowners, and the Quakers' abandonment of their founding principles the spiritual death knell of the religion, he thought. If George Fox was Quakerism's Moses, Benjamin Lay was its Jeremiah.

Benjamin Lay,
Quaker abolitionist,
by W. Williams (no
date) (Society Portrait
Collection, Historical
Society of Pennsylvania)

We pretend not to love fighting with carnal Weapons, nor to carry Swords by our sides, but carry a worse thing in the Heart, as will I believe appear by and by; what, I pray and beseech you, dear Friends, by the tender Mercies of our God, to consider, can be greater Hypocrisy, and plainer contradiction, than for us as a People, to refuse to bear Arms, or to pay them that do, and yet purchase the Plunder, the captives, for Slaves at a very great Price, thereby justifying their selling of them, and the War, by which they were or are obtained; nor doth this satisfy, but their Children also are kept in Slavery, *ad infinitum*; is not this plainly and substantially trampling the most Blessed and Glorious Testimony that ever was or ever will be in the World, under our Feet, and committing of Iniquity with, both Hands earnestly? Is this the way to convince the poor Slaves, or our Children, or Neighbours, or the World? Is it not the way rather to encourage and strengthen

them in their Infidelity, and Atheism, and their Hellish Practice of Fighting, Murthering, killing and Robbing one another, to the end of the World?[56]

Woolman was sixteen when Franklin published Lay's indictment of Quaker hypocrisy, seventeen when Philadelphia Yearly
Meeting confirmed its disownment of Lay, which he may have witnessed. There is no telling what Woolman thought of Lay, whom he
likely saw on any number of occasions, possibly met, and surely
heard about. John Smith, the Burlington diarist who was Woolman's
friend, ridiculed Lay as "the comi-cynic philosopher," but whether
Woolman shared Smith's disdain, as seems unlikely, or read Lay's
book, he may have been influenced by the abolitionist's passion.
Within the tangle of his words, and despite the eccentricities of his
appearance and his extreme tactics, Lay's theological reasoning was
convincing and sound.[57]

W OOLMAN closes the part of the *Journal* that concerns his
first twenty-three years with a summation of the person he
had become. In retrospect, he was pleased with the spiritual progress
he had made, which came in stages associated with personal events:
being inspired to read Revelation at seven, dreaming about the sun
worm when he was nine and killing the birds at about the same age,
challenging his mother's discipline in his twelfth year, pursuing vain
social relations during his teens, surviving a life-threatening illness
and embracing the spiritual resolve that he found, suffering through
an emotional breakdown and spiritual awakening thereafter, writing
the bill of sale for a slave, and emerging as his own spiritual man. "In
the management of my outward affairs, I may say with thankfulness
I found Truth to be my support," he writes. In other words, Woolman was satisfied that for the first time in his life his spirit began
consistently to rule over his nature. He heard the quiet voice of God
inside him and tried to act as it directed.

About the twenty-third year of my age, I had many fresh and
heavenly openings in respect to the care and providence of

the Almighty over his creatures in general, and over man as the most noble amongst those which are visible. And being clearly convinced in my judgment that to place my whole trust in God was best for me, I felt renewed engagements that in all things I might act on an inward principle of virtue and pursue worldly business no further than as Truth opened my way therein.

His real life, his true experience, was not in the visible world. He dwelled in the spirit, a state he found impossible to describe: "While I silently ponder on that change wrought in me, I find no language equal to it nor any means to convey to another a clear idea of it." Only those who shared his spiritual state could possibly understand what had happened to him.[58]

Woolman tried to suspend his will and to surrender to God's. When he achieved an ascendant spirit, he no longer initiated his own actions. God troubled him at Christmas, a holiday that Quakers did not celebrate any more than they celebrated others, when so many people spent their time drinking in taverns and engaging in "vain sports, tending to corrupt one another." He wished the burden of such sinful behavior fell to someone else: "I considered I was young and that several elderly Friends in town had opportunity to see these things, and though I would gladly have been excused, yet I could not feel my mind clear."[59]

In such an agitated spiritual state, Woolman read from the Bible (Ezekiel 33:7–9) about God's appointing the prophet as a watchman.

So, you, mortal, I have made a sentinel for the house of Israel; whenever you hear a word from my mouth, you shall give them warning from me. If I say to the wicked, "O wicked ones, you shall surely die," and you do not seek to warn the wicked to turn from their ways, the wicked shall die in their iniquity, but their blood I will require at your hand. But if you warn the wicked to run from their ways, and they do not turn from their ways, the wicked shall die in their iniquity, but you will have saved your life.

Woolman understood that he had the same job as Ezekiel. He went to the tavern, sought out the owner, and asked to speak to him privately. "So we went aside," he explains, "and there in the fear and dread of the Almighty I expressed to him what rested on my mind, which he took kindly, and afterward showed more regard to me than before." This conversation made him feel better, especially since a few years later the man died in middle age, "and I often thought that had I neglected my duty in that case it would have given me great trouble." (The last draft before the published *Journal* says "remorse" rather than "trouble.")[60]

In the *Journal*, Woolman reversed the chronological relationship between his failure to act on behalf of the female slave and his modest confrontation with the tavern owner, so that his moral failure about the slave occurs *after* the period of profound spiritual growth. This reversal in the narrative sequence elevates slavery's standing in his autobiography. Since slavery will become a major focus of his life and the rest of the *Journal*, he places the account of his guilt at an important transitional point. Slavery is the problem for which Woolman will be responsible as an adult—after he has achieved dominance of his spirit over his nature and not until he has fully surrendered his will to God's.

5

Charity

1743–53

WHEN it formally recognized John Woolman as a minister at the age of twenty-three, Burlington Monthly Meeting gave him new roles. Over the following decade it chose him as a representative to Quarterly and Yearly Meetings and assigned him to "clearness" committees, which explored the fitness of several men who wanted to marry under the Meeting's authority (committees of women examined the prospective brides); committees considering the establishment of a school in Northampton and a Meeting for Worship in Mount Holly; and committees investigating charges that individuals had breached Quaker discipline by drunkenness, by bearing arms in war, or by marrying gentiles. Most important, it endorsed his traveling ministry—that is, his personal journeys, formally recognized as led by the will of God—to the South and New England.[1]

In 1743, Woolman accompanied the Quaker minister Abraham Farrington (1691–1758) to places in central and eastern New Jersey that had no Quaker Meetings—New Brunswick, Perth Amboy, Woodbridge, Rahway, and Plainfield—where Farrington preached a half dozen times. Born in Bucks County, Pennsylvania, Farrington was a convert to Quakerism who had moved to Burlington in the 1730s. He traveled in his ministry for more than forty years and was to die in London on such a journey. Once, when Woolman was with him, he preached in a tavern, where "the room was full and the people quiet"; this suggests that Farrington had smaller, less attentive crowds elsewhere. Once he preached in a courthouse, with members of the New Jersey Assembly in attendance. Farrington may have spoken on similar themes each time, but he ministered by inspiration, as the spirit moved him, rather than on a predetermined subject from a prepared text.[2]

Woolman studied the older man, fifty-two at the time. He wrote in the *Journal*:

> My ancient companion was enlarged in the love of the gospel . . . my beloved companion was frequently strengthened to hold forth the Word of Life amongst them. As for me, I was frequently silent through the meetings, and when I spake, it was with much care that I might speak only what Truth opened. My mind was often tender and I learned some profitable lessons.

Woolman was still an apprentice in the matter of public ministry. He listened; he learned; he waited for the spirit to move him. Conscious always of a hierarchy of age and wisdom, he edged into his public role as a minister cautiously.[3]

In the *Journal* he recalls that a conflict erupted among several Quaker families from his Meeting, causing widespread discomfort and lingering bad feelings. He thought that "one valuable Friend got off his watch," by which he meant that the man was in the wrong, but Woolman held his tongue and waited modestly for others to intervene. When some time had passed and tempers had cooled, he felt moved to say something.

> I had great regard for him and felt a strong inclination after matters were settled to speak to him concerning his conduct in that case, but I being a youth and he far advanced in age and experience, my way appeared difficult. But after some days deliberation and inward seeking to the Lord for assistance, I was made subject, so that I expressed what lay upon me in a way which became my youth and his years; and though it was a hard task to me, it was well taken, and I believe was useful to us both.[4]

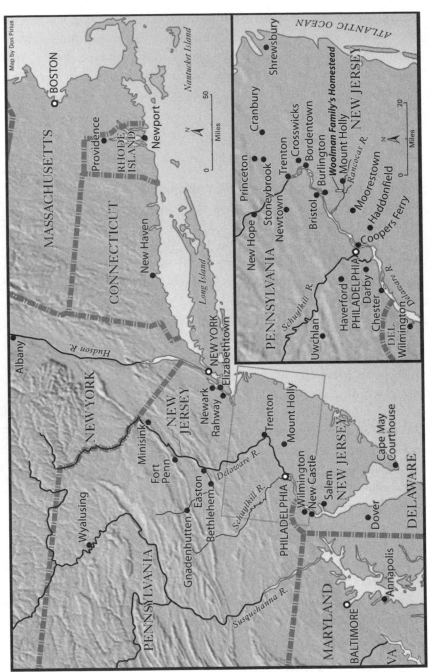

John Woolman's home and the areas covered in his American ministry

The point of juxtaposing the two stories—about going with Farrington and speaking to the Friend he believed in the wrong—is to illustrate a process that unfolded over time. Woolman grew by small steps. He wanted readers to know that his continuing spiritual growth warranted humility, that its fragility often left him unsure of the difference between the Light within him and his own flawed nature, that he was not certain he could act consistently in the right way.

After several years working in the shop in Mount Holly, Woolman was also considering a career change. Being a tradesman offered opportunities for big profits, but it was risky. Since he lacked the ambition to become rich like the fathers of his friends the Smiths, Pembertons, and Logans, and because the work sapped his time and energy, he sought an alternative way of life. Moreover, shopkeeping could be morally compromising. Could Woolman sell in good conscience what he believed customers did not need or accept their judgments about the quality and quantities they bought when he knew they were flawed? Could he avoid stocking merchandise that was tainted by links with slavery and other injustices to people or animals?

Woolman lacked the capacity to compromise his principles to engage in the commerce of the world. He could not overlook the little things as others did. The complexity of some transactions overwhelmed him. He had to take moral stock of the goods in the store, their places of origin, production, transportation, and sale; he had to know the customer, including her financial condition, and to judge her "real" needs, whether she might be in danger of spending too much for questionable ends. Then, or perhaps even first, he had to assess his own motives in making a sale; he had constantly to calculate where he was in relationship to the line between providing sustenance for his family, which was warranted, and seeking economic security or material prosperity, which was intolerable to him.

Advertisements in the *Pennsylvania Journal* reveal the unavoidable connections among the various types of merchandise. One Joseph Marks offered goods that could well have all come to Pennsylvania on the same ship: "a Parcell of likely Negro Boys and Girls, also rum, claret, and preserv'd Tammerans." Another advertised sugar, cloth, and Irish linen along with black children. A third offered "two stout likely negro men," sugar, and "an assortment of dry goods." The sugar, cloth, and dry goods could not be separated from the slaves. Slaves produced the sugar, loaded the ship, and became valuable cargo that made feasible the transportation and sale of the dry goods at competitive prices. The web was sticky and strong; there was no escaping once the shopkeeper and his customers bought anything that had come to New Jersey on a ship in the West Indies trade.[5]

Woolman continued to simplify his life and was learning to get along with ever-fewer worldly possessions. As he explains in the *Journal*, "My mind through the power of Truth was in a good degree weaned from the desire of outward greatness, and I was learning to be content with real conveniences that were not costly, so that a way of life free from much entanglements appeared best for me, though the income was small." The logic Woolman applied to leaving his work at the store is a refrain of his concern as a teenager about the lifestyles of his friends. Rather than exploiting his association with the merchant families of Burlington and Philadelphia, the way to success in his world, he rejected the wealth pursued by them.

> I had several offers of business that appeared profitable, but did not see my way clear to accept of them, as believing the business proposed would be attended with more outward care and cumber than was required of me to engage in. I saw that a humble man with the blessing of the Lord might live on a little, and that where the heart was set on greatness, success in business did not satisfy the craving, but that in common with an increase of wealth the desire of wealth increased. There was a care on my mind to so pass my time as to things outward that nothing might hinder me from the most steady attention to the voice of the True Shepherd.[6]

Although the published *Journal* explains Woolman's decision to seek "some other way of business" in purely moral terms, a draft suggests an earthly motivation: "I was thoughtful of some other way of business [in case I should settle], perceiving merchandise to be attended with much cumber in the way of trading in these parts." The bracketed, expunged phrase suggests that the idea of settling—marrying and having a family—was part of the impetus for his search for a new job.[7]

Since it was another five or six years before Woolman married, he may not yet have had a particular woman in mind as a prospective wife or he courted slowly. Nonetheless, the deleted phrase gives a rare insight, and its deletion is consistent with his pattern of leaving domestic information out of the *Journal*. We are left to wonder whether he experienced any tension between an ambition to marry and the intention to live apart from the world. It would be curious if he had decided in principle to forge new worldly attachments before he had a specific woman to woo. Such thinking runs against his usual self-characterization. Perhaps he was more worldly, more distracted by desires of the flesh, than he acknowledges. How he thought that work that would pay less was consistent with planning a family is a question the *Journal* raises but does not answer.

Another deleted passage acknowledges that the business in the shop Woolman managed was "growing slack." No wonder, then, that he imagined a tradesman's life too unpredictable for supporting a family unless done with the dedicated energy of such men as John Smith and John Pemberton, and only with luck. But to accept a position with one of them would be to commit to a life like theirs, and that was not the life he aspired to.[8]

For all these reasons, Woolman decided to become a tailor. His employer, though now a shopkeeper and baker, had started out as a tailor and still had a servant in that business. "I began to think about learning the trade," Woolman explains, "expecting that if I should settle, I might by this trade and a little retailing of goods get a living in a plain way without the load of great business [and have opportunity for retirement and inward recollection]." "Great business" and economic insecurity were the Scylla and Charybdis of the mercantile life, and he could sail past both by supplementing a "little retailing of goods" with a tailor's trade.[9]

During slow times in his work Woolman took lessons from the tailor indentured to his employer. "I believed the hand of Providence pointed out this business for me," Woolman writes, "and was taught to be content with it, though I felt at times a disposition that would have sought for something greater." A tailor's station in life was lower than the one Woolman was born to and certainly beneath the alternative open to him if he accepted the patronage of his wealthy friends. But even though he might occasionally have yearned "for something greater," he took a servile place, making and repairing clothing. As the place of his friends grew higher, his sank lower. All this he accepted as a gift from God, because he believed that the humble life helped him deepen his religious commitment. "Through the revelation of Jesus Christ I had seen the happiness of humility," he writes, "and there was an earnest desire in me to enter deep into it; and at times this desire arose to a degree of fervent supplication, wherein my soul was so environed with heavenly light and consolation that things were made easy to me which had been otherwise."[10]

What was in some ways a sacrifice for others helped Woolman fulfill spiritual ambitions. What complicated his life also simplified it. What lowered him socially raised him spiritually. Where his life may have appeared harder than the one he gave up, it was actually easier, for which he gave thanks. He lost material wealth he did not need and gained the spiritual growth he craved. These may have seemed like strange choices to those around him; perhaps acquaintances felt judged. No earthly judgment deterred Woolman, however.

When Woolman's employer retired in 1746, Woolman bought the shop and continued to work there on his own. Self-employment and living alone gave him freedom to pursue his higher calling: "I then wrought at my trade as a tailor, carefully attended meetings for worship and discipline, and found an enlargement of gospel love in my mind and therein a concern to visit Friends in some of the back settlements of Pennsylvania and Virginia." He was no longer an apprentice in either facet of his adult life.[11]

Isaac Andrews (?–1775), a resident of Little Egg Harbor and a member of Haddonfield Meeting, was to be his traveling companion on his next trip. Andrews's grandfather was a proprietor (a founding owner) of West Jersey and a kinsman of the New York governor Sir Edmund Andros (the spellings "Andrews" and "Andros" were interchangeable in the seventeenth century); his grandmother was the maid who had accompanied Margaret Brewster to Boston in 1658 to care for her baby but was whipped and expelled just like her mistress. Having ascertained that godly inspiration, what Friends called a leading, drew Andrews and Woolman to visit Quakers in the backcountry of Pennsylvania, Maryland, Virginia, and North Carolina, Friends gave the two men a "minute" (a letter of introduction to other Quakers) and their blessing.

Woolman and Andrews rode through southeastern Pennsylvania, passing through Lancaster and Chester counties, on their way to crossing the Susquehanna River into Maryland. Their first stop was in Chester, southwest of Philadelphia on the Delaware River. In *Letters from an American Farmer* (1782), J. Hector St. John de Crèvecoeur describes a Quaker Meeting for Worship in Chester that might well have been set in a meetinghouse where Woolman worshiped and preached on this journey.

> When I entered the house where the Friends were assembled, who might be about two hundred men and women, the involuntary impulse of ancient custom made me pull off my hat; but soon recovering myself, I sat with it on, at the end of a bench. The meeting-house was a square building devoid of any ornament whatever; the whiteness of the walls, the conveniency of seats, that of a large stove, which in cold weather keeps the whole house warm, were the only essential things which I observed. Neither pulpit nor desk, font nor altar, tabernacle nor organ, were there to be seen; it is merely a spacious room, in which these good people meet every Sunday.

Crèvecoeur's farmer was struck by the service as well as the architecture, which he found of a piece; he was also impressed by a woman who rose from the silence to preach.

> A profound silence ensued, which lasted about half an hour; every one had his head reclined and seemed absorbed in profound meditation, when a female Friend arose and declared with a most engaging modesty that the spirit moved her to

entertain them on the subject she had chosen . . . Her discourse lasted three quarters of an hour. I did not observe one single face turned toward her; never before had I seen a congregation listening with so much attention to a public oration . . . As soon as she had finished, every one seemed to return to their former meditation for about a quarter of an hour, when they rose up by common consent and after some general conversation departed.[12]

Andrews and Woolman continued west into Lancaster County, crossing a rural landscape that the Swedish botanist Peter Kalm wrote about a few years later.

We continually saw at moderate distances little fields which had been cleared of the wood. Each one of these was a farm. These farms were commonly very pretty, and a walk of trees frequently led from them to the highroad. The houses were all built of brick or of the stone which is found here everywhere. Every countryman, even the poorest peasant, had an orchard with apples, peaches, chestnuts, walnuts, cherries, quinces and such fruits, and sometimes we saw vines climbing in them. The valleys were frequently blessed with little brooks of crystal-clear water. The fields by the sides of the road were almost all mown and of grain crops only.

Few Indians had occupied southeastern Pennsylvania when the Quaker settlers arrived in 1680, and there were even fewer by the mid-eighteenth century; the ones there were principally Iroquoian and, as in central New Jersey, Unami (Delaware) speakers. By this time the region had a mix of German, Scots-Irish, Welsh, and English settlers, with the German population growing the most quickly. There were about twenty-one thousand settlers in 1700 and more than one hundred thousand when Woolman and Andrews passed through. The ethnic mix was greater than what they knew in New Jersey, with the large German presence most striking.[13]

Most of the men were farmers or artisans; the middling (what we would call middle) class predominated, and there was a growing number of landless laborers. The size of farms ranged from 100 to 500 acres, with the average about 125, and lessening as land values rose and splitting (partible) inheritances contributed to the shrinkage from generation to generation. Quakers and Mennonites were generally more successful than the unchurched and members of other faith communities—Lutheran, Reformed, Anglican, and Presbyterian.

Like the settlers of central New Jersey, southeastern Pennsylvanians raised crops for export, mainly wheat; the major markets were Philadelphia, Baltimore, and Europe. Farmers also grew rye, oats, barley, buckwheat, and Indian corn; the oats were generally for their own horses, and the corn fed their pigs. They also grew a variety of grasses for animal feed as well as flax and hemp for fiber and oil. On average, there were three or four horses per farm and five to ten pigs; farmers also kept chickens and a few cows. As Kalm attests, orchards of 150 or more trees—principally apple, peach, and cherry— were common, as were house gardens for vegetables and herbs. After 1750 they also shipped iron to England and lived in the most productive flour-milling region on the continent. The fences, orchards, and fields of southeastern Pennsylvania could have reminded Woolman and Andrews of home; the landscape was hillier than central New Jersey, but the soil, crops, and animals were much the same.[14]

When they crossed the Susquehanna River into Maryland, the countryside changed. They now visited Friends in what Woolman terms "remote deserts" and "wilderness." This overstates the remoteness and difficulty of the terrain, but not the primitiveness of the living conditions.

It is the poorer sort of people that commonly begin to improve remote deserts. With a small stock they have houses to build, lands to clear and fence, corn to raise, clothes to provide, and children to educate, that Friends who visit such may well sympathize with them in their hardships in the wilderness; and though the best entertainment such can give may seem coarse to some who are used to cities or old settled places, it becomes the disciples of Christ to be content with it.[15]

The planters lived farther apart, often a quarter mile or more, in contrast with the farms in southeastern Pennsylvania and central New Jersey, which were adjacent, with clearly marked boundaries, geometrically shaped fields, and fences. The buildings were often ramshackle, and the houses suggested a lack of commitment: when the fields played out (the tobacco farmed extensively there was hard on the land), those who could afford to leave did; those who could not afford to move got poorer. Lancaster and Chester County farmers built barns to last, and some of them are still standing, functioning testaments to workmanship and the materials the builders used; the same is not true in the rural Maryland the two Quakers visited. Tobacco led the southern economy; small grain fields were laid out in irregular shapes and not plowed into neat rows. Chesapeake planters used hoes to grow maize in hills, Indian style, and wheat was mainly for domestic consumption. Mixed agriculture was not yet commonplace.

Wealth was more stratified than Andrews and Woolman were used to. When they crossed the Susquehanna, they left a middling-class world for one that lacked a clear middle; rich whites, poor whites, and slaves defined Chesapeake society. The tobacco economy created a permanent underclass of bound laborers, first servants in the seventeenth century and then slaves. Tenancy had increased, and permanent landlessness had become more common. Not until later in the eighteenth century did Maryland planters grow maize and grains for the international market. Only about 2 percent of Maryland land had been cultivated by 1720; by 1800, 40 percent had been cleared and planted.

The two men made their way through the Maryland settlements and eventually reached older ones in Virginia, where Woolman found Friends less welcoming and, to his mind, less spiritually sound: "So we took the meetings in our way through Virginia, were in some degree baptized into a feeling sense of the conditions of the people [the pure lamb-like nature of Jesus Christ being too much departed from by many of them], and our exercise in general was more painful in these old settlements than it had been amongst the back inhabitants." The passage suggests tension and judgment and also implies that Woolman encountered resistance or even hostility to the message he preached. He took solace in the "sincere-hearted" souls they met and "some honest-hearted Friends who appeared to be concerned for the cause of Truth among a backsliding people." Principally, though, the three months of rough travel was "hard labour" among Friends who had lost touch with the Truth, Friends who "baptized" Woolman and Andrews with their defense of slavery.[16]

Woolman is always a disappointing travel writer. Where are the heat, mud, dust, and mosquitoes; how did it feel? The gorgeous Chesapeake landscape and the stunning Virginia hills are entirely missing from his account. There is no wildlife, not a heron, eagle, fox, or crab. There is no endless, majestic bay, no river or stream, and not a tree to behold in his *Journal* and scant correspondence. He reports the squalor and ruins of slavery—tumbledown barns, dilapidated dwellings, and down-at-the-heel planters—but is blind to the larger landscape. No birds sing, no crickets chirp, brooks do not burble, and the wind does not rustle through the trees. He is deaf to, or at least mute about, the wonders of nature. There are cranky Quakers, down-and-out farmers, self justifying patriarchs on palatial estates, and pathetic slaves, but no people experiencing the full range of human existence. There are no smiles, no wonder, no joy, and not even physical pain; nobody sings or cries, winces or laughs. Everyone he meets and everything he sees are an abstract, anonymous symbol of spiritual squalor, of interior decay; the exteriors are never concrete.

In his *Journal*, Woolman recalls two lessons he learned during this trip. The first is that accepting hospitality from people "who lived in ease on the labour of their slaves" made him "uneasy." The second is that he "saw in these southern provinces so many vices and corruptions increased by this trade and this way of life that it appeared to [him] as a dark gloominess hanging over the land; and though now many willingly run into it, yet in future the consequence will be grievous to posterity!"[17]

W ITNESSING the evils of slavery in the South led Woolman to ponder the chain of connections back to the Quaker merchants he knew. Woolman's discomfort with the knowledge that the Smiths, Pembertons, and Logans all had trafficked in slaves deepened. These genteel Quaker families who had welcomed him in his youth had perpetrated horrors from which they largely isolated themselves. The Logans had corrupted the southerners who owned slaves. The Pembertons were responsible for the "heavy burdens" borne by slaves laboring for harsh masters. The Smiths had profited from the violence that stole people. Therefore, Woolman reasoned, so had he. The Smiths' food, the Pembertons' tea, and the Logans' books had been purchased with blood money. No one was pure; the blood of Africans stained them all.

By this logic, Woolman had not committed his first act in support of slavery when he drafted the bill of sale for a slave. Wearing clothes made from fabric that his parents had bought from a merchant who also sold West Indian rum was tantamount to engaging in the slave trade. The questions became, as he rode back to New Jersey with Andrews in June: What would he do? What could he do? What did God want from him?

What Woolman did first was to write his thoughts down. In the second half of 1746 he drafted an essay that was published eight years later as *Some Considerations on the Keeping of Negroes*. In it he articulated the connections between good, family-centered ambitions of people he knew and the evil done to others who seemed remote from them. As was his nature, Woolman did this gently, even obliquely, in ways designed to avoid giving offense. But he made his case powerfully and in terms new to antislavery writing. He showed that evil derived not just from bad people committing immoral acts but also from well-intentioned but mistaken attempts to do good. He argued that even something as natural as loving one's children could be a sin. He warned good people, but with love for them in his heart.

The best case for portraying Woolman as an Enlightenment figure comes from his pamphlets, like this one, whose abstract quality can be read as an adoption of the tone of rational rather than mystical religion. Woolman engages in an "impartial enquiry," encourages "close thinking" and "wise and judicious consideration," thereby using the Enlightenment language of reason, rationality, and, ultimately, rights. He does not judge slaveowners: "My inclination is to persuade and entreat, and simply give hints of my way of thinking." He specifically describes as "a contradiction to reason" the argument about acquiring slaves to teach them Christianity. And he makes several neutral, even positive references to nature that ring of natural rights literature of the time: "If I purchase a man who hath never forfeited his liberty, the natural right of freedom is in him." Woolman also advances ideas consistent with the eighteenth-century theory of benevolent Providence and moral self-interest as paths to earthly happiness; the Sermon on the Mount, he writes, "contains a short but comprehensive view of our duty and happiness." Woolman even seems to echo Alexander Arscott and his book *The Present State of the Christian Religion* in applying major themes of rational religion: "If the Christian religion be considered, both respecting its doctrines and the happy influence which it hath on the minds and manners of all real Christians, it looks reasonable to think that the miraculous manifestation thereof to the world is a kindness beyond expression."[18]

Woolman's indictment of slavery has the previous abolitionists' moral perspective, but he was aiming for more fundamental reform than the Pennsylvania Assembly or Philadelphia Yearly Meeting had ever endorsed. Woolman built his argument on different New Testament passages from the ones Quaker reformers had used previously; a dismissal of the authority of tradition, which none of them made; and a radical social perspective that none of them shared. His fundamental premise was that slavery arose from parents' customary and "natural" attachment to children, that the root causes of slavery were deeply embedded in Judeo-Christian beliefs about parental responsibility. Popular opinion about loving families led even good people who did not own slaves into attachments that benefited no one, defied rules that governed the natural world, and produced unanticipated consequences that upset the balance of nature.

> Customs generally approved and opinions received by youth from their superiors become like the natural produce of a soil, especially when they are suited to favourite inclinations. But as the judgments of God are without partiality, by which the state of the soul must be tried, it would be the highest wis-

dom to forego customs and popular opinions, and try the treasures of the soul by the infallible standard: Truth.[19]

Woolman believed that if you ask people why they behave in a particular way, they generally plead common practice—it is how things are done. If you press them further, they make some reference to the past—it is the way things have long or always been done. But neither explanation justifies the behavior as right. Woolman thought that this logic of common practice and tradition was a barrier to clear thought, and not only in regard to slavery. Slavery is ubiquitous: everyone does it. Slavery is traditional: Old Testament law accepts it; Israelites were slaves and owned slaves at different points in their history; and ancient Romans, including Christians, also enslaved criminals and captives.

In the first paragraph of *Some Considerations on the Keeping of Negroes*, Woolman cleared the decks of this justification by past practices. His reasoning rings of the Enlightenment philosophy that was to inform the American revolutionaries like Thomas Jefferson—"the earth belongs in usufruct to the living"—and the Englishman Thomas Paine, whose opening sentences of *Common Sense* express similar sentiments: "A long habit of not thinking a thing *wrong*, gives it a superficial appearance of being *right*, and raises at first a formidable outcry in defense of custom . . . Time makes more converts than reason." Woolman, like Paine, worked with traditional biblical tools. Timeless Truth, though, rather than inalienable rights, was Woolman's justification for throwing over customs. Nor would Woolman determine Truth by a vote of the people, however republican the method of discerning the popular will.[20]

Simply put, Woolman's thesis in *Some Considerations* is that parents love their children too much: "Natural affection needs a careful examination. Operating upon us in a soft manner, it kindles desires of love and tenderness, and there is danger of taking it for something higher." But we should not mistake love for another human—spouse, parent, sibling, or child—for love of God. Such an error distracts from our central purpose in life, which is to secure our place in the hereafter, and it also produces positive evils.[21]

Woolman could have absorbed this concept of "natural affection," which predates the ancient Greeks, from anywhere. Thomas Tryon used it in his 1684 antislavery tract *Friendly Advice to the Gentlemen-Planters of the East and West Indies*, in reference to masters who raped and impregnated their female slaves. Enslaving one's own children struck Tryon as an unnatural act. "The fathers, being without natural affection," he observes, "though they are their own seed, do expose them, and make them perpetual slaves."[22] More recently, Anthony Ashley Cooper, the Third Earl of Shaftesbury (1631–1713), one of the most influential philosophers of his day, had written that "those affections of earliest alliance and mutual kindness between the parent and the offspring, known more particularly by the name of *natural affection*," were the foundation of all ethical action, the root of moral living, extending from the self to family and charitable relationships with the world. Natural affection was the source of all that is humanly good.[23]

Most eighteenth-century usages of the term derive from Shaftesbury's optimistic alternative to Thomas Hobbes's indictment of humanity's dark natural inclinations. Woolman, however, considers natural affection the generating source for violence and evil in the world. He is not harking back to Hobbes or any other modern thinker; his usage is not even derived from Locke's warning to parents lest they love their children too much, coddling them and doing them an ill service in a hostile world, though it is consistent with Lockean principles about child rearing. It comes from another, more spiritual, source, once again Thomas à Kempis.

Both the language and philosophy of Woolman's antislavery argument are consistent with the Christian ascetic tradition and were directly inspired by his reading of *The Imitation of Christ*. The same advice that inspired Woolman to separate from his friends and seek his own solitary, contemplative way in the world led him to view the natural affection that parents have for children as a restraint on the spiritual growth of all family members. Nature, for Woolman as for Kempis, is a force in opposition to spirit and therefore an attachment to be resisted with all one's spiritual strength. "Nature finds pleasure in having many friends and relatives," Kempis writes, and "glories in family estate and its genealogical trees." That was precisely Woolman's point.[24]

Where Shaftesbury saw nature as the inspiration for moral impulses that ultimately transcended it, Kempis and Woolman identified nature as a fleshly enemy. *The Imitation of Christ* embodies a
litany of nature's faults. Nature is concerned with outward forms
rather than the "inward reality" of grace. Nature is misguided; grace
is not deceived. Nature is "cunning and seductive," obsessed with
self, acts always in its own interest, pursues honor and homage,
loves leisure, focuses on the temporal, including "terrestrial gain,"
and is greedy. "The more nature is curbed and conquered," Woolman read in *The Imitation of Christ*, "so much the more is Grace infused into the soul."[25]

If the origin of natural affection is self-love, as Kempis writes,
then nature is the source of the human instinct to self-preservation,
Woolman believed, from which springs the desire to protect our
children as an extension of ourselves. In moderation, such natural
love is a good thing. It leads birds to care for their young until the
fledglings can fly, bears to teach their cubs to fish, and parents to
educate their children and secure them trades. It kindles tenderness and develops within us the capacity to love others. But unrestrained, unconquered by grace, this attachment to individuals
is, according to Woolman, "productive of evil by exciting desires
to promote some by means prejudicial to others," just as Kempis
says.[26]

This was a major challenge to the family-centered religion of
Quakers. Making families the primary institutional unit ran the danger of diminishing love and a sense of responsibility for those outside
the relational group. "Our blessed Saviour seems to give a check to
this irregular fondness in nature," according to Woolman, "and, at
the same time, [establishes] a precedent for us." The effort must
be made to transcend nature, to achieve a higher—supernatural—
spiritual state. The goal is to love all creation equally, as an extension
of our primary love of God, not to elevate our love of family above
our affection for other creatures.[27]

The Bible tells us that one day when Christ is preaching, someone alerts him to the presence of his mother and brothers, who are
waiting at the edge of the crowd to speak with him. Christ replies
with a rhetorical question—"Who is my mother, and who are my

brothers?"—and then points at his disciples and says, "Here are my mother and my brothers! For whoever does the will of my Father in heaven is my brother and sister and mother" (Matthew 12:46–50). Woolman understood this lesson to teach that "earthly ties of relationship are comparatively inconsiderable to such who, through a steady course of obedience, have come to the happy experience of the Spirit of God bearing witness with their spirits that they are his children." He parenthetically terms the higher supernatural connection that transcends mere natural ones "the more noble part of true relationship."[28]

The final step in Woolman's logic, connecting the love of parents for their children to the accumulation of wealth, mirrors Kempis's words when he claims that nature "glories in family estates." Woolman writes: "In our present condition, to love our children is needful; but except this love proceeds from the true heavenly principle which sees beyond earthly treasures, it will rather be injurious than of any real advantage to them. Where the fountain is corrupt, the streams must necessarily be impure." According to Woolman, Quaker parents justified their accumulation of wealth beyond what they needed to support their families by their desire to have their children be "eminent amongst men" after their deaths, and then rationalized slavery as necessary to achieve that goal, adding the traditional argument that slavery was also conducive to the slaves' Christian conversion and good for them. This chain of logic pitted parents' love for their children against slaves' freedom, and it placed the children above all. This was, for Woolman, a contravention of the Golden Rule, which led him to make arguments like those of the abolitionists who preceded him: that theft is theft, that good intentions do not justify sin.[29]

But *Some Considerations* breaks new ground; implicit is a critique of the underlying drive to accumulate capital. This ascetic strain in Woolman's writing is not central to earlier abolitionist thought (although Lay, following Tryon, adopted an eremitic lifestyle that also permeated the philosophy of their antislavery writings). Woolman cites no biblical authority for his disdain for material gain, although he might have: "You cannot serve God and wealth" (Matthew 6:24); "Look at the birds of the air; they neither sow nor reap nor gather into barns, and yet your heavenly Father feeds them. Are you not of more value than they?" (Matthew 6:26); "Blessed are you who are poor, for yours is the kingdom of God" (Luke 6:20). His readers knew these teachings on wealth and charity well.

Since Woolman was familiar with the writings of John Locke, he could have supplemented the biblical evidence with Lockean philosophy: "Covetousness and the desire of having in our possession and under our dominion more than we have need of, being the root of all evil, should be early and carefully weeded out and the contrary quality of a readiness to impart to others implanted." Locke's respect for kindness, liberality, and civility to others was informed by the same biblical tradition that Woolman knew, expressed in Enlightenment terms. But Woolman did not cite the Bible or Locke. His argument embodies its own authority, as those of Old Testament prophets do; he was delivering biblically steeped prophecies to *his* fallen people, the Quakers around him.[30]

Like Locke, Woolman believed that parents should rule children with a firm but gentle hand. He thought it a mistake either to give youngsters too much or to expect too little of them. Being overly protective only made them vulnerable and fragile rather than strong and mature. Woolman thought one should guide by example rather than physical discipline, that children should be taught to take care of themselves. Those raised according to such methods would become independent adults who would not need, expect, or desire financial legacies to make their way in the world. Slaveowners were, perhaps, guilty of coddling, indulging, domineering, and overprotecting their progeny. Love that did not prepare the fledgling to leave the nest flew in the face of nature's laws. It led to unnatural relations between parent and child and perverted labor relations by enslaving workers rather than paying them as independent actors governed by God and their own free will. Indulging the natural parental instincts, according to Woolman, had actually led humans to devolve from nature rather than transcend it gracefully. Human nature had led to unnatural acts.

Woolman's introduction to *Some Considerations*, in which he makes this argument, is composed in gentle, humble terms and avoids an accusatory tone. He instructs rather than denounces; he pleads rather than threatens. He aims for a genuine expression of empathy that would make the message palatable to Quaker slave-owners and slave traffickers. This persuasive approach is another departure from the heavy-handed yet unsuccessful arguments made by his abolitionist predecessors. When he claims to write "with reluctance," the apologetic pose is one that is common to the abolitionists, and when he explains that "the hints given are in as general terms as my concern would allow," he is trying to avoid giving offense. His approach is that of a Quaker minister preaching with the authority of his religion rather than against those in authority. Unlike Keith, Sandiford, and Lay, Woolman worked within institutional structures rather than as a disowned exile assaulting Quaker "hypocrisy" from the outside. He presents himself humbly, as a meek, flawed, Quaker ascetic.[31]

To accuse slaveowners of loving their children too much is to couch criticism in terms that might feel like praise. The familiar reproach of being heartless, unfeeling wretches is absent; Woolman instead identifies with parents who want to nurture their offspring as best they can. He simply warns them of the dangers of excessive affection. The problem is not that slaveowners are uncharitable but that they need to expand their realm of charitable responsibility. It is not that they are unloving but that they need to love more widely and moderately.

Extension of charity to strangers had always been an issue among Quakers, just as it had been in England going back to the Reformation. As long as England had one national church, charity was distributed through it to all subjects of the kingdom. But the struggle between Roman Catholics and Anglicans during the sixteenth century, the fragmentation of Anglicanism brought about by the Puritan movement, and the proliferation of Dissenting sects in the mid-seventeenth century created uncertainty about the locus of charitable responsibility. Ultimately, many charitable tasks that had once been carried out by the church devolved to the government, but during the long transition preceding the rise of the welfare state, people were not sure who was responsible for whom.[32]

Quakers and other Dissenters defined charity as caring for the members of their Meetings, churches, and chapels; partly this was because their resources were limited, but partly it was a function of their antipathy to other Christians. The persecution that Quakers had endured between 1650 and 1689 left them with little spirit for giving charity to outsiders, and they dedicated no resources to it. They believed all they could do was care for the families of imprisoned, widowed, and orphaned Friends and support the poor within their ranks. Conversely, though, their persecution by Puritans and Anglicans led Quakers to sympathize with the plight of prison inmates and the poor around them, whoever they might be. Their eventual commitment to penal reform, opposition to capital punishment, and support for the rehabilitation of prisoners were linked to firsthand knowledge of prisons during the formative era of their faith.[33]

In their colonies of Pennsylvania and West Jersey, Quakers aimed to avoid the punitive laws they associated with an established church. For this reason, they instituted laws and governance that recognized the community's social responsibility and tried to focus the work of their Meetings internally. They rationalized that in order to avoid offending non-Quakers, they would take care of themselves; they had the power and resources to reach out, to define community more inclusively, but they did not. They accepted William Penn's definition of charity as "the love of God, which first made us love one another." The Meeting as a gathering of families was the focus of their charity.[34]

Quakers, Anglicans, English Nonconformists, German Pietists, and American Puritans all began to redefine their responsibilities to outsiders during the eighteenth century. Cotton Mather tried to revitalize the piety of New England Puritans by advocating voluntary associations that would reform morals, stamp out vice, and assist the poor. In 1698 Anglicans created the Society for the Promotion of Christian Knowledge, and in 1701 the Society for the Propagation of the Gospel in Foreign Parts, as a way of looking outward and thus transcending their own doctrinal disputes.[35]

American Quakers considered that benevolence toward neighbors was essentially an ethical responsibility. They should be no less honest with, should practice universal love toward, and should not sell to outsiders anything they disapproved of using themselves.

These were the values of their economic morality, and it gave them a reputation as fair traders; it also built relationships of trust in financial transactions.[36]

Moral responsibilities toward Native Americans were another matter, however. Quakers did not think that the assumption that the other party to a financial transaction could look out for his own interests applied to trading with Indians or purchasing their land, because the other party was always in a weaker position. For example, Quakers decided, after some experience, that selling liquor to Indians was wrong because Indians drank to excess. They defined any moral problem as theirs when their dealings with "primitive" peoples created difficulties, and they held themselves accountable, through Monthly and Yearly Meetings. But then they compromised this moral stand by casting a blind eye on liquor sales to Native Americans by non-Quaker fur traders, which their political enemies saw as hypocrisy.[37]

The Quaker governments of Pennsylvania and New Jersey, which took responsibility for the purchase of land from the natives, tried to ensure that the transactions were fair and in the legitimate interests of the sellers. At the same time, Meetings made sure that Quakers settled only on land that had been obtained in this way. But governments and Meetings cast the same blind eye on land transactions by non-Quakers. The Quaker definition of benevolence toward the native tribes was limited and self-serving, then, but the Quaker colonies enjoyed better relations with them than other English colonies did.[38]

Servants and slaves, as members of Quaker families, fell under the umbrella of Quaker charity. By the late seventeenth century the status of slave had been clearly differentiated from that of servant, and benevolence toward the perpetually bonded slave was recognized as a different matter from that toward non-Quaker servants, for whom education, exposure to Christianity and Quakerism, and fair treatment were considered essential acts of charity.

Some Quakers thought they would always live among permanent outsiders, but this was only slowly acknowledged by the Quaker collectivity. They never agreed theoretically to a permanent exclusion of Indians and slaves; American Quakers recognized that including them in the Quaker community would come, at best, over the long term, which might be shortened by taking on charitable responsibility for these unique outsiders. Education, although not essential to discovery of the Light within, would facilitate their "awakening" through access to the Bible and other spiritually inspiring literature. And Quakers eventually became leaders in establishing charitable schools for Indians and African Americans, just as they were in the primary education of their own children.

Quaker abolitionists had always inquired about the appropriate expression of charity toward slaves. By the mid-eighteenth century, though, they were turning away from the moral indictment of masters that such reformers as Sandiford and Lay had expressed and toward a more loving concern for slaves *and* masters. Woolman represented this new approach, but he did not labor alone.

Right from the start, Woolman's genius was to combine his vision of Truth with a disarming expression of his love for masters as well as slaves. "I know it [slavery] is a point about which in all its branches men that appear to aim well are not generally agreed," he writes in his generous, self-deprecating vein, "and for that reason I chose to avoid being very particular." He avoids "particular" criticism that would strike close to the bone and tries to open the minds of "candid" people who share his values but may disagree with him. In 1762, when the shifting ground of debate dictated a change in strategy, Woolman was to suggest that this conciliatory language be dropped from a new edition of his pamphlet. In the first edition, though, he tried not to point fingers but to spread arms in a gesture of openness and affection that he believed was the Truth.[39]

S HORTLY after he drafted *Some Considerations on the Keeping of Negroes*, Woolman's eldest sister, his emotionally closest sibling, died. Elizabeth, named for their father's sister, succumbed to smallpox in the early winter of 1746–47. She was thirty-one years old, had never married, and had lived in Haddonfield, where she worked as a seamstress.[40]

Woolman mentions none of his other siblings or his daughter by name in the *Journal*, and names his wife and parents only in passing, but he devotes five paragraphs to Elizabeth. "She was from her youth of a thoughtful disposition," Woolman recalls, "and very compassionate to her acquaintance in their sickness or distress, being ready to help as far as she could." He admired her asceticism and tried to emulate her dutiful obedience to their parents. She had lived a "self-denying, exemplary life, giving herself much to reading and meditation." Elizabeth was a model for him, perhaps even in his decision to become a tailor.[41]

At her first awareness that her illness was mortal, Elizabeth "was in great sadness and dejection of mind," Woolman writes, not because she feared death but because she regretted her life. She thought she had already repented her "wanton and airy" girlish ways but still felt guilty. In her last days, though, as she recovered her knowledge of God's favor, despondency turned to gratitude. She traveled an emotional path from disconsolation to hope, and rested in peace as disease wracked her body. "'I have had a hard night,'" Elizabeth explained to a friend, "'but shall not have another such, for I shall die, and it will be well with my soul.'" As she predicted, Elizabeth passed before the night ended. She lived a good life and died well, inspiring her brother to include her story in his.[42]

John and his brother Asher were coexecutors of their sister's estate, which had a value of £194.6.8 (194 pounds sterling, 6 shillings, and 8 pence), a substantial sum for anyone then, but especially for an unmarried woman. Among the accounts to be settled was one with "Negro Maria," who was paid 6 shillings in goods for work she had done for Elizabeth; she also received a bequest of 18 shillings and 9 pence. We can assume in light of the will that Maria and Elizabeth had a working relationship of some duration, but Woolman, not surprisingly, mentions nothing about Maria in the *Journal*.[43]

Other experiences affected Woolman's spiritual development in these years. But in his *Journal* he does not weigh the relative significance of events or mention the contexts of those that bore on his life or his decision to publish his antislavery pamphlet. As he tells the story throughout, he was internally motivated rather than externally moved. The carnal world around him was of no moment, and the spirit within him was motivator and guide.

In the spring of 1747, Woolman and his neighbor Peter Andrews

(1707–56), who was Isaac's brother and was also to die in England, traveled in their ministry to Long Island, Connecticut, and Rhode Island, where Friends now worshiped free of the anti-Quaker laws they had encountered in the seventeenth century. On Long Island, the two Friends met with Presbyterian converts who had abandoned what they considered the lax practices of their own church and were "humbly led to take up the cross of Christ," some as reformers of their own sect and others as Quakers. Woolman valued the company of these spiritually intense young people; he and Andrews may have been in the wake of the Great Awakening's enthusiastic religion, witnessing the flowering of spirituality and reformist temperament that swept through the colonies. In New England, Woolman and Andrews endured spiritually fallow meetings amid "seasons of refreshment wherein the power of Truth prevailed." This was all part of Woolman's spiritual growth, cultural broadening, and emotional maturing. He continued to seek, and sometimes to find, the spirit that defined him. He became more confident as he grew humbler, he honed his public ministry as he focused inwardly, and he listened patiently.

> In this journey I may say in general we were sometimes in much weakness and laboured under discouragements, and at other times, through the renewed manifestations of divine love, we had seasons of refreshment wherein the power of Truth prevailed.
>
> We were taught by renewed experience to labour for an inward stillness, at no time to seek for words, but to live in the spirit of Truth and utter that to the people which Truth opened in us.[44]

In 1748 came another trip. Woolman sojourned in Delaware and Maryland's Eastern Shore with John Sykes (1682–1771), a Quaker minister who had settled in Bordentown, New Jersey, after emigrating from Hull, Yorkshire. As in Woolman's first trip to the South, the "declining condition" of Quakerism in that region, both a decrease in numbers and the moral decline brought by slavery, discouraged him. "Our exercise at times was heavy," he later recalled, "but through the goodness of the Lord we were often refreshed." Hope, faith, patience, and resignation to the will of God gave Woolman peace amid the spiritual turmoil he found.[45]

Consistent with Woolman's focus on his interior life, he did not even mention in the first draft of the *Journal* that he married in October 1749, though eventually he added a sentence where it fit chronologically. Perhaps he had noticed the inconsistency of referring to his wife later in the *Journal* without having previously mentioned that he had one. Possibly Sarah or some other reader, an overseer or a friend, called his attention to what he had left out. In any event, Woolman inserted a sentence in a blank space between two chapters, writing with a different ink. For some reason, the correction did not stick, and Woolman either forgot to include the information in the subsequent draft or again decided to omit it. The overseers who edited his revised manuscript put the sentence back, and it appeared in the published version. The emphasis, as always with Woolman, is on the spiritual inspiration behind the event: "About this time believing it good for me to settle, and thinking seriously about a companion, my heart was turned to the Lord with desires that he would give me wisdom to proceed therein agreeable to his will; and he was pleased to give me a well-inclined damsel, Sarah Ellis, to whom I was married the 18th day, 8th month, 1749."[46]

Jehovah decided, "It is not good that the man should be alone; I will make him a helper as his partner" (Genesis 2:18). So God created Eve. The Lord told the prophet Hosea to take a wife, and he married Gomer. Woolman believed that God had chosen for him this orphaned young woman, born one year after him. Her father had been lost at sea shortly after her birth, and her mother died when Sarah was seventeen, after which she lived with relatives near Mount Holly. She traveled in the same circles as John and attended the same Meeting, where her name appears in committee minutes throughout her adulthood. So John had known Sarah all her life. Maybe Woolman's ambivalence about the sentence mentioning her derived from a nagging doubt, conscious or not, that he had not married Sarah for purely spiritual reasons; perhaps he was not sure his motives were chaste and the decision was entirely God's.

A little more than a year after the wedding, John's father, Samuel, died "with a fever, aged about sixty years." Woolman offers a brief eulogy in the *Journal*, where he celebrates Samuel's nurturing of his children's spirituality: "In his lifetime he manifested much care for us his children, that in our youth we might learn to fear the Lord, often endeavouring to imprint in our minds the true principles of virtue, and particularly to cherish in us a spirit of tenderness, not only toward poor people, but also towards all creatures of which we had the command." The recollection is of a gentle man, kind to children and animals, a teacher at heart, who governed his household with love.

John had admired and loved his father, who had returned the sentiments. On Samuel's deathbed he asked John about the essay on slavery written four years before. Back in 1746 John had shown a draft to his father, who "perused the manuscript, proposed a few alterations, and appeared well satisfied that I found a concern on that account." Now that he was dying, Samuel inquired about the essay and John's intentions for publication. "I have all along been deeply affected with the oppression of the poor Negroes," John quotes Samuel as saying very close to his death, "and now at last [in my last days] my concern for them is as great as ever."[47]

Samuel was at peace toward the end, according to his son, sensible of his imperfections but also certain of Truth's power and the goodness of God: "he had no doubt but that in leaving this life he should enter into one more happy." Shortly after Samuel announced that he was ready to go, his sister Elizabeth, John's aunt, told him that their sibling Ann had recently died. Samuel asked whether she thought Ann had felt ready to leave the world, to which Elizabeth replied affirmatively. "'I also am free to leave it,'" Samuel remarked, "and being in great weakness of body said, 'I hope I shall shortly go to rest.'"[48]

Woolman reports on Samuel's interest in the antislavery pamphlet with pride in his father and perhaps also in himself. But the fatherly revisions, inquiry, and deathbed endorsement were nonetheless insufficient spurs. John still held back the revolutionary document, and he does not tell us why. What he reports on instead are additional personal ministries to northwestern New Jersey and Bucks County, Pennsylvania.

Woolman also does not mention that he and Sarah became parents on December 18, 1750, less than three months after Samuel's death. They named their daughter Mary (1750–97), perhaps because her birth came only a week before Christmas. The joy of parental life, which began so soon after Samuel's death, did not bear reporting. In fact John never mentions Mary at all, though she was his only child to live to adulthood. Some readers may interpret this familial absence as evidence that Woolman was an unaffectionate, uncaring husband and father, but it could also demonstrate the opposite: that he feared he loved them too much. When Burlington Monthly Meeting memorialized Woolman after his death, Friends recalled that he was "a loving husband [and] a tender father." This could have been boilerplate or it may have been true.[49]

I N 1753, Woolman and Henry Paxson, the Quaker sheriff of Mount Holly for many years, served as coexecutors of the estate of Thomas Shinn (1694–1753), a judge of the Court of Common Pleas, a New Jersey assemblyman, and an elder of Mount Holly Meeting. In 1762, nine years later, when they finally settled Shinn's estate, Woolman noted that "the one hundred pounds to be reserved for the Negroes is in Henry's hands and the affairs relating to the administration I believe are nearly accomplished." This hundred pounds was likely a bequest the coexecutors administered in behalf of the "Negroes" for whom they were responsible. Colonial New Jersey required a two-hundred-pound bond for each released slave to ensure that he or she did not become a burden on taxpayers, but this transaction appears nowhere in Woolman's book of executorship or in his accounts.[50]

One year after Shinn's death, Woolman wrote an indenture for "Negro James . . . to serve 21 years, that is till 2d. 1 mo. 1775." He makes no mention of the first transaction in his *Journal* covering 1753–55, but when he writes about 1769, he refers to an indenture he wrote at an unspecified time in the past that could have been this one.

As persons setting Negroes free in our province are bound by law to maintain them in case they have need of relief; some who scrupled keeping slaves [for a] term of life (in the time of my youth) were wont to detain their young negroes in their service till thirty years of age, without wages, on that account. And with this custom I so far agreed that I, as companion to another Friend in executing the will of a deceased Friend, once sold a Negro lad till he might attain the age of thirty years and applied the money to the use of the estate[, which lad at dating this note is upward of twenty-four years of age and now a servant and frequently attends the meeting I belong to].⁵¹

The context for writing in 1769 about this manumission was the evidence in Woolman's life of the unnamed "free" black man who still attended Mount Holly Meeting. This man was twenty-four in 1769, so he could have been James, whose stated age in 1754 would fit the dates. His attendance at Mount Holly Meeting for Worship suggests that Woolman and his coexecutor indentured the boy, who grew to manhood before their eyes, to a fellow Quaker. This would mean that year after year, on the morning and possibly afternoon of First Day (Sunday) and the evening of Fifth Day, Woolman saw the young man sit in the tiny twenty-foot-square building that Quakers used for Meetings for Worship during his lifetime. Woolman sat on the facing bench of presiding elders and often preached, and the young man was in Woolman's field of view.

Why did Woolman erase the bracketed phrase? Erasure rather than his usual cross-out suggests anguish rather than a simple attempt to excise repetition. He goes on to record the guilt this "youthful" error caused him: "With abasement of heart I may now say that sometimes as I have sat [in the uppermost seat] in a meeting with my heart exercised toward that awful Being who respecteth not persons nor colours, and have looked upon this lad, I have felt that all was not clear in my mind respecting him." Until recently, Woolman continues, he could not think how to make restitution for his commission of the injustice: "And under this sore affliction my heart was softened to receive instruction, and here I first saw that as I had been one of the two executors who had sold this lad nine years longer than is common for our own children to serve, so I should now offer a part of my substance to redeem the last half of that nine years."⁵²

New Jersey law mandated that orphaned white children who had no living relative to take responsibility for them would be indentured to a trade until they were twenty-one. This is what the coexecutors of the Shinn estate did for the deceased man's sons Aquilla and Gamaliel. But they had dealt with the freed slaves differently. Woolman now determined to pay for the remaining half of the nine-year extension for the black man, being half responsible as one of the two executors.

Woolman aimed for justice, at least consciously. His stated concern was whether he had been fair to the young man's master— "what to candid men might appear equitable for the last four years and a half of his time." This was an honest complication and showed Woolman applying universal love to the problem at hand. Any change would have to be fair to master and servant, equal in God's and now Woolman's eyes. The erasures, oversights, and errors suggest a tension, though, between the story that Woolman tells readers and what he felt in his heart. Unresolved guilt made for a barrier between Woolman and the Light within him.[53]

We do not know what happened to the one or more additional slaves freed in the settlement of the estate. Perhaps any other slaves were already dead in 1769. Or Woolman "forgot" the freed slave in the same complicated way that he garbled chronology and facts. Or if the others were older and their indentures therefore shorter, the transactions involving them may not have burdened him with guilt. Or Woolman may have consciously suppressed part of the story for other reasons. But the omissions make sense as evidence of the psychological complexity of this story. In any case the indenturing of James may have affected his decision to publish his antislavery pamphlet.

When Woolman drafted *A Plea for the Poor* during 1763 and 1764, he criticized the custom of indenturing manumitted slaves for nine years longer than white orphans: "To keep Negroes as servants till they are thirty years of age and hold the profits of the last nine years of their labour as our own, on a supposition that they may sometime be an expense to our estates, is a way of proceeding which appears to admit of improvement." This is a very gentle dissent from the practice, but it is clear that he already had the moral insight that festered inside him. "My heart is infected with sorrow while I write on this subject," Woolman says in *A Plea*. At this time, though, he does not admit, perhaps to himself, a personal connection to injustice that saddens him.[54]

In the *Journal* he implies that sale of the indenture occurred "in the time of my youth" before he was a responsible adult with fully formed views of racial justice. Leaving the story out of its chronological place and misstating when it actually happened reveal more than a forthright inclusion would. We can only glimpse the guilt that continued to haunt his dreams.

O VER the decade after Burlington Monthly Meeting recognized Woolman as a minister in 1743, Woolman's responsibilities were not unusual for a man active in Meeting affairs, where duties were widely distributed among members. And after ten years he was appointed clerk, the Meeting's most responsible position. For sixteen years beginning in 1753, he facilitated ("clerked") Meetings for Business, took the minutes, and fulfilled the coordinating and leadership roles. His hand is all over the Meeting records, the details revealing his dedication and the high standards he set for himself and his Meeting.[55]

The time of Woolman's rise to leadership corresponded to a period of deep reform within the Society of Friends on both sides of the Atlantic. At the local level, where Woolman focused his institutional energies in the 1740s, the reformers wanted to tighten Quaker discipline and bring Friends back from modern corruptions to the founding generation's faith. The reformers, who coalesced into a veritable movement, thought Friends had become extravagant, prone to excesses of consumption (especially of alcohol but also of food), ostentatious in their displays of wealth, and inattentive to testimonies that defined their faith. Quakers, in sum, had become vain, and their Meetings full of "dead, lifeless members," which left the church in "ruinous heaps." The number of formal complaints against "delinquent" Friends dramatically increased.[56]

When Monthly Meetings received such reports, they appointed committees to visit the accused and ascertain their responses to the charges. The technical accuracy of the accusations was not the principal focus. All could be forgiven if an accused Friend accepted the discipline and responded meekly with a guilty plea and a pledge of reform. Repeat offenses were more difficult to forgive, of course, and chronic breaches, drunkenness being the most intractable, were also causes for formal disownment. This was not a bar to attendance at Meetings, except in such unusual cases as that of Benjamin Lay, who had intentionally disrupted worship. Often, though, accused Friends simply distanced themselves from Meeting and refused to appeal for forgiveness.[57]

The most complaints were lodged against members who had married outside the religion. Here an admission of error for not marrying a Quaker in good standing, or for failing to obtain sanction of the union through the approved process, and an apology were generally sufficient to restore Friends to the good graces of Meeting. But committees investigated accusations of a host of other infractions: drunkenness; bearing arms in war or becoming a militiaman; poor attendance at Meetings for Worship; loose conduct, which could be flirtatious or overtly sexual; profanity; attending an unsanctioned wedding; incessant quarreling; participating in such entertainments as card playing, attending theatrical productions, or paying to watch jugglers and magicians; gambling; keeping bad company; questionable business ethics; excessive debt; fraud; theft; taking oaths; lying; theological deviations; Sabbath breaking; assault; slander; and overt sexual misconduct, such as fornication, incest, and adultery.

The attempt to tighten discipline at the local level reached a peak in the 1750s and 1760s, when Woolman was clerking Burlington Monthly Meeting. But the early stages of reform are visible in minutes from the 1740s, just as Woolman became a minister. It is more than his handwriting that is all over those records. His universal love, high moral standards, and open heart are there too.[58]

6

Nightmares

1754–55

D URING the night of February 7, 1754, John Woolman dreamed about walking in an orchard. He reports that in the dream two lights, which had a "dull and gloomy aspect," appeared to him in the east. One shone halfway between earth and the celestial meridian and looked like the sun; the other was north of the first and lower on the horizon. The sky caught fire. Flames engulfed the orchard but left Woolman unscathed, and he remained at peace. As he watched the firestorm, he became aware of a friend who was frightened by the conflagration. Woolman attempted to calm the man by reminding him of their shared mortality and the peace enjoyed by those who submit to God's will.

> Then I walked to a house hard by, and going upstairs, saw people with sad and troubled aspects, amongst whom I passed into another room where the floor was only some loose boards. There I sat down alone by a window, and looking out I saw in the south three great red streams standing at equal distance from each other, the bottom of which appeared to stand on the earth and the top to reach above the region of the clouds. Across those three streams went less ones, and from each end of such small stream others extended in regular lines to the earth, all red and appeared to extend through

at this unusual appearance, my mind felt calm, and I said to my Friend, we must all once die, and if it please the LOrd that our death be in this way it's good for us to be resigned : then I walked to a house hard by, and going up stairs saw people with sad and troubled aspects, amongst whom I passed into another Room, where the floor was only some loose Boards, there I sat down alone by a window, and looking out I saw in the South, three great red Streams, standing at equal distance from each other, the bottom of which appeared to stand on the Earth, and the top to reach above the region of the Clouds : across those three Streams went less ones, and from each end of such small Stream others pointing in regular lines to the Earth, all red and appeared to extend through the whole Southern Firmament like this figure,

I do not want this
figure printed
J Woolman

There then appeared on a green plain, a great multitude of men in a military posture some of whom I knew, these came near the house and passing on westward some of them looking up at me, exprest themselves in a taunting ... way, to which I made no reply : soon after an old Captain of the Militia came to me, and I was told these men were assembled to Improve in the discipline of war. —

Woolman's sketch to explain a dream he had, in a manuscript draft from his journal, 1754 (John Woolman Papers, Collection No. 737, Historical Society of Pennsylvania)

the whole southern firmament. There then appeared on a green plain a great multitude of men in a military posture, some of whom I knew. They came near the house, and passing on westward some of them, looking up at me, expressed themselves in a scoffing, taunting way, to which I made no reply; soon after, an old captain of the militia came to me, and I was told these men were assembled to improve in the discipline of war.[1]

The editorial committee excised this dream and a primitive sketch in black ink that accompanied it in his draft before publishing the *Journal*. Woolman himself had wanted to exclude the drawing—he wrote in the manuscript's margin: "I do not want this figure printed J Woolman"—but not the dream, which he thought enhanced his spiritual autobiography. In retrospect, he believed it had prophesied the French and Indian War.[2]

During the 1740s and early 1750s, English colonists moving north from Virginia and west across Pennsylvania and New York knew they were intruding on territory claimed by France and threatening its monopoly on the fur trade in the continent's interior. Not only that, but they were clearing forests that had been hunted by Indians for millennia. The century-long worldwide conflict between the French and British empires was coming to a head, not just in North America but first and decisively there; the opening shots of this world war were fired on the Pennsylvania-Virginia frontier and were aimed at a young militia major named George Washington. The British decision in 1754 to build a fort in western Pennsylvania as a symbol of their territorial claim and to defend the region against French and Indian incursions, and its subsequent loss to the enemy, led directly to war. Skirmishes, brush fires that needed only an ill wind to spread, increased in frequency. Soon the frontier was aflame, just as the orchard was in the dream. Woolman feared for everyone but himself. He remained calm when blood flowed in streams above and around him.

More than a year after Woolman had his dream, English Maj. Gen. Edward Braddock left Fort Cumberland in Virginia with an expeditionary force of British regulars and colonial militia on June 10,

1755, after numerous delays—some a function of his incompetence, some out of his control—having alienated his Indian allies and colonial officials by his arrogance and disinterest in their advice. The troops moved slowly, hindered by wilderness conditions, their commander's inexperience, and the weight of ordnance and supplies. They were sitting ducks for a combined force of 123 French soldiers, about 100 militia, and 600 Indians, who ambushed the British regulars and Virginia militia from the high, forested ground as they crossed a creek on July 9. A three-hour battle turned into a rout, with the British suffering catastrophic losses; more than two-thirds of the enlisted men and three-quarters of the officers were wounded or dead, including Braddock, who was quickly buried on the field of combat.

After routing Braddock's forces, Indians raided the Pennsylvania and Virginia frontier with impunity. Thousands of settlers fled, creating a refugee problem in the colonies; more than fifteen hundred died, and more than a thousand were captured. As the frontier burned, the Pennsylvania Assembly fiddled; it was weakened by factionalism and slow to address the catastrophe. It took several years for the colony and Great Britain to implement an effective response, in the process breaking Quaker political dominance and strengthening the colony's government.

Other Pennsylvanians blamed Quakers for their inadequate defense against Indians, and Quakers themselves were divided—the two lights of Woolman's dream—over how to maintain public responsibilities without abandoning their peace testimony. The second story of the Quakers' house, the society they founded in Pennsylvania and New Jersey, had loose boards, it was in disrepair. They were sad and troubled in the dream and in conscious life; Woolman felt alone as he sat placidly by the window with a full view of the scene in clear light. The dream's militia headed west, toward the frontier to kill Indians. Woolman radiated a pacific temperament and argued against war, making him vulnerable to the harsh words of those who, like the militia captain in the dream, fought the French and Indians in defense of the British colonies, while Quakers seemed indecisive, hypocritical, cowardly, and irresponsible in the face of an enemy's threat. They cowered in a ramshackle house as flames burned around them rather than pitching in to help extinguish the fire and repair their home. Woolman asserted his principles and apparently felt alienated from both sides, the fearful and the bellicose.

Quakers had long disagreed about application of the peace testimony to particular cases, but few had embraced pacifism as uncompromisingly as did the reformers of the 1750s. The war was the precipitating event for their reconsideration of the peace testimony. But Woolman's prophetic dream reveals that the question absorbed him even before its first battle.

The story of conflict between the Quaker community's politics and its ethics reaches back to the founding of Pennsylvania. Right from the beginning, Quakers had controlled Pennsylvania's thirty-six-man assembly and therefore triumphed in any conflict with the governors, who represented the Penns. Sixty percent of the assemblymen were Quakers in 1730, more than 80 percent in 1740, and 75 percent in the early 1750s. To be sure, during some periods, such as the schism in the 1690s led by George Keith, the Quakers did not present a united front, but in the early 1740s they ruled amicably and in concert largely because others—the Penns, the governors, and some ambitious non-Quakers—challenged their dominance.[3]

The issue around which the Quakers' opponents coalesced was the assembly's reluctance to support Great Britain's war against Spain, its other principal imperial competitor. The war was called the War of Jenkins's Ear after an English sea captain who famously testified before Parliament in 1738 that his ear, which he displayed pickled in a jar, had been cut off by a Spanish coastguardsman in 1731. The ceaseless trade disputes between the two imperial powers were the occasion for both the amputation and the war, which began in 1739. The Pennsylvania governor George Thomas had requested establishment of a provincial militia, recruitment for the regular British armed forces, and appropriations for war supplies, all of which the assembly declined to endorse. Opponents attacked Quaker control of the assembly on two fronts: mounting political campaigns against their reelection in 1741 and 1743 and appealing to the king and Parliament in London to ban them from holding office in Pennsylvania. These assaults failed. Quakers won reelection to office easily; forty-one of the fifty-two men who served in the assembly during the 1740s were Quakers, and the minority generally voted with them. The king lacked authority to intervene, according to the Privy Council, and Parliament saw no looming threat to the empire in the electoral politics of Pennsylvania.

Quaker reformers were also critical of their delegates, but from the opposite ideological direction. They rightly viewed politics as a world of compromise, and they were not inclined to barter principles. Far from finding the assembly too pacific, they believed it too accommodating of war. Still, Quaker legislators consistently opposed a draft, thereby protecting Quakers, Mennonites, and other pacifists from having to choose between waging war or challenging authority, and they also refused to support the costs of military operations directly. But there lay the reformers' problem: the Quaker assemblymen supported war indirectly. They refused to allocate money for specific purposes—weapons, ammunition, food, or housing of combatants, for example—but did vote for unrestricted funds "for the king's use," thereby rendering unto Caesar the things that were Caesar's with full knowledge that some of the money would be spent for war.

Quakers had governed Pennsylvania by this sort of ethical sleight of hand for more than seventy years. The beginning of the French and Indian War in 1754, Braddock's death and the disastrous defeat of his expeditionary force in 1755, and the flaming Pennsylvania frontier that made an official declaration of war inevitable in 1756 left Quaker politicians no place to hide. Some of them withdrew from public life as a matter of conscience, splitting from those who remained active in the face of increasing criticism from Friends. When six Quaker pacifists resigned their seats in 1756, special elections replaced them all with non-Quakers. In the regular election that same year, twelve Quakers won, but four resigned under pressure initiated by the reformers; thus only eight of the thirty-six assemblymen were Quakers when there had been twenty-six, a strong and controlling majority, before the war.[4]

These large political and military crises were but part of the context of Woolman's dream about a burning orchard. The placement of the dream in the *Journal* exposes its symbolic role in his life: between two personal references to slavery. First, he writes that in 1753 a Quaker of some standing—a "weighty" Friend, in Quaker parlance—asked him to write a will for the man's seriously ill brother. Woolman knew the sick man owned slaves and inquired what the disposition of them would be in the will. The man answered that the slaves would be left to his brother's children.

> As writing is a profitable employ, as offending sober people is disagreeable to my inclination, I was straitened in my mind; but as I looked to the Lord, he inclined my heart to his testimony, and I told the man that I believed the practice of continuing slavery to this people was not right and had a scruple in mind against doing writings of that kind: that though many in our Society kept them as slaves, still I was not easy to be concerned in it and desired to be excused from going to write the will.[5]

As Woolman feared, the weighty Friend took offense and walked away in silence. Woolman had insulted him by judging his dying brother's life and, Woolman tells us, because he "had some concerns in the practice"—that is, owned slaves himself. Woolman had lost a friend, reluctantly but self-righteously: "In this case I had a fresh confirmation that acting contrary to present outward interest from a motive of divine love and in regard to truth and righteousness, and thereby incurring the resentments of people, opens the way to a treasure better than silver and to a friendship exceeding the friendship of men."[6]

Woolman's account of his dream follows right before a one-sentence paragraph on *Some Thoughts on the Keeping of Negroes.* So in the narrative as he presents it, the dream precedes his submission of the manuscript: "The manuscript before-mentioned having lain by me several years, the publication of it rested weightily upon me, and this year I offered it to the Overseers of the Press, who, having examined and made some small alterations in it, ordered a number of copies thereof to be published by the Yearly Meeting stock and dispersed amongst Friends." The reference to 1754 seems clear, but it is inaccurate; he actually submitted the manuscript to the overseers in 1753, before he had the dream and before the beginning of the war.[7]

Yet the larger point of the juxtaposition is true. Woolman saw a relationship between slavery and war, and he made it manifest not only in the *Journal*'s composition but in the argument of another abolitionist text he wrote for Yearly Meeting, *An Epistle of Caution and Advice, Concerning the Buying and Keeping of Slaves*. He drafted this document before he had dreamed the dream and before the first battle of the war. If the sequence was jumbled in his mind, it is because the war and the publication of his first two abolitionist writings all came in 1754.

The Quaker press published "An Epistle of Caution" in the fall of 1754 over the names of twelve Friends who signed as representatives of Philadelphia Yearly Meeting, since epistles are considered collective endeavors representing the shared sense of believers. Woolman was not even one of them, so his authorship was buried in anonymity, and there was no personal renown in his antislavery testimony. He had rightly recognized that previous antislavery reformers Lay, Sandiford, Keith, et al.—had made slaveowning Friends defensive, hostile, and closed to changing their minds.[8]

Shrewdly, Woolman had asked his friend Anthony Benezet to read the epistle to Philadelphia Monthly Meeting in January of that year, so during 1754 Friends grew accustomed to its pointed arguments before the text came to Yearly Meeting in the fall. Then, when Delaware Valley Friends considered communicating the epistle to other Yearly Meetings in London, Dublin, New England, Maryland, Virginia, and North Carolina, Woolman was neither the center of attention nor in a position to defend his words. It would be difficult to overstate the significance of this low-key, almost invisible approach. In the history of the abolition movement there was no more effective advocate by virtue of submerging his ego in the interests of the cause. Woolman led by appearing to follow; he argued by listening; he dissented with consensus in mind.

Woolman was not a voice in the wilderness either. He was part of a movement within Quakerism that made the environment receptive to antislavery reform. The compromisers who dominated the Philadelphia Yearly Meeting through the 1740s were gradually being replaced by moral purists. The Quaker version of the Great Awakening, quieter but of a piece with intense spiritual outbreaks across the Atlantic world, reached its climax in 1754–56, when Samuel Fothergill (1715–72), an English Friend, ministered to American Quakers. His preaching corresponded in time and success with that of the Anglican revivalist George Whitefield, whose emotional style Quakers rejected.

The philosophical basis for the reformers' abolitionism was a belief in the equality of all souls before God. Quakers shared a testimony on equality, but Woolman began to extend it universally. Since Quakers focused on the family, they based their traditional extension of philanthropy on an expansive definition that included their servants and slaves. In a Quaker family, slaves would be exposed to Christianity, have food, clothing, and shelter provided, be educated, and be treated humanely; they were less likely to suffer physical violence and harsh working conditions. But in fact the relationship between Quaker masters and slaves remained oppressive. To rationalize that the owners were social superiors who recognized the spiritual equality of master and slave was a sincere delusion for some, lip service to Quaker principles for others, and may have had an effect on the humanity of the Quaker masters. But it was total rot in the face of the psychological horrors of enslavement, the destruction of slaves' families, and the legacy of violence that endured across generations. Woolman rejected the theory of benign mastery and embraced Quakers' seventeenth-century understanding of equality, which corresponded with the social theory of John Locke, the only secular philosopher that we know he read.

Philosophers and historians debate whether Locke opposed slavery. They point, on the one hand, to his investment in the slave colony of North Carolina and the work he did in helping draft its charter and, on the other, to the social implications of his writings. But Locke's inconsistency, hypocrisy, or inner struggle does not bear on how a Quaker reader might have understood him in the 1740s and 1750s. The better question is whether his *Essay Concerning Human Understanding* and *Some Thoughts Concerning Education* contributed to an environment in which abolitionism drew adherents.[9]

English Dissenters of the seventeenth century had inspired Locke's writings on equality, so the influence was reciprocal or circular. Locke imbibed some of his ideas from Quakers, and Quakers later found in his writings intellectual and psychological support for their faith. Equality was a radical concept in seventeenth-century England, where belief in the divine right of kings to govern, a hierarchical church to impose its beliefs and practices on the unconvinced, and patriarchs to rule with unquestioned authority over their families were generally accepted, against which the Dissenting sects opposed their egalitarian radicalism. What English subjects debated and fought over in the seventeenth century was which king and which church would rule, but not whether civil and ecclesiastical authority was absolute. Quakers believed in equality right from the beginning, but they were less social levelers than spiritual ones. The distinction was lost on those who believed that both secular and spiritual equality was a threat to order, an understandable interpretation of the turmoil of the 1650s. Anglican and royal officials, as well as Cromwell's army, perceived challenges to either formulation of authority as threatening anarchy.

Locke accepted equality as a theological axiom, which he applied to his philosophy of family, childhood development, society, and the state. His sources and rationale were Christian from the Dissenting perspective. His reading of Genesis disputed whether God assigned Adam authority to rule over Eve and, by implication, whether men had the God-given role of patriarch in their families. Locke was elusive and inconsistent on the issue, but he came close to advocating gender equality—not as close as Quakers did, but much closer than most. He and Quakers believed that the Fifth Commandment applied equally to fathers and mothers:

> [The term] *Paternal Power* . . . seems so to place the power of parents over their children wholly in the *father*, as if the *mother* had no share in it, whereas if we consult reason or revelation, we shall find she hath an equal title. This may give one reason to ask, whether this might not be more properly called *parental power*. For whatever obligation nature and the right of generation lays on children, it must certainly bind them

equal to both the concurrent causes of it. And accordingly
we see the positive law of God everywhere joins them together, without distinction, when it commands the obedience of children.

Like Quakers, who reject sacramental baptism, Locke minimizes
the significance of sin and punishment passed down through the
generations. Whether he even believed in original sin is unclear.[10]

In his political works, Locke clearly postulates the equality of all
human beings without racial or gender qualification. His contention
that "all men by nature are equal" eliminates race as a qualifier, and
he is consistent on this point. He finds nothing in the Bible to justify the dominance of one group over all classes of another. Every
man has an "equal right . . . to his natural freedom," according to
Locke. His qualifiers are age and mental capacity. Children need
the protection of their parents until they reach adulthood, their in-
equality in respect to their parents being therefore not a permanent
condition, while lunatics, idiots, and madmen need to be sheltered
by society. "Thus we are born free, as we are born rational," Locke
writes, "not that we have actually the exercise of either: age that
brings one, brings with it the other, too."[11]

Locke's baseline for equality is quite low, requiring only the capacity to reason from the abstract concept of God to one's own corporeal state. Differently said, you have to be able to see yourself
within a spiritual universe. The key here is capacity. It is not essential that you actually see yourself in this way, but it is necessary that
you are capable of such reasoning. Locke made only one other exception to universal equality, and that concerned the condition of
slaves. As utter and lifelong dependents subject to the authority of
their masters, slaves have no claim on the equality enjoyed by other
rational humans. But this exception is strictly limited.

Woolman and other reform-minded Quakers could find in Locke
arguments against the institution of slavery as it existed in the
British colonies. Men lack the power to enslave themselves, Locke
says, because their power over themselves does not extend to personally forfeiting their own lives. Since "the *natural liberty* of man is
to be free from any superior power on earth," then our right "is to be

under no other restraint but the law of nature." The only just slavery, Locke goes on, "is nothing else, but *the state of war continued, between a lawful conqueror, and a captive.*" He believed that only captives taken in a just war can be enslaved legitimately. And this right to enslave captives is not transferable to others. Since New Jersey and Pennsylvania slaves were not prisoners of war, and none of them had been the slaves of enemy combatants, slavery in the Quaker colonies was illegitimate by both the philosophical logic of Locke and Woolman's moral calculus.[12]

Woolman's inspired belief in equality extended to all humans and, in due course, to animals as well, and without Locke's qualifiers for rationality. Onto the abolitionism that sprang from this belief he also grafted an abhorrence of violence, an ascetic sensibility, a mystical temperament, and a valuation of universal love over natural affection.

We have only a vague knowledge that Woolman, Benezet, and others—Israel Pemberton, Jr., John Churchman, and Daniel Stanton, to name three—were instrumental in the revival among Delaware Valley Quakers in the 1750s and 1760s, but abolitionism was one dimension of the moral reformation that inspired them. Strict pacifism, absolute devotion to the Golden Rule, enforcement of marriage within the religion, and renunciation of temporal ambitions again became working principles for the Quakers as they strove to reform their institutions. The impetus for stricter devotion to Quaker discipline came from both the periphery and the center—from local Meetings and Meetings from which no written records survive as well as from Yearly Meetings in Philadelphia and London. Much of the most effective advocacy came from the peripheries.[13]

Woolman's epistle of 1754 took the forthright tack of summarizing the traditional reform Quaker argument against buying and selling slaves. It did not matter where slaves were born; purchase and sale furthered a system that kidnapped people, exposed them to cruelty, separated them from spouses and family, and deprived them of the liberty to learn about God. Knowledge of the Golden Rule should be enough to convince all Christians, let alone inheritors of the apostolic church, that slavery was contrary to Christ's

teachings. Inevitably, owning slaves evoked the displeasure of
heaven and corrupted masters' souls.

> What dreadful scenes of murther and cruelty those barbarous
> ravages must occasion in these unhappy people's country, are
> too obvious to mention: Let us make their case our own, and
> consider what we should think, and how we should feel, were
> we in their circumstances. Remember our blessed Re-
> deemer's positive command, *To do unto others, as we would*
> *have them do unto us*, and that, *with what measure we mete, it shall*
> *be measured to us again*. And we intreat you to examine,
> whether the purchasing of a *Negroe* either born here, or im-
> ported, doth not contribute to a further Importation; and con-
> sequently to the upholding all the evils above mentioned,
> and promoting man-stealing, the only theft which by the *Mo-*
> *saic* Law was punished with Death.[14]

He invites Quaker readers to imagine themselves in the slaves'
place, to explore the unanticipated effects of slavery on even the
best masters, as well as their implication in the cruelest manifesta-
tions of forced bondage, no matter how remote in time, place, or circumstance. He challenges rationalizations and insists that it is not
possible to be a good slave master in any moral sense of the word.
Slavery is not right under any circumstances. His epistle makes a
plea for masters to act in their own spiritual self-interest. Doing
right by slaves promotes saving themselves. Freedom is socially responsible. No matter how unfortunate the outcome for freed slaves,
masters are obliged to prepare them for independence. Yes, African
Americans should read the Bible and have skills to support themselves, but that is no excuse for perpetual bondage. Look into your
soul, the epistle says; are you motivated by economic ambitions?
Question the judgments you make for material reasons; fear being
judged yourselves.

> Finally Brethren, we intreat you, in the Bowels of Gospel
> Love, seriously to weigh the cause of detaining them in
> bondage: If it be for your own private gain, or any other mo-

tive than their good, it's much to be feared, that the love of
God, and the influence of the Holy Spirit is not the prevailing
principle in you, and that your hearts are not sufficiently redeemed from the world.[15]

The dream came to Woolman after Benezet had read the epistle
to fellow Quakers and after Woolman had submitted *Some Considerations on the Keeping of Negroes* to the newly enlarged board of overseers of the press. A confluence of external and internal motives led
him to publish the long-moldering pamphlet eight years after he
wrote it, but the dream was not one of them, though as Woolman recounted it, the act of submission—*of* the manuscript and *to* God and
the overseers of the Quaker press—derived from the dream.

Woolman's account of his dream makes no mention of slavery,
it should be noted, not even a recognizable symbol of enslavement, unless the three vertical red streams signify slave, white,
and Indian blood; that it was a premonition of war, of the spilling
of French, Indian, and English blood, makes better sense. The
dream's obscurity may have perplexed the overseers, or they may
have rejected Woolman's mystical understanding of it as a message
from God.[16]

The key to Woolman's intended interpretation of the dream can
be found in *Some Considerations on the Keeping of Negroes* itself, in the
chain of logic that leads from parental love to slavery's sin: "the state
of mankind was harmonious in the beginning; and . . . sin hath introduced discord." Woolman shared Robert Barclay's understanding
that Adam's sin passes down to all humanity in the depravity of our
natures. There is nothing natural about the Light and nothing good
about our nature. Nevertheless, this is not what some Christian traditions call original sin: "This seed is not imputed to infants until
by transgression they actually join themselves therewith." Escape
from our evil nature comes through union with the divine Light. It
is sin deriving from our evil natures in rejection of the Light that
leads to war, and war is a punishment for sin in Woolman's moral
equation.[17]

The reasoning was not unique to Woolman. Thomas Tryon had
used it too; Benjamin Lay, making the point dramatically in the

1730s, had worn in Meeting a military uniform to dramatize the connection between slavery and war. John Churchman (1705–75), a Quaker from Chester County, Pennsylvania, who traveled with Woolman in the colonies and without him to England and the Continent in his ministry, also believed that the war with France was God's punishment for stealing fellow humans. In 1755, after an Indian raid on the west bank of the Susquehanna River, militiamen carried several corpses back to Philadelphia, where they displayed them in order to incite the populace to vengeance. Indeed, the sight of the mutilated bodies did lead to outcries against both the Indian perpetrators of such atrocities and Quakers who were not supporting the war effort. About seven hundred frontiersmen paraded through Philadelphia to protest the assembly's resistance to allocations for frontier defense. The intimidation worked, and in November 1755 the assembly authorized the formation of volunteer militias to meet the French and Indian threat.[18]

The bodies and rage displayed on city streets shocked Churchman. He considered strife a punishment for sin and contemplated which sins provoked God's ire. Surely the general depravity of society—the prevalence of drunkenness, profanity, and pride—warranted reprisal. Bloodshed on the frontier indicted Philadelphians as well as British settlers of the backcountry.

The weight of my exercise increasing as I walked along the street; at length it was said in my soul, *This Land is polluted with blood, and in the day of inquisition for blood, it will not only be required at the frontiers and borders, but even in this place where these bodies are now seen.* I said within myself, "How can this be? Since this has been a land of peace, and as yet not much concerned in war;" but as it were in a moment mine eyes turned to the case of the poor enslaved Negroes: And however light a matter they who have been concerned with them may look upon the purchasing, selling, or keeping those oppressed people in slavery, it then appeared plain to me, that such were partakers in iniquity, encouragers of war and the shedding of innocent blood, which is often the case, where those unhappy people are or have been captivated and brought away for slaves.[19]

This was the Truth that had enlightened Woolman in 1754, the inspiration coming to him in a dream as it did to Churchman in a flash of insight as he contemplated the Philadelphia street scene in 1755. Churchman and Woolman both concluded that slavery had bloodied Quakers' hands; slavery was the moral cause of violence on the frontier.

The unnamed friend in Woolman's dream believed the conflagration was a heavenly reprisal; he needed reminding about the relationship between submission and interior peace. The man was a Quaker—a Friend and a friend. If he had a clear conscience and trusted his fate to God, there was nothing to fear. But guilt agitated him. The man symbolized most Quakers, average people who followed the earthly crowd and were precisely the sort whom Woolman addressed. Quakers were responsible for the war and for slavery, because they knew better if they only followed the Light. They had failed New Jersey and Pennsylvania, Indians, Africans, and themselves. Worst of all, they defied the Truth that God had revealed to them.

The dream friend was likely Woolman too. His fearless, saintly self witnessed the conflagration along with the guilty part of him that feared God's judgment more than death. All his mistakes, oversights, and conflicted behavior flooded the bloody streams around him. It was his house too that was in disarray and vulnerable to the flames licking its foundations. Vanity consumed him.

> To conclude, 'tis a truth most certain that a life guided by wisdom from above, agreeable with justice, equity, and mercy, is throughout consistent and amiable, and truly beneficial to society. The serenity and calmness of mind in it affords an unparalleled comfort in this life, and the end of it is blessed. And, no less true, that they who in the midst of high favours remain ungrateful, and under all the advantages that a Christian can desire are selfish, earthly, and sensual, do miss the true fountain of happiness and wander in a maze of dark anxiety, where all their treasures are insufficient to quiet their minds. Hence, from an insatiable craving they neglect doing good with what they have acquired, and too often add oppression to vanity, that they may compass more.

Vanity, greed, oppression, and violence are the links that chain slaveowners and the society that suffers slavekeeping, to earth. War is the social consequence; turmoil is the personal experience; spiritual desolation is the soul's loss. War with the French and Indians derived from unbridled consumption and the moral depravity of slavery. There was no spiritual escape for souls tethered to earth by possessions, who blindly careened about in a maze of anxiety.[20]

W OOLMAN's dream suggests that the relationship between the external events of the years 1746–54 and his internal spiritual development was closer than he acknowledges in the *Journal*. In that same year of 1754 Woolman's wife, Sarah, gave birth to William, named for John's grandfather. The birth may have been difficult for mother and infant; the boy died within two months, and Sarah bore no more children, even though she was only thirty-three when she delivered this one. John nowhere mentions the pain of this loss, just as he does not acknowledge in print the joy of Mary's arrival. William's name does not appear in the *Journal*, account books, or personal correspondence. The only record of him is in Burlington Monthly Meeting's register of births and deaths.

The greatest nightmare a parent can live is the death of a child. No loss rends the soul with such despair. We are not left entirely to imagine how deeply Woolman understood this, because he wrote a condolence letter to John Ely and his unnamed wife at around this time. He knows firsthand, he says, the suffering of a parent whose child dies: "The wounds and agonies that seize a parent's heart on such an occasion cannot be thoroughly communicated to one who never felt them or scarce ever be forgotten by one who has had so long a share in them as I have had, so that nature as well as Christian Duty leads me to mourn with you that weep."[21]

We are left to wonder about Woolman's "long share" of such tragedy, which implies more than one death. For the date on the letter is May 9, 1754, three months *before* his infant son William was born and five months before his death. Perhaps there were earlier miscarriages or stillbirths, which would also account for the passage of four years since the birth of Mary. Such events were not noted in the Meeting records, so this is the only clue we have to what John and Sarah may have suffered from 1750 to 1754.

Woolman does not minimize the loss or understate the blessing that the Elys' son had been when alive. The boy was "in the beginning of the bloom of life whose sweetness of temper with a complication of desirable endowments of nature crowned with a virtuous and pious turn of mind, seemed to promise much comfort to you and a blessing to the church of Christ in days to come." The unnamed boy's nature was admirable, but the parents must now resist their own grieving "animal nature." Woolman names here with clarity and grace the great life struggle that he knew within himself. Life is spirit at war with nature, and when spirits are low, nature rears its animal head, "but now alas the smiles of the morning sun are obscured by dark and sable clouds; the curtains of midnight and the shadow of death overspreads your tabernacle." The poetic sensibility shown here is absent from anything Woolman wrote in the *Journal* or pamphlets. Do not submit, do not forget the prosperity bestowed on us by God's gift of grace, he advises. Do not succumb with Job, who felt that God had abandoned him after torments greater than ours.

> Job again took up his discourse and said:
> "O that I were as in the months of old, as in the days when God watched over me; when his lamp shone over my head, and by his light I walked through darkness; when I was in my prime, when the friendship of God was upon my tent; when the Almighty was still with me, when my children were around me; when my steps were washed with milk, and the rock poured out for me streams of oil!" (Job 29:1–6)[22]

Woolman's heartfelt consolation also warns against indulging in grief. "He who gives has a right to take away and we ought in humility to bless his holy name," Woolman wrote. The Elys should trust to God and accept His will. They should count themselves blessed and be grateful that they are not among those without hope. "Your child though parted from you for a season; you may (I believe) justly hope to meet hereafter in the shining realms of paradise where there is no more death, sorrow nor crying nor any more pain." Woolman shares the pain, sheds the tears, and cannot forget, but he places his trust in God and his hope for reunion in the afterlife. The parenthetical reservation—"(I believe)"—expresses his humble knowledge that only God can judge the Elys' worthiness.[23]

In what is apparently the first and only draft of this letter, the unedited, emotionally unrestrained Woolman uses remarkably lyrical language. He is not calculating his effect for many readers or honing his style to achieve the requisite Quaker simplicity. This unrevised Woolman feels life's pain even as he strives to rise above his nature's limitations. Such a letter shows us a new aspect of him, and its very survival attests to the importance of Woolman's words for the bereaved Elys and to their gratitude for his empathy.

But the dream about a fire and the condolence letter reflect inner turmoil. Spiritual tumult was shaking Woolman's confidence that he could discern the quiet voice of God. He does not acknowledge emotional torment, but something was disquieting his soul. We do not know whether a melancholy cloud hung over him, his wife, and their four-year-old daughter or whether other stresses propelled him away from home. But we can wonder whether his traveling in the months after William's death reflected a disregard for his wife or a return to life that they both welcomed. We cannot know whether he felt unable to face his wife and daughter after their loss or mourned deeply with them. We cannot judge whether his behavior was detached, indeed callous, or whether he was more attached than he wanted readers to know.

Travel put Woolman's edginess in motion but did not by itself resolve the crisis. He thought God wanted him to visit Chesterfield Monthly Meeting, in Burlington County, but when he arrived, he was confused about why he was there. In a perplexed state, Woolman considered going back home but decided to ponder the question overnight and await spiritual clarity. By the next morning, after what may have been a sleepless night, he "felt easy to proceed on the visit, being very low in my mind."[24]

By "low in my mind" Woolman did not mean that he was melancholic, but rather that he was high-spirited, that his spirit was in ascendance over his nature, his soul over his mind. This restored his confidence that he was in communion with God. "And as mine eye was turned to the Lord," he writes, by which Woolman means, as he gazed inward, God "was pleased graciously to afford help." The deity offered Woolman grace, "so that we had many comfortable opportunities and it appeared as a fresh visitation to some young people." In other words, for the first time those young Friends experienced the transcendent, and Woolman was pleased to have served as the conduit. This flash of Light from Woolman's inner darkness revived his spirit and led him to make other trips over the winter months following his son's death.[25]

As Woolman recovered inner peace, he had occasion again to witness against slavery, now within the context of war and his first published abolitionist writings. In 1755 an older man from Mount Holly asked Woolman to write his will for an estate that included slaves. Woolman still struggled with saying no, for he did not relish offending his neighbors and was uncomfortable about questioning the moral character of men senior to him who had a "fair reputation." He was sensitive to the weight of custom yet convinced that traditional practice was no authority for doing what was wrong. He was sympathetic to the difficulty people had changing their ways, but that did not lessen the responsibility to make moral choices: "Deep-rooted customs, though wrong, are not easily altered, but it is the duty of everyone to be firm in that which they certainly know is right for them."[26]

Woolman therefore explained his scruple against writing wills that bequeathed slaves. He knew the slaveowner meant well, and he delivered praise rather than indicting, embarrassing, or angering him.

A charitable, benevolent man, well acquainted with a Negro, may, I believe, under some certain circumstances keep him in his family as a servant on no other motives than the Negro's good; but man, as man, knows not what shall be after him, nor hath he any assurance that his children will attain to that perfection in wisdom and goodness necessary in every absolute governor. Hence it is clear to me that I ought not to be the scribe where wills are drawn in which some children are made absolute masters over others during life.

The man was flattered to hear himself described so generously, and he found another scribe. Several years later, births and deaths in the same man's family dictated rewriting the will, and he asked Woolman again, telling him that his son was now sober, apparently believing that his son's character was what had led Woolman to decline the first time. But when Woolman had said that the children might not share their parents' "perfection in wisdom and goodness," he had meant his judgment to apply universally, not specifically to a "libertine" son. Woolman explained again that he still would not write the will.[27]

The man went away as he had before, bewildered but flattered by what he understood to be Woolman's high view of his charitable motives for owning slaves. This time, though, he returned a few days later to request that Woolman rewrite the will with a clause that freed the slaves. This Woolman gladly did, and they parted amicably.

At about the same time, Woolman bled a neighbor who had received a bad bruise; this was the common medical treatment for a variety of ills, the theory being that the letting of "bad" blood restored the body's balance and enabled it to fight off injury or infection. Believing he was close to death, the man asked Woolman to write his will and in the course of dictating his intentions named an heir for his female slave. Woolman wrote the will but left out the offending clause; he told the man that he would charge nothing for the service and that someone else would have to fill in the blank space left for disposition of the slave. After talking about it for some time, the man agreed to free his slave, and Woolman completed the will dictating manumission upon the master's death.[28]

Convincing two men to disinherit their children by freeing slaves was a real accomplishment. Woolman might have pressed further to encourage the men to release the slaves in their own lifetimes, taking on the financial burden of a salved conscience themselves. He must have calculated that such a recommendation would not prevail and settled for the best he could do. This willingness to soften his message for tactical reasons distinguishes Woolman from the confrontational abolitionists who came before and after him; it is also a key to any explanation for his comparative success in breaking the generational chain that passed slaves and their offspring through white families in perpetuity. Each master convinced in this way freed not just one slave but also the slave's lineal descendants born in freedom.

Small successes with large implications were gratifying but insufficient. By 1755 Woolman had become convinced that progress against war, slavery, and poverty would require challenging his own church. Freeing one slave at a time was important work, but freeing Quakers from slavery's moral taint was the bigger job that he believed God meant for him. As was his nature, Woolman frames this insight subtly, indeed obliquely, in the *Journal*. He introduces the subject as an aside, a one-sentence paragraph that is not fully integrated into a discussion of his opposition to war taxes.

Woolman's decision about tax resistance pitted his conscience against his respect for authority, creating a familiar emotional torment. Tax resistance was especially troubling because in recommending it, he was departing from a long-standing consensus among Quakers, though he was not a lone dissenter. Still, he was a step ahead of the other reformers who advocated loftier ideals and a stricter adherence to principle than the Society of Friends had shown since its early years.[29]

When Woolman first experienced pangs of conscience about paying war taxes in the mid-1750s, he could find no authority to support him in the Bible, Quaker tradition, or common practice among his coreligionists.

I was told that Friends in England frequently paid taxes when the money was applied to such purposes. I had conference with several noted Friends on the subject, who all favoured the payment of such taxes, some of whom I preferred before myself; and this made me easier for a time. Yet there was in the deeps of my mind a scruple which I never could get over, and at certain times I was greatly distressed on that account.

From a strictly theological perspective, Woolman needed no external validation for divine revelation, but he did need to be sure that the inspiration came from God. And even if he was convinced, as he was, the burden of building a consensus among believers remained: "I all along believed that there were some upright-hearted men who paid such taxes, but could not see that their example was a sufficient reason for me to do so, while I believed that the spirit of Truth required of me as an individual to suffer patiently the distress of goods rather than pay actively."[30]

Woolman was not seeking a precedent for principled resistance to lawful government or even to war, since he knew scores of examples in the history of church-state conflict dating back to early Christianity, the Reformation, and Quaker martyrdom on both sides of the Atlantic. He wanted authority to challenge his own church. In the *Journal* he cites two thinkers whose experiences comforted him, both of whom had stood against received ecclesiastical wisdom. One dissenter, who paid with his life, was the Bohemian reformer Jan Hus (ca. 1369–1415); the other was Thomas à Kempis.[31]

Hus was an enthusiastic supporter of the ideas of the English cleric John Wycliffe (ca. 1329–84), who had become well known on the Continent for his belief that the church should secularize its properties and remove itself from temporal governance, for his questioning the authority of the pope and asking whether the office should be abolished, for his denials of the priestly power of absolution, and for his renunciation of the whole system of confession, penances, and indulgences. (Eventually he even rejected the central dogma of transubstantiation, belief in the actual transformation of bread and wine into the body and blood of Christ.) He emphasized the importance of inward religion over outward forms, and he was a prolific writer. Hus read Wycliffe's work—composed in Latin, of course—and adopted it, often verbatim, as his own. The Vatican excommunicated Hus when he refused to cease his public advocacy of Wycliffe's teachings, and despite strong public support, the Council of Constance imprisoned him and called upon him to recant; when he refused, he was tried, condemned, and burned at the stake.[32]

Woolman understood from John Foxe's *Acts and Monuments* that Hus "contended against . . . errors [that] crept into the church." According to Woolman's reading, Hus "modestly vindicated the cause which he believed was right, and though his language and conduct toward his judges appear to have been respectful, yet he never could be moved from the principles settled in his mind." Woolman believed that Hus had been executed for following the Light within him, which challenged the outward forms of church practice. One may dispute the subtlety of Woolman's understanding or even see it as a caricature of the actual history of fourteenth- and fifteenth-century reform efforts within the church, but this is how Foxe tells the story and how Woolman derived a meaningful moral from it.[33]

Thomas à Kempis also advocated the authority of conscience over earthly powers, as Woolman understood him. Kempis, according to Woolman, "appears to have laboured, by a pious example as well as by preaching and writing, to promote virtue and an inward spiritual religion." Whether Woolman got the orthodox Kempis right from a Catholic theological perspective is beside the point. For him both Hus and Kempis were "sincere-hearted followers of Christ" and worthy of emulation, models of resolve in the face of contrary opinion within the church and, in Hus's case, also in the face of state authority. Woolman did not risk his life, as Hus did; the worst that Quakers might do would be to disown him, but Woolman took that possibility seriously. He respected those "noted Friends" who disagreed with him, "some of whom I preferred before myself," but he had to follow his own conscience rather than theirs and take the consequences within and possibly outside his church.[34]

Woolman was on what he hoped was an upward-spiraling path, inward toward social action and outward from his church toward its reform. Withdrawal brought him into increasing contact with the world; humility led him to challenge those above him; pacifism put him in conflict with fellow pacifists. He was leading where no one had ever followed God before. Woolman's advocacy of tax resistance and of abolition of slavery were two sides of the same moral coin. The source for both leadings was internal, even mystical, but more than he knew, external influences affected Woolman's comprehension of the spirit that moved him. Few would have interpreted his dreams and meditative inspiration as injunctions to act as he did, and fewer still would have followed such leadings so devotedly.

THE delegation of work for epistles from Yearly Meeting varies depending on the relationships and recognized gifts of committee members. The process for a series of epistles in the 1750s differed somewhat, though, as a deleted passage in a manuscript draft of Woolman's *Journal* shows. At first he wrote of an epistle he composed in 1755 on the subject of the French and Indian War: "It came upon me to write an Epistle to Friends which I took to our General Spring Meeting and passed to some Elderly Friends to have it inspected and signed by a number of the brethren on behalf of the meeting." Comparison of Woolman's handwritten drafts of the epistle with the final text shows that the only revisions were minor ones for style, clarity, and nuance, so the committees were endorsing material that truly expressed his personal vision. But then Woolman deleted this sentence from his *Journal* and substituted one that hid him from view: "An epistle to Friends went forth from our General Spring Meeting, which I thought good to give a place in this Journal." Including the 1755 epistle in his published *Journal* makes more sense when we know that he drafted it.[35]

The epistle of 1755 is a reminder of the traditional Quaker principles that inform the peace testimony. The meaning of Christ's life and personal sacrifice is to bring peace on earth; this is Christ as Redeemer, not the warrior with a sword in his hand. The sacredness of God's creation makes violence a breach of the deity's will. Submission to the higher order means working toward God's peaceable kingdom, signs of which are already evident. The triumph of spirit over nature can be achieved only by eschewing the meaningless conflicts of the world. Acts of violence lead to collective retribution: "And if for the chastisement of wickedness and the further promoting his own glory, he doth arise even to shake terribly the earth, who then may oppose Him and prosper." The war was both retribution for the colony's earlier violence and an opportunity to reverse course, to rekindle God's favor or to invite further reprisals: "To meekly suffer by our lawful rulers seems to me like placing the Light on the candlestick and adding our mite to help forward toward that mountain where they shall no more hurt or destroy."[36]

The network of precepts on which Woolman drew was complex. There was no conflict for him where others might have experienced a jangle of thoughts. The key to coherence for Woolman was mystical experience, his unfailing guide to what he read and to what he gleaned from his readings, whether they were in Locke, Quaker theologians, Catholic ascetics, Continental mystics, French quietists, or the Bible. He applied them all to the Quakers' responsibility for violence, slavery, and war.

7

Taxed

1756–57

SINCE their settlement of Pennsylvania and New Jersey, the Quakers' peace testimony had evolved. American Quakers had long sought to avoid complicity in war, but this was a far cry from taking a public stand against all violence. George Fox and other early articulators of the peace testimony had declared it to be divine revelation; they had not quoted scripture to support it. And they extended their pacifism to all humanity, not just to fellow Quakers. But the next generation, including William Penn, had also argued on secular and humanitarian grounds that violence is destructive of all combatants. Then, by the end of the seventeenth century, Friends were quoting the New Testament in support of the peace testimony and declaring war inconsistent with Christ's teachings.

Early in the eighteenth century they were focusing inward, expressing the peace testimony as a concern for their own spiritual purity. They abandoned their earlier ecumenical humanitarianism and New Testament universalism for a tribal vision of Quaker responsibility; they accepted the short-term inevitability of war, and though they declined to participate as combatants or as purveyors of weaponry, they supported general taxation measures, including allocations for combat troops. This was the insular, rhetorical pacifism that Quaker reformers challenged in the 1750s.[1]

In 1756 Woolman wrote a parable that shows the process by

which he worked out his position on resistance to taxes that financed war and searched outside himself for authority to support the inner voice he heard. As he had before, Woolman reached into the past for models; and though he used the New Testament parable form, he used Old Testament figures—Nimrod, Sheba, Shem, and the sons of Ham—in a story about the origins of government and the dilemma of Christians taxed to support war.

Significantly, the general assumption in eighteenth-century Anglo-America was that the biblical Canaan, the son who bore the curse for the sin of Ham, was black. Such an interpretation of Genesis 9:18–25 had Arabic, Hebrew, and ancient Greek and Roman sources; it gained authority from a misunderstanding of the etymological origins of Ham's name as part of an attempt to justify the social status quo in which black Africans were enslaved. Using circular logic, people called on Genesis to explain slavery, and the enslavement of blacks provided grounds for interpreting the biblical passage.

> And Ham, the father of Canaan, saw the nakedness of his father, and told his two brothers outside. Then Shem and Japheth [Noah's other sons] took a garment, laid it upon both their shoulders, and walked backward and covered the nakedness of their father; their faces were turned away, and they did not see their father's nakedness. When Noah awoke from his wine and knew what his youngest son had done to him, he said, "Cursed be Canaan; a slave of slaves shall he be to his brothers."

Woolman explicitly rejected the popular reading of God's curse on Canaan as a justification for black slavery; there is no reason to believe, and every reason to doubt, that he thought the descendants of Canaan were black. But in any case Canaan and his sons are free men in Woolman's parable.[2]

One hundred years after the Flood, in Woolman's story, Ham's sons are fighting among themselves, so they resolve in open council to choose a king and annually elect a minister to head the government. Nimrod, the monarch, and Sheba, his minister, submit rules of conduct to them for approval, and the brothers agree to abide by them. Monarch and minister distribute charity to the needy and "view with the spirit of a parent the situation of their family, abridge the schemes of individuals so far as they interfere with the public good, and give light and encouragement to their honest and industrious children." The brothers cheerfully pay taxes to support their government. They annually reelect Sheba as minister, and the two rulers are universally beloved.

But over time the hearts of Nimrod and Sheba are "lifted up because of their beauty, and their wisdom corrupted by reason of their brightness." By degrees they grow rich, greedy, oppressive, and corrupt. They levy more taxes for their own benefit, well beyond the community's real needs.

A man named Shem and his family live a short distance away. He is righteous and rules his family peacefully. In "the integrity of his heart" Shem condemns Nimrod's apostasy, and King Nimrod cannot bear this criticism because of his haughty spirit and because he knows that what Shem says is true. So Nimrod bides his time, looks for an opportunity, and fabricates a threat to his kingdom that he claims Shem represents. He stirs up his people with lies and an impassioned call to arms. With the sons of Ham aroused by the patriotic cry for war, Sheba demands four times the taxes necessary to conduct domestic affairs, collects them, and "hires men who are zealous for their prince though ignorant of the merits of his cause." The army marches across Shem's border and presents him with an ultimatum, which he cannot accept because he "serves God and trusts in Him, and cannot bow to a cruel hunter."[3]

A number of men in Nimrod's kingdom who "love Truth and Justice" recognize Sheba and Nimrod for the corrupt tyrants they have become. They sympathize with Shem's position. The question for these men is whether they should pay the taxes demanded by their monarch or stand up to tyranny.

The story's anachronisms are distinctively eighteenth-century Anglo-American. Woolman calls the two texts that frame Nimrod's government articles of agreement and laws; acceptance of the former binds the sons of Ham to obedience to the latter—that is, the articles have precedence over laws, a view that was an American innovation in political theory. During the 1760s and 1770s this distinction was to become a source of dispute between the Americans and Parliament when colonists claimed that their founding charters were written constitutions, which prevailed over laws enacted by Parliament that might be unconstitutional and therefore void. Britons on the other side of the Atlantic held the traditional view that no single document embodied the British constitution, made up as it was of parliamentary acts, judicial decisions, bureaucratic edicts, and traditional practices; to them, the Americans were introducing a nonsensical notion of divided sovereignty.

True, the colonists believed that Parliament in London was sovereign in matters relating to the administration of the empire, but they were also sure that their own colonial legislatures were sovereign over local affairs. They came to believe that the charters embodying this local authority had a constitutional standing higher than acts of Parliament, edicts of colonial administrators, or provincial laws. Not the king or Parliament or their governors-in-council could contravene rights protected by the charters, they thought. For Britons, sovereignty resided in the king in Parliament, and it balanced the three interests of society—monarchy, aristocracy, and democracy—in the three institutions of king, House of Lords, and House of Commons. They had arrived at this resolution after spilling much blood in the seventeenth century, and they were not about to renegotiate such hard won constitutional relationships.[4]

In the Old Testament there are no written constitutions, only God's covenant with Israel and the Ten Commandments. Nor does one find a model for the code of conduct Woolman describes or for frames of government, and Moses did not submit the commandments to the Jews for ratification. But the distinction between compact and law is such a commonplace in Anglo-American colonial thought that it appears even in the writing of a Quaker tailor who was not educated in constitutional law or pleading a special case in the colonies' behalf, and even before the constitutional crisis of the 1760s and 1770s. It is also noteworthy that Woolman views government as a contract between rulers and ruled from which the sons of Ham are released when their rulers break the compact by their corruption. Like his fellow Americans who were to declare their contract broken and their constitution breached after the political disputes of the 1760s, Woolman believed that power was corrupting and that corruption was the principal threat to good governance.

Woolman could have gleaned this contract theory from John Locke's writings on child rearing and education. He did not listen to ballads and popular music, and as far as we know, he did not read political pamphlets, newspapers, novels, plays, poetry, almanacs, or other popular literature; but contract theory permeated colonial American popular culture. His conscious focus was elsewhere—on the moral obligation to resist war—and the political theory that informs his story is simply a cultural commonplace, which is what makes it interesting.

At the end of his parable Woolman draws out the lesson, which elevates spiritual values above earthly politics by appealing to the authority of a higher law with precedence over civil legislation. The duty of a righteous man is clear, whether the leaders who start wars are corrupt or simply misguided. War is wrong no matter what the cause and no matter how good or bad the intentions, how clouded or clear the judgments of rulers who make the call to arms.

> If those men of wisdom and honesty whose characters and beauty to his [the monarch's] kingdom contribute to his designs cheerfully, he has no real help from their honest hearts and better understandings. If from their firm attachment to virtue they conscientiously refuse to contribute actively, but with meekness and fortitude submit to the penalty, Nimrod on this occasion seeing their conduct, may likely make profitable reflections on his own. However that be, they keep a good conscience and maintain their characters. They may be considered as persons disaffected to government and their little kingdom as divided against itself. Yet where honesty, meekness, and fortitude is united, hard words can not move it. "There is no good in unity except unity be in goodness."[5]

In John Woolman's eyes, the next worse thing to fighting a war or profiting from it is to pay taxes that support it. A pacifist in the Quaker tradition defies earthly authority forthrightly and accepts the consequences for such actions. During his lifetime, as today, the decision to put Truth before self-interest could be emotionally wrenching. War resisters suffered ridicule, charges of hypocrisy, loss of neighbors' goodwill, and arousal of patriotic ire that sometimes made them victims of the violence they abhorred. They might have their properties confiscated or be personally subject to a retributive draft or imprisonment, any of which would devastate their families.[6]

Sometimes, depending on their personal inclinations, the authorities made allowances for Quaker beliefs. Among Quaker populations or when the tax collectors were Quakers themselves, the laws were sometimes enforced gently. Joshua Evans, a contemporary of Woolman's who lived near him in Mount Holly for a time, endured "much reproach" for his war tax resistance and feared worse, given the political environment.

> Thus I had to pass through reproach, because I had enlisted under his banner who declared his kingdom was not of this world, or else his servants would fight. When my goods were taken to answer demands of a military nature, (which I was not free to pay voluntarily) and sold perhaps much under their value, some would pity me, supposing it likely I should be ruined. Others would term it stubbornness in me, or contrary to the doctrine of Christ, concerning rendering to Caesar his due.

Evans was fortunate that he did not suffer a worse fate, as some did, but he and Woolman were not physically assaulted or imprisoned. Then the war against the French and Indians offered them the chance to take a principled stand modeled on those of the early Friends whose lives Woolman had found so inspiring as a child, and Woolman seized it personally and advocated it to others of his faith.[7]

In the end, the assessment on Woolman was not for a direct cash payment. Instead, he was ordered to house two soldiers when the army barracked them in Mount Holly. An officer explained that the government would pay six shillings a week for each man's room and board. Woolman was taken aback by the order, which he had not anticipated.

I was fully convinced that the proceedings in wars are inconsistent with the purity of the Christian religion, and to be
hired to entertain men who were then under pay as soldiers
was a difficulty with me. I expected they had legal authority
for what they did, and after a short time I said to the officer,
"if the men are sent here for entertainment, I believe I shall
not refuse to admit them into my house, but the nature of the
case is such that I expect I cannot keep them on hire." One
of the men intimated that he thought I might do it consistent
with my religious principles, to which I made no reply, as believing silence at that time best for me.

The extremity of his pacifism surprised the officers. When one of
them tried to pay him for boarding a soldier in April 1758, Woolman
explained that he "could not take pay for it, having admitted him
into my house in a passive obedience to authority." As they parted,
the captain said he was "obliged" to him. This too worried Woolman, who apparently feared that his motives had been misunderstood. He did not want anyone to think that he provided the service
gratis out of a sense of patriotic duty, so he rode to the captain's
quarters and explained more fully why he had declined payment.[8]

Woolman has inspired generations of war tax resisters, but most
of them lack the courage to follow in his uncompromising steps. He
beautifully expressed his spiritual genius with an artful, sensitive
resistance, and without anger or stridency, sympathizing with, rather
than demonizing, the officers who led soldiers into war. "Amongst
the officers are men of understanding," he writes, "who have some
regard to sincerity where they see it; and in the execution of their
office, when they have men to deal with whom they believe to be
upright-hearted men, to put them to trouble on account of scruples
of conscience is a painful task and likely to be avoided as much as
may be easily."[9]

Woolman's identification with the position of those who had not
yet seen the Light, his universal love, applied to soldiers, Indians,
politicians, and slaveowners. They were not enemies, as he had no
enemy but his own nature, so it was not a matter of loving his enemies as himself; but he embraced strangers, fought his nature, and

valued the best in others. His modesty disarmed those who might have taken offense. He convinced others because he did not judge them more harshly than he judged himself, and his flaws humbled him, his standard of moral purity being so high.

Woolman's friend Anthony Benezet also took a gentle approach to reform, and he derived it from some of the same sources, although Benezet did not identify with the prophets, was not so extreme in his practices, and judged others more gently. He too believed that a "true Christian . . . is willing to take up his daily cross, to be crucified to his own desires, to renounce the world, the flesh, and the devil." He too dwelled on "Christ's redeeming grace" and renounced the "deep and subtle corruptions of nature." And he too focused on "true charity," which he considered

> the love which was in Christ . . . If this love prevailed, it would certainly manifest itself by fruits as well as words. Self-denial, mortification, sympathy and benevolence, to do good and to communicate, to seek judgment and relieve the oppressed, and to the utmost of our power to bind up the broken-hearted would naturally flow as water from the fountain.[10]

W OOLMAN's selective reading of the Gospels and devotional books emphasized his quietist leanings, and those clearly influenced his approach to reform: Barclay's *Apology*, Kempis's *Imitation of Christ*, and the works by French quietists Jeanne Marie Guyon (1648–1717) and François Fénelon. Guyon, a Frenchwoman widowed at the age of twenty-eight, devoted her life to helping the poor and cultivating her spiritual "perfection." Catholic officials in a number of European cities, including Geneva, Turin, Grenoble, Nice, Genoa, and Paris, denounced her as a heretic for her mystical quietist beliefs, and she was imprisoned a number of times for her advocacy of quietism. Assertions that a believer communicated directly with God were seen, as they often had been in the past, to threaten the authority of priests, ceremonies, sacraments, and doctrines. She became a central figure in the movement for "holy living," and her writings inspired mystics across sectarian lines. Fénelon, a bishop who advocated the liberal education of women, tutored the grandson of King Louis XIV, and was appointed archbishop of Cambrai in 1695, wrote *Explanation of the Maxims of the Saints on the Interior Life* (1697) as a defense of Madame Guyon's quietism. The book was extremely controversial within the Catholic Church and was condemned by the pope; it too was as influential outside the church as within it, Guyon's and Fénelon's books circulating widely among Protestants.

The spiritual core of quietism is a distrust of human nature, a call for annihilation of the self, and a belief that the triumph of spirit over nature invites manifestation of the divine. The quietist phase of Quaker history ran its course for about a hundred years after 1725, with its greatest effect some years after Woolman's death. But his *Journal* is infused with quietism's language of purity, its belief in the possibility of attaining spiritual perfection on earth, and its passive approach to prayer. His writings disseminated quietist principles among Quakers and magnified their influence.

Quietists were prone to ecstatic experiences that overcame them during long periods of silent contemplation. They could meditate on the essence of God for hours at a time, physically unmoved and spiritually focused, far longer than other Christians practiced. Their meditative states were close to those of fellow mystics from other religious traditions, such as Buddhist monks. Quietism influenced American evangelicals in the early years of the nineteenth century with what critics thought were their "fanatical" beliefs and practices shared by "enthusiastic" exemplars of Quakerism and abolitionism. Woolman's quietism was remarkable both for his close embrace of its greatest challenges and for his application of its values and vocabulary to his antislavery writings.[11]

That quietists thought of prayer as a passive act was a key to their affinity with Quakers. "The reason the inward silence is so necessary," Madame Guyon said in *A Short and Easy Method of Prayer*, "is because this is a proper disposition and requisite for receiving into the soul the Word, which is the eternal and essential speech." Although theologians could parse the differences between her idea of the soul's reception of a message external to it and the Quakers' belief that the Light dwelled within, Quaker readers understood her concept well enough. "The hearing is a sense more passive than active," she wrote; "it receiveth, but doth not communicate." Both quietists and their Quaker admirers focused on "external silence," developing the "internal" senses, and waiting in "loving silence and retirement" for the voice of God.[12]

Fénelon too dwelled on the "inward teacher." He wrote:

The Holy Spirit is the soul of our soul. We cannot frame a thought, or create a desire, but through him . . . We make account as if we were by ourselves in this *inward* sanctuary, but on the contrary, God is there more nearly and intimately than we ourselves are. We must silence every creature and ourselves, too, to hear in a profound stillness of the soul, this inexpressible voice of Christ.[13]

A S Woolman continued reading in the quietistic vein, he honed his ministry to slaveowning Quakers, which kept him on the road. In May 1756 he spent almost a month at Quaker Meetings on Long Island, ministries he found quite successful. Now in his midforties, he was not so deferential as he had been in addressing patriarchs who were not much his senior. He had once lacked the confidence to challenge authority with Truth, but no more. In the *Journal*, Woolman compares himself during this period with the prophet Jeremiah: "I saw at this time that if I was honest to declare that which Truth opened in me, I could not please all men, and laboured to be content in the way of my duty, however disagreeable to my own inclination." He was still temperamentally disinclined to confrontation—gentle, self-deprecating, and humble in his address—but he believed he was delivering God's Truth without equivocation.[14]

Again, as so often, it is unclear how he assessed his family responsibilities. We do not know what his wife and daughter thought of his going off on these trips. Surely most of the household work fell on Sarah: looking after the orchard, garden, domestic animals, and perhaps even customers. Mary was six years old, and her emotional needs would have had to be filled by Sarah in his absence. Thomas Jefferson left his motherless daughters repeatedly for months at a time; Benjamin Franklin abandoned his family for years. These comparisons do not absolve Woolman or even explain his behavior, but the idea of surrender to a higher calling—whether God's, war's, or government's—was accepted among the men of eighteenth-century America and for many generations thereafter. Woolman's family may have understood their sacrifice as a calling from God or they may have resented it, but the circumstantial evidence we have supports the former and not the latter.

Woolman may have shared Anthony Benezet's views about women's ministry as Benezet expressed them in his letters. Once, in 1751, Benezet explained to a female correspondent, Susanna Pyrleus, and her husband that public ministry was man's work: "Whether it be, or be not, his duty at this time to go abroad on this errand we will leave to the great Judge and tryer of hearts. But as to our Sister Susanna," who wanted to go along with her husband,

> we must declare our dislike and our *dis-union* with her intended voyage. It is certainly her duty to take care and watch over the children that God has given her. Whether it is her duty to leave them & go abroad must certainly be a matter of grave doubt, even with her. Let people say what they will, none are so proper to watch over the wants and weaknesses of children as their own mother. We do not believe that any service, civil or religious, calls her to leave her tender children, and cross the seas. We look upon it rather as a snare, and suggestion of the enemy of her soul, who would keep her busy and employed in other men's vineyards, while her own remains uncultivated.

Benezet's certain knowledge about the woman's duty and place derived from his unshakable beliefs about a gendered division of responsibility in the home. Benezet and perhaps Woolman accepted only grudgingly the idea of a ministry for spinsters, widows, and other women. In any event, Susanna Pyrleus rejected Benezet's advice and accompanied her husband, taking their children along. If Woolman's wife or daughter ever raised the possibility of going with him, there is no surviving record of the discussion.[15]

On his way home from Long Island, Woolman thought about

another trip to the South, but this raised questions about how he would handle his now successful tailoring and merchandising businesses. He had begun to stock trimmings for garments and had expanded into selling clothes and linens. With the shop showing promise of additional growth, Woolman became concerned about how much time it required. The demands of the two related businesses were "cumbersome," and he felt a "stop" in his mind about the consequences of his success. It was time to follow his leadings and simplify his life yet again, he thought, as he had when he left the farm. Woolman was content with plain living, his family was small, and he did not need much money. "The increase of business became my burden," Woolman writes in the *Journal*, "for though my natural inclination was toward merchandise, yet I believed Truth required me to live more free from outward cumbers, and there was now a strife in my mind between the two."[16]

Woolman had another problem, which he addressed indirectly. He had a concern that his trade was contributing to customers' living less simply than Truth warranted, to their increasing indebtedness, and to their consuming immoderate quantities of alcoholic beverages. Woolman applied a chain metaphor to illustrate such connections. Quakers and other seventeenth-century Dissenters had challenged the Elizabethan hierarchical metaphor of the Great Chain of Being, which reached down from the heavens and assigned a link to each creature in the universe, and they turned the metaphor on its side. They liked to describe parallel relationships based on equality that stretched across creation rather than vertically from the heavens to earth. If God is within us, all creatures are linked by a chain that explains causal relationships as well as those of affinity.

> In the time of trading, I had an opportunity of seeing that too liberal a use of spirituous liquors and the custom of wearing too costly apparel lead some people into great inconveniences, and these two things appear to be often connected one with the other. For by not attending to that use of things which is consistent with universal righteousness, there is an increase of labour which extends beyond what our Heavenly Father intends for us. And by great labour, and often by much

sweating in the heat, there is even amongst such who are not drunkards a craving of some liquors to revive the spirits.

Driven by debt, which merchants encouraged or at least suffered, customers worked too hard, and then they would drink. This in turn could lead to neglect of their social and family responsibilities, and from there the spiral continued down through diminished spiritual acuity and even into lawsuits.[17]

But as a merchant Woolman tried to be helpful to his customers. He advised "poor people to take such goods as were most useful and not costly." He stocked products that were sturdy, inexpensive, practical, and of simple style and use. Nonetheless, Woolman had to sue a customer once (and apparently only once) to collect money from an "idle man who I believed was about to run away." Since merchants did business by credit in his community, even the cautious Woolman found inevitable conflicts over payment, which concerned him, particularly in light of his growing disillusionment with trade and commerce throughout the empire.

Though trading in things useful is an honest employ, yet through the great number of superfluities which are bought and sold and through the corruption of the times, they who apply to merchandise for a living have great need to be well experienced in that precept which the prophet Jeremiah laid down for his scribe: "Seekest thou great things for thyself? Seek them not" [Jeremiah 45:5].[18]

As Woolman grew more ascetic, the incompatibility between selling and his quietistic convictions became stark. As hard as he tried as a retailer, he could not avoid the international commerce he disapproved of. By 1756 he may not have fully comprehended the moral challenges of selling textiles, but he did grasp the implications of debt and increased consumption, and he eventually found a moral taint even in the dyes used to color the cloth he sold.

Woolman now reversed professional direction and decided to move back to the farm life he had left as a young man. His shop and house were on Mill Street in Mount Holly's central business district, across the road from a grain mill and next to the Three Tuns Tavern. Nearby was the town square, with its whipping post and stocks. In a few years Quakers were to build their Little Meeting House, which was also their school, on the other side of Woolman's property. But in 1753 he had sold this Mill Street property to his mother, who apparently moved into the house while he continued to use the attached shop for another three years.[19]

In 1747 Woolman had purchased eleven acres on the King's Highway, less than a mile from the center of Mount Holly, from his friend Peter Andrews, who had bought it the previous year from Elizabeth Haddon-Estaugh. Woolman built a house there and later built another close by for his daughter, Mary, when she was grown and married. The earliest depiction of Woolman's house is a sepia drawing from almost a century after his death, by which time the residents had enlarged the house, but the orchard he planted nearby is still visible in the rural setting. Later still, owners moved the building off site, and it lost its distinctive identity as Woolman's dwelling. Woolman apparently made a "noon mark" on his floor and perhaps hour lines as well, to tell time by the sun. The house was simple, perhaps overshadowed by the cultivated glory of his orchard.[20]

In the summer of 1756 Woolman left his shop, which his mother may have rented out, and focused on tailoring and tending his orchard. One immediate manifestation of his refocused energies was that he started composing the famous *Journal*, which he then kept for the remaining sixteen years of his life, writing ever more closely in time to the experiences recounted. Woolman believed that it was worth sharing the path he had traveled. He had been taking notes, for how long is unclear, which he worked with now but did not preserve. The three drafts of the *Journal* that survive, then, all are at least once more removed from any original written conception of the *Journal*'s contents. He could begin to write in his mid-thirties because the journey he recounted was an internal one; whatever external events were to mark the rest of his days, they would not change the denouement.

It would have been uncharacteristic of Woolman to decide on his own to enter into such a project of public reflection. He does not say

A nineteenth-century sketch of John Woolman's house (Cox-Parish-Wharton Family Papers, Collections No. 154, Quaker Scrapbook No. 1, p. 303, Historical Society of Pennsylvania)

whether the impetus for writing came from within or was suggested by others; had he experienced the inspiration as coming uniquely from God, he would have likely said so. But whatever the source, he would not have begun unless he believed the work sanctioned by God.

Woolman's role on the public stage now changed, for he became a self-conscious character in his own narrative. He was watching himself from the outside, an embodied observer of his spirit and nature, of how God graced him and how he connected with the material world. The *Journal* added another mirror for Woolman's self-reflection, with a new angle and a different distortion.

Settling into his house in the country affected more than Woolman's disposition of time. Solitary tailoring and outdoor husbandry replaced the bustle of his shop; he became even more reflective. In a letter to a friend recovering from a serious illness during the winter of 1756–57, he writes of a Truth that left him "more fully acquainted with that way which the world esteems foolish." This oblique reference to Woolman's own brush with death as a teenager and the spiritual rebirth it brought him suggests the blessing of recovery after giving up hope and attachment to life—enlightenment. Woolman imagined that his friend now felt "the clothing of divine fortitude" against the snares of worldly wisdom. "There is a love clothes my mind while I write, which is superior to all expressions," Woolman concludes. Words do not capture the transcendent experience that the two friends now share, but tailoring metaphors come to him.[21]

This new composure opened Woolman to a higher plane of spiritual receptivity. It is no coincidence that it was now that he had a mystical experience. As he reports it in the *Journal*, after he had gone to bed at the home of a friend in Burlington, he slept, woke after a while, meditated prayerfully, fell asleep again, and then woke once more soon thereafter.

It was yet dark and no appearance of day nor moonshine, and as I opened my eyes I saw a light in my chamber at the apparent distance of five feet, about nine inches diameter, of a clear, easy brightness and near the center the most radiant. As I lay still without any surprise looking upon it, words were spoken to my inward ear which filled my whole inward man. They were not the effect of thought nor any conclusion in relation to the appearance, but as the language of the Holy One spoken in my mind. The words were, "Certain Evidence of Divine Truth," and were again repeated exactly in the same manner, whereupon the light disappeared.[22]

Woolman offers no analysis of this, only the basic information intended to establish credibility. He was in good health, so fevered hallucination could not explain it away; there was no moonlight or sunlight, and the light was only a few yards from him; he received words in his "inward ear," passively. He knows as well as anyone that disbelieving readers will not be convinced by his assurances. But the details are intended to show, for those open to revelation, that he approached the vision, which he knows happened, soberly, critically, but with conviction.

This incident opens chapter 4 of the *Journal*, suggesting that it marks a new beginning, and it is followed by Woolman's account of his second trip to the South, in 1757. The juxtaposition of the two conforms to the established structural pattern, in which spiritual enlightenment precedes decisive action. Whether this was a rhetorical device, a trick of memory, a conviction, or the recording of literal facts, its clarity suggests that it was likely intended self-consciously. It is the way Woolman understood and explained what he did: he acted how and when the spirit inspired him, and he was less decisive when he lacked such guidance from the Light within.

This time, Woolman traveled part of the way with his brother Uriah, who had business in North Carolina.* The spiritual growth he had experienced in the decade since his first southern journey in 1746 had sensitized his conscience, but new problems presented themselves. Traditionally, Friends provided free hospitality to traveling Quakers. But Woolman was conscience-stricken by the knowledge that where the hosts owned slaves his presence added to their, not the hosts', burdens. To accept free hospitality was tantamount to forging a link with the master and against the slave: "Receiving a gift, considered as a gift, brings the receiver under obligations to the benefactor and has a natural tendency to draw the obliged into a party with the giver." Since he felt an equal connection to the slave and to the master, he could not endure favoring the one over the other in this way.[23]

Woolman worried about this problem even before he began his journey, anticipating the moral conflict. He decided to resolve the dilemma by insisting on paying for his keep. Paying the slaves for their services would have no effect on the institution of slavery unless it induced guilt in the masters, but this was apparently Woolman's intent. "I spoke to one of the heads of the family privately," he writes, to avoid public embarrassment that might make the slaveowner intransigent. When possible, he gave the money in silver coins of small denominations and asked his host to decide how to distribute it among his slaves. If the master declined the money, though, or if Woolman sensed that his request for dispersal of the

*Uriah pops up unannounced in his role as traveling companion and then disappears from the *Journal* without description or elaboration (and without Woolman's having previously mentioned that he had a brother named Uriah), another one of the ghosts who pass as external ephemera in Woolman's story of his inner life.

funds would not be honored, he paid the slaves himself for the extra work he caused them.[24]

Even with this resolution of the dilemma, the journey was difficult for him. He was uncomfortable with conflict, and southern Friends challenged what he said about slaves and slavery at Meetings he visited. They argued that blacks were a backward people and that as bleak as their lives might appear to Woolman, bringing them from Africa had improved their condition. But they had not bought slaves for the Africans' good, Woolman argued to the planters: "I was troubled to perceive the darkness of their imaginations, and in some pressure of spirit said: 'The love of ease and gain are the motives in general of keeping slaves, and men are wont to take hold of weak arguments to support a cause which is unreasonable.'" If they had imported or kept the slaves in order to improve them, Friends would treat them better, educate, feed, and clothe them as befitted a fellow human, and they would not overwork or physically abuse them. No, they bought slaves to profit from the labor of those who were unable to resist the violence perpetrated against them.[25]

Other Friends contended that Africans were the descendants of Cain, and their race was a curse that marked them for their ancestor's sin of murdering his brother. They misread the Bible, Woolman replied, mistaking chronology and ignoring the fact that all humans descended from Noah, the evil and cursed of our single race having been obliterated from the earth by the flood. "I further reminded them how the prophets repeatedly declare that the son shall not suffer for the iniquity of the father, but every one be answerable for his own sins."[26]

Woolman now explicitly identified with Jesus' apostles when he was on this traveling ministry, spreading the Truth revealed to him by God. But his standard of conduct had to be different. "As the disciples were sent forth without any provision for their journey and our Lord said the workman is worthy of his meat, their labour in the gospel was considered as a reward for their entertainment, and therefore not received as a gift; yet in regard to my present journey I could not see my way clear in that respect." The difference was that Quakers looked after him as an act of civility because of his reputation, not out of any unity with his ministry. The apostles moved the hearts of men and women who then welcomed them into their homes; Woolman's hosts claimed to share his principles, but their actions contradicted their words and showed they had rejected his message from God.[27]

Although Woolman believed that he had rhetorically bested his critics, he was not pleased. He labored under "some pressure of spirit," by which he means that he was engaged, even angry, when disputing with southern defenders of slavery, and it was difficult for him to accept these emotional limitations in himself. He believed that such passion was counterproductive, but his ambition for the cause had agitated him: "I have had renewed evidences that to be faithful to the Lord and content with his will concerning me is a most necessary and useful lesson for me to be learning, looking less at the effects of my labour than at the pure motion and reality of the concern as it arises from heavenly love." His ministry could not be goal-oriented; it was not for Woolman to be concerned about the effect of his message on those who heard him. He should trust God and deliver Truth, not debate.[28]

Frustrated with himself, critical of his errors of judgment, lack of faith, and ascendance of nature over spirit, Woolman retreated into silence toward the end of his trip and left the work of moving souls to God.

> I was silent during the meeting for worship, and when business came on, my mind was exercised concerning the poor slaves, but did not feel my way clear to speak. And in this condition I was bowed in spirit before the Lord and with tears and inward supplications besought him to so open my understanding that I might know his will concerning me, and at length my mind was settled in silence.

What happened next was extraordinary. A Friend rose in one Meeting for Worship that Woolman attended to indict himself and others for not educating their slaves. Another stood to express concern about the slaves' religious instruction. In short, the spirit rose from the Meeting without a word from Woolman. The hand of God worked with or without him. It was a humbling experience for which he was grateful.[29]

Later, on the road back home, lying awake under the stars and unable to sleep because of mosquitoes, Woolman had another insight. Even though God had banished Adam and Eve from the Garden of Eden and given them no tools, food, clothing, or shelter, even though they had disobeyed him, he was still their father and watched over them and their descendants.

> To provide things relative to our outward living in the way of true wisdom is good, and the gift of improving in things useful is a good gift and comes from the Father of Lights. Many have had this gift and from age to age there have been improvements of this kind made in the world. But some, not keeping to the pure gift, have in the creaturely cunning and self-exaltation sought out many inventions, which inventions of men, as distinct from that uprightness in which man was created, as in the first motion it was evil so the effects of it have been, and are, evil.

In other words, God had given the first parents all they needed to live well, yet they sought more; their ambition exceeded their spiritual grasp, and they fell from grace. Humans should care for basic needs with the materials and skills God provided and should not overtax themselves or others in an endless quest for what they did not need and would be better off without. Woolman already knew this, but he learned it anew when he accepted that ambition for success had been distracting him. To have effected a change was a gratifying outcome, but it was not the point of his ministry.[30]

Woolman knew, after all, that even his home Meeting was not free from slavery. Burlington Monthly Meeting minuted in 1757 that all its members were "clear of importing negroes or purchasing them for term of life; several have been purchased for a term of years. They are generally well fed and clothed. Some are taught to read and taken to meetings, but others are taken little care of in these respects." Philadelphia Yearly Meeting had established a Meeting for Sufferings the year before (modeled on one that early

Quakers organized to give counsel to activists, record "sufferings" for public discussion, and care for the families of martyred or imprisoned Friends), and Woolman was a member of it. One of the first acts of this new committee was to suggest that relief funds be sent to settlers on the Pennsylvania frontier who were suffering because of the war. This extension of charity to non-Quakers was a good sign that reformers' pleas for universal love were having an effect.

For decades the Quaker-controlled assembly of Pennsylvania had moved in two directions: it had tried to limit the importation of slaves while guarding against slave uprisings and also increasing the punishment of slaves who created trouble. The defensive measures clearly suggest that self-protection rather than humanitarianism was the motive. Similarly, when conservative members of Yearly Meeting now responded to the moral pleas of the reformers, they did so by making self-serving concessions while they resisted changes that would have challenged their economic interests.[31]

The Society of Friends did not regularly undertake charitable endeavors for the benefit of nonmembers until later in the century, after Woolman's death. (This change was at least partly due to their withdrawal from politics; when they had controlled the government purse strings, they had used public means for charitable ends. When they no longer dominated the assembly, they formed private charities, such as the Pennsylvania Hospital in 1751.) But this action in 1756 showed that they were reconsidering the relationship between their church and the community in light of the war. Friends now followed two apparently antithetical lines of corporate development: intensified asceticism, greater sectarian exclusivity, and group solidarity, on the one hand, and a commitment to addressing the world's problems, on the other.[32]

F OR most of humanity, morality is culturally and temporally relative; people define what is good within the standards of their time and place. Woolman faced the challenge of this kind of moral complacency at each stage of antislavery reform. And the defense of perceived economic self-interest did not deter him; he was unwilling to make social compromises. He had higher ambitions for humankind.

Woolman also knew from his experiences as a scribe and an estate executor about the laws regulating slavery in the Quaker colonies. The front lines of the abolitionist battle included the Pennsylvania and New Jersey legislatures, as well as the docks, shops, and Quaker Meetings. True, slavery had always been less visible in Pennsylvania than in the colonies bordering it—New York, New Jersey, Delaware, and Maryland—and in 1780 the abolition movement Woolman helped start was to achieve a dramatic triumph in the state's Act for the Gradual Abolition of Slavery. But in the century before then, the legislative process was not a progressive one.

In New Jersey the government responded even more slowly to demands for reform. A 1774 petition supporting emancipation was presented to the assembly, which responded by adopting a law that would have effectively eliminated the importation of slaves but that the Council vetoed. It was not until 1788 that the state adopted a halfway measure prohibiting slave ships from fitting out—docking for supplies and repairs—and providing that no slave who had resided in New Jersey for a year could be removed without his or her consent.

Dutch and Swedish settlers had held slaves in the region even before the Quakers arrived. Then, in 1664, after the English had gained control of the Delaware Valley, the Duke of York's Laws, the new legal code now extended to the mid-Atlantic colonies, prohibited the enslavement of Christians. Enslaving non-Christians was evidently just fine, and that is how the colonists interpreted the law, which also took care to protect the property rights of masters whose slaves converted to Christianity: "This Law shall not extend to sett at liberty Any Negroe or Indian Servant who shall turne Christian after he shall have been bought by Any Person." The law also distinguished between a "person," on the one hand, and a black or Indian, on the other, capturing the essence of race relations at the time.[33]

In 1682, laws largely drafted by William Penn and then adopted by the founding Quaker settlers of Pennsylvania superseded the Duke of York's Laws, but de facto slavery continued uninterrupted since there were few sanctions against it. Records of purchase and sale of blacks survive from the 1680s. By the turn of the century the legal distinctions between all blacks, slave or free, and all whites had become clearer; black and white servants were treated differently; blacks could not bear witness against whites in court, and they were publicly whipped for theft rather than incarcerated and fined. They were also prohibited from carrying weapons.[34]

The Quaker majority in Pennsylvania's assembly moved against slavery in 1700 by levying a tax on imported slaves, which in 1705 and 1710 it increased. Then, in 1711, importation of slaves into the colony was prohibited. The British disallowed these efforts to limit or abolish the international merchandising of Africans, claiming they overreached the colonial assembly's authority. After all, both the British Empire and British merchants made money from the slave trade, and they were not about to let one colony run by religious Dissenters make public policy. The assembly in Philadelphia never moved to abolish slavery in Pennsylvania or to prohibit the buying and selling of slaves who already resided there, but even this attempt to halt the importation of slaves ran afoul of financial interests more influential than reform-minded Quakers.[35]

In 1725–26 the Pennsylvania Assembly passed the Act for the Better Regulation of Negroes, which, among other provisions, directed compensation to the masters for slaves executed for the commissions of crimes. But perhaps the most dramatic clauses in the new law were those concerning free blacks. "Experience" showed the legislature that "free negroes are an idle, slothful people, and often burdensome to the neighborhood and afford ill examples to other negroes." For these reasons, and to ensure that a freed black person did not become a financial burden on the colony, the law required surety of thirty pounds from any master who manumitted a slave. The predictable result was that fewer slaves were manumitted. The same law gave magistrates license to bind out—sell into servitude—any free black who was deemed an idler or a public nuisance and inclined to "misspend" time. It *required* the binding out of *all* children of free blacks to the age of twenty-one for girls and twenty-four for boys, in effect instituting a rotating labor force of black servants bound for long terms.[36]

Like politicians throughout the colonies, Pennsylvania's leaders feared slave revolts, and they found South Carolina's Stono Rebellion in 1739 and the New York slave conspiracy in 1741 horrifying.

They were also sensitive to issues of labor supply and demand, trying to avoid having a surplus of slaves, which would threaten the market in indentured servants (white immigrants who worked for a given number of years to pay off their passages from Europe to the New World) while encouraging slavery when labor shortages recommended it. In 1726, when the assembly raised the duty on imported slaves to ten pounds, the slave trade in Pennsylvania came to a virtual halt, but in 1729 the assembly lowered the duty to forty shillings, which opened up the market again. Moral questions raised in Philadelphia Yearly Meeting may have also affected the assembly, but Pennsylvania's safety and economy were priorities of elected officials.[37]

What about the economic motives of the Quaker reformers? The information we have shows only that they were moved by moral concerns, and no one has ever suggested that men such as Lay, Sandiford, Woolman, and Benezet had a financial interest in the abolition of slavery. Still, one must acknowledge a connection between the economic and moral motives of the Quakers' response to the call for reform. It is likely that the conservative leaders of Yearly Meeting who at first resisted reform did have economic interests in slavery. Then the balance of power shifted to the reformers; the twenty years between the mid-1730s and the 1750s became the contested terrain onto which Woolman strode. The ultimate victory of the reformers over mercantile interests was neither economically determined nor inevitable, and it happened not without conflict and the loss of significant numbers who left the church or were disowned when they refused to accept the Quaker discipline.

In the last fifteen years of his life, Woolman traveled to bring his prophecy to more Quakers, widen his horizons to include sailors, miners, and wage laborers, and to identify more of the consumer goods that were complicit in slavery's horror. He broadened his vision, and the message of the Quaker abolitionists who had come before him, to include children, Indians, wage laborers, and animals in his understanding of responsibility for strangers. He was to dream, write, and preach, but first and always he focused on his personal need to purify.

8

Pure Wisdom

1758–59

E ARLY in 1758 John Woolman and a fellow traveler heard
about a woman who had become disconsolate in the wake of a
dream "wherein death and the judgments of the Almighty after
death were represented to her mind in a moving manner." Woolman
tells us in the *Journal* that his unnamed companion detoured to pray
with the dreamer while Woolman continued home. The woman, her
husband, and the visitor had "some religious conversation" that affected the three of them, and they shed "many tears" together. The
man then resumed his journey back to Mount Holly but drowned
fording a river.[1]

Woolman leaves his *Journal*'s readers to draw their own conclu-
sions. The dreamer apparently did not know whose death her
dream foretold. Was the moral that the man would have lived had he
stayed with Woolman, who apparently had no problems crossing the
same river? Or was the man's death fated, and did his meeting with
the prophetess prepare him for the inevitable? What about Woolman's own fate had he visited the dreamer too, or his charitable
responsibility for the sick woman, let alone his friend? Did he perhaps have a premonition that warned him away? This story about
prophetic dreaming, the uncertainty of life, the proximity of death,
and the imminence of judgment comes right after the passage in the
Journal on Woolman's anguished decision to resist paying taxes in

support of the French and Indian War. In that context, it seems to emphasize the importance of living with a clear conscience in preparation for death and divine judgment, which may come without warning.

For Woolman, a prophetic dreamer himself, this story struck close to home. He identified with the Old Testament prophets, drew on them, and frequently returned to the accounts of their prophecies. Two-thirds of Woolman's biblical citations are to the Old Testament, and he quoted the prophets nearly as often as he quoted all other passages combined. The seventeenth-century Quakers George Fox, Robert Barclay, and William Penn had referred to the New Testament twice as much as to the Old, in contrast, and in Woolman's own day American Quakers and other colonists also cited the New Testament more often than the Old, since Enlightenment liberalism found the New Testament more companionable. Woolman's against-the-grain emphasis on the prophets was consistent with his distinctively backward-reaching Protestantism.[2]

Great Britain in the seventeenth century had been awash in self-proclaimed prophets, and another wave swept the island in the early eighteenth century, when the Camisards, French Huguenots battling King Louis XIV's banishment of Protestants, became famous; but their notoriety as fanatics tainted all prophetic claims on both sides of the Atlantic for decades thereafter. Of the hundreds of prophetic voices heard in England and America during the eighteenth century, most were those of evangelical millenarians predicting an imminent end to the world.[3]

The Quakers shared with other Protestants a confidence in ongoing revelation. Johannes Kelpius (1673–1708), a young German mystic, added to the mix when he immigrated to Pennsylvania with a small group of followers in 1694. Samuel Keimer, an English printer influenced by the French prophets, arrived in Philadelphia in 1718, declared himself a Quaker (without the sanction of the Society of Friends), and advocated vegetarianism. These mystically inclined individuals shared a belief in what anthropologists call spirit possession, which could manifest itself in sleep or a trance, in a vision or dream, the line between the two not always being discernible. When an individual experienced the divine, it was often called a mystical event. When the mystic communicated God's word, it was prophecy—no matter what the nature of the message—and a revelation of Truth.[4]

The Christian mystic is a Christian first, and his mysticism, with its roots in Jewish and Hellenistic beliefs and practices, derives from his religion rather than the reverse. The mystical experience itself, then, is not necessarily the mystic's defining characteristic. Ethereal visions, voices, dreams, or raptures that anticipate and prepare for otherworldly experience are not essential for an encounter with God. Consciousness of the immediate presence of God can manifest itself in bewildering as well as unremarkable ways and to various states of mind.[5]

Preparation for the direct experience of God can be achieved in ascetic and meditative practices, formulaic or extemporaneous prayer, sacramental rituals, or the reading of sacred texts, sometimes in prescribed ways. The text's authorial intent or historically revealed meanings are not as important as the mystic's understanding of them. So when John Woolman read Revelation, he participated in a mystical tradition of preparation that complemented his way of life and his ability to elicit meanings significant to him. He was experiencing a tradition dating back to several centuries before the birth of Christ, in which God speaks not through human agents but from a fixed written text, which itself has then taken on mystical meaning.[6]

Theologians contend that early Christian mystics insisted that communion with the divine was not experiential, that their mystical experiences were internal. For them, the locus of mystical experience had moved from the material world to the Bible. They did not claim to have seen a burning bush, to have heard a heavenly choir, or to have witnessed bodily ascents to heaven, but they believed the biblical accounts of such phenomena and had their own mystical experiences when reading the texts. Even Teresa of Avila should perhaps be understood to have rejected the possibility of continuing revelation by direct communication between God and humans.[7]

But this was not the only way that Quakers, among other Dissenting Christians, experienced the divine. Quakers' faith continued the mystical tradition without concern for such theological distinctions. Quakers believed they could come to know God personally and directly and that they spoke prophetically when God spoke through them.

Mysticism and prophecy arrived on American shores with the first settlers and during the eighteenth century reflected a spirit that was rekindling across religions and continents. God spoke through evangelicals and Moravians in the Americas, Jews and Muslims in southeastern Europe, Jansenist Convulsionaries in France, Catholic and Protestant peasants all over Europe, and Britons on both sides of the Atlantic. Between 1700 and 1800 seventy-four Quaker women, thirty-one of them British and forty-three of them American colonists, sailed the Atlantic to share their prophecy, and about twice as many male prophets also made the crossing. These all were recognized ministers, who had the endorsement and financial support of their home Meetings.[8]

Perhaps the ubiquity of these "prophets" and their association with an evangelical, even lunatic fringe is one reason why Woolman never identified himself as a prophet. There was nothing to be gained and much to be lost by identification with the outliers of religious practice.

Like other prophets of his day, Woolman spoke in the idiom of the marketplace, and he did not seem to be affected by the transformation of the political landscape around him. His isolation from Pennsylvania's and New Jersey's political culture is consonant with Quakers' collective withdrawal from politics and his own personal alienation from civic life. He was not quintessentially modern, as evangelical prophets were in the form, if not the content, of their communications, adopting a rhetorical style that also affected popular politics. He was neither deluded nor unique in the context of his religious culture, but he was extreme.

It is common to associate Old Testament prophets, warriors for the Lord, with patriarchal Calvinists rather than with quietistic Quakers. The radical abolitionist John Brown is an example of the prophetic Calvinist figure who believed himself preordained to make war as part of an inspired warning to a society that tolerated slavery. Brown typifies the linkage of prophecy with violence, radical reform with shrill zealotry, and refusal to compromise principle with a rigid personality.[9]

But Woolman identified with Jeremiah as a fellow pacifist, with

Isaiah's promise of peace, with Hosea's indictment of the wealthy, and with Habakkuk's endorsement of prayerful silence. True, the prophets had delivered warnings and predicted doom if the people of God did not mend their ways, but it was their messages of hope and redemption that Woolman cited. God told Jeremiah, "Amend your ways and your doings," and everything will be fine. "If you will indeed obey this word," there is nothing to worry about. Isaiah spoke God's promise that "the effect of righteousness will be peace, and the result of righteousness, quietness and trust forever." Jeremiah did not believe that divine retribution was inevitable any more than Woolman did, and he delivered revelation for a loving God. "Return, faithless Israel," was Jeremiah's message; "I will not look on you in anger, for I am merciful, says the Lord; I will not be angry forever. Only acknowledge your guilt." Isaiah anticipated the day when "justice will dwell in the wilderness, and righteousness abide in the fruitful field." Woolman also quoted Isaiah's expectation that "because everyone will do what is right, there will be peace and security forever." The prophets predicted a time without sin, which the founders of Quakerism proclaimed achievable on earth.[10]

The Old Testament prophets—preachers, social critics, and moralists, just as Woolman was—felt fiercely and acted passionately. When Woolman preached against the moral deficiencies of common practice, he focused on the flawed nature of human beings and on injustices that others accepted as inevitable. The behaviors that concerned Woolman and the prophets do indeed continue today: greed has not succumbed to charity, nor has humility conquered pride or love triumphed over racism, tribalism, and xenophobia. Small injustices committed out of oversight, ignorance, and callousness have proliferated as much as the blights of bigotry and war.

For Woolman, prophets were solitary, detached souls who made no concessions to human frailty. They reminded God's people that even when few are guilty, all are responsible for immoral acts. True, Isaiah prophesied a coming war, Jeremiah bore witness to utter desolation and foresaw peace only after the annihilation of a doomed Israel. But although they warned about the consequences of God's anger, Woolman quoted Jeremiah, Isaiah, Habakkuk, and Hosea as men of peace. One day the Lord would "judge between the nations, and shall arbitrate for many peoples," Isaiah prophesied; "they shall beat their swords into plowshares, and their spears into pruning hooks; nation shall not lift up sword against nation, neither shall they learn war any more." Woolman, a pacifist who pruned his own apple trees, quoted the passage confidently.[11]

Woolman believed that he was following Isaiah when he denounced worldly wisdom and interpreted pride and arrogance as impeding spiritual growth. "Those who are wise will turn out to be fools," Isaiah predicted. Habakkuk, like Quakers after him, found words inadequate and envisioned all creation as a temple of God. "Let all the earth keep silence before him," the prophet advised.[12]

Not surprisingly, the passages that Woolman quoted from the prophets often contained horticultural images of seeds, vineyards, fertile and fallow fields, orchards, and diligent tillers of the earth. But he also quoted the prophets on the personal burden of mystical experience, noting Isaiah's lament that "I am bowed down so that I cannot hear, I am dismayed so that I cannot see. My mind reels, horror has appalled me; the twilight I longed for has been turned for me into trembling." Woolman too felt blessed that God had chosen him to share revelation, but he was unsettled, awestruck, and sometimes overwhelmed by the responsibility.[13]

Woolman acknowledged that his work was to deliver, not to argue, God's message, but this was often frustrating. "To whom shall I speak and give warning, that they may hear?" Jeremiah asked the Lord. "See, their ears are closed, they cannot listen. The word of the Lord is to them an object of scorn; they take no pleasure in it. But I am full of the wrath of the Lord; I am weary of holding it in." Woolman seldom became angry, and we know of only a few occasions when he got into an argument. But like Jeremiah, he felt the sting of public deafness to his call. He tried not to measure the effect of his interventions, knowing that it was largely lost to him and wasn't the gauge of success in any event. Simple affirmation was another source of authority, after all. "It is the Lord who sent me to give you this warning," Jeremiah asserted. Either you believed or you didn't. Woolman delivered God's message and left it at that.[14]

Woolman was sensitive to the skeptic's grounds for disbelieving him; that is why he articulated so carefully his rationale for eliminating all other possible sources than God for his words. He wanted readers to know that he had been awake when he saw the ball of light in the night and that he had been alone when he heard the voice speak his name. The prophet anticipates resistance to the message and ridicule of the messenger. He expects rejection, which gives him another form of authority. Perhaps Woolman welcomed unpopularity. "I have become a laughingstock all day long," Jeremiah told the Lord; "everyone mocks me." Taunts could be reassuring, and when Woolman went on his traveling ministries, he endured glorious pain in God's name.[15]

It was important too that prophets distinguish their voices from God's. Proving (most importantly to themselves) that they did not benefit from their work was a kind of evidence that the divine inspiration was not being manufactured. They needed to show that they were disinterested witnesses to the experience that flowed through them. Woolman thought he should share the loneliness the Old Testament prophets felt.

The Old Testament prophets always claimed that their messages were not new. They appealed to the authority of past knowledge and practice; they told their congregations that they would know God's word better if they recalled past revelations. Woolman's rhetorical strategy was similar. Jeremiah instructs his people in the name of the Lord to "ask for the ancient paths" before deciding where to go. Woolman understood that tradition is true but that revelation is open. And Truth was itself evidence for the divine source of prophecy. The words are consistent with God as the people knew him from past revelations. "'Let those who boast boast this,'" the Lord instructs Jeremiah, "'that they understand and know me, that I am the Lord; I act with steadfast love, justice, and righteousness in the earth, for in these things I delight.'" If Woolman had a boast, this was it; he knew the Lord and his revelations were consistent with what God had already said.[16]

There was nothing unorthodox about John Woolman's faith or his interpretation of the prophetic tradition. What distinguished his ministry was the way he combined truths—revelations built on theologically sound foundations—expressed insights, and offered an uncompromising vision that transcended Quaker practice. He advocated perfection and believed it achievable, just as the first Quakers had believed themselves redeemed from sin, and he articulated a philosophy challenging human nature's resistance to spiritual growth.

Woolman had a positive plan for right living that was redemptive, reforming first individuals and then the world around them in concentric circles spreading outward from the revelatory pebble that he dropped into the pond of material life. Several short essays that the Quaker press published in 1758—*Considerations on Pure Wisdom and Human Policy; on Labour; on Schools;* and *on the Right Use of the Lord's Outward Gifts*—collectively present his unified vision of personal and social reform. The foundation of Woolman's philosophy was that pursuit of wealth overtaxes the body, mind, and soul. The place to break the chain that binds the world in violence and woe is at the beginning, at the personal source of it all. Reform yourself first, Woolman proclaims; accept responsibility with all due humility rather than lay blame, and work from there. This first step is the most difficult one: to elevate spirit over nature, universal love over ambition, simplicity over vanity, and compassion over selfishness.

Woolman had often enough risen from the silence of Meeting for Worship to share revelations, and he had already put some of them in unpublished drafts of the *Journal* and in *Considerations on the Keeping of Negroes*. But his array of social criticisms was published together here for the first time in one place, sharpening his public challenge to the Quaker community.

The Quakers' focus on earthly achievement was particularly troubling to Woolman, so he began the collection with a classic lament on its soul-corrupting consequences: "My mind hath often been affected with sorrow on account of the prevailing of that spirit, which leads from an humble waiting on the inward teaching of Christ, to pursue ways of living, attended with unnecessary labour." This inordinate emphasis on work leads to ambition for "outward power" and strivings for wealth, which could result only in evil ends. This was familiar ground, and Woolman applied the same logic that he adhered to throughout his life, crediting his insights to the "mercies of our Heavenly Father, who, in infinite love, did visit me in my youth, and wrought a belief in me, that through true obe-

dience a state of inward purity may be known in this life." God had
taught Woolman to "love mankind in the same love with which our
Redeemer loveth us, and therein learn resignation to endure hardships, for the real good of others." This was the "universal love"
that Woolman extended to Native Americans, African Americans,
and all cultures, faiths, and creatures.[17]

Woolman tried to achieve the virtues extolled in the Sermon on
the Mount, and he welcomed persecution as Christ directed:
"Blessed are you when people revile you and persecute you and utter all kinds of evil against you falsely on my account. Rejoice and
be glad, for your reward is great in heaven, for in the same way they
persecuted the prophets who were before you." Confronting the injustices that are produced by "selfish desires" angrily or violently
only kindles more injustice, however, and is equally selfish: "Where
violent measures are pursued in opposing injustice, the passions
and resentments of the injured frequently operate in the prosecution of their designs: and after conflicts productive of very great
calamities, the minds of contending parties often remain as little acquainted with the pure principle of Divine Love as they were before." With all good intentions, it is possible to make matters worse
by provoking anger on top of the injustice that requires reform.[18]

Yet Woolman never lost hope. *Considerations on Pure Wisdom* laid
out a plan for self-reform that would help fulfill the prophecy that
Woolman quoted from Isaiah 2:4: "A time, I believe, is coming,
wherein this divine work will so spread and prevail, that 'Nation
shall not lift up Sword against Nation, nor learn War any more.'" He
anticipated the triumph of God's kingdom on earth, a time of peace
that he believed would precede the end of the world.[19]

Thus does Woolman reach the millenarian crossroads, but there
he chooses a different path. Engagement with the sources of desire
is, according to Woolman, the first important step. The plan is to
trust God, eschew desire, and live in the spirit contentedly; in a
state of pure wisdom people can focus on the "root and original
spring of motions and desires." Woolman's idea of the correct ascetic regimen is akin to the one that Thomas à Kempis prescribed for
contemplative monks, but he recommends meditation as a way of
engaging in rather than retreating from the world's problems.[20]

True wisdom, as opposed to the "wisdom of this world," informs the spirit, and humility leads to happiness, not to deprivation: "Small treasure to a resigned mind is sufficient. How happy it is to be content with a little." True wisdom also keeps us from sloth, neglect, and abdication of work or responsibility that might otherwise plague the soul.[21]

Predictably for Woolman, the next rut on the road of desire is ambition for the power by which we mistakenly believe we can control the future. Efforts to secure our children's lives after our death are mired in delusion and fraught with dire consequences: "If, in acquiring wealth we take hold on the wisdom which is from beneath, and depart from the leadings of truth, and example our children herein, we have great cause to apprehend that wealth may be a snare to them; and prove an injury to others over whom their wealth may give them power."[22]

The moderate exercise that Woolman recommends is connected to the same spiritual program and the same economic reasoning. A body-mind-soul connection that facilitates right thinking and meditative communion with the divine "opens the pores, gives the blood a lively circulation, and better enables us to judge rightly respecting the portion of labour which is the true medium." Physical activity inspired by true wisdom makes for health and happiness; overwork dulls reason, induces weariness, and increases the desire for liquor—in short, leads to crankiness, drunkenness, and impaired judgment. And it frustrates spirituality.[23]

One example of such a downward spiral is that of a landlord who, whether because of greed, thoughtless materialism, or a misplaced desire to build an estate for his children, sets his rents higher than is purely just. His tenants must then overwork to meet his demands, and that leads them down the path to dissipation: driving animals and employees too hard, perhaps hiring or purchasing and abusing slaves to increase productivity, and contributing to an environment in which violence becomes common. The ultimate end for masters, slaves, and members of societies that tolerate slavery is of course materialism, violence, war, pestilence, plague, and the whole range of calamities wrought by those who live contrary to pure wisdom.[24]

The ambitious landlord who cannot see that he is responsible for slavery or war even though he owns no slaves and himself raises no weapon misperceives his place in the world. He also misunderstands where reform should begin. And when he blames others—masters, tenants, Indians, foreigners, and political or military leaders—he only makes matters worse by offending them, producing more anger and ubiquitous violence. When he holds himself up as a model of probity and peace because he does not drink too much, or personally abuse his animals or employees, or vote for warmongering politicians, he misses the point. Consuming expensive imported liquor and food, wearing fine clothes, furnishing a mansion stylishly, and enjoying other displays of wealth leave blood on his hands as surely as if he wielded a sword. And his evil traits are then passed down to the next generation.

Neglecting or bungling the education of children also contributes to nature's ascendancy over spirit, and this too is a consequence of worldliness. It is folly, according to Woolman, for parents to let estate building for the benefit of their children distract them from teaching pure wisdom to them. And Woolman advocates closer supervision of children than has been the rule among Quakers he knows. He grieves about the poor condition of education in the Quaker colonies, which he thinks is due to the same focus on making money that undermines society in other ways. Moreover, living for praise inspires pride and an untoward external focus on the "wisdom of this world," as he put it. And if teachers are not themselves inspired by pure wisdom, their effect on children is worse than the children having no education at all; small classes given by inspired teachers are the only way for students to focus on pure wisdom. A "humble, plain, temperate" lifestyle is the key to personal and then collective reform, and it is its own reward.

> Meditating on the situation of schools in our provinces, my mind hath, at times, been affected with sorrow; and under these exercises it hath appeared to me, that if those who have large estates were faithful stewards and laid no rent nor interest nor other demand higher than is consistent with universal love; and those in lower circumstances would under a moderate employ shun unnecessary expense, even to the smallest

article; and all unite in humbly seeking to the Lord, he would graciously instruct us and strengthen us to relieve the youth from various snares in which many of them are entangled.[25]

Arm children with "wisdom from above," and instill in them strength to resist the "wisdom of the world." Teach them to live on little and in a state of true resignation to the will of God. Show them that the real comforts of life are not diminished by living simply. Know that the problems of the world and their solutions are embodied in small things that are within our control: "Where people depart from pure wisdom in one case, it is often an introduction to depart from it in many more: and thus a spirit which seeks for outward greatness, and leads into worldly wisdom to attain it and support it, gets possession of the mind." Simplicity is a small, liberating step to spiritual freedom. Love is the heart of peace and reform. Look inward, act outwardly, and accept responsibility. You have no enemies but only fellow creatures who reflect what you display.[26]

AT the core of Woolman's diagnosis and prescription for cure is a sharpened criticism of the social effects of trade and commerce. His tone is more critical than it was in *Considerations on the Keeping of Negroes*, the argument more fully developed, the accusations more pointed and less forgiving. He hones ideas that he had expressed piecemeal into a holistic philosophy depicting a way of life.

The overseers of the Quaker press were not in harmony with Woolman's prophecy, though, at least inasmuch as it dissented from the commercial culture that had brought American Quakers so much success. They could live with Woolman's indictment of worldliness up to a point, but the full argument was more than the censors could bear. In all humility, Woolman put his best face on their rejection of an additional twelve-paragraph essay he showed them entitled "Serious Considerations on Trade," which the overseers excised before approving publication of the rest of the pamphlet. He explained in a private notation that though the overseers "did not reject this chapter, yet expressed some desire that the publication of it might at least be deferred," he "felt easy" with this decision.[27]

Yet Woolman preserved the deleted paragraphs, evidently hoping that the overseers would eventually publish the complete argument. But they never relented, and the lack of any surviving copies of the first, truncated edition suggests that only a few were printed. (The earliest known copies of the text are of an English edition that appeared the year after Woolman's death, which London Friends retitled *Serious Considerations on Various Subjects of Importance.* There was no second American edition of this pamphlet published until the nineteenth century.)[28]

The opening sentence of the deleted chapter aims indirectly, in Woolman's usual nonconfrontational style: "As it hath pleased the Divine Being to people the earth by inhabitants descended from one man; and as Christ commanded his disciples to preach the gospel to distant countries, the necessity of sometimes crossing the seas is evident." The implicit idea is that the numbers of people who make transatlantic trips should be few, on God's business, and then only when divine inspiration compels the journey. Embedded in the sentence is a strongly negative view of international trafficking in people and goods.[29]

When revelation propels immigrants to the wilderness on God's journey, they will at first need to supply themselves from abroad while they are "improving" the new land, Woolman continues. Some members of their "family," by which he means "community," will need to cross the seas repeatedly for material necessities while the first generations clear fields, build homes, and plant, tend, and harvest crops. This peripatetic commerce should end, though, once the settlers can support themselves. Woolman reflects abstractly here on the state of humanity and concretely on the Quaker experience in New Jersey and Pennsylvania:

> When lands are so improved that with a divine blessing they afford food, raiment, and all those necessaries which pertain to the life of a humble follower of Christ, it behooves the inhabitants to take heed that a custom be not continued longer than the usefulness of it, and that the number of that calling

who have been helpful in importing necessaries be not greater than is consistent with pure wisdom.

The time when transatlantic trade furthered the Quakers' religious goals has long passed, and the amount of transatlantic traffic and the quantity of goods are no longer justifiable in spiritual terms. The Quaker merchant class was no longer offering a useful or morally sound service to the holy experiment. The fathers of Woolman's old friends and the friends themselves were among those who undermined the godly enterprise by acting contrary to pure wisdom. They "alienate the minds of people from their truest interest," tempting them with vanities and nonessential possessions.[30]

If merchants craved great wealth, it mattered little whether they used their surplus riches to buy land they rented out or to invest in more ships and merchandise; the result was the same for the community. Woolman had already described the chain of consequences driving high rents, and expansion of Quaker business only exacerbated the problems.

The colonists were perfectly capable of meeting their real needs without hazarding the treacherous seas; they should cease endangering themselves and others and stop creating debt relationships that forced ever more work and ever less spiritual contemplation on everyone. The value of true relationships was then reversed: "For brethren to visit each other in true love, I believe, makes part of that happiness which our heavenly father intends for us in this life; but where pure wisdom direct[s] not our visits we may not suppose them truly profitable." This last sentence melds mystical revelation of God's will with quietistic concepts expressed in the vocabulary of the marketplace. "Profit" is calculated on a spiritual balance sheet enriched by the light of pure wisdom and true love.[31]

Yet Woolman the farmer, shopkeeper, and tailor was as much a creature of the marketplace as were the Quaker merchants whose ships plied the seas. He was speaking with assurance about a life and values that he knew at first hand. And the end result, he insisted, was the oppression of laborers—which included slaves—violence, and war. If Quakers took their pacifism seriously, lived by their testimony on simplicity, and practiced pure love, they would abandon all this.

Woolman's rhetoric builds as his charges become specific, indeed horrible to contemplate. Blood is on the hands of participants in the expanding market that Woolman describes, and this is the passage the overseers could not let pass:

> By giving way to a desire after delicacies and things fetched far, many men appear to be employed unnecessarily, many ships built by much labour are lost, many people brought to an untimely end; much good produce buried in the seas; many people busied in that which serves chiefly to please a wandering desire who might better be employed in those affairs which are of real service, and ease the burdens of such poor honest people, who to answer the demands of others are often necessitated to exceed the bounds of healthful, agreeable exercise.

Rather than being peacemakers, Quakers were misallocating resources; wasting produce that could be used by the poor, including Indians and African slaves, and they were also responsible for the deaths of sailors lost at sea on trivial crossings. Surrendering to a "desire" for wealth expressed a selfish logic built on a foundation of worldly wisdom. Violence was the predictable end.[32]

Woolman blamed everyone who participated in the global economy, but Quaker merchants more than anyone else. The chain of responsibility started with the likes of the Logans, Pembertons, and Smiths and continued with the eager participation of lesser merchants and their customers. Woolman understood how far and wide the guilt about slavery reached, for it bound consumers to this global economy—whether or not they ever saw a slave—if they ate eggs laid by chickens fed on grain harvested by slaves, if they wore jackets colored by indigo produced by slaves, if they drank rum transported in a ship that had carried slaves, or if they rode in coaches pulled by horses driven too hard by men who needed money to pay rents that were set too high.

Woolman recognized how difficult it was in his day, as we know it is in ours, to break the chain of injustice that mistreats laborers anywhere in the world. To people who would have preferred to remain ignorant (and whom the overseers of the Quaker press did not want to offend), he made it clear that cruelty to animals, abuse of workers, and accumulation of wealth all were corruptions of the marketplace motivated by earthly desires in conflict with pure wisdom, true brotherhood, and universal love.

On Labour cut close to Quaker bones. There is little in this essay that Woolman had not expressed in his earlier ones, but the implacable logic burdened Quakers with inescapable responsibility in a newly fierce way. It addressed specific behavior, rather than offering a general philosophy of life that could be morally instructive even for those who did not live by Woolman's high standards. We have met the enemy, Woolman was saying, and they are we, to paraphrase a modern-day philosopher. The overseers' "deferral" of the essay's publication shows that they got the point and were confident that other American Quakers would too.

G OD used other punishments besides violence to smite those who ignored his voice. Natural disasters, pestilence, and disease were consequences that Woolman, like the biblical prophets and Christians throughout history, predicted would surpass the tragedy of war if Quakers did not heed warnings already delivered. Within this context of belief, smallpox was much on Woolman's mind in 1759.

The disease struck Mount Holly again that year, bringing fear and death close to home. Some neighbors died from inoculations, leading Woolman to think about the purpose of bodily afflictions in the divine plan. When he meditated on the subject, he decided that smallpox was an act of God that it was futile to resist. Since you could die either way—because of an inoculation or without one—it was better to trust God than to have faith in medical science. "The more fully our lives are conformable to the will of God, the better it is for us," he writes in the *Journal*. "I have looked at the smallpox as a messenger sent from the Almighty to be an assistant in the cause of virtue, and to incite us to consider whether we employ our time only in such things as are consistent with perfect wisdom and goodness."[33]

Woolman believed that there *are* things we can do to protect ourselves that are consistent with God's will. We can build houses to shelter us and barns for the animals in our care. We can dress appropriately for the climate and season, eat wisely, and live sensibly. We can take care not to work too hard or sleep too little, and try to live unselfishly. The goal of conquering the self, living against ambition and ultimately without ego, is difficult to reach because of the influences of personality and circumstance and because of conditions out of our control. To suppress vanity and desire and to cultivate humility require constant vigilance and improvised responses to events that advice books on diet, exercise, and child rearing cannot anticipate.

Each of us must sort out what is God's business and whether we are following the Light or pursuing our own selfish ends. Even apparently moral acts require close scrutiny to discern our true motives. No behavior is objectively good; a rigorous assessment of why we do something—attend church, donate to the poor, or care for the sick—is essential to discover whether we act selflessly, and we are the only ones who can know that about ourselves: "If I go to a religious meeting, it puts me athinking whether I go in sincerity and in a clear sense of duty, or whether it is not partly in conformity to custom, or partly from a sensible delight which my animal spirits feel in the company of other people, and whether to support my reputation as a religious man has no share in it."[34]

Woolman believed that it is in our hands to live in harmony with God's will: "Was no business done, no visits made, nor any assembling of people together but such as were consistent with pure wisdom, nor any inoculation, there would be a great alteration in the operation of this disorder amongst men." His approach to the prevention of disease, as well as his diagnosis of its cause, were antidotes, he thought, to the secularization of society going on around him. But his view of disease as punishment and of moral behavior as a physical cure rang of the past. It dissented from the new science of medicine and from Enlightenment rationality, which together were finding biological causes and surgical, chemical, and environmental cures in the world the philosophers knew. In this respect, Woolman was a throwback, a survival, a conservative voice in more ways than one. He was out of step, but not out of touch, with the changes that promised a better, wealthier, healthier society by controlling the material world.[35]

Worldly wisdom is what Woolman called the rationalizations of the secular worldview. He was not one of the self-styled "curious" men of his day, who tried to understand better the laws of nature and the nature of the physical world. Perhaps the overseers of the Quaker press were more in tune with the modernizing forces around them, and that would explain why they deleted the sentence about public health. Declining to be inoculated was a symptom of Woolman's spiritual approach to the physical world and his rejection of secularization.

Let no one fear for his life while on God's business, Woolman proclaimed. He surrendered to the divine will and continued his public ministry during the smallpox outbreaks. He weighed each act carefully to be sure that it was necessary and that his motives were pure. He continued to visit slaveowning members of Philadelphia Yearly Meeting, sometimes along with other Friends who were also assigned this duty.

He also began to teach school in 1759. A remembrance added to the *Journal* after his death by Burlington Monthly Meeting noted that Woolman "several times opened a school in Mount Holly, for the instruction of poor Friends' children and others, being concerned for their help and improvement therein." One oral tradition has it that he taught students in a small structure (twenty by twenty-four feet) on New Street in Bridgetown, which Friends built in September 1759. (Six years later twenty-five men subscribed a total of nine pounds, ten shillings, and six pence for a stove to heat the school and to make repairs.) Other traditions place Woolman's school in Mount Holly's Quaker meetinghouse, the Brainerd Street Schoolhouse, or his tailor's shop. But there is no direct evidence to support any of these claims.

Surely, he reasoned, education pursued for the right reasons is God's work; just as certainly, schooling small children is no way to avoid contagions. He traveled to Monthly, Quarterly, and Yearly Meetings to await the Truth. He became even more conscious and cautious about speaking when silence would suffice: "In three hundred minutes are five hours, and he that improperly detains three hundred people one minute, besides other evils that attend it, does an injury like that of imprisoning one man five hours without cause."[36]

Late in 1759 Woolman attended Quarterly Meeting in Bucks County, just across the river from Burlington and northeast of Philadelphia, and saw the ministers and elders who gathered there. He was confident that he came on God's bidding and not by his own choice; his "heart was enlarged in the love of Jesus Christ and the favour of the Most High was extended to us." One elder said he planned to visit some slaveowning Friends elsewhere in the county, so Woolman went home to Mount Holly, prayed on the subject, and "put things in order" before returning to the home of Samuel Eastburn (1702–85) to begin the visitations with him. The smallpox epidemic still raged. Again, Woolman was pleased that he had made the right choice, following God's will rather than his own nature, when "the descendings of the heavenly dew" comforted him. He had prepared as best he could.[37]

"In private my prayers at times were put up to God," Woolman writes, "that he would be pleased to so purge me from all selfishness that I might be strengthened to discharge my duty faithfully, how hard soever to the natural part." In other words, he prayed for the strength of spirit to overcome the physical challenges: the cold of winter, the threat of smallpox, his fear of death, the discomforts of unseasonable travel. Eastburn and Woolman visited active members who owned slaves. The trials were "great," and the work was "hard to nature, yet through the strength of that love which is stronger than death, tenderness of heart was often felt amongst us in our visits, and we parted from several families with greater satisfaction than we expected."[38]

N OT even success in his ministry to slaveowning Friends and the assurance that he labored as God directed were enough to satisfy the self-critical Woolman that he and fellow ministers abided with the spirit over their natures. During attendance at Meetings for Business, when they considered matters "related to the testimony of Truth," Woolman believed they worked too hastily, rather than waiting silently for divine guidance. An impatience to move on to the next item on the agenda "prevented so weighty and deliberate a proceeding" as spirit required. "I believe that it is the will of our heavenly Father that we, with a single eye to the leadings of his Holy Spirit, should quietly wait on him, without hurrying in the business before us."[39]

Woolman was also concerned that those who accommodated Friends who came from afar for Yearly Meeting business were too lavish in their hospitality. If "the leadings of Truth were faithfully followed," prevailing custom would be abandoned and expenses reduced. "Many" of the hosting Friends "under an outward show of a delicate life are entangled in a worldly spirit, labouring to support those expensive customs, which they at times feel to be a burden." The expenditures, which had arisen "from a conformity to the spirit of this world," lay as a "heavy burden" on Woolman's mind. He was confidently on God's rather than his own business, but he feared that he was still complicit in the network of customary relationships that he had decried in his *Considerations on Pure Wisdom and Human Policy*. His viable options were to decline the hospitality or, at least, accept less of it—in quantity, quality, and kind—and encourage the hosts to give less. Woolman tried to convince wealthy Friends to transform their lives along the lines he had advocated in the pamphlet until they lived "conformable to the simplicity that is in Christ, where we may faithfully serve God without distraction, and have no interruption from that which is against Truth."[40]

A letter in which Woolman raises his concern about extravagant hospitality is neither dated nor addressed. Possibly it is not a letter at all, but a template for oral presentations that he made to his hosts. We can see from the *Journal*, pamphlets, and correspondence that the relationship between Woolman's oral and written ministries was fluid. When he stayed true to his inspiration, as he tried to do, the writings were recorded revelations, second, third, or subsequent drafts of mystically derived insights that he first delivered orally. This "letter" addressed to an anonymous Friend may well have been an intermediate stage in the process between revelation and face-to-face presentation of a concern. When Woolman honed his written language, it was to modulate the tone, not the content, and he was wary of losing the inspired message as he transmitted it.

God appoints each of us to "different offices in his work," he writes, which is why Woolman was in the uncomfortable position of seeming to lecture from a moral high ground. God may give each messenger the task of testifying to a different Truth. Neither Woolman nor God elevated the messenger over his hosts except in respect to this particular revelation. The messenger was uniquely gifted or burdened but not necessarily favored over the recipient. (There were biblical examples where the opposite was true.) All are equally unworthy; none sees the whole picture, about which individuals may have partial knowledge. Woolman wanted to be inoffensive and to deliver God's message humbly as an act of love, wanting to solicit Friends' help to further by example Christ's ministry and Quakers' testimony on simplicity.[41]

The sentiments of *Considerations on Pure Wisdom and Human Policy* appeared again in an epistle sent from Philadelphia Yearly Meeting in 1759 to its constituent Quarterly and Monthly Meetings. The original draft is in Woolman's hand, and the words are his. Like his parable, the epistle has a structure echoing passages of the Old Testament. The story he tells in it about the Quakers' settlement of New Jersey and Pennsylvania is not a biblical allegory, but its resolution is similar to those drawn in what Christians call the Pentateuch or the Five Books of Moses, Jews the Torah.

The epistle begins by placing Quakers in the whole history of humanity. "The empires and kingdoms of the earth are but branches of his family," Woolman writes in Old Testament fashion, but here Quaker colonists play the part of peripatetic Jews. God "hath been to us a most gracious and tender parent and dealt bountifully with us even from the days of our fathers." It was God who "strengthened them to labour through the difficulties attending the improvement of a wilderness, and made way for them in the hearts of the natives, so that by them they were comforted in times of want and distress."[42]

Friends had now reached a juncture, though, reminiscent of the ever-backsliding Old Testament Jews, in which they had not, exercising their free will, made the right choices. Now the future of their progeny was at stake, as was the fate of their holy experiment in the New World. Despite God's favor and clear instruction on Truth, Quakers risked his just wrath.

> And though the Almighty does not at all times suddenly exe-
> cute his judgments on sinful people in this life, yet we see by
> many instances, that where men follow lying vanities they
> forsake their own mercies and as proud selfish spirit prevails
> and spreads amongst a people. So partial judgments, oppres-
> sion, discords, envy and confusions increase, and provinces
> and kingdoms are made to drink the cup of adversity as a re-
> ward of their own doings.[43]

Quakers remained deaf to God's voice, which he raised louder for their benefit. The signs were clear, the warnings apparent, and retribution had already begun. No longer were Quaker provinces escaping the plague of war as they had in the past. The once-welcoming natives now tortured and killed Pennsylvanians in their homes on the frontier; colonists lost spouses and children to Indian kidnappers, who spirited them into the wilderness. Pennsylvanians and New Jerseyans died in battle, and military officers were drafting young Quakers. All this reversed the fortunes of a people who considered themselves God's chosen and had benefited so bountifully from his grace.

In Woolman's first antislavery essay he had traced the connections among violence, slavery, and war back to parents' unrestrained natural love for their children. Subsequently, he wrote of a chain with links that began with vanity and led to greed, violence, slavery, and war. Now Woolman described the cycle of violence that exploited animals and manual laborers (only some of whom were slaves). If Quakers had focused less on accumulating wealth and building estates for their children's benefit and more on devoting their energy to Christian charity to Indians, the epistle said, the violence that took settlers' lives would not have occurred. If Quakers now refocused their attention away from "worldly treasures" and toward giving Indians justice, the warfare would cease.[44]

The epistle instructs Friends that God deals justly with his people, and even as their New World enterprise once benefited from his providence, so now they are suffering from his displeasure. Difficult as the first Quaker settlers found "labouring for the necessaries of life," they still had time "to promote piety and virtue in the earth and educated their children in the fear of the Lord." Their reward was God's blessing, and their legacy was peace. A misguided focus on worldly pursuits for some time had distracted them from the spiritual ambitions that were in the best interest of the Indians, themselves, and their children. If they really felt "affectionate regard for posterity," they would seek the spiritual rather than the material prosperity of their children. From any practical perspective, their children would be better off if parents gave them models for piety and virtue, and "let them see that we really value" those qualities over any others. Quaker children would grow up in a safer environment, have more comfortable lives, and benefit from God's blessings rather than his curse if they abided Truth: "In all our cares about worldly treasures, let us steadily bear in mind that riches possessed by children, who do not truly serve God, are likely to prove snares that may more grievously entangle them in the spirit of selfishness and exaltation which stands in opposition to real peace and happiness and renders them enemies to the Cross of Christ."[45]

THE first indication that Woolman was extending his ministry to Indians had come two years earlier, when he became a founding member of the New Jersey Association for Helping the Indians. We can see his hand in the articles of that association, dated April 16, 1757. It collected contributions for purchasing two thousand acres of land bordering the Pine Barrens in central New Jersey, where the Indians could live without charge. The goal was to "try to keep them from being in contact with 'foreign' Indians and prevent foreign Indians from settling in NJ, funds solicited from Quakers only."[46]

There were charitable motives for making an Indian reservation that controlled the movements of native people who had welcomed the Quakers less than a century before. The intentions were humane within the context of the times, when non-Quaker settlers often stole rather than bought Indian land. The association wanted to enhance relations with the natives and to do so charitably, giving the increasingly impoverished Indians an opportunity that they were in theory free to decline but that had the potential to benefit them. From the signatories' perspective, if not from our modern retrospective one, the Quakers were treating the Indians with justice and love.

The articles were the first in a series of three Woolman texts, which included the pamphlet published the following year and the epistle that Yearly Meeting sent out a year after that. Indians were integral, then, to Woolman's vision of universal love and of the grave consequences of denying the spirit's leading. The articles recall the friendship that Indians extended to the first Quaker settlers in New Jersey, just as the epistle alluded to the settlement of the Pennsylvania frontier. Indians, who had outnumbered Quakers by a hundred or more to one, could have dealt a decisive blow to them right at the start, "but so far were they from any thoughts of that kind that they promoted their welfare in almost every instance where it lay in their power, cherished them through many distressing intervals and greatly contributed under Providence to render an otherwise inhospitable wilderness even pleasant to the European strangers."[47]

Now, though, chiefly through the Indians' "own bad conduct," they had fallen on hard times. Securing a place for them to live together, hunt, fish, and raise crops would repay their earlier generosity and make New Jersey safer. Perhaps it could learn from the bad example of Pennsylvania, where the frontier was aflame, and bring peace through Christian charity to a people who, in league with Indian allies from afar, might otherwise lash out violently. Safety came not from accumulating wealth but from sharing it with less fortunate beings.[48]

By 1758 the French and Indian War had reached the environs of New Jersey, with continuing skirmishes of Indian tribes allied with France challenging English settlements in Pennsylvania, New York, and then across the Delaware River and into New Jersey. In June Delawares attacked the family of Nicholas Cole in Walpack, a settlement in the hilly northwestern part of the colony about a hundred miles from Mount Holly and near the Pennsylvania line. The

Delawares killed and took captives in retaliation for the murder of the sachem Weequehelah. The assault stunned New Jerseyans, who had believed themselves immune to the violence on the Pennsylvania frontier. The assembly had already appointed a commission to investigate the treatment of Indians in New Jersey, listen to grievances, and report back their findings. It had also passed laws banning the sale of alcoholic beverages to Indians, forbidding the imprisonment of Indians for debt, limiting the size of animal traps set by non-Indians, and voiding all leases and sales of Indian land obtained contrary to regulations. The commissioners had also been given authority to purchase Indians' land and establish a reservation south of the Raritan River.

The commission held a series of conferences with Indians to exchange views. Land, animal traps that depleted game, and alcohol were the recurring issues. At one conference, called shortly after the attack in Walpack, they assured the Indians that the incursions by other Indians from Pennsylvania had not lessened their own regard for those who resided in New Jersey. The natives tried to explain that the settlers' methods of measuring land were alien to them, that they did not understand or trust their surveying methods but instead preferred to mark boundaries by topographical features: streams, hollows, and nameless hills. For this reason, even in land transactions involving people of goodwill on both sides, there were often misunderstandings that led to violence. Specific cases were discussed in detail.

The Minisinks of New Jersey believed that whites had robbed them of land, and this gave them common cause with other aggrieved tribes, including the Delawares who had crossed the river to attack Walpack. The governor and commissioners of New Jersey offered the Minisinks a cash settlement for their land claims. The Indians negotiated successfully for a larger sum. The governor of Pennsylvania made a similar settlement with Delaware Indians on the upper Susquehanna River near the New York line, the Indians agreeing to exchange prisoners, return to peace, and rest content with the lands they received.[49]

In this atmosphere of hope and fear New Jersey established in Burlington County the first North American Indian reservation. The reasons that Quakers, including Woolman, were attentive to fair dealing for Indian land included their testimony on the extension of charity to peoples of other races and cultures, as well as wanting to avoid any violence that might challenge their peace testimony or threaten them. It is also worth considering whether the Quakers' understanding of the spiritual significance of place, which differed not only from those of the Indians but from those of fellow Christians, affected their approach to spatial relationships with those around them.

People often re-create their environment symbolically with sacred places. Vertical connections with ascendant spirits affect horizontal relations with people, animals, and the earth. Belief that the mythological place of their origins is the center of the earth, and architectural expressions of connections between heaven and earth, such as sacred poles, raised altars, and church spires, sacralize space. When Quakers saw themselves as a chosen people, they unselfconsciously connected their sect to this ancient and shared spiritual history of humanity.

By insisting that all space is sacred because God created it, Quakers established the potential for distinctive relationships with nature, architecture, and humanity. When Woolman traveled to the South in his ministry, walked long distances rather than ride a tired horse, wrote *Considerations on Keeping Negroes* and *Considerations on Pure Wisdom*, and stood on the threshold of his father's house in the sun worm dream, he occupied the sacred space between the house of God and the natural world where humanity dwelled. As Mircea Eliade explains in *The Sacred and the Profane*, "the threshold, the door *show* the solution of continuity in space immediately and concretely; hence their great religious importance, for they are symbols and at the same time vehicles of *passage* from one space to the other." Woolman reminded humanity of what the prophets revealed: that all life is sacred and that we can pass from the material to the spiritual realm.[50]

9

Words

1760–63

JOHN Woolman wrote "15th day, 6th month," stopped, and stuck a pin in the page; it was 1763. The point marks time (day and month but not year), place, and life's intrusion on solitude in a manuscript draft of his *Journal*. It was a tailor's absentminded act, treating paper as cloth, quill as needle, and ink as thread. Pins can fix the end stitch of a half-finished seam but do not keep a story from unraveling.[1]

Woolman wrote with his tailoring tools at hand, pins protruding accessibly from his cuff, scissors close by, needles arrayed in a cushion, selvage before him, and scraps on the floor, his profession and avocation on the table where he composed. He cut cloth with paper, ink, and memories surrounding him. It was a seamless life, which had been his goal when he left farming and retired from shopkeeping—fewer distractions, but still some, it seems. Woolman was an experienced craftsman in his early forties and could prick the margins unconsciously. Habit dictated the act; distraction accounts for the oversight. Woolman was no longer young when he wrote about his life in 1763, so myopia may have affected his hindsight too.

During the 1760s Woolman recorded transactions in a small account book—selling a pair of gloves for five shillings, for example. He continued a financial relationship with Aquilla Shinn, the son of the late Thomas Shinn, whose will he had coexecuted; it took a decade (1753–63) to settle the estate. Aquilla contracted with Wool-man to "take the North end of my orchard next year and to put on what dung his stable affords and hath now in his hands." We can wonder, but not know, if Woolman found earthy humor in a literal reading of this entry. James Dobins paid eighteen shillings' rent for that fertilized field. Aquilla also established credit with Woolman by repairing leaky barrels that needed new hoops, for which Woolman paid him eleven shillings and six pence in April 1763.[2]

A pair of linen breeches (or britches) suitable for summer cost Aaron Barton three shillings. They fitted tightly below the knee and had a two-button flap that opened in front. Linen was inexpensive, breathable cloth that allowed air to circulate through the garment. Woolman also stitched leather breeches, which wore well for hard labor, and others made of sheepskin for winter work. He used tanned leather to make shoes for women and men; he cut and sewed cloth shoes for children. There was a hat for his daughter, a jacket for Timothy Sullivan, and shifts, dresses, and mittens for other customers.[3]

Bleached white cambric, a finely woven plain linen like that used today for high-quality handkerchiefs, was the principal fabric Wool-man used for women's garments. Aprons, caps, and the visible parts of shifts were made of cambric. Wool, cotton, and cotton flannel were also the natural materials of a country tailor's trade: flannel shirts; jackets of fustian—Woolman wrote "fustin" or "fistin"—a plain, strong, mid-weight cotton; breeches of holland (a heavy linen); and many different garments of osnaburg or osnabrig (an inexpensive, coarse, scratchy unbleached cotton).[4]

The key word is "plain." Woolman sewed functional clothes, only what worked. He did not use imported linens or silk, no broadcloth, chintz, drouguet, or lustring for gowns and fashionable men's suits. His rich friends in Burlington and Philadelphia had more ambitious tailors design garments for their families. On the other hand, Woolman apparently had little use for plains, the rough woolen weaves imported from England for slaves; or linsey-woolsey, another plain-woven textile most often used for the clothing of sailors, day laborers, servants, and other "lower sorts." There is no mention of them in his account books. He did make a coat for an unnamed servant and charged four shillings, and he made a pair of trousers for "Cupid," whose name suggests a slave; but the prices were consistent with what he charged his usual customers for similar items.[5]

It appears that Woolman's transactions with African Americans were direct, not through third parties. For example, he credited "Negro Sam" three shillings and nine pence for "scowering my ditch" and forgave him a debt of one shilling and eleven pence. Perhaps Sam was a slave who lacked a surname; possibly he worked to purchase his freedom, which would explain the financial forgiveness. For chopping cordwood on Woolman's pineland, "Negro Baccus" received a credit against existing debt.[6]

A master asking Woolman to make clothes for a slave might well have invited an unwelcome sermon and burdened him with a moral dilemma, so it is unlikely to have happened often. Woolman usually responded to such challenges by asking for time to consider the proposal; pray in silence, seeking a resolution true to his principles, including his concern for the physical welfare of the slave and for the master's spiritual fate; and, upon reaching clarity, deliver his decision forthrightly, humbly, and lovingly.

He surely included an attempt to convince the slaveowner to divest himself of human chattel, but Woolman would also consider the slave's need to be protected from the elements by seasonally appropriate clothes. He could choose to accept such a commission and payment but turn the money over to the slave, although he might not wish to arouse anger with such a provocation. More likely, he could make the garment at cost, giving his time and labor as a sacrifice for the slave's well-being and as testimony to the master's need for moral reform. Whatever the master did thereafter would then be in God's hands. It was a question of free will exercised in the face of Truth, possibly with the gift of grace to hear the words differently this time. Woolman's manner and heartfelt, perhaps even tearful, comments might shame the slaveowner, who would recall the warnings every time the slave wore Woolman's garments. If all went well, the experience would open the slaveowner's heart rather than closing it down in defensive anger.

Woolman made many dresses and other garments for women, all of them in the fashion of the time. He sewed a "calomink" gown for Achsak Matlack, for example, calamanco being a worsted wool, for which he charged three shillings and six pence, and other gowns from poplin, calico, and homespun (an American-produced textile usually made of mixed cotton and wool). Gowns made up a good part of his work in the early years of his trade, but he also furnished jackets, cloaks, coats, breeches, and stomachers, these last being detachable decorative panels for women's dresses shaped as a triangle with the point down and stretching from the breasts to just below the waist. Over the course of a pregnancy, a woman would need progressively larger stomachers, which accounted for some of the trade. He also sewed women's undergarments stiffened with whalebone, like corsets and waistcoats, which were undervests that tied in front; for these he sometimes used quilted cotton cloth, which added warmth and flexibility. "Flaring" waistcoats, which he sewed for Martha Matlack and Thomas Robson, were in a style that accommodated wide hips in both men and women. Short gowns worn over shifts like long blouses were an extra layer of clothing. He also mended clothes and cut leather and cloth for customers who sewed their own garments.[7]

Woolman probably learned only a few basic stitches, but that would have been all he needed. He knew how to oversew, using a stitch for piecing cloth together that kept the seam flat so that it wouldn't chafe. And he could hem, folding over the cloth and stitching slantwise across the weave to finish the edges with maximum strength and durability. He used an awl to poke regularly spaced holes through leather, which he sewed with waxed linen thread, and he probably knew the traditional Indian method of sewing with a specially fashioned animal tendon as a needle. He would not have bothered to gather shirt cuffs and collars for the sake of appearance or to make invisible seams, even if he knew how.[8]

Woolman continued to weave his traveling ministry into the tailor's trade, practicing one or the other as the spirit moved him. In the spring of 1760 he "laboured under some discouragement" in Woodbridge, Rahway, and Plainfield, New Jersey, with his fellow abolitionist Samuel Eastburn. They also went to Meetings on Long Island, where Woolman wrestled with his sociability, "being jealous over myself, lest I should speak anything to make my testimony look agreeable to that mind in people which is not in pure obedience to the cross of Christ." He later recalled that the "spring of the ministry was often low" during this trip, which reflected the same troubled mood he had been in when he hemmed and sewed before the journey.[9]

"As the present appearance of things is not joyous," Woolman wrote to his wife from Long Island, he was "much shut up from outward cheerfulness," which may understate his frame of mind. He worried about Sarah and Mary getting smallpox, which was then striking communities all over Pennsylvania and New Jersey, and his concern for himself was also a "trial": "Yet I often remember there are many widows and fatherless, many who have poor tutors, many who have evil examples before them, and many whose minds are in captivity, for whose sake my heart is at times moved with [such] compassion that I feel my mind resigned to leave you for a season, to exercise that gift which the Lord hath bestowed on me." But he knew that whenever he left his family, he put them all in jeopardy; whether he went the short distance to his shop or journeyed far from home, he increased the likelihood of his exposure to smallpox and the possibility that he might infect Mary and Sarah when he returned.[10]

Eastburn and Woolman persisted on their northern sojourn to Connecticut, sailing the thirty miles across Long Island Sound to New London in a large open boat. When a strong wind blew up, Woolman felt in peril. Later he recalled battling his fear of death by trying to resign himself to God's will; he considered himself to be living on "lent" (what we would call borrowed) time. Our use of the active voice, "borrowed," is a modern conceit, giving us the illusion of agency and control, while Woolman's "lent" expresses his surrender to God's will. Reflecting back after the trip, he wrote, "The journey has appeared difficult, but my mind was turned to Him who made and commands the winds and the waters, and whose Providence is over the raven and the sparrows." Woolman's terrifying experience at sea became for him a metaphor for life's journey and for a spiritual quest more fraught than the discomfiting trip to New England.[11]

Woolman's correspondence during that trip has an air of finality: "Farewell my dear friend," he concludes one letter, and all the others dwell on the imminence of death. To feel the hand of mortality upon him was understandable, given the diseased environment he traveled in, but the gloom came from within him and was not just a reflection of external circumstances: "My life from one minute to another is sustained by Him." He felt himself clinging to the world by a thread, as a loose button hangs from a coat. Imagining his family to be "lonesome" in his absence, he expressed his own pain of isolation more than he usually did.[12]

Woolman had heard from an acquaintance, but not from Sarah's letters, that she was ill, and he was not feeling so well himself: "I am not so hearty and healthy as I have sometimes [been]." The threat of smallpox was never far from his mind. He wished he could be home with her and their child, but the "weight of the work I am engaged in, and such [are] the baptisms with which I have been baptized that I see necessity for all nature to stand silent." What a powerful thought, so poetically put, and reaching back to the early traditions of the Christian church—at least to the fourth-century liturgy of St. James. The prophetic task assigned by God required that Woolman, as a messenger delivering Truth, silence the voice of nature within him, override the natural affection that he felt for his family, and get on with God's work. Woolman believed that nature should have no impact on his actions, and he knew that his spirituality caused pain to the ones who loved him.[13]

In Rhode Island, Woolman and Eastburn attended five Meetings in Narragansett before going on to Newport, where their "deep exercises . . . were mortifying to the creaturely will." Woolman felt drawn to meet privately with Quaker slaveowners there, at least partly out of frustration with the reception his message was given in public forums. Such private engagements made him "singular," he wrote, by which he meant peculiar, odd, unusual, or different, and this attracted harsh criticism of him. He struggled to accept that God "assigned" him an "unpleasant" task that needed to be done. It was the fate of the prophet to suffer such isolation, and Woolman identified with Habakkuk's pain: "I hear, and I tremble within; my lips quiver at the sound." Woolman had "many cogitations" similar to Habakkuk's and "was sorely distressed."[14]

Rhode Island farmers prospered, some by raising tobacco with Indian and African slaves, but it was Narragansett Bay that brought wealth to Newport, Providence, Bristol, East Greenwich, Warren, and Warwick. The bay was well located for coastal trade and contained six excellent small harbors suitable for launching ships. Commercial fishing supplied local markets and Boston as well.

Newport was one of the wealthiest cities in eighteenth-century North America, although not very large, for it was a bustling shipbuilding and international shipping center. Its merchants had more than a hundred large ships at sea by 1739; by 1769 at least twice that many had a home port in Narragansett Bay. In the seventeenth century Rhode Island traders had supplied planters on Barbados and other West Indian islands with staple goods—beef, chicken, mutton, corn, butter, cheese, and wool. In the eighteenth century the ships continued to carry staples to the West Indies, rum to Africa, slaves back to the West Indies, and then molasses home. It was not until 1774 that Rhode Island barred the importation of slaves; in 1784 the state freed all newly born children of female slaves, beginning the gradual process of abolishing slavery there. Into the nineteenth century, though, Rhode Island's merchants trafficked in slaves. Between 1804 and 1807, 59 of the 202 slave ships, carrying 8,238 slaves and docking in Charleston, South Carolina, were from Rhode Island.[15]

It was no surprise, then, that Rhode Island Quakers were deeply invested in slaves. One member of Newport Yearly Meeting imported a "large number" of slaves from Guinea, West Africa, and sold them publicly. But when Woolman drafted a petition to the Rhode Island Assembly on the slave trade, which Friends agreed to read to Yearly Meeting, he was gratified that "many expressed their unity with the proposal." He was also moved to speak at Newport Yearly Meeting against lotteries, as it "appeared very clear . . . that the spirit of lotteries was a spirit of selfishness, which tended to confusion and darkness of understanding." Woolman became agitated during the ensuing debate, and his own assessment was that his words were "not enough seasoned with charity, and after this I spake no more on the subject."[16]

The particular Friend to whose remarks Woolman had responded heatedly was a man of some years, and the forty-year-old Woolman remained as ever deferential to his elders, so this dispute particularly troubled him. Since "milder language" would have been more appropriate, Woolman rose to explain himself "in some degree of creaturely abasement," which he thought well received and a calming influence after the "warm debate."[17]

Mercy Redman (1721–78), from Haddonfield, New Jersey, was another sojourning Friend attending Newport Yearly Meeting, and she reported that Woolman also addressed the women's Meeting on the subjects of child rearing and education, then joined some of the women one evening to continue the conversation on these subjects close to his heart. In an apparent reference to the subject of slaveholding, Redman perceived "great openness and tenderness in the minds of some friends in that place."[18]

As always in his *Journal*, Woolman is vague about time, but he spent several days at Newport, during which he sought another route to Quaker consciences on the subject of slavery, a "secret, though heavy, exercise in regard to some leading active members about Newport being in the practice of slave-keeping." One morning a Friend arranged a "private conference" for Woolman and these merchants in a member's home. There followed, according to the *Journal*, "a free conference upon the subject," and he was pleased by the exchange of views occurring "in a calm and peaceable spirit." When he left, he was sure that some would now release their slaves in their wills and relieved that others had at least heard the message.[19]

But it was not easy to instruct those who entertained him so graciously in their homes, since it could feel like a breach of manners or even disrespectful to criticize a host while accepting his hospitality. Still, Woolman believed that affability should not "hinder us from the Lord's work." Such challenges were "hard labour" but nonetheless essential. "Superficial friendship" must not stand in Truth's way. He often felt humbled yet "content to appear weak or as a fool for his [Christ's] sake." Affability might seem a virtue or, at worst, a sometimes irritating character flaw, but "to see the failings of our friends and think hard of them, without opening that which we ought to open, and still carry a face of friendship—this tends to undermine the foundation of true unity." His office was particularly "weighty," since "watchmen"—a prophetic role that Woolman believed he shared with Ezekiel—were responsible to "guard against the snares of prosperity and an outside friendship" resulting from natural attachments.[20]

From Newport, Woolman and Eastburn continued north to the Massachusetts towns of Newton, Cushnet, Long Plain, Rochester, and Dartmouth, after which they sailed to Nantucket Island in the company of Mercy Redman and Ann Gauntt (1710–?) of Little Egg Harbor, New Jersey, Quaker ministers traveling together. Woolman thought the work on Nantucket Island was, again, hard labor, and he detected an "evil spirit" among Friends that led to strife. When he left the island—on a ship, with about fifty passengers, that was becalmed when the winds changed—Woolman retired to the solitude of a cabin, where, after "some hours" of prayerful silence as they waited for favorable weather, his heart filled "with the spirit of supplication, my prayers and tears were poured out before my Heavenly Father for his help and instruction in the manifold difficulties which attended me in life."[21]

In this frame of mind, opened emotionally to receiving the spirit, he contemplated the nature of island living as he had experienced it on Nantucket, where the weather was harsh, the soil infertile, the timber harvested to extinction, and the whale fishery the only profitable pursuit left to its inhabitants. But whales were already being overhunted and had become scarce, surviving whales were wary of human predators, and both conditions dictated longer and more dangerous journeys for the whalers.

> I considered that the formation of the earth, the seas, the islands, bays, and rivers, the motions of the winds and great waters, which cause bars and shoals in particular places, were all the works of him who is perfect wisdom and goodness; and as people attend to his heavenly instruction and put their trust in him, he provides for them in all parts where he gives them a being.[22]

At Monthly Meeting for Business on Nantucket, Woolman had shared his insights on islanders' lives with Friends "in the fresh spring of pure love." If they focused inwardly, attended to the "pure guidance of the Holy Spirit," educated their children to true humility and "disuse of all superfluities," then their conflict with nature would be replaced by greater harmony with the world around them. The more plainly and simply they lived, the less danger the island's men would have to endure to furnish their needs. He encouraged the young women to keep their homes and themselves in a plain, humble fashion. Where people were content with a plain way of life, they enjoyed "more true peace and calmness of mind" than those who aspired to "greatness and outward show." Noticing that there were few slaves on Nantucket, Woolman encouraged islanders to be content without them, "making mention of the numerous troubles and vexations which frequently attend the minds of people who depend on slaves to do their labor."[23]

From Nantucket, Eastburn and Woolman sailed to Sandwich, then headed south through Rhode Island and Connecticut to New York, then Rahway, New Jersey, where the two men parted as each headed for home after four months on the road. Toward the end of the trip Woolman began to feel better about himself and his work. "That poverty of spirit and inward weakness with which I was much tried the forepart of this journey has of late appeared to me as a dispensation of kindness" he wrote, and he now saw his melancholic mood "as a kindness from the Lord."[24]

Back from New England, Woolman again cut cloth and sewed buttons, seams, and hems in the quiet he craved. Sensitive soul that he was, he contemplated his tailoring materials within the spiritual realm where he dwelled. For fifteen years he had been measuring, threading, and writing in the same chair, and over the years a small concern grew to an internal conflict that he later described as a "sadness" causing him "distress." He was led to see moral mountains in bolts of cloth.

Woolman describes in his *Journal* this inner tumult, which led uncomfortably to personal crises in 1761 and 1762. He had noticed that undyed cloth was stronger and cleaner and better resisted soiling than dyed fabric. The observation likely came from mending torn garments, noting the comparative durability of his clothes, and knowing the quality of the bleeding dye that stained his hands. "The thoughts of my wearing hats and garments dyed with a dye hurtful to them," he recalled, "has made lasting impressions on me."

"Hurtful" is an emotionally hot, extreme word to describe cloth weakened by dye, but it is certainly appropriate to explain Woolman's own state: "From my early acquaintance with Truth I have often felt an inward distress occasioned by the striving of a spirit in me against the operation of the Heavenly Principle, and in this circumstance have been affected with a sense of my own wretchedness, and in a mourning condition felt earnest longings for that divine help which brings the soul into true liberty." What might have been a passing, casual observation of another tailor became a spiritual crisis for Woolman, one that echoes St. Paul's battle between flesh and the spirit. "Distress" and then "wretchedness" left him desperate for rescue from the imprisonment of his spirit. He could not act on this insight; he lived in conflict with Truth. He knew better than to defy God, as the prophet Jonah did to his peril, but was unable to make the principled change dictated by the spirit within him: "And sometimes in this state, retiring into private places, the spirit of supplication hath been given me, and under a heavenly covering have asked my gracious Father to give me a heart in all things resigned to the direction of his wisdom."[25]

The same process of discernment, internal crisis, and resolution accompanied by mournful distress, desperation, and divine rescue occurred "often" to Woolman. The specific account of how he purified his clothes illustrates how he believed that God reformed him time and again, and offers another example of how apparently small conflicts with Truth could lead to moral chaos if unaddressed: "In visiting people of note in the Society who had slaves and labouring with them in brotherly love on that account, I have seen, and the sight has affected me, that a conformity to some customs distinguishable from pure wisdom has entangled many, and the desire of gain to support these customs greatly opposed the work of Truth."[26]

The pressure of social conformity was the curse of humanity, as Woolman had already explained. Only by rising above the ways of the world can we detach from nature and achieve the spiritual triumph that unites our spirit with Truth. When he was in closest touch with the Inner Light, Woolman realized that he must "in all things attend to his wisdom and be teachable, and so cease from all customs contrary thereto, however used amongst religious people."

No matter whether every Quaker on earth wore dyed garments of whatever color, it was wrong.[27]

Because he feared what others might think if he discarded his dyed clothing, he tormented himself with painful images of men crippled in war, women and children taken captive, and wounded soldiers in agony. "Thinking often on these things," he explains, "the use of hats and garments dyed with a dye hurtful to them and wearing more clothes in summer than are useful grew more uneasy to me, believing them to be customs which have not their foundation in pure wisdom."[28]

On May 31, 1761, Woolman fell ill, was feverish and "in great distress of body," and in his sickness there was "a cry raised" in him that revealed why. God was punishing him for not resolving the conflict between Truth and wearing dyed clothes: "And in the continuation of the exercise [i.e., practice] I felt all the powers in me yield themselves up into the hands of him who gave me being and was made thankful that he had taken hold of me by his chastisement, feeling the necessity of further purifying." The illness was, then, a punishment and a blessing, and Woolman learned to surrender his need for approval to the Truth, which brought him "calm resignation" and "inward healing." In the clarity of his fevered state, Woolman reached a new understanding.[29]

Woolman reasoned that it would also be wrong to dispose of serviceable garments. So he continued to wear dyed clothing but replaced each item when it wore out with an untinted one, a process that took nine months to complete, suggesting that he owned very few clothes, wearing out a pair of trousers, a jacket, and a hat, perhaps; he may have already been wearing natural cotton shirts. He was still uncomfortable in his new clothes, and because he knew that undyed fur hats were becoming stylish, he anticipated that Friends might think he was "affecting singularity" in his dress. During a spring Meeting in 1762, Woolman prayed on the subject and resolved to "speak for a hat the natural colour of the fur" when he got home.[30]

As Woolman feared, his new clothes led some Friends to "carry shy" of him. The hat, the first item in his new wardrobe, raised questions about his apparent bow to fashion. Woolman explained to those who inquired about his "affected singularity" that he was led by the spirit and was not following his own will. But not everyone was convinced, and perhaps some Friends were eager to dismiss him as a hypocrite. But Woolman reasoned that the loss of "superficial" friendships was a "providential kindness" that broke some of the ties binding him to earth. He decided to resist the impulse to explain himself, to bear the looks and silent judgments as purifying sacrifices, and to accept that in time God would "open the hearts of Friends" toward him.[31]

The fur hat raises the issue of Woolman's sympathy for abused animals, but there is no record of his feeling guilty about killing them for fur, skin, or meat. He advocated kind treatment of living animals but butchered hogs that he raised for his family's consumption. Although we have no evidence that Woolman ever advocated vegetarianism on moral grounds, he apparently adhered to a meatless diet for reasons of health during at least the last year of his life.

Vegetarianism was fashionable during Woolman's lifetime. The seventeenth-century English antislavery pamphleteer Thomas Tryon had promoted it, inspiring Benjamin Franklin (a brief experiment) and Benjamin Lay, among others, to reject meat eating as unnatural. Adam and Eve were commonly thought of as vegetarians by those who saw the biblical grant of dominion over animals as an injunction against killing them, because of the very next thing that God said: "See, I have given you every plant yielding seed that is upon the face of all the earth, and every tree with seed in its fruit; you shall have them for food" (Genesis 1:29). By this same reading, God changed the human-animal relationship after the Flood: "Every moving thing that lives shall be food for you; and just as I gave you the green plants, I give you everything" (Genesis 9:3). On both sides of the Atlantic there were people who believed that recovery of the prelapsarian state linked vegetarianism and pacifism; eating only vegetables and grains was the sort of gentle, kind dominion that Woolman advocated in his writings on animals, slavery, and war.[32]

Perhaps it was vegetarianism's very fashionableness that put Woolman off; but it was one of those practices that crossed the line between Enlightenment liberals and religious conservatives, and its biblical rationale was decidedly Old Testament. Possibly he resisted its nonviolence, simplicity, and potential to break market relationships only because he was more a man of the countryside, with a farmer's complex relationship with animals. It could have been more appealing to urbane professional men who had never decapitated a living chicken or butchered a hog. Woolman was apparently more comfortable practicing than advocating dietary cures designed by vegetarian doctors, whose specialty swept Europe during the eighteenth century. But Woolman might simply have been inconsistent, resisting what others who thought a lot like him embraced as a moral Truth, one that had not been revealed to him.

In adopting white raiment, which Woolman eventually did, he located himself within Revelation's prophecy. When Christ appears to the prophet John, "his head and his hair were as white as white wool, white as snow." To the angel of the church in Sardis, John sends a warning to the people to turn from their sins.

> Wake up, and strengthen what remains and is on the point of death, for I have not found your works perfect in the sight of my God. Remember then what you received and heard; obey it, and repent. If you do not wake up, I will come like a thief, and you will not know at what hour I will come to you. Yet you have still a few persons in Sardis who have not soiled their clothes; they will walk with me, dressed in white, for they are worthy. If you conquer, you will be clothed like them in white robes, and I will not blot your name out of the book of life.

John also advises believers, through the angel of the church in Laodicea, to buy "white robes to clothe you and to keep the shame of your nakedness from being seen."[33]

The focus on cleanliness and the less than obvious description of wool as white are in Revelation. The specific association of clothing with the soul—"not soiled their clothes"—and redemption are there as well. Though Woolman would not have called himself worthy, he embraced John's prophecy and followed the directive to wear white. In displaying the prophecy, he manifested the difference between the prophet's purity of spirit and his fallen people, modeling purity without uttering an unnecessary word.

The prophet Isaiah walked the streets of Jerusalem in a slave's scanty clothes to communicate an unspoken warning. In Woolman's own time, Benjamin Lay had worn a military uniform to dramatize the linkage between slavery and war. Woolman, in a more subtle but equally stunning display, dressed in white for the last ten years of his life. The obstacle that his eccentricity raised to his ministry was an additional challenge that he welcomed with humility. The pain it caused him to look different, to offend, and to be misunderstood was a cross that he thanked God for the privilege to bear. He became ever more sure that he was abiding the spirit, abiding the message of the Sermon on the Mount and Revelation, and following the example of the Old Testament prophets.

Whiteness testified to "pure" wisdom and love. Wearing white was not a claim to embody perfection but a symbol that he was aspiring to a sinless state. It spoke for Truth and against the small compromises that are morally entangling. The progression from dyed to natural to bleached cloth expresses Woolman's quest for purity literally and metaphorically. It shows that he was unwilling to settle for nature, that he went from unnatural to natural and then on to a spiritual or supranatural state, not a supernatural one but a step past the physical world. Purity became Woolman's personal and social ambition, and it took him past simplicity and mere concern about being "hurtful" to clothes. Colorlessness expressed his hopes for a race-neutral, classless society, which could not be accomplished simply and would be hurtful to those at the top.

Whiteness was not natural; bleaching weakened the fabric and was time-consuming work.

> To whiten cloth, take a tub with a plug at bottom. Lay the cloth or yarn in it. Spread a coarse cloth over the tub and lay ashes in it. Then pour on boiling water and let it stand all night. In the morning draw off the lye, make it boil and pour it on again and again. Then throw away the lye, and with hot water make the cloth or yarn middling clean. Then lay it in the sun and wet it. So proceed as the case requires.

So the wearer of white sacrificed simplicity for dramatic effect, and indeed, Woolman's garments made his point. By embodying his message, he could speak less and to greater effect during his last decade; the white hat was only a start.[34]

For most of 1761 Woolman continued to work at home and traveled only locally. During the spring he headed southwest toward Haddonfield, but he made no definite plan about the duration and destinations of his trip, "concluding in my mind to seek for heavenly instruction and come home or go on, as I might then believe best for me; and there through the springing up of pure love I felt encouragement and so crossed the river." In Pennsylvania thereafter, Woolman attended two Quarterly and three Monthly Meetings, where he "laboured" with some "noted" Friends who owned slaves, and then he went home. At the end of the summer, he again left his needle and quill and went northeast to Shrewsbury, where he discharged the same duty, relieving his conscience that he had delivered the message entrusted to him.[35]

During this time Woolman wrote a second part to his *Considerations on the Keeping of Negroes,* and the overseers approved it for publication in 1762. He solicited comments on his draft from his fellow reformers John Churchman and Israel Pemberton, but smallpox had broken out in Philadelphia, and that slowed communication. "I am a little cautious of being much at thy house on acct. of the smallpox," Woolman wrote to Pemberton on the subject of the manuscript, "but would gladly meet thee at such house as thou thinks suitable to have a little conversation with thee." He knew he could count on Pemberton's friendship and influence within Philadelphia Yearly Meeting and on Churchman's dedication to radical reform. The former would advise restraint; the latter would support the quest for purity without compromise. Churchman had traveled widely in America and Europe in his own ministry, opposed war taxes, visited Quaker slaveowners with Woolman, and held Friends to some of the same high moral standards. In the first draft of his *Journal,* Woolman quoted extensively from Churchman's spiritual autobiography. Pemberton and Woolman had worked together to secure fair treatment of Indians, and Pemberton, an old friend, was now a rich businessman and philanthropist, a major figure in

Philadelphia's Quaker community whose support would be invaluable.[36]

The overseers offered to publish the pamphlet at Yearly Meeting's expense, but Woolman gratefully declined and paid for the printing himself. He thought Quaker slaveowners would not want the cost to be paid from the Meeting's general funds to which they contributed, and he anticipated that people would value, and hence take more seriously, a text they purchased themselves. Woolman believed that a privately published pamphlet approved by the Meeting would have a larger, more attentive audience and be less provocative to those who were not open to its message. He made sure that some copies were bound separately from the essay's previously published first part, since frugal readers who already owned Part One would be more likely to purchase Part Two if it stood alone.[37]

The larger audience Woolman ambitiously hoped for is signaled in the subtitle of the second part, *Recommended to the Professors of Christianity of Every Denomination.* Part One had made the case that all Quakers were guilty; Part Two now argued that all Christian slaveholders who aimed to profit from the labors of others were responsible parties. The changed goal suggests how the abolitionist cause was evolving: Woolman had first wanted to convince all Quakers of their responsibility for slavery whether or not they owned slaves; now he wanted to enlist all nonslaveholding Christians in the antislavery movement developing within the Society of Friends.

Woolman's opening appeal for universal love to all who professed faith in Christ aimed beyond sectarian bounds. With a conventional warning against idolatry, he reminded his readers that they all were Christians, whatever their sectarian differences.

> The apostles and primitive Christians did not censure all the Gentiles as wicked men (Rom. 2:14; Col. 3:2), but as they were favoured with a gift to discern things more clearly respecting the worship of the true God, they with much firmness declared against the worshiping of idols and with true patience endured many sufferings on that account.

Great numbers of faithful Protestants have contended for the Truth in opposition to papal errors and with true fortitude laid down their lives in the conflict, without saying that no man was saved who made profession of that religion.

Although in principle Woolman might have included Catholics, as an eighteenth-century Briton he was apparently incapable of the gesture; it was easier for him to extend universal love to non-Christians.[38]

He explains in a softer tone that there is no moral right for a Christian to own slaves for the purpose of realizing economic gain from their labor; the fact that so many Christians kept slaves does not make it right, "for as justice remains to be justice, so many people of reputation in the world joining with wrong things do not excuse others in joining with them nor make the consequence of their proceedings less dreadful in the final issue than it would be otherwise." The long tradition of slave keeping among Christians is no reason for the evil to endure: "Where unrighteousness is justified from one age to another, it is like dark matter gathering into clouds over us." Only weakness keeps those who know slavery is wrong from speaking out against tradition and against the self-interested practices of those around them. Christians endure whatever suffering comes from testifying to Truth.[39]

Yet again Woolman drew on the Old Testament prophetic tradition to explain himself and to encourage other Christians to renounce slavery. The prophets had made it clear that when Truth warranted it, God commanded his people to act contrary to their economic interest. He cites, as he does so often, God's message to Jeremiah: "'Do not be afraid of them, for I am with you to protect you'" (Jeremiah 1:8). "'Speak to them all the words that I command you; do not hold back a word. It may be that they will listen, all of them, and will turn from their evil way, that I may change my mind about the disaster that I intend to bring on them because of their evil doings'" (Jeremiah 26:2–3). Ezekiel heard the same thing: "'And you, O mortal, do not be afraid of them, and do not be afraid of their words, though briers and thorns surround you and you live among scorpions; do not be afraid of their words, and do not be dismayed at the looks, for they are a rebellious house. You shall speak my words to them, whether they hear or refuse to hear; for they are a rebellious house'" (Ezekiel 2:6–7).

This was Woolman's charge, and the message he delivered: stand up for your beliefs, for what you know in your heart is right; love universally and purely. Tell the world that slavery is wrong. People of African descent are humans, were not put on earth to serve white men, and need guardianship no more frequently than those of other races. Masters who mean well are responsible for educating their slaves in religion and literacy and then setting them free. The slave trade is not only morally unjustifiable but detrimental to the economic prosperity of the nations that ply it.[40]

Slaves who came to American shores as prisoners—that is, convicts—were still a threat, but "the innocent children ought not to be made slaves because their parents sinned." Jeremiah and Ezekiel renounce holding the child responsible for the crimes of the parent. "It is the one who sins who will die," as Woolman explains Ezekiel; "a son is not to suffer because of the father's sins, nor a father because of the sins of his son. A good man will be rewarded for doing good, and an evil man will suffer for the evil he does." Equally, slavery could not be justified by a parent's desire to provide economic security for his offspring. This would be to teach the children sinful behavior and leave them with inadequate moral instruction as well as the blood of slaves on their hands.[41]

Woolman addresses each of the biblical passages that Christians usually cited to justify slavery, explaining what he believed are misunderstandings and faulty reasoning. He makes it clear that the slavery found in the Old Testament is morally unjustifiable on Christian terms: "It appears that the great men amongst the Jews were fully resolved to have slaves, even of their own brethren. Jer. 34. Notwithstanding the promises and threatenings of the Lord." Furthermore, there is no moral justification for enslaving strangers of different faiths or of no religion: "The mind, when moved by a principle of true love, may feel a warmth of gratitude to the universal Father and a lively sympathy with those nations where divine light has been less manifest."[42]

Christians have a responsibility to share the gospel with those ignorant of the word but no right to kidnap gentiles for profit, a cruel practice showing "narrow self-love." Enslavement degrades the slaves in their masters' eyes, creating a class of people deemed sub-human and treated as such in a circular logic passed down through generations. Overworking the slaves and acting violently toward them in turn make them violent and thus a social threat. The slaves of greedy masters are chronically exhausted, dirty, hungry, and poorly clothed and housed; they are denied literacy and knowledge of God. The owners' desire for profit trumps all humanitarian impulses and guides all decisions. Families are sundered—husbands kept from wives and fathers from children—only encouraging licentiousness and denying children loving parental care.[43]

The illogic of race has poisoned slavery, according to Woolman, "and where false ideas are twisted into our minds, it is with difficulty we get fairly disentangled." People become fixed in error as in truth, and the linkage of blackness with slavery and whiteness with liberty is a clear and vicious example: "The colour of a man avails nothing in matters of right and equity." Again, it is self-love, arrogance, and greed that cause bigotry. If Christians chose a "plain, simple way of living," if they renounced "superfine clothes, silks, and linens," the consumption of "delicious foods," and residence in "stately buildings," they would have no need for slaves.[44]

Americans who live in luxury, Woolman thought, had much in common with the ancient Picts who once inhabited Scotland. The Picts had themselves tattooed from head to toe, a painful, bloody procedure, and, with their vanity thus indulged and indeed amplified by body art, went naked in a cold climate so they could admire themselves and arouse the envy of others. Not surprisingly, their culture was now extinct. The artifacts of modern life are no more sensible than the Picts' tattoos, according to Woolman. The price of self-indulgence was high when the culture required a pumped-up economy to feed the consumers' vanity.[45]

Then Woolman addresses himself to the brutalities of the slave trade and, indeed, all international commerce. Christians who participate in the slave traffic are perpetrating violence and fostering the barbarity of others. They are just as bad as, and sometimes worse than, the Catholics who persecuted Protestants in France during the sixteenth century. Here he cites John Foxe's *Book of Martyrs*, describing what happened when "great numbers of people fled to the wilderness, amongst whom were ancient people, women great with child, and others with babes in their arms, who endured calamities grievous to relate; and in the end some perished with hunger, and many were destroyed by fire and sword."[46]

This was part of Foxe's account of atrocities committed against French Protestants in 1545, when French troops brutally enforced a decree against the Provençal village of Mérindol for heresy. Soldiers incinerated hundreds of women and children in the village church; militia trapped two dozen women and children in a cave, sealed its mouth, and set a fire that filled the cave with smoke and suffocated all inside; and random mass arrests greatly exceeding the authority of the warrants were made of men throughout the region, along with summary executions. More than six hundred peasants were imprisoned in conditions that led to the deaths of about two hundred of them. Altogether, about two thousand people, most of them women and children, died, and an unspecified number of captives were sold into slavery.[47]

Woolman avoided details he thought "too grievous to relate": elderly people dragged through the streets until dead; a man hung by the armpits while pincers tore flesh from his body; a boy burned at the stake until blistered and scorched and then snatched from the flames while still alive; women tortured with hot irons, raped, and tormented by the sight and sounds of their starving babies. But he equated them with the details of Africans kidnapped and bound hand and foot in chains, women raped, their babies snatched from their arms, and other horrors of the Middle Passage. His reference to the notorious French actions against Protestants was a canny move in the circumstances, given New Jersey's and Pennsylvania's Francophobia during the French and Indian War and the traditional English anti-Catholic bigotry.[48]

His point was that Anglo-American Christians had no better excuse for brutalizing Africans because of their race than Saul, Herod, or French Catholics had had for tormenting people because of their faith.

Many who are parties in this trade by keeping slaves with views of self-interest, were they to go as soldiers in one of these inland expeditions to catch slaves, they must necessarily grow dissatisfied with such employ or cease to profess their religious principles. And though the first and most striking part of the scene is done at a great distance and by other hands, yet every one who is aquainted with the circumstances, and notwithstanding joins in it for the sake of gain only, must in the nature of things be chargeable with the others.

Those who did not oppose slavery were "present as spectators," however far from the actual scenes of torment. Everyone was responsible for the wars that the slave trade had kindled to flames. Think of slaves' children when you care for yours, Woolman pleaded: "Our children breaking a bone, getting so bruised that a leg or an arm must be taken off, lost for a few hours, so that we despair of their being found again, a friend hurt so that he dieth in a day or two—these move us with grief." Such was the imagination we must bring to the suffering of slaves; such was the sympathy that Christians must have for those innocent people torn from their families and homes.[49]

Masters who claim that slaves born in America are not victims of the slave trade are wrong, according to Woolman. This simply extends an injustice across generations, making it still more horrific: "The upright in heart cannot succeed the wicked in their wickedness, nor is it consonant to the life they live to hold fast an advantage unjustly gained." An estate built on the labor of slaves is theft, and its wealthy master owes much to those who have worked for its creation, growth, and preservation. The innocent are due liberty, and workers should earn the product of their labors.

He that has a servant made so wrongfully, and knows it to be so, when he treats him otherwise than a free man, when he reaps the benefit of his labour without paying him such wages as are reasonably due to free men for the like service (clothes excepted), these things, tho' done in calmness without any show of disorder, do yet deprave the mind in like manner and with as great certainty as prevailing cold congeals water.

(Woolman the tailor thought to deduct the cost of their clothes from the wages due them.)[50]

Woolman suggests no alternative Christian path. There is only one way to "Perfect Goodness," and it dictates a change of course: "Negroes are our fellow creatures and their present condition amongst us requires our serious consideration." He implores his readers to recall the Sermon on the Mount: the haughty shall be humbled; the meek shall inherit the earth. Masters should follow the "God of love," who is both "gracious" and "mighty." He cares for his "smallest creatures" and for all humanity. Whether one looked to the Bible, like Woolman, or to the Enlightenment's expansive notions of "sympathy," the message was essentially the same: with an introspective sense of self, imagine your way into the experience of others, share their pain, and act rightly in recognition of the rights of others and what is morally right.[51]

I N 1763 the same impulse to extend his ministry beyond the Society of Friends led Woolman to the Pennsylvania wilderness and to meet with Indians. During his last journey to the South two years earlier, Woolman had met some Delaware Indians who hailed from Wyalusing, a village about two hundred miles northwest of Philadelphia on the east branch of the Susquehanna River, not far from the New York border, and talked with them through an interpreter. He was impressed: "I believed some of them were measurably acquainted with that divine power which subjects the rough and froward will of the creature; and at times I felt inward drawing toward a visit to that place, of which I told none except my dear wife until it came to some ripeness."[52]

Woolman had kept Wyalusing in mind for more than two years, but the continuing hostility with the French and Indians had made it difficult to go there. The European nations had finally agreed to peace terms in February 1763, with Great Britain victorious over the French and their Indian allies, but the Treaty of Paris did not bring peace to the American frontier. After only a few months during which Indians contemplated the consequences of defeat for their French allies, the wilderness was once again set ablaze in Pontiac's War, an uprising of Indian tribes against the British led by the Ottawa chief Pontiac. Woolman knew that tensions remained high and that sporadic violence continued. But he secured the endorsement of his Monthly and Quarterly Meetings for the trip and waited for an opportune time, which presented itself in June.[53]

Then Woolman began to have second thoughts, born, he decided, of weakness and fear: "After I had given up to go, the thoughts of the journey were often attended with an unusual sadness, in which times my heart was frequently turned to the Lord with inward breathings for his heavenly support, that I might not fail to follow him wheresoever he might lead me." He knew that some of Christ's apostles "suffered death by cruel men." The thought that "whatever befalls men while they live in pure obedience to God, as it certainly works for their good, so it may not be considered an evil as it relates to them," gave him some inner peace but did not entirely erase from his mind the stories of recent torments inflicted by Indians on settlers, and he knew that Indians still seethed with anger at the injustices perpetrated against them.[54]

June 6, 1763, the day before Woolman was to leave on his trip, in the Sunday afternoon Meeting, "my heart being enlarged in love, I was led to speak on the care and protection of the Lord over his people and to make mention of that passage where a band of Assyrians, endeavouring to take captive the prophet, were disappointed, and how the Psalmist said, 'The angel of the Lord encampeth round about them that fear him'" (Psalm 34:7). He identified with the prophet and saw a parallel between the Indians of the forest and the Assyrians. He apparently did not doubt their violence or expect that they would welcome him, and he was incapable of defending himself (as a pacifist he wouldn't even try) and so had to trust to heaven's protection. That night he went to bed early and fell asleep quickly, only to be awakened by a man calling at his door. The messenger may have been Daniel Jones, a Mount Holly innkeeper who was not a Quaker but was the brother of one, Rebecca Jones, a good friend of Woolman's.[55]

He dressed quickly and followed the man back to the Three Tuns Tavern, where his old Quaker friends Israel and John Pemberton were waiting. They had ridden quickly to share news that had just reached Philadelphia from Pittsburgh: Indians had scalped and killed settlers in "divers places" on the frontier. In his *Journal*, Woolman explains that "some elderly Friends in Philadelphia, knowing the time of my expecting to set off, had conferred together and thought good to inform me of these things before I left home that I might consider them and proceed as I believed best." The news rattled him, but he returned home and slipped into bed without waking his wife. "My heart was turned to the Lord for his heavenly instruction," Woolman writes, "and it was a humbling time to me." The next morning, when he told his wife the news, she was "deeply concerned," but he nonetheless decided that it was his "duty" to go, following the "pure spirit of Truth" on the journey. He expected to die serving the Lord, but found some peace in resignation, took leave of family and friends in what apparently was a heartrending departure, and rode off with the Pembertons.[56]

Woolman's first stop was Burlington, where there was Monthly Meeting that day. The next morning brought another round of goodbyes, and then the three men led their horses onto a ferry and crossed the Delaware River to Bristol. From there they rode to Philadelphia, where Woolman spent the night in the home of Israel Pemberton; the next morning John Pemberton accompanied Woolman to the Bucks County home of Samuel Foulke, a Quaker and prominent political figure two years younger than Woolman, who was one of the few Quakers still serving in the Pennsylvania Assembly; he also served as the clerk of Richland Monthly Meeting.[57]

Foulke supported Woolman's journey, and two other Quakers—Benjamin Parvin (1727–?), a surveyor and coroner in Berks County, and William Lightfoot (1731–97), a member of Uwchlan Monthly Meeting and Parvin's cousin—turned up too, intending to go with him to Wyalusing. Woolman tried to dissuade Pemberton, Lightfoot, and Parvin from undertaking the full journey with him, but they all left Foulke's together.

In his *Journal*, Woolman mentions in passing that arriving at Foulke's home, "I met the before-mentioned Indians, and we were glad to see each other." These were the same Indians he had met two years previously, the very ones who inspired his trip. He does not say how this meeting was arranged, but the coordination suggests advanced planning by others. The Indians accompanied Woolman and the other Quakers when they left Foulke's; they were still with him after two of his three Quaker companions returned home before the party reached Wyalusing. They undoubtedly served as guides, translators, and shields, who by their very presence protected the white men from becoming the victims of indiscriminate retaliation for past wrongs and ongoing offenses committed by others of their race.[58]

Two days later Woolman wrote to his wife from Bethlehem, by which time the men had agreed that Pemberton would leave the following morning and Lightfoot would go the additional twenty miles to Fort Allen. But Parvin felt called to accompany Woolman the rest of the way: "And as to Benjamin, his mind at present seems so engaged that he shews no inclination to leave me," Woolman wrote to Sarah. "When I parted with them," Lightfoot wrote to Sarah, "they seemed well and cheerful."[59]

The most difficult part of the trip lay ahead. Woolman recalled for his *Journal* that after they left the English settlements, they had

only a narrow path, which in many places is much grown up with bushes and interrupted by abundance of trees lying across it, which together with the mountains, swamps, and rough stones, it is a difficult road to travel, and the more so for that rattlesnakes abound there, of which we killed four   that people who have never been in such places have but an imperfect idea of them. But I was not only taught patience but also made thankful to God, who thus led me about and instructed me that I might have a quick and lively feeling of the afflictions of my fellow creatures whose situation in life is difficult.[60]

Continuing northwest from Fort Allen, Woolman, Parvin, and the unmentioned Indians crossed paths with a trader returning from Wyalusing. Their conversation led Woolman to ruminate on the sale of rum to Indians, which he considered "a great evil." From Bethlehem, he had written to his wife:

I am humbly thankful to the Lord that my mind is so supported in a trust of Him that I go cheerfully on my journey and at present apprehend that I have nothing in my way to fear but a spirit of disobedience which I trust through divine help I may be delivered from . . . First, they being thereby deprived of the use of their reason and their spirits violently agitated, quarrels often arise which end in mischief, and the bitterness and resentments occasioned hereby are frequently of long continuance. Again, their skins and furs, gotten through much fatigue and hard travels in hunting, with which they intended to buy clothing, these when they begin to be intoxicated they often sell at a low rate for more rum; and afterward when they suffer for want of the necessaries of life, [they] are angry with those who for the sake of gain took the advantage of their weakness.

This story of overworked Indians seduced by harmful trade goods was another variation on Woolman's indictment of market relations. Greedy traders sold the Indians rum, thus extending the chain of violence that reached from the slave-based sugar plantations to frontier warfare: "To sell that to people which we know does them harm and which often works their ruin, for the sake of gain, manifests a hardened and corrupt heart and is an evil which demands the care of all true lovers of virtue to suppress."[61] The same greedy hand of commerce struck down the settlers, who had encroached on Indian lands, venturing

to the outside of a colony that they may live more independent on such who are wealthy, who often set high rents on their land, being renewedly confirmed in a belief that if all our inhabitants lived according to sound wisdom, labouring to promote universal love and righteousness, and ceased from every inordinate desire after wealth and from all customs which are tinctured with luxury, the way would be easy for our inhabitants, though much more numerous than at present, to live comfortably on honest employments, without having that temptation they are often under of being drawn into schemes to make settlements on lands which have not been purchased of the Indians, or of applying to that wicked practice of selling rum to them.

Landlords along the seaboard, then, many of whom were Quakers, shared the guilt of slavery and the responsibility for violence on the frontier even if they did not own slaves or participate directly in the slave trade, or sold no rum to Indians, or endorsed fair trading for Indian land. The real blame lay at the feet of comfortable colonists who had never set foot west of the Schuylkill River. Those who blamed the settlers for provoking violence had blood on their own hands, for they benefited from an economy that drove impoverished immigrants into a region where they had little recourse but to seize land from and sell rum to the Indians.[62]

Parvin and Woolman left Fort Allen with their Indian guides on June 10. They used canoes to cross an upper branch of the Delaware called the Great Lehigh, traded some biscuits for deer meat with an Indian they met on the trail, and talked with several Indian men and women who were leaving the environs of Wyalusing with a cow, a horse, and the rest of their worldly possessions. Woolman believed they made a good impression on the Indians, which he found encouraging, but the terrain ahead was as daunting as the possibility of a hostile reception in the forest. They had thus far ridden their horses over cleared land and rolling hills but now faced a rugged, steep, rocky, forested landscape.

> So going on we pitched our tent near the banks of the same river, having laboured hard in crossing some of those mountains called the Blue Ridge. And by the roughness of the stones and the cavities between them and the steepness of the hills, it appeared dangerous, but we were preserved in safety, through the kindness of him whose works in those mountainous deserts appeared awful, toward whom my heart was turned during this day's travel.[63]

As the trees blocked the sun and the forward movement slowed, he experienced the darkness as grim. His fear grew in the waning light, a deprivation he experienced spiritually as much as or more than he did physically. As he rode and sometimes walked the faltering horse, Woolman considered his chain of sympathy and blame; this led him to contemplate the numerous red marks he saw carved on large trees along the trail, symbols used by Indian warriors to communicate with one another. Many of these Indians had journeyed far under harsh conditions to protect their families; some had died, in battle or from exposure or disease, shortly after leaving the marks that recorded their place in the "histories" told by the trees. Their fatiguing lives were yet another example of the way harshness of livelihood led to hardness of spirit and in turn to violence and hatred among warring nations. Camping in the cold, damp forests brought Woolman some peace in the knowledge that his fate was in God's hands and that he traveled with an important message: "During these meditations the desire to cherish the spirit of love and peace amongst these people arose very fresh in me."[64]

On their first night sleeping in the woods, "being wet with traveling in the rain, the ground and our tent wet, and the bushes wet which we purposed [to] lay under our blankets, all looked discouraging." On June 11 they met up with a Moravian missionary and his Indian translator who were headed to the same place and continued on with them. (The Moravian was a lay, not an ordained, minister, whose message emphasized Christian unity, personal piety, and singing hymns.) Woolman thought about the message he had to give: "Love was the first motion, and then a concern arose to spend some time with the Indians, that I might feel and understand their life and the spirit they live in, if haply I might receive some instruction from them, or they be in any degree helped forward by my following the leadings of Truth amongst them." He believed God had chosen the difficult destination and traveling conditions, and therefore they were signs of divine pleasure: "When by reason of much wet weather traveling was more difficult than usual at that season, I looked upon it as a more favourable opportunity to season my mind and bring me into a nearer sympathy with them."[65]

The Indians had once lived contentedly, Woolman believed. Those by the sea had fished waters teeming with creatures; in the mountains they had hunted prolific game. There had been berries and roots to eat and good soil to till on the forests' edges; the rivers had allowed them transportation over long distances. Now, though, many had lost their land by the colonists' sharp dealings with them or had been driven off by superior force. Life was harsh, resources were sparse and scattered, and the labor required to feed a family had increased mightily. As white settlers pressed westward, they were driving tribes closer together, and violence ensued. Where subsistence had once been easy, survival was no longer assured.

> And a weighty and heavenly care came over my mind, and love filled my heart toward all mankind, in which I felt a strong engagement that we might be obedient to the Lord while in tender mercies he is yet calling to us, and so attend to pure universal righteousness as to give no just cause of offense to the Gentiles, who do not profess Christianity, whether the blacks from Africa or the native inhabitants of this continent.[66]

Woolman searched his heart for evidence of guilt in the wars that racked Africa and North America. Was he complicit in them? He resolved to be more attentive in the future to the "pure Truth and live and walk in the plainness and simplicity of a sincere follower of Christ." He would weed out the "seeds" that grew into oppressions, and he would deliver the message to those who shared his faith.[67]

It was still raining on June 12; the sun broke through the treetops on June 13, and they arrived at the Indian settlement of Wyoming. The atmosphere there was tense. An Indian runner had arrived the previous night with two English scalps in hand and news that war with the English had resumed. Another Indian drew a hatchet from his cloak as he approached Woolman, who explained, first by himself and then through an interpreter, the purpose of his visit. The conversation disarmed the man, who Woolman came to believe had meant only to defend himself, not to attack. Nonetheless, the news and the personal experience intensified Woolman's fears.

> I thought that to all outward appearance it was dangerous traveling at this time, and was after a hard day's journey brought into a painful exercise at night, in which I had to trace back and feel over the steps I had taken from my first moving in the visit. And though I had to bewail some weak-

ness which at times had attended me, yet I could not find that I had ever given way to a willful disobedience. And then as I believed I had under a sense of duty come thus far, I was now earnest in spirit beseeching the Lord to show me what I ought to do.

Woolman spent a restless night considering whether to persist or go home. Resolution came in the dark, and he "again strengthened to commit my life and all things relating thereto into his heavenly hands; and getting a little sleep toward day, when morning came we arose."[68]

On June 14, Woolman tried to visit "all the Indians hereabouts." To his relief, but also to his concern, only "some of them appeared kind and friendly." The party dined with Jacob January and his family, who were about to travel upriver to escape the dangers of the renewed war. Woolman's party swam their horses across the Lackawanna River and set up a tent in a light rain. There he "lay down in a humble, bowed frame of mind and had a comfortable night's lodging." The next morning they rode until afternoon, when it began to storm, which led them to camp for the night. On June 16 their progress was slowed by trees that had fallen in the storm's heavy winds. "I had this day often to consider myself as a sojourner in this world," Woolman wrote in his *Journal*, "and a belief in the all-sufficiency of God to support his people in their pilgrimage felt comfortable to me, and I was industriously employed to get to a state of perfect resignation."

They met up with Job Chilaway, an Indian from Wyalusing who spoke English and who told them that three warriors bent on fighting the whites had recently passed. Woolman felt weak from the exertion and rough weather, "and the news of these warriors being on their march so near us, and not knowing whether we might not fall in with them, it was a fresh trial of my faith . . . And my cries for help were put up to the Lord, who in great mercy gave me a resigned heart, in which I found quietness."[69]

They reached Wyalusing on the afternoon of June 17. It was, Woolman reported, a town of about forty split-plank houses approximately eighteen by thirty feet set closely together on the east bank of the Susquehanna. The first Indian Woolman met there was a woman who had in her arms, according to different drafts of his *Journal*, either a "babe" or a "bable." "Bible" would make sense given that the woman extended a greeting to the Quaker and Moravian missionaries, if she suspected that was what they were. Perhaps it was obvious to her that the one dressed in white was a man of God. The editorial committee resolved the discrepancy between the two drafts with "bible" in the *Journal*'s first edition; the modern editor chose "babe." Woolman may have conflated "Bible" and "babe"; "Babel" and "babble" are other variations that neither editor chose, though the confusion of strange tongues and totemic towers in the Indian village could have impressed the biblically steeped Quaker with an image of Babylonian idol worshipers.[70]

Woolman and his Indian interpreter then sat down on a log "in a deep inward stillness," acording to the *Journal*. As Woolman meditated on the spirit within, the "poor" Indian woman sat down with them: "Great awefulness coming over us, we rejoiced in a sense of God's love manifested to our poor souls." This awe, joyfully achieved, reduced differences of race, gender, and standard of living to insignificance; the three were spiritually equal.[71]

It had been a stressful journey for Woolman, with a hatchet drawn on him and with news of hostile warriors nearby and settlers' scalps being waved in the air. As night fell, he was still agitated, making it hard for him to find calm in the spirit of his prophecy. As the others slept, he struggled to recover his inner peace, and he began to doubt his motives for persevering in the face of danger. It occurred to him that he was possibly becoming proud of his courage; he may have had a previously undetected ambition for people to think of him as brave. He searched his soul, realizing that such impure motives as these would require him to abandon the mission. But he worked through his inner conflicts over the course of a restless first night at Wyalusing and was "again strengthened to commit my life and all things relating thereto into his heavenly hands; and getting a little sleep toward day, when morning came we arose."[72]

On June 18, Woolman tried to smooth any potential conflict that might occur between the Quakers and the Moravian missionary, whom he sought to reassure: "I found liberty in my heart to speak to the Moravian and told him of the care I felt on my mind for the good of these people, and that I believed no ill effects would follow it if I sometimes spake in their meetings when love engaged me thereto . . . whereupon he expressed his good will toward my speaking at any time all that I found in my heart to say." Near evening, when the Indians gathered to listen to the white men, Woolman asked an interpreter not to translate word for word, praying instead for inspiration. After he finished, John Papunhank—a Mahican who was a spiritual leader among the Delawares, a Christian convert, and a voice for peace—explained to the interpreter, "I love to feel where words come from." Without comprehending Woolman's English, he had grasped its spirit and felt the preverbal source of pure wisdom.[73]

Papunhank was himself considered a prophet, whose visions had brought the Delaware, Munsee, Nanticoke, and Conoy Indians together at Wyalusing under the protection of the Pennsylvania government. He had past associations with the Moravians and Quakers and had been wounded in his efforts to broker peace among the Indians. His followers did not fight in Pontiac's War, and they had informed the colonists about the movements of hostile warriors. It is unclear whether Woolman knew that Papunhank was a prophet or, if he did, whether he took the Indian's prophecy seriously.[74]

On the morning of June 19, Woolman again preached to the Indians: "I spake to them awhile by interpreters, but none of them being perfect in the work," communication was minimal. Woolman asked them to be quiet and, "feeling the current of love run strong, told the interpreters that I believed some of the people would understand me, and so proceeded, in which exercise I believe the Holy Ghost wrought on some hearts to edification, where all the words were not understood." Woolman believed that he had reached people who did not comprehend his words, that even the interpreters were "spirited up" by the experience, and that they translated the substance of his remarks for their own edification. That evening, after the meeting had broken up and people were settling in for the night, Woolman witnessed Papunhank speaking to fellow Indians in a "harmonious voice" and asked an interpreter what he was saying: "He was expressing his thankfulness to God for the favours he had received that day, and prayed that he would continue to favour him with that same which he had experienced in that meeting."[75]

Woolman sat quietly through two meetings on June 20. The next morning, he reports in his *Journal* that in them his "heart was enlarged in pure love amongst them, and in short plain sentences [I] expressed several things that rested upon me, which one of the interpreters gave the people pretty readily, after which the meeting ended in supplication."

After five days Woolman finally felt "at liberty" to go home; he believed he had delivered the message God had sent with him. He took care to part amicably both with the Indians who had attended his meetings and with those who had not. He and Parvin had expected two Indians to go back with them as guides but discovered that a large contingent was packed to carry furs to Bethlehem for trading. Woolman reasoned that it was "the troubles westward, and the difficulty for Indians to pass through our frontier" that led so many of them to travel with the white men. The Indians insisted that the two Quakers travel by canoe, for although the creeks were swollen by heavy rains, and dangerous, that was safer for them than walking on horseback; meanwhile Indians more experienced in wilderness travel brought their horses overland. That evening the party camped together and ate a deer shot by an Indian hunter. They reached Wyoming by nightfall on June 22; the next day fourteen of them made it halfway to Fort Allen and again slept on the ground; Woolman was weary at day's end and came down with a cold during the night.[76]

On June 24, an exhausting day in which they forded the west branch of the Delaware River three times to avoid the steepest climbs through the Blue Ridge, they passed Fort Allen and again slept in the woods. On June 25 they reached Bethlehem, where the Quakers took leave of the Indians. The next day Parvin and Woolman arrived at Richland, Bucks County, and parted. Woolman reached home on June 27, after three weeks away, and found his family "middling well." Sarah, Mary, and his friends were joyful that he had returned safely, but he tried to restrain himself from celebrating a safe end to his journey. "I was careful," he writes in his

Journal, "lest I should admit any degree of selfishness in being glad overmuch, and laboured to improve by those trials in such a manner as my gracious Father and Protector intends for me."[77]

After the trip Woolman was a potential source of information about the Indians' intentions, but his friend John Pemberton, who interviewed him for this purpose, got precious little useful intelligence. Woolman had steered clear of conversations with the Delawares about frontier troubles because that was not his concern and he did not want them to suspect him of being a spy. Nor did he want to be questioned on subjects about which he was ignorant or be in the position of "casting some blame on the English." He had also been "cautious of questioning the Indians for prudential reasons," Pemberton wrote; "he apprehended it might beget some jealousies in the minds of some." According to Pemberton, Woolman reported that "in every place where they understood his errand [the Indians] rejoiced and [were] very kind, and he did not perceive in any an evil disposition towards the English."[78]

L ATER in 1763, Woolman again had occasion to extend his ministry outside the Society of Friends. This time it was a juggling and magic show that aroused his spiritual concern for humanity. The magician had posted a broadside advertising "many wonderful operations" that he would perform at a Mount Holly tavern. (It may have been the Three Tuns, just down Mill Street from Woolman's shop, but there were also two other taverns in town at that time.) He saw the advertisement only the day after the show had occurred, when he heard that "this man at the time appointed did by sleight of hand sundry things which to those gathered appeared strange"; the performance was to be repeated at sunset to meet popular demand, and Woolman felt "an exercise on that account."[79]

He went to the tavern and informed the tavern keeper that he had an "inclination" to spend part of the evening there, which the man indulged. So Woolman sat by the door and warned spectators of the sinful nature of such performances. The seats filled, but he was undeterred, engaging arrivals in conversation meant to "convince them that thus assembling to see those tricks or sleights-of-hand, and bestowing their money to support men who in that capacity were of no use in the world, was contrary to the nature of the Christian religion." One man argued with him but eventually "gave up the point." Woolman continued fruitlessly for about an hour before "feeling my mind easy" and going home. In believing that supporting performers in a useless profession was a sin, Woolman reflected traditional Quaker values, but it is also likely that magic and juggling especially troubled him, even when people knew that the sleight of hand was an illusion and not a manifestation of supernatural, unnatural, or frivolous toying with the universe.[80]

10

Travels

1764–69

A CCORDING to William James, the saint is fallible, irresponsive to "reason," and impractical, a fool to some, an irritant to many, selfish, prudish, gullible, morbid, and scrupulous to excess. In his positive and negative traits, John Woolman was a model of such an ideal type of saint. He had always been exceptional, but he grew increasingly eccentric. Religion burned for him as an "acute fever" rather than as the "dull habit" that it was for most believers. He was a "genius," according to James, with spiritual capacities that surpassed those of others around him, the religious equivalent of a Mozart, Michelangelo, Newton, or Shakespeare.

> Invariably they have been creatures of exalted emotional sensibility. Often they have led a discordant inner life, and had melancholy during a part of their career. They have known no measure, been liable to obsessions and fixed ideas; and frequently they have fallen into trances, heard voices, seen visions, and presented all sorts of peculiarities which are ordinarily classed as pathological.[1]

James admired Woolman's courage in the face of death, his detachment from the material world, his "abandonment of self-responsibility"—that is, his ability to surrender to the will of God, overcome personal interests, and enjoy freedom from "inner friction and nervous waste." Having only the *Journal* and no contextual sources, James perceived in Woolman an absence of internal conflict; although he got much about Woolman right, he could not understand him fully. In fact, as we have seen, Woolman feared death and experienced internal conflict throughout his life; his spiritual triumphs were achieved despite fears and inner turmoil.[2]

Saints, as James describes them, harbor positive "spiritual emotions" at the center of their personalities. They live without selfish interests, their spiritual convictions transcend the intellectual, and they *know* God in a mystical sense. This description seems apt for Woolman. He experienced unusual elation and freedom, but also depths of despair and increasing melancholy. His emotional core continued to shift away from the ego-centered life that most humans live. He moved toward total surrender, a state that enabled him to respond positively to external demands that the rest of humanity might reflexively reject. As James put it, "where others excuse ourselves on ego-centered grounds—as too tired, cold, otherwise engaged, uninterested, sick, in pain, or whatever—the saint without conflict or hesitation responds affirmatively."[3]

Saints can seem irresponsible, James knew; to them, "father and mother, sisters, brothers, and friends are felt as interfering distractions; for sensitiveness and narrowness, when they occur together, as they often do, require above all things a simplified world to dwell in." Attachments to people as well as to things distract the saint from his devotion to God. Saints are also unsociable, unwilling to play, imbibe, relax, or even enjoy lighthearted company. That was Woolman. Others pay a high price for associating with them. That was Woolman too.[4]

"The saints are authors, *auctores*, increasers of goodness," James writes, not only accepting of the sacredness of all creatures but acting on this belief. They are extravagantly tender, good, and kind, as well as generally pacific and forgiving. They tend to see the best and the worst in others, even where others do not see it in themselves. The world is better for the saints' presence, but humanity never lives up to the example.

Whoever possesses strongly this sense comes naturally to think that the smallest details of this world derive infinite significance from their relation to an unseen divine order. The thought of this order yields him a superior denomination of happiness, and a steadfastness of soul with which no other can compare. In social relations his serviceability is exemplary; he abounds in impulses to help. His help is inward as well as outward, for his sympathy reaches souls as well as bodies, and kindles unsuspected faculties therein. Instead of placing happiness where common men place it, in comfort, he places it in a higher kind of inner excitement, which converts discomforts into sources of cheer and annuls unhappiness. So he turns his back upon no duty, however thankless; and when we are in need of assistance, we can count upon the saint lending his hand with more certainty than we can count upon any other person.[5]

James was brilliantly insightful about this personality type, and his typology did not reduce saintliness to a psychological state. He saw no conflict between religious belief and a recognition of the characteristics that saints share. There is therefore a real analytical gain to be made in viewing Woolman through James's prism. Also, Woolman was inspired by the saints who came before him, self-consciously copying their approaches to spirit and nature, sharing their ambitions and mystical states. When he dreamed, and when he wrote about his dreams, Woolman knew about the dreamers who had come before him. Consider this example from his *Journal* one year after returning from Wyalusing:

> 26th day, 7th month, 1764. At night I dreamed I was abroad on a religious visit beyond the sea and had been out upward of two months, and that while I was out on the visit the people of the country where I was and those of a neighboring kingdom, having concerns together in affairs abroad had difference which arose so high that they began to fight; and both parties were preparing for a general war.

This nocturnal event was not a vision; Woolman reports on the locale, purpose, and duration of his "visit," and the repeats of "out" and "abroad" show the tentative, transitional state of a true dream, as well as the distance and foreignness.[6]

"I thought there was no sea between them, but only bounded by a line, and that the man who was chief amongst the other people lived within a day's journey of where I was," he continues. Woolman dreamed he was close to the border, in a liminal spot, the dream itself being a liminal state of consciousness. "Chief" and "kingdom" fuse Indians and empire in ways that were familiar.[7]

The possibility that Woolman had Chief Pontiac on his mind is reinforced by his saying that he felt a "desire" in the dream "to go and speak with this chief man and try to prevail on him to stop fighting, that they might enquire more fully into the grounds of their disagreement and endeavour to accommodate their difference without shedding more blood." The "chief," it seems, had started the war; this was not to comment on his grievances but to say that it was he who needed to stop fighting and to him that a peacemaker must go. So Woolman sets off with a "pilot," an important figure in his dream world; it was the word he had used to describe his Indian guides to Wyalusing.

The two men travel "some time in the woods" before they come upon "other people" at work with guns close by. Woolman and his guide startle these laborers, who quickly recognize them as coming from the enemy's country. The woods and the visual recognition are consistent with Indians at war with white men, as is Woolman's labeling them "other people." Woolman holds up his hands in peace and goes forward to shake hands in greeting and explain the reason for his visit, but his pilot pulls a gun, shocking him; he would not have knowingly traveled in the company of an armed man. Fortunately, the "other people" respond to Woolman's peaceful gesture, and the guide disappears from the dream, perhaps captive or dead, of no more use or a counterproductive force.[8]

One of the workers offers to take Woolman to the chief, and this new pilot leads him southeast on a path through woods and swamps. The guide, in "broken English," encourages Woolman to speak his mind freely to the chief and shows him their common verbal greeting (unspecified in Woolman's account) but discourages him from shaking hands. Handshakes were indeed alien to Indian cultures before Europeans introduced the practice, so Woolman was dreaming good advice; the guide was correcting his earlier mistake in having approached strangers with an extended hand. The "chief man" is not a king, but he commands soldiers and heads local affairs. Eventually the two men find his house, which stands alone in a clearing and has a "good garden with green herbs before the door," where Woolman waits while the guide speaks with the chief.

> As I stood alone in the garden my mind was exercised on the affair I came upon, and presently my pilot returned, and passing by me said he had forgot to tell me that I had an invitation to dinner. Soon after him came the chief man, who having been told the cause of my coming looked on me with a friendly countenance, and as I was about to enter on the business I awoke.

In the dream, Woolman leads the first guide and is "foremost" when they enter the clearing, startling the armed laborers. The second pilot leads Woolman and offers more than geographical expertise, instructing Woolman in etiquette, translating for him, and introducing him—a successful strategy that elicits a dinner invitation and a "friendly countenance" from the chief.[9]

If the dream guide is the dreamer, then Woolman resolved internal conflict, overcame a lapse of judgment, and learned from his mistakes. He also carried a heavy burden of responsibility for leading the peace effort. Indeed, in real life this was the role he accepted in the antislavery cause and hoped he could bring to Anglo-Indian relations.

The dream account survives on a leaf of the same paper that Woolman used for the second draft of his *Journal.* He never integrated it into the *Journal,* but since he recalled and recorded it, we know it had some meaning to him, even if it did not belong in his spiritual autobiography. The crisis was evidently unresolved: "As I was about to enter on the business I awoke." After all, the trip and the connection with the chief were not the "business" he had started out on. But the dream expresses an expansion of Woolman's mission across the seas, the direction in which his unarticulated ambitions were taking him.

Woolman had this dream after his agitation about the juggler and apparently in the same year that he drafted *A Plea for the Poor*, a more aggressive, comprehensive work on social relations than he had previously attempted. He broke little new philosophical ground but addressed himself to a larger audience, writing more plainly and extending the implications of his prophecy. The logic was again that of a chain: small injustices lead to larger ones, and this is true in racial, labor, and class relations. (This is the pamphlet that most appealed to the Fabian Society a century later, when members read it as a Christian Socialist indictment of capitalist market relations.)

Wealth desired for its own sake obstructs the increase of virtue, and large possessions in the hands of selfish men have a bad tendency, for by their means too small a number of people are employed in things useful; and therefore they, or some of them, are necessitated to labour too hard, while others would want business to earn their bread were not employments invented which, having no real use, serve only to please the vain mind.[10]

Woolman now asks questions not just about the greed of individual landlords but about the social system that supports them. Has the world forgotten that "the Creator of the earth is the owner of it"? Woolman disputes the very notion of possession, asserts the obligations of stewardship, and describes subsistence through moderate labor almost, but not quite, as a right: "As he is kind and merciful, we as his creatures, while we live answerable to the design of our creation, we are so far entitled to a convenient subsistence that no man may justly deprive us of it." If Woolman had used the language of rights, which he did not, he would have been saying that moral rights to a just proportion of the fruits of the earth supersede any contractual right to possession of property.[11]

Fine garments and furniture are kindling for the fires of oppression, slavery, and war, greed the first cause of catastrophic social ills: "This is like a chain where the end of one link encloses the end of another. The rising up of a desire to attain wealth is the beginning." The inheritor of wealth is obliged to calculate the most socially effective way to dispose of it, but "to lay aside curious, costly attire, and use that only which is plain and serviceable, to cease from all superfluities and too much strong drink, are agreeable to the doctrines of our blessed Redeemer." The landlord who charges high rents to support vanities and the enlargement of his estate "puts the wheels of perfect brotherhood out of order."[12]

Each generation borrows the world anew. Encumbering the earth's resources and trying to control property from beyond the grave is to steal from those who come after us: "Are great labours performed to gain wealth for posterity? Are many supported with wages to furnish us with delicacies and luxuries? Are monies expended for colours to please the eye, which renders our garments less serviceable? Are garments of a curious texture purchased at a high rate, for the sake of their delicacy?" Ornamentation on apparel and furniture forges the first link of a chain that chokes the earth. Asceticism is a moral requirement. In a dramatic escalation of his prophetic mission, Woolman writes now for everyone and holds all to the standards he sets for himself.[13]

Woolman's moral philosophy pits heavenly law against human injustice. "We ought to obey God rather than men," he writes, echoing Peter in Acts 5:29: "We must obey God rather than any human authority." Slaves, servants, and hired laborers should always obey God: "As the pure principle of righteousness is the foundation whereon the pure in heart stand, so their proceedings are consistent herewith; and while they encourage to an upright performance of every reasonable duty on one hand, they guard on the other against servants actively complying with unrighteous commands."[14] This argument encourages resistance to injustice and implicitly rejects Paul in Romans 13:1: "Let every person be subject to the governing authorities; for there is no authority except from God, and those authorities that exist have been instituted by God. Therefore whoever resists authority resists what God has appointed, and those who resist will incur judgment."

To be sure, Woolman only implies his message that slaves might lawfully resist their bondage, that if slavery itself is "unrighteous," then the master-slave relationship is sinful and a slaveowner's commands have no moral authority. Nineteenth-century abolitionists were to draw out these implications explicitly in what they called a higher law argument, reasoning that God's law was higher than humankind's. So many unrighteous demands were made of slaves that if they followed Woolman's prophecy, they would resist the violence, the attempts to divide their families, the denial of adequate food, clothing, shelter, and education that were their right as God's children and would suffer the consequences as martyrs would.

Woolman copied out this *Plea for the Poor* in 1769, ensuring that at least one of the copies would survive him: "I could not be easy without entering it at large [in full], nearly as I had wrote it at first in an unbound book." He left no record of submitting it to the overseers of the Quaker press, and it was published only in 1793, thirty years after Woolman had written it and long after his death. Retitled *A Word of Remembrance and Caution to the Rich*, this is Woolman's most quoted pamphlet and generally acknowledged to be his best.[15]

In the plea, as in Woolman's other writings, educating children was a principal concern and a key to reform. Like Anthony Benezet, Woolman believed that everyone had a responsibility for educating children whatever their race, gender, religion, or social condition. For both men, teaching school was an important part of their ministries. Benezet's words on the subject could well be Woolman's:

> Although by engaging in the education of youth we should be deprived of some of those things so desirable to nature, which we might better enjoy and accumulate in the way of trade, and thereby look upon ourselves under affliction, yet may we not hope that it will be termed for righteousness' sake, and therefore should not we have thereat to rejoice, and be exceeding glad, and even leap for joy?[16]

Benezet and Woolman were exceptional teachers, known for their gentle handling of students in an age when non-Quaker schoolmasters often brutalized their pupils. One illustrative story about Benezet has it that two boys pilloried a mouse and left it on his desk with a note that read, "I stand here, my honest friends, for stealing cheese and candle-ends." If the goal was to provoke their teacher, the mischievous students failed. Benezet identified the culprits easily, complimented them before the class for their compassionate decision not to execute the mouse for his crimes, and set the animal free. Such was the philosophy that informed both men's teaching. (Though Benezet lived in Burlington for about a year in the mid-1760s, we know little more about their collaboration on abolition or teaching.)[17]

Woolman continued to teach intermittently during the 1760s, but we do not know how many children he taught. His general accounts show that he billed fourteen different men for tuition; Burlington Meeting's memorial implies that he tutored some without charge. During 1766 and 1767, Jabez Eldridge paid for two children's education and the paper they used and also provided his share of wood for heating the school. It appears that he paid seven shillings and a penny for each child, one of whom was a girl, but it is unclear for how many months each attended. A standard fee is not discernible in the accounts Woolman kept; some paid by the month, three months, or more at a time, and barter relationships also obscure costs. Woolman billed his brother Asher two pounds and nine shillings for teaching his daughter from February through May 1769, but only one pound, two shillings, and six pence for June through September of the same year, suggesting that she boarded with her uncle and aunt only in the winter and spring.[18]

In 1764, Woolman turned over his school account book (now lost) to his brother Asher to settle a debt between them: "4 mo 5 1764 to leaving the school book in which the employers were indebted to me with directions for them to pay thee which thou accepted as cash from me 08 00 00." The entry suggests that after this point Woolman no longer kept the school accounts separately. We know that Thomas Bispham paid in March 1766, 1767, and 1768 for the education of his children: the first year nine shillings and six pence for tuition and paper, in 1767 thirteen shillings and ten pence, and in 1768 another nine shillings and tuppence. We do not know how many children Bispham had in Woolman's school or why the cost of their supplies varied.[19]

It made sense to keep the school accounts in the general books because the transactions intertwined with Woolman's other business. He billed Aaron Barton in 1769, for example, for schooling, a spelling book, and a pair of breeches. Other transactions balanced the school accounts with hay, veal, and pasturing a cow. Bispham and Woolman also exchanged wood and apple trees in addition to their arrangement for Bispham's children. So Woolman traded for what his animals and orchard required and produced; for bleeding a man; tanning hides; making clothes; addressing a drainage problem; repairing the same window twice; painting a bedstead and bench; haymaking; selling stone; and buying needles, thread, cloth, hides, a looking glass, an ivory comb, and a copper kettle. All were part of the network of connections that kept his family clothed, housed, and fed.[20]

The account books suggest that Woolman relied on two or three texts for his teaching. He compiled his own spelling book or primer, which he prepared in three editions, the third one "enlarged" from the first two. He also purchased "J Griffiths books" and "Elizabeth Jacobs Epistles in quantity," the latter of which was standard fare for eighteenth-century Quaker teachers. We do not know if he sold these books, loaned them to students, or gave them away; indeed, we cannot be sure that he intended Griffith's work for his classes. In 1768 he bought a dozen copies of the 1757 London edition of Jacob's *Epistle* and six copies of John Griffith's *Some Brief Remarks on Sundry Important Subjects*, which had appeared in 1764. A year later he purchased an additional six dozen copies of Griffith's book and three dozen of Jacob's, at the same time as he received four dozen copies of his own antislavery pamphlet. So Woolman was surely distributing these books as part of his ministry, and he may well have been reselling them.[21]

Woolman had students write in their primers, so he had one for each child. Instructions suggested that they were to "deface" the alphabet on the first page, tear out the leaf, turn it over, paste it on the cover, and perform the same exercise on the obverse. It appears as if small children traced the upper- and lowercase letters, for there was not enough empty space to copy them out on the page. Since the primers were destroyed by use, it is no surprise that only one copy (of the third edition) is known to have survived. Little distinguished this spelling book from the one Woolman had used as a student forty years earlier. Anthony Benezet also wrote a primer titled *A First Book for Children* that took a similar approach, with different biblical passages but working the same ground. It was not uncommon for teachers to publish their own primers. Some supplemented their teaching incomes by selling the texts; Benezet and Woolman used them to further their moral pedagogy.[22]

Woolman's early lessons in writing and reading moved from letter recognition to two-letter combinations—an, en, in, on, un—to three-letter combinations and words—bit, fit, hit, nit, pit—interspersing short reading exercises at each stage in the progression: "The sun is up my boy, get out of thy bed, go thy way for the cow, let her eat the hay. Now the sun is set, and the cow is put up, the boy may go to his bed. Go not in the way of a bad man; do not tell a lie my son." The book continued with four- and five-letter words.[23]

Literacy for these students was founded on moral precepts: "The dove doth no harm, the lamb doth no harm, a good boy doth no harm. The eye of the Lord is on them that fear him. He will love them, and do them good. He will keep their feet in the way they go, and save them from the paths of death." Most of the aphorisms concerned boys, but both "the good boy and the good girl learn their books." The morbid focus on death was not unique to Woolman, Quakers, or the times: "O my child love the Lord, and strive to be good, that it may be well with thee when thou dies." The threat of a wandering soul's finding "no rest in the other world" was in fact a gentle version of the hellfire and damnation preached by other sects. The positive, hopeful focus of Woolman's aphorisms reflects his times and his faith: "The Lord is good to them that wait for him, to the soul that seeketh him . . . The earth is full of the goodness of the Lord."[24]

For one long reading passage Woolman included the parable of the Good Samaritan; another was the parable of the beggar Lazarus and the rich man. The Samaritan teaches universal benevolence extended to anyone in need; the parable about Lazarus shows the responsibility of the rich for the poor. Woolman also used aphorisms for handwriting practice. Some of them survive in an account book, and again they reveal a fluid relationship among a variety of business endeavors and teaching school.

> If anger burns, stand still.
> Meekness is a pleasant garden.

Kindness in the heart feels pleasant.
The wounds of a friend need no plaster.
A lamb took by fraud is an ill sacrifice.
Religion without righteousness profits not.
A rose in the spring smells sweet.
Let the dainty man try abstinence.
An easy life, a delicious cook, and the doctor.

The aesthetic is that of a cultivated garden as imagined by a man who has savored time spent tending his orchard. The physical regimen is one of work and abstinence. The values are integrity, righteousness, meekness, kindness, and peace. As Woolman grew older and simplified his personal philosophy, it became easier to distill for the children in his care.[25]

We do not know when Woolman first read Elizabeth Jacob's *Epistle in True Love* (1712), which was published before he was born; it may have influenced the perspective he took on his own childhood and young adulthood when he began composing the *Journal* in 1756. He was closely attuned to Jacob's advice against the "spirit of the world, pride, covetousness, fleshly ease with self-interest." He was surely influenced by her counsel to establish a "holy discipline" in households and to raise children to follow the leadings of their own inner guides. Before Woolman and other reformers of his generation, she lamented the "great declension" of Quakerism "from the primitive plainness, simplicity, and sincerity which Truth led our faithful elders into," an enduring reprise among self-critical Christians.[26]

Jacob, just like Woolman, advised parents to model Christian conduct for their children, "for surely it is by this power of love that we are enabled to order our families rightly both in life and manners." Children were her greatest hope for the redemption of Quakerism, "for you He hath chosen." Choose good over evil, obey those in authority over you, and try never to lie. Seek and speak Truth at all times. Reject fashion, covet nothing, and display simplicity in your clothes. Avoid friendship with non-Quakers, but love all equally: "Shun bad company as infectious both to soul and body, and let your spare hours be spent in religious company, or retirement, reading or meditating on heavenly subjects." Woolman wrote such lessons himself. Much of Jacob's *Epistle* was vintage Quaker wisdom, but she wrote in a distinctive voice that complemented Woolman's later work.[27]

John Griffith (1713–76) was a Welsh Quaker who migrated with his family to Pennsylvania at the age of thirteen, settled in Darby, and began his ministry in 1734, when he was twenty-one (Woolman was then fourteen). French privateers attacked the ship on which he was crossing the Atlantic back to Great Britain in 1747 and took him, some of the crew, and other passengers captive. He had some harrowing experiences as a prisoner of war but, eventually escaping from Spain, showed up at London Yearly Meeting in 1748. He recounts these adventures in his autobiography, which did not appear until seven years after Woolman's death and which presents him as a sensitive kindred spirit to Woolman, whom he knew. (Their paths crossed on Long Island in 1747, but they were already acquainted by then, as Woolman notes in the *Journal*.) Griffith's *Some Brief Remarks on Sundry Important Subjects* appeared in London in 1764 and in Dublin a year later.

Like Jacob, Griffith lamented the backsliding among modern Quakers: "That many of these descendants [of the early Christians] in this day of outward peace and plenty, inclining to false liberty and ease do shun the cross of Christ, which would crucify them to the world, is a mournful truth, too obvious to be denied." He thought Friends had lost the zeal of the founding generations, and if the sect was to survive, young people must recover the spirit that had escaped their parents and grandparents. Thus, like Jacob, he founded his moral system on the education of children. Parents teach best by modeling virtue, he observes, using the familiar Lockean approach: "That which is likely to have the greatest influence upon their tender minds, is a steady circumspect example." With Woolman, Griffith believed that it is "much more desirous they should possess a heavenly than an earthly inheritance"; that children are as likely to be morally ruined by parents' "imprudent indulgence" as by abuse or neglect; that parents should teach them to resist cravings and work hard, keep them from associating with non-Quakers, and teach them obedience and the Bible.[28]

The destruction of Quakerism, according to Griffith, came in a secular flood: "a mournful inundation of undue liberties." He preached spirit over intellectual enlightenment, self-restraint in an age that worshiped liberty, and withdrawal in an era of engagement. Like Woolman, Griffith was out of step with the times but in league with other mid-century Quaker reformers.

> It greatly behooves you to look diligently to the footsteps of Christ's companions, who walked with him through many tribulations, having washed their robes and made them white in the blood of the lamb. Be truly contented with that low, humble, self-denying way which you see they walked in; you can never mend it. If you seek more liberty than that allows of, it will only bring upon you darkness, pain, and vexation of spirit.

Woolman would not have missed the clothing metaphor drawn from Revelation 7:14: "They have washed their robes and made them white with the blood of the Lamb." Both men directed readers to first principles, to the primitive church, and to the writings of the early Quakers. They both saw a "natural, unrenewed state" as spiritually inhibiting; the goal was to overcome "nature" rather than conform to the ways of the earth.[29]

But Woolman's precepts extended beyond those preached by his fellow Quakers. The key to coherence for Woolman was mystical experience, his unfailing guide. We have seen that, for him, the Hebrew prophets were optimists and pacifists, not fire-and-brimstone doomsayers, as others painted them, and it was their mystically derived Truth that led him to interpret them as messengers of good news.

Woolman writes in his *Journal* that at Yearly Meeting in 1764 an eighty-year-old Friend delivered a valedictory sermon in which he indicted "many" Friends for making a "spacious appearance in the world, which marks of outward wealth and greatness appeared on many in our meetings of ministers and elders." In the published *Journal*, the editorial committee substituted "some" for "many," whether because its members thought that Woolman had exaggerated the elderly Friend's remarks, that both men were wrong, or that the charge was too incendiary, we do not know, but the point is the same: Woolman moved further to the fringes of Friends' practice even as the society reformed along lines he advocated. He was less satisfied with progress, less appreciative of change, and perhaps even less hopeful about Quakers' recovering the purity of the primitive church. "The powerful overshadowings of the Holy Ghost were less manifest in the Society," he writes; there had been a "continued increase of these ways of life even until now, and that the weakness which hath now overspread the Society and the barrenness manifest amongst us is matter of much sorrow."[30]

By example and prophecy, Woolman wanted to help Quakers "of the foremost rank in our Society" to remove the "obstacles" that stood in the way of their salvation. When he wrote that for himself, he sought to rid his home of anything that might tempt a poor man to steal from him, implying that the rich, "grievously entangled in expensive customs," are to blame for theft because they create poverty and inspire jealousy. His disdain for money was increased by his growing concern for laborers who mined the minerals used to make coins. He now was uncomfortable even touching money, whatever it bought, because of the harsh, dangerous conditions in the Spanish silver mines of South America: "And though I sometimes handle silver and gold as a currency, my so doing, is at times, attended with pensiveness, and a care that my ears may not be stopped against further instructions." By the late 1760s, then, he was anticipating the call to renounce a cash economy entirely.[31]

Sometime during 1764, Woolman had a talk with a hired man who had been a soldier in the French and Indian War and been captured by Indians. The captors tortured two of his companions, "one of which, being tied to a tree, had abundance of pine splinters run into his body and then set on fire," which the Indians continued for two days until the captive died. "They opened the belly of the other," Woolman heard, "and fastened a part of his bowels to a tree, and then whipped the poor creature till by his running round the tree his bowels were drawn out of his body." The horror of this story made a strong impression on Woolman, and he retired that evening with it on his mind, saddened by what he had heard and discomfited in his wish to remain sympathetic to the Indians.[32]

Woolman woke the next morning much relieved, though, to a "fresh and living sense of divine love . . . spread over my mind, in which I had a renewed prospect of the nature of that wisdom from above which leads to a right use of all gifts both spiritual and temporal, and gives content therein." Once again he had brooded on his own complicity in the violence and asked how his fellow Quakers and other colonists could have provoked such hatred. He concluded this time that vanity was the cause; the effort to satisfy many wants unknown to other creatures turned jealousy to malice, which in turn became a quest for revenge. "Take heed," Woolman warned himself and those who would listen to him, "that no weakness in conforming to expensive, unwise, and hard-hearted customs, gendering to discord and strife, be given way to." Conquer vanity, personally and socially, and violence would pass from the world.[33]

In the spring of 1766 Woolman felt moved to travel again, and his lifelong friend John Sleeper (1731–?), a Mount Holly carpenter descended from Quakers persecuted in New England, independently felt the same call, so they set off together on a mission to slaveowning Quakers in Maryland. This time they walked.

> An exercise having at times for several years attended me in regard to paying a religious visit to Friends on the eastern shore of Maryland, such was the nature of this exercise that I believed the Lord moved me to travel on foot amongst them, that by so traveling I might have a more lively feeling of the condition of the oppressed slaves, set an example of lowliness before the eyes of their masters, and be more out of the way of temptation to unprofitable familiarities.[34]

It was not out of tenderness for abused animals that Woolman began his walking ministry in the South, then; as he had previously explained in the *Journal*, he was profoundly uncomfortable making extra work for the slaves who would care for his horse. The decision also fitted his self-styling as a prophet, walking because Christ, the apostles, and the Old Testament prophets walked. Although he was too self-effacing to describe himself explicitly as a prophet, his adoption of symbolic clothing and a more exhausting form of travel purified him and physically represented the messages he delivered about simplicity, self-denial, and disentanglement from worldly attachments. From here on out Woolman walked.

The early May weather was hot and dry; the walking ministry was exhausting. "I grew weakly," Woolman recalled. It discouraged him until he decided that he shouldn't hurry from one point to the next: "I now saw that I had been in danger of too strongly desiring to get soon through the journey, and that this bodily weakness now attending me was a kindness to me." Again, his own nature had led him to focus unduly on ends rather than process; he needed to learn to be content in the moment of his mission, not to be overwhelmed by ambitions for success measured in earthly terms. Not only did his exhaustion help him figure this out, but he felt blessed to have a personal experience of the suffering of slaves.[35]

Woolman knew something about the history of Quakers in colonial America that accounted for the profound differences between Friends in the middle colonies and those in the South. Few Quaker immigrants had settled in the South; Quakers there were largely converts from Anglicanism brought into the society by the ministry of English Friends. The early generations of southerners were bellicose people, Woolman thought, "grounded in customs contrary to the pure Truth." Conversion may have softened them, made them less violent and more enlightened, but they were still not as peaceful as the Quaker immigrants to Pennsylvania and New Jersey. "It is observable in the history of the reformation from popery," Woolman writes, "that it had a gradual progress from age to age." The same might reasonably be hoped for southern Quakers: "Amongst an imperious warlike people supported by oppressed slaves, some of these masters I suppose are awakened to feel and see their error and through sincere repentance cease from oppression and become like fathers to their servants, showing by their example a pattern of humility in living and moderation in governing, for the instruction and admonition of their oppressing neighbors."[36]

In light of their progress and their good example to other slave-owners, Woolman was not inclined to judge the southern Quakers too harshly. Confident that God understood their progress in the same way, Woolman saw himself as helping in this process, moving the "hearts of people to draw them off from the desire of wealth and bring them into such a humble, lowly way of living that they may see their way clearly to repair to the standard of true righteousness." He persuaded himself that he had performed his task as appointed and to some good effect.[37]

One year later Woolman walked off again, this time alone on a monthlong journey south to the western shore of the Chesapeake Bay, first taking a ferry across the Delaware to Philadelphia, spending the night at a friend's in Darby, then on to Concord, New Garden, Nottingham, and Little Britain, still in Pennsylvania. He found traveling on foot "wearisome to my body" but "agreeable to the state of my mind." He felt "weakly," traveled "gently," by which he apparently means slowly, and "was covered with sorrow and heaviness on account of the spreading, prevailing spirit of this world, introducing customs grievous and oppressive on one hand, and cherishing pride and wantonness on the other."[38]

He crossed the Susquehanna River on April 26, 1767, possibly at Susquehanna Lower Ferry, and reached Gunpowder, Maryland, in time for Quarterly Meeting, where he found "people who lived in outward ease and greatness, chiefly on the labour of slaves." Witnessing such injustice moved him to sadness rather than anger, and he was unsure what he should do in this setting: "In this lonely walk and state of abasement and humiliation, the state of the church in these parts was opened before me, and I may truly say with the prophet, 'I was bowed down at the hearing of it; I was dismayed at the seeing of it'" (Isaiah 21:3). He spoke at Meeting with "bowedness of spirit" and "much plainness of speech" on the subject of slavery, which he saw as a fulfillment of the prophecy of Isaiah 66:18: "For I know their works and their thoughts, and I am coming to gather all nations and tongues; and they shall come and shall see my glory, and I will set a sign among them." By "plainness of speech" (he erased "of speech" from the last manuscript draft, but it is still visible on the page), he means that he held nothing back. The passage from Isaiah suggests either that he saw himself in white array as a "sign" or that he embodied a warning that judgment of his people was imminent.[39]

Once again Woolman recalled the apostles and early Christians who suffered death to convert gentiles, so very different from the Quakers who now oppressed their slaves.

Through the humbling dispensations of Divine Providence, my mind hath been brought into a further feeling of the difficulties of Friends and their servants Southwestward and being often engaged in Spirit on their account, I believed it my duty to walk into some parts of the western shore of Maryland, to pay them a Religious visit: And having obtained a Certificate from Friends of our Monthly meeting, I took leave of my Family under the heart tendering operation of Truth

A page from a manuscript draft of John Woolman's *Journal* (John Woolman Papers, Special Collections and University Archives, Rutgers University Libraries)

Here the sufferings of Christ and his tasting death for every man, and the travels, sufferings, and martydoms of the apostles and primitive Christians in labouring for the conversion of the Gentiles, was livingly revived in me; and according to the measure of strength afforded, I laboured in some tenderness of spirit, being deeply affected amongst them.

The next day, in another Meeting, he was "deeply engaged in inward cries to the Lord for help" and prayed aloud for resignation to the state of the world in which such injustice ruled, in which God's people were the instruments of unrighteousness: "And I was mercifully helped to labour honestly and fervently amongst them, in which I found inward peace, and the sincere were comforted."[40]

Woolman reports in his *Journal* that from Gunpowder he walked through Red Lands to Pipe Creek, Maryland, a journey of about fifty miles, but says nothing about the trip except that he had "several meetings amongst friends in those parts" at which his "heart was often tenderly affected." At that point he was three miles south of the Pennsylvania line and thirty miles southwest of York, more than a hundred miles from home as the crow flies.[41]

After praying and bearing witness among Quakers on the western shore, Woolman returned, stopping first in Pennsylvania's Western Quarterly Meeting, where he was "mercifully preserved in an inward feeling after the mind of Truth, and my public labours tended to my humiliation, with which I was content." He then felt "drawn" to attend the women's Meeting for Business, which he describes as "full" and where "the humility of Jesus Christ as a pattern for us to walk by was livingly opened before me, and in treating on it my heart was enlarged, and it was a baptizing time."[42]

According to his *Journal*, then, it was toward the end of his trip that he understood himself to be walking in the steps of Christ; previously he may have seen his connection to the apostles and prophets or he may not even have known why he walked but just that he was called to do so. He then walked to Meetings in Concord, Middletown, and Providence, before crossing the Delaware back to New Jersey. He stopped to attend a Meeting at Haddonfield before returning home in late May, where he found his family well. Four months later Woolman, back on the road to visit Friends in Berks and Philadelphia counties, attended eleven Meetings in two weeks. During the winter of 1767–68 he, as a member of a group of Friends, visited Burlington Meeting families, "in which exercise the pure influence of divine love made our visits reviving."[43]

Woolman returned in May 1768 to Maryland, where he attended Yearly Meeting at West River, south of Annapolis on the Western Shore. This was about 160 miles by land from Mount Holly. Again, "to proceed without a horse looked clearest to me." The task remained the same as in previous trips, the physical challenges unchanged, and the inner struggle for peace in the face of injustice as great a trial for Woolman as ever. But he believed this was his call: to testify in his white clothes, on foot, by his witness and by words as God moved him. Even if he could see no progress or could measure his effect only by the number of people who were kind to him, Friends knew who he was and why he was there; even, perhaps especially, in silence they heard the message he delivered to them.[44]

To suspend judgment of slaveowners even while judging their acts was difficult for Woolman, but he tried to maintain an open heart.

> It was a journey of much inward waiting, and as my eye was to the Lord, [a] way was several times opened to my humbling admiration when things had appeared very difficult. In my return I felt a relief of mind very comfortable to me, having through divine help laboured in much plainness, both with Friends selected and in the more public meetings, so that I trust the pure witness in many minds was reached.

By June 11, he reports in his *Journal*, the "labour of heart" under which he had lived for years was lifting. "I find peace," he writes, in his communication with the owners of slaves. Nonetheless, there was no rest for his weary soul; even as he contemplated his ministry with some satisfaction, he found another reason to judge his own behavior harshly, which was a harder cross to bear than the message that he carried to others.[45]

It was in 1769, in the context of these missionary travels, that

Woolman confronted anew his own complicity in evil, his having apprenticed the young freed slave of Thomas Shinn until he was thirty years old, nine years longer than white orphans served. Buying the young man out of four and a half of those nine years had not brought him peace. Witnessing the sins of others in Maryland reminded Woolman again of his own failings and his own guilt. Traveling brought his sins home.

11

Growth

1769–72

12th, 3rd month, 1770. Having for some years past dieted myself on account of a lump gathering on my nose, and under
this diet grew weak in body and not of ability to travel by land
as heretofore, I was at times favoured to look with awfulness
toward the Lord, before whom are all my ways, who alone
hath the power of life and death, and to feel thankfulness incited in me for this his fatherly chastisement, believing if I
was truly humbled under it, all would work for good.

Perhaps it was a cancerous tumor; the diet might have been a vegetarian regimen of the sort favored by Benjamin Lay and Anthony
Benezet and tried by Benjamin Franklin. Walking long distances
rather than riding had weakened him further, and dehydration during his long trip in rural Maryland in the late spring and early summer may have hastened his decline. But in any case the weakness
may well have contributed to Woolman's melancholy state and mystical experiences. Woolman tried an herbal remedy in May 1769 (for
what his *Journal* does not say), but the growth on his nose and his
general physical debility continued to trouble him.[1]

Yet later that same year, still exhausted in body and spirit, ever
aware that death could be at hand, he decided to sail to the West
Indies as an extension of his ministry against slavery. In October he

inquired about ships scheduled to leave Philadelphia for Barbados. Unsure whether God intended him to make such a dangerous voyage, he prayed on the question: "And upward of a year having passed, I walked one day in a solitary wood; my mind being covered with awfulness, cries were raised in me to my merciful Father that he would graciously keep me in faithfulness, and it then settled on my mind as a duty to open my condition to Friends at our Monthly Meeting."[2]

Woolman secured letters endorsing the journey from Monthly, Quarterly, and Yearly Meetings and "believed resignation herein was required of me." He began anew the process of detaching himself from worldly connections, making him feel "like a sojourner at my outward habitation." He put twenty pounds for the journey in the hands of a friend, "to be ready when I want it," and after shopping for a mattress to use on board, he decided to make one himself. He mentions his failure of conscience over Thomas Shinn's young slave for a second time, which in this context suggests that Woolman may have thought of sailing to Barbados as a penance, perhaps as an opportunity to cleanse himself of the sin.[3]

In November Woolman learned that a ship owned by his childhood friends John Smith and James Pemberton was set to sail for Barbados. Woolman met with Smith in Burlington to discuss passage, returned home, and then went to Philadelphia to see Smith again and give him a written explanation for his anticipated journey. This document dwells on Woolman's responsibility and that of others in supporting the slave trade. Despite Woolman's disclaimer— "I do not censure my brethren in these things"—the document was clearly meant as a judgment against the two merchants' long-standing and profitable West Indies trade. In his usual style of address, Woolman began with an indictment of himself.

> I once, some years ago, retailed rum, sugar, and molasses, the fruits of the labour of slaves, but then had not much concern about them save only that the rum might be used in moderation; nor was this concern so weightily attended to as I now believe it ought to have been. But of late years being further informed respecting the oppressions too generally exercised

in these islands, and thinking often on the degrees that there are in connections of interest and fellowship with the works of darkness (Eph. 5:11), and feeling an increasing concern to be wholly given up to the leadings of the Holy Spirit, it hath appeared that the small gain I got by this branch of trade should be applied in promoting righteousness in the earth.[4]

Smith and Pemberton would have understood what Woolman meant when he referred to the "temptations of my fellow creatures labouring under those expensive customs distinguishable from 'the simplicity that there is in Christ.'" It was merchants such as they whom Ezekiel chastises when he declares that "they have strengthened the hands of the wicked," and Woolman quoted the prophet. Those who looked for profits by trafficking in goods produced by slaves made the slaveowners "more easy respecting their conduct than they would be if the cause of universal righteousness was humbly and firmly attended to by those in general with whom they have commerce."[5]

Woolman's prophetic sermon built to a final charge against the two Quaker merchants, whom he had known all his life. Buying and selling slave-produced goods in effect subsidized passage on ships to the West Indies, he reasoned; in other words, if it were not for the profits from what he considered an illicit trade, the fees charged passengers would be higher. For this reason, Woolman concludes: "I should not take the advantage of this great trade and small passage money, but as testimony in favour of less trading should pay more than is common for others to pay, if I go at this time."[6]

Smith read this document; then he and Woolman delivered it to Pemberton, who read while the other two waited. When he was done, the three men had what Woolman considered a "solid conversation," which made him feel his "soul bowed in reverence before the Most High." This is how Woolman writes about it in his *Journal*, though without mentioning Smith's name. But the discussion unsettled him: "At length one of them asked me if I would go and see the vessel, but I had not clearness in my mind to go, but went to my lodgings and retired in private." Clearly the conflict with his old friends had raised doubts and confusion. "I was now under great exercise of mind," Woolman recalled not long after, "and my tears were poured out before the Lord with inward cries that he would graciously help me under these trials."[7]

He was unsure whether God wanted him to sail on this or any ship. He was "resigned" but "did not feel clearness to proceed." He was "tossed as in a tempest," and he thought of the passage from Matthew 6:34: "Take no thought for the morrow." He left Philadelphia on foot, hoping to achieve spiritual "stillness" before the ship sailed; crossed the Delaware, walking east; and eventually wandered past Mount Holly and all the way to the Jersey shore. "And as I lay in bed the latter part of that night," he wrote, "my mind was comforted" by deciding to go home.[8]

But Woolman "still felt like a sojourner with my family." Unsettled, alone, and feeling out of place with his wife and daughter, he took off again, still unsure where he would go but clear on the Truth God wanted him to speak. On the road another biblical passage occurred to him, this time Ezekiel again. "Withersoever their faces were turned, thither they went," he remembered. (Woolman conflated several lines here, the original, "Each moved straight ahead; wherever the spirit would go, they went, without turning as they went," is very close to what he meant [Ezekiel 1:12].) Ezekiel is describing a vision of a windstorm surrounded by brilliant light. In the vortex is a fire in which there are four living creatures, each with four human faces, four wings, the legs of a man, and the feet of a calf. The spirit pulled Woolman, but his nature was unsure which of the four compass points he should go to. He was undecided—two-faced, if not four—but had to act with resolve, resignation, and trust in the higher power that guided him. It was Woolman's fate to wander wherever God led him as a prophet, but he was less comfortable following the spirit on the high seas.[9]

Then God almost took him away. On December 13, 1769, a few weeks after his tortured decision against sailing to Barbados, Woolman attended his brother Asher's wedding (one of the very few times that we learn anything from the *Journal* about one of his siblings) even though he had a cold and didn't feel well. He sat through the long Meeting, made the several miles' trip to Asher's house and the old family homestead on the Rancocas River, partook dutifully of the meal, and returned—on horse or in a horse-drawn wagon, one presumes—through the winter weather. By the time he got home, he was suffering from fever and chills. We can imagine his by now chronically weakened immune system undermined by the stresses of his peripatetic ministry. Then there was that bulbous growth on his nose. By morning his illness was no longer a cold but pleurisy, and this infection of the lungs struck him down. Still, Woolman instructed his wife not to send for a doctor. Since the treatment for high fever at that time was copious bleeding, which would have weakened him more, this decision may have saved his life, although the intent was to put himself in God's hands.

Friends spelled his wife and daughter at nursing for the next weeks. They gathered at his bedside in a rotation organized by Mount Holly Meeting—"the following Friends are desired to meet at the house of John Woolman at 10:o'clock . . ."—met, prayed, and held Meeting for Worship at his bedside. They sat with him through the nights and took care of him while his wife and daughter got some sleep, giving him a cup of water, in a tin or ceramic vessel, of course, helping him with a call of nature or of the spirit, such as a revelation that he wanted someone to write down, or a wet cloth to cool his fevered brow.

Woolman told everyone that he was resigned to die. He was forty-nine years old; given his age, condition, and the state of medical knowledge then, this expectation was not unreasonable. He drifted in and out of consciousness, and when his mind was clear, he asked those around him to write his thoughts down. The fever, which persisted for weeks, made Woolman feel closer to the inspired state in which insights became clarified. Before dawn on January 4, 1770, he dictated to Caleb Carr (1719–83), a lifelong friend—a "solid Friend," according to the *Journal*—who had been sitting with him through the last hours of that night.

I have seen in the light of the Lord that the day is approaching when the man that is the most wise in human policies shall be the greatest fool, and the arm that is mighty to support injustice shall be broken to pieces. The enemies of righteousness shall make a terrible rattle, and shall mightily torment one another. For he that is omnipotent is rising up to judgment and will plead the cause of the oppressed. And he commanded me to open the vision.

Abolitionists such as John Greenleaf Whittier later read this passage as a prophecy of the Civil War. It is certainly composed in the language of imminent retribution generally associated with the Old Testament prophets, a warning of apocalyptic reprisal that rattles the earth, a "rising up to judgment" that manifests itself in "torment." Woolman believed that God "commanded" him to deliver the warning to Quakers—to "open the vision"—so that their fate would rest on free will.[10]

Several additional crises marked the progress of Woolman's illness, and the patient was at the mercy of fever-induced surges of resignation and hope. With the tides of illness sweeping over him, Woolman's expectations rose and fell. On more than one occasion he thought he was living his last day.

One night in particular my bodily distress was great: my feet grew cold, and cold increased up my legs toward my body, and at that time I had no inclination to ask my nurse to apply anything warm to my feet, expecting my end was near. And after I had lain, I believe, near ten hours in this condition, I closed my eyes, thinking whether I might now be delivered out of the body; but in these awful moments my mind was livingly opened to behold the church, and strong engagements were begotten in me for the everlasting well-being of my fellow creatures. And I felt in the spring of pure love that I might remain some time longer in the body, in filling up according to my measure that which remains of the afflictions of Christ and in labouring for the good of the church, after which I requested my nurse to apply warmth to my feet, and I revived.[11]

In the aftermath of that emotional descent and climb, Woolman again despaired. His daughter, Mary, recorded a message he dictated to her.

I feel a pure and Holy Spirit in a weak and broken constitution: this Spirit within me hath suffered deeply and I have born my part in the suffering, that there may come forth a church pure and clean like the New Jerusalem, as a bride adorned for her husband. I believe my sufferings in this broken Nature are now nearly accomplished, and my Father hath showed me that the holy Spirit that now works within me, may work in young lively constitutions and may strengthen them to travel up and down the world in the feeling of pure wisdom, that many may believe them and the purity of their lives and learn instruction.

His nature was dying, then, but the spirit was strong; he had suffered to purify the church, but more work remained to be done. Having his daughter in the sickroom inspired Woolman to bequeath her his mission, an apostolic legacy from a feverish prophet: "taken from the mouth of my Father as he uttered it in my hearing on a first day meeting while dying." (The last word in Mary's shaking hand is almost illegible; only the "ing" is clear.)[12]

Aaron Smith, a member of Mount Holly Meeting, attended Woolman during the night of January 12–13. At about 3:00 a.m., "having for some time lain like a man a dying," Woolman asked for water, saying that his tongue was dry and he needed to speak. After drinking, he told Smith that "the forepart of the same night he had very great horrors on his mind for departing from the purity of his Testimony, in relation to the West India traffic." The guilt was consuming him; he could not forgive himself, and now he believed that the decision not to sail contravened God's intention.

Under this anguish of soul, evident to all about him, he stood up on his feet, though weak, and with a lamentable voice cried mightily to God that he would have mercy upon him, a miserable sinner for that he had lately, under extreme weakness, given up the purity of his Testimony against the West India trade, in partaking freely of rum and molasses. After long conflict with these horrors, he appeared more easy, as believing God would be gracious to him. He now informed us he had found the mercies of God to be toward him, and that he had an evidence of inward peace, and that God had accepted of his great conflict with the power of darkness the fore part of this night. Uttered by John Woolman's lips and wrote by Aaron Smith.[13]

Woolman had once sold rum, molasses, and dyed cloth, and this had made him complicit in others' sins. He had stopped this business, but eliminating rum and molasses from his own personal consumption was a step long overdue by his moral calculus. The problem now was not God's forgiveness but Woolman's self-absolution; his saintly, ascetic temperament left him prostrate before his own conscience. Once Woolman accepted his nature and humbly petitioned for mercy, he could return to the road to perfection. The saint could accept nothing less from life, so he worried about dying before he achieved the goal.

But Woolman did not die from pleurisy in 1770. To everyone's surprise, as he himself continued sometimes to doubt that he would live, he began to recover. As he slowly regained strength and buoyancy of spirit, Woolman was thankful that God had heard the prayers uttered silently in his room.

The place of prayer is a precious habitation, for I now saw that the prayers of the saints was precious incense. And a trumpet was given me that I might sound forth this language, that the children might hear it and be invited to gather to this precious habitation, where the prayers of saints, as precious incense, ariseth up before the throne of God and the Lamb. I saw this habitation to be safe, to be inwardly quiet, when there was great stirrings and commotions in the world.

Prayer at this day in pure resignation is a precious place. The trumpet is sounded; the call goes forth to the church that she gather to the place of pure inward prayer, and her habitation is safe.[14]

God had another job for Woolman, then, and therefore spared him. Woolman saw the saints' spiritual petitions received by God as "precious incense" burned in their sacrifices for him, and Woolman makes a humble but hopeful identification of his life with those of other saintly souls. He believed that the prayers of saints sounded like trumpets in God's ears and that God made him an instrument in order to sound prophecy in Quaker hearts. "Pure resignation," likewise a "precious place," is the highest achievement of prayerful silence and the greatest gift God can bestow. Having delivered the message, the saint returns to "pure inward prayer" in the safe habitation within, which is the spirit, the Light, and the last resting place of the soul.

After he had recovered fully, Woolman added this note: "I believe it will be felt by feeling living members, that that which hath been uttered by my lips had proceeded from the Spirit of Truth, operating on mine understanding, and I meddle not with the fever." He hoped, then, that Quakers would not interpret his statements as deriving from nature rather than spirit, from fever rather than God. Woolman's concern was to distinguish spiritual Light from bodily heat.[15]

As with his life-threatening illness during his adolescence, pleurisy at forty-nine inspired a spiritual breakthrough for Woolman. He did not write about it until two and a half years later, when he was in England, putting some distance between him and the event. He had been "brought so near the gates of death that [he] forgot my name," he writes. He recalled being conscious, but then he recounted a dream, or dreamlike experience that he had had in a fevered state.

> Being then desirous to know who I was, I saw a mass of matter of a dull gloomy color, between the South and the East, and was informed that this mass was human beings in as great misery as they could be and live, and that I was mixed in with them and henceforth might not consider myself as a distinct or separate being. In this state I remained several hours. I then heard a soft, melodious voice, more pure and harmonious than any voice I had heard with my ears before, and I believed it was the voice of an angel who spake to other angels. The words were, *"John Woolman is dead."* I soon remembered that I once was John Woolman, and being assured that I was alive in the body, I greatly wondered what that heavenly voice could mean. I believed beyond doubting

that it was the voice of an holy angel, but as yet it was a mystery to me.[16]

It took him many long months to comprehend fully this near-death experience. Woolman felt that it was real, not dreamy or feverish, and that he had crossed over into a place where distraught souls dwelled. Perhaps their recent deaths disoriented people he believed were alive. He lost his own identity within the experience but felt conscious and saw himself singled out; despite the declaration of his death by an ethereal authority, he recovered a sense of self and was "assured" that his death was not biological. But this simply left him confused.

The vision continued in a new setting.

I was then carried in spirit to the mines, where poor oppressed people were digging rich treasures for those called Christians, and heard them blaspheme the name of Christ, at which I was grieved, for his name to me was precious. Then I was informed that these heathens were told that those who oppressed them were the followers of Christ, and they said amongst themselves: "If Christ directed them to use us in this sort, then Christ is a cruel tyrant."

With these otherworldly mines, apparently silver mines, Christians were responsible for their own spiritual downfall and for the physical suffering of gentiles whom they oppressed: that much was clear. Rather than convert gentiles, as Christ required, Christians had perverted God's charge.[17]

But there was still the "mystery" of the angel's pronouncing him dead. What did this mean?

In the morning my dear wife and some others coming to my bedside, I asked them if they knew who I was; and they, telling me I was John Woolman, thought I was only lightheaded, for I told them not what the angel said, nor was I disposed to talk much to anyone, but was very desirous to get so deep that I might understand this mystery.[18]

Possibly Woolman's fever had broken, and he was fully conscious, in which case his question sprang not from confusion about who he had been during the night but who he was when he awoke. He was unclear about how much time had passed, although he estimated that the vision lasted two hours, and was uncertain in what dimension he dwelled. Yet he never doubted that the angel was real and its statement was true.

> My tongue was often so dry that I could not speak till I had moved it about and gathered some moisture, and as I lay still for a time, at length I felt divine power prepare my mouth that I could speak, and then I said: "I am crucified with Christ, nevertheless I live; yet not I, but Christ that liveth in me, and the life I now live in the flesh is by faith in the Son of God, who loved me and gave himself for me" [Gal. 2:20]. Then the mystery was opened, and I perceived there was joy in heaven over a sinner who had repented and that that language *John Woolman is dead* meant no more than the death of my own will.[19]

Death of his conscious will left Woolman alive to the spirit, which led him to hope that he would no longer struggle to know God's desire and to suppress his own. Quite possibly he believed that his own internal conflict over his planned Barbados trip was the cause of his pleurisy, with his becoming ill from body-rending guilt over his decision against sailing. He resolved not to allow trepidation to stand in Truth's way again. As he had throughout his life, Woolman recognized Christ the Redeemer, the Christ of the cross, as the spirit inhabiting him.

Woolman believed that during the experience of his vision he had transcended nature, and it took a biological event to return him to the physical world. As a visionary he gained spiritual insight that he lacked when he was his normal self; restored to his natural state, he could translate the message into human terms. Then a new burden flashed before him.

> Soon after this I coughed and raised much bloody matter, which I had not during this vision, and now my natural understanding returned as before. Here I saw that people getting

silver vessels to set off their tables at entertainments was often stained with worldly glory, and that in the present state of things, I should take heed how I fed myself from out of silver vessels.

Soon after my recovery I, going to our Monthly Meeting, dined at a Friend's house, where drink was brought in silver vessels and not in any other. And I, wanting some drink, told him my case with weeping, and he ordered some drink for me in another vessel.[20]

Who was this unnamed Friend? As with the discussion of the Barbados ship Woolman does not mention John Smith's name, but the references are clear, and his identity was confirmed almost a century ago. The unnamed man in both stories thus frames the *Journal*'s presentation of the death of Woolman's will, yet not consciously, since he tells part of the story at the point it happened in 1769 and the rest when he wrote about it in 1772, the pleurisy and the vision becoming autonomous events in the telling, though spiritually connected. His open confrontation with John Smith in this scene evoked pity or embarrassment, but evidently Woolman believed that Smith was not offended by this repudiation of his silver teapot and servers.[21]

On January 20, 1770, during his convalescence, Woolman had written a short statement explaining his ministry against silver vessels, a document that was not intended for the *Journal* and not sent or delivered to anyone as far as we know. He wrote that he was calling people to account in their homes and in public for their silver teapots and place settings. Envisioning oppressed miners had clarified God's will for Woolman, linking slavery to the mining of precious metals that were used in coins of the realm and for tea services in the houses of wealthy Quakers. When he wrote the statement, Woolman felt an opening to "pure wisdom," which directed him to record "the council of the Lord to this generation respecting these things. He that can receive it let him receive it. There is idolatry committed in the use of these things, and where this is the case if they are sold they may be idols to others."[22]

Not only was Woolman's ministry becoming more direct, perhaps even aggressive—"He that can receive it let him receive it"—

in the style of George Keith and Benjamin Lay, but he felt called to record revelations in writing that would leave the prophecy behind when he died. He believed he was adding to the Bible, to the word that is God's. And this particular warning reflected on Jacob's ministry to destroy his people's idols, as reported in Genesis 35:1–14. Woolman was repeating Old Testament Truth already revealed for a generation of Quakers who had forgotten its lessons. The evil of silver vessels was clear to him, though not to successful Quakers in an era of ever more available and lavish household goods. As always, the line between a cup and an idol was in the eye of the beholder, and Woolman was still stretching the boundaries of responsibility and simplicity for complacent Friends.

By the end of March 1770, Woolman was back in his orchard grafting apple trees and probably gratified to be alive. That spring, while visiting Crosswicks Meeting, Woolman had a most unusual dream:

THE FOX AND THE CAT: A DREAM

On the night between the 28th and 29th, 5th month, 1770, I dreamed a man had been hunting and brought a living creature to Mount Holly of a mixed breed, part fox and part cat. It appeared active in various motions, especially with its claws and teeth. I beheld and lo! many people gathering in the house where it was talked one to another, and after some time I perceived by their talk that an old Negro man was just now dead, and that his death was on this wise: They wanted flesh to feed this creature, and they wanted to be quit of the expense of keeping a man who through great age was unable to labor; so raising a long ladder against the house, they hanged the old man.

One woman spake lightly of it and signified she was sitting at the tea table when they hung him up, and though neither she nor any present said anything against their proceedings, yet she said at the sight of the old man a dying, she could not go on with tea drinking.

I stood silent all this time and was filled with extreme sorrow at so horrible an action and now began to lament bitterly, like as some lament at the decease of a friend, at which lamentation some smiled, but none mourned with me.

One man spake in justification of what was done and said that the flesh of the old Negro was wanted, not only that this creature might have plenty, but some other creatures also wanted his flesh, which I apprehended from what he said were some hounds kept for hunting; I felt matter on my mind, and would have spake to the man, but utterance was taken from me and I could not speak to him. And being in great distress I continued wailing till I began to wake, and opening my eyes, I perceived it was morning.[23]

About this dream, Woolman wrote in the margin of the *Journal* manuscript: "A fox is cunning; a cat is often idle; hunting represents vain delights; tea drinking with which there is sugar points out the slavery of the Negroes, with which many are oppressed to the shortening of their days." Thus did Woolman link tea, silver, and slavery. During a time when tea consumption and the number of tea services in the colonies were growing exponentially, when colonists equated tea with taxes, boycotts of imported consumer goods with patriotism, and their own political relationship to Great Britain with the exaggerated imagery of "enslaved" subjects who lacked representation in Parliament, tea and tea services were becoming potent political symbols for Americans. Ceremonies associated with tea drinking were also opportunities to display class pretensions. Consumer politics did not affect Woolman, but he did challenge the culture of consumption. He questioned the tastes of Quakers in the middling and upper classes whose aesthetic style and personal behavior broke from the testimony on simplicity as he understood it.[24]

Witnessing the hanging ruined the woman's appetite, at least for tea and for the time being; whether her disaffection from the commodity was temporary or permanent was not reported. Likewise, the meaning of Woolman's speechlessness in the dream is unclear to the reader, as it may have been to the dreamer. In tandem double meanings, the woman's tastelessness was manifested in her temporary inability to drink, and the dreaming Woolman's ineffectual preaching left him unable to preach. So the dream of the fox-cat dramatized the callousness of wealthy colonists, including the tea-drinking woman, who displayed and used commodities extracted by the African slaves in the West Indies and the shackled Indian silver miners in South America. The dream also raised questions about capitalism's celebration of productivity, which treated laborers as expendable resources.

The leading that brought on Woolman's vision of lost souls and mines, his challenge to the use of silver vessels, and the dream of the fox-cat also led him to write *Considerations on the True Harmony of Mankind, and How It Is to Be Maintained*, which is the most biblically centered of his writings and the most theologically driven; it is also his most morally demanding vision of Christian responsibility. The overseers of the Quaker press approved its publication in 1770. By this time Woolman was one of the overseers, about which he makes no written comment. He drafted an advertisement that the Committee for Sufferings circulated to each Monthly Meeting under the care of Philadelphia Yearly Meeting, announcing its availability for two shillings per dozen.

Woolman's vision of the good life is a traditional bucolic one, which such contemporaries as Rousseau and Jefferson shared in their secular Enlightenment perspective. But for the Enlightenment philosophers, worldly wisdom and minds attuned to nature were redemptive, liberalizing forces, while Woolman considered both nature and worldly wisdom seductive, retrograde evils. Jefferson believed the rural idyll politically redemptive, while Woolman emphasized the soullessness of urbanity. Rousseau and Jefferson celebrated nature as morally uplifting, while Woolman continued in his un-Enlightened sensibility to view nature as opposed to spirituality: by "desiring to support their families in a way pleasant to the natural mind, there may be danger of the worldly wisdom gaining strength in them, and of their departure from that pure feeling of Truth, which if faithfully attended to, would teach contentment in the Divine will, even in a very low estate."[25]

For Woolman, true profits accrue not from commerce and exploitation but from self-denial—"the profitableness of true humility." Here he quotes William Cave's *Primitive Christianity* and those whom Cave cited—Tertullian, for instance, on the value of setting an example for others: "It is not enough that a Christian be chaste and modest, but he must appear to be so." Presenting oneself as a model is both a ministry in itself and a path to escape worldly ways. This is quite different from Benjamin Franklin, who thought of public display of virtue as an opportunity for an entrepreneur to make his way in the world: "I sometimes brought home the paper I purchased at the stores through the streets on a wheelbarrow. Thus being esteemed an industrious thriving young man, and paying duly for what I bought, the merchants who imported stationery solicited my custom . . . and I went on swimmingly."[26]

Woolman quotes from Cave on the matter of clothing: "'The garments we wear . . . ought to be mean and frugal. That is true simplicity of habit, which takes away what is vain and superfluous; that [is] the best and most solid garment, which is the furthest from curiosity.'" Woolman may have seen this as endorsing his abandonment of dyed clothes, but others might as easily have seen it as a critique of a Quaker tailor whose strange attire made him into a "curiosity"; one man's simplicity could be another's ostentation, though Woolman did not view it in that light.[27]

The gap between rich and poor is most visible and the excesses of material display are most shocking in the cities, Woolman asserts. He suggests that those in "some branches of business" should listen carefully for leadings to change their jobs and go elsewhere: "Where the holy Leader directeth to a country life, or some change of employ, he may be faithfully followed." Christians should flee "from the entanglements of the spirit of the world" and "restore mankind to a state of true harmony" with their faith.[28]

Compromise puts one on a slippery slope of moral decline, Woolman reminds his fellow Quakers: "Though the change from day to night is by a motion so gradual as scarcely to be perceived, yet when night is come we behold it very different from the day." In full daylight "customs rise up from the spirit of this world," and the next thing you know, without even perceiving the change, you are living in impenetrable darkness. The appropriate lesson for Christians to learn from this metaphor is never to take even a step toward the darkness that looms ahead. Reject "unsavory employments," possessions and experiences that are "pleasant to the natural mind" but that are not in one's best moral interest or that oppress others, and the wealth necessary to "uphold a delicate life"; focus on "true Love" for humanity, "healing," and "true harmony." Recall the Golden Rule and live by it. Do not forget the experience of "Babel or Babylon," which its inhabitants built as a "place of business." Be warned of the dangers that lurk in such mercantile centers.[29]

Woolman also buttresses his recent decision to cease riding over long distances with biblical references to walking: "Walking is a phrase frequently used in Scripture to represent our journey through life, and appears to comprehend the various affairs and transactions properly relating to our being in this world." He advocates "true Christian walking" and quotes an apostolic injunction that he has adopted: "'He that saith he abideth in Him ought also to walk even as He walked.'" "True harmony" can be facilitated or perhaps even achieved by a Christian's "harmonious walking." This language is more than metaphor for Woolman. The scriptural passages he quotes here are, as the Bible always was in Woolman's recounting, endorsements rather than inspirations for his revelations. The Bible was not what moved him consciously to act as he did—prayer, visions, voices, and dreams express the Truth from within—but he drew on it for assurance and authority. Whether he actively searched for passages supporting his testimonies or they simply leaped off the page for him, the effect was the same.[30]

Woolman writes, as ever, in the language of confrontation between nature and spirit. Satan is not the real enemy, the biggest challenge, or the worst phantom of his dreams; rather, it is our "imperfect natures" and the "wisdom of the world." God chose to embody himself as one of us, with a flawed nature, rather than to adopt the "nature of angels" or keep his own. That Christ achieved "infinite love" with a human nature teaches us that we can do the same. He was "perfectly sincere, having the same human nature which we have," meaning that any compromises we make with Truth are less than what we are capable of achieving.[31]

Woolman was accommodating, if not patronizing, to Quaker merchants in this pamphlet. He was willing, albeit grudgingly, to accept the legitimacy of a merchant's work; even when buying and selling were a "duty," though, they remained a trap. Christian merchants have to be careful to carry their business no further than God intends. He did not cite any specific Christian merchants and evidently believed that the day had passed when traders could justify their business as a community service.[32]

Although he may have entertained the possibility that Truth and capitalism were compatible, he believed that in practice merchants led self-indulgent lives of moral squalor. If a person was found guilty of stealing goods from a shop or accepting stolen goods from a thief, he suffered a loss of reputation for the first offense and of his good name entirely if caught and convicted of a second or third offense. He would be considered dishonest and shunned by people of good repute, "but where iniquity is committed openly, and the authors of it are not brought to justice, nor put to shame, their hands grow strong." This, Woolman believed, was the case with the leading businessmen he knew.[33]

The danger was the spreading of a "general corruption," such as that of the Jews before the Chaldean conquest, a time of great anxiety and self-indulgence during which prophets delivered their messages. He cites Jeremiah: "'Were they ashamed when they had committed abominations? Nay, they were not at all ashamed, neither could they blush.' Jer. vi. 15." Then Ezekiel: "'Thou hast defiled thy sanctuaries by the multitude of thine iniquities; by the iniquity of thy traffic.' Ezek. xxviii. 18." Finally, Isaiah: "'They walk righteously, and speak uprightly,'" "They" being those who encourage their people back to the true path. What Woolman says, none too subtly, is that the leaders of his faith had grown corrupt by trafficking in slaves and slave-produced commodities and by their indulgence in superfluous goods, the products of oppression and the vessels of vanity. The corruption was spreading unchecked by law, custom, or moral suasion. He cites Isaiah again:

> "They walk righteously, and speak uprightly." By *walking* he represents the journey through life, as a righteous journey; and *by speaking uprightly*, seems to point at that which Moses appears to have had in view, when he thus expressed himself: "thou shalt not follow a multitude to do evil; nor speak in a cause to decline after many to wrest judgment." Exod. xxiii.2.[34]

Quakers in America were not heeding the lessons of Isaiah and Moses. They followed traditional practices rather than their consciences; they closed their eyes to blood and their ears to cries of pain. They followed the desire for gain rather than the way of the cross. They were caught in the "snares of unrighteous gain." If only they followed the prophets, who had "an inward sense of the spreading of the Kingdom of Christ," they would lead the heathen to God rather than pursue profits to their own destruction and that of their church.[35]

God had sent numerous warnings to his people since they had crossed the Atlantic: "Though from the first settlement of this part of America, he hath not extended his judgments to the degree of famine, yet worms at times have come forth beyond numbering, and laid waste fields of grain and grass, where they have appeared." He had sent other "devouring creatures," whose work was invisible beneath the soil, "tempests of hail," and drought. Woolman noted the drought in 1770: "I have beheld with attention from week to week how dryness from the top of the earth hath extended deeper and deeper, while the corn and plants have languished." Quakers should experience quenching rain as a blessing and not tempt God's hand. They should use their blessings wisely, always with an eye to divine intentions. If they did not, then they should expect the warning of the prophet Jeremiah to apply.

"Hast thou not procured this unto thyself, in that thou hast forsaken the Lord thy God, when he led thee by the way? Thine own wickedness shall correct thee, and thy backslidings shall reprove thee: know therefore and see, that it is an evil thing and bitter, that thou hast forsaken the Lord thy God, and that my fear is not in thee, saith the Lord God of hosts." Jer.ii. 17, 19.[36]

WOOLMAN'S *Journal* tells us nothing about the two years of his life between the springs of 1770 and 1772. The editorial committee deleted his dream about the fox-cat, just as it eliminated all the other dreams, so his story, as told in the *Journal*'s first edition, leaps from his recovery from pleurisy in the winter of 1770 to his preparations for going to England in 1772. During those twenty-four months he drafted and published *Considerations on the True Harmony of Mankind*, had a house built for his daughter, revised the *Journal* three times, saw his brother Abner through his last illness, continued to preach and teach (although he stopped traveling), and copied Abner's essay on the West Indies trade and his spiritual autobiography so it could be circulated among Friends.

Also, John Smith had died in March 1771. Was there a deathbed scene involving Woolman? Had he convinced his merchant friend to repent for living lavishly (by Woolman's standard) off profits from the West Indies trade? We can only speculate about whether Smith, as an unnamed Friend, would have become an object lesson in the *Journal* had Woolman lived to write about the two years leading up to his final journey. Smith's death would have been a fitting denouement, though, for his anonymous role in the *Journal*'s story.

We do not know why Woolman did not address any of these experiences in the *Journal* or why he tells readers nothing more about his daughter, his brother, or other family members. Had he survived the English journey on which he was about to embark, he might have written about these years, but there is no reason to suspect that he would have written any more about the people who meant most to him. In any case, we know from other sources that Woolman made a wedding present of a new house to his daughter, Mary, when she married John Comfort (1745–1803) in 1771—a simple structure where the first seven of their ten children were born and lived until 1787, when John's widow, Sarah, died. At that point the family moved to the Comfort family's farm in Morrisville, Pennsylvania. Mary died there from smallpox in 1797 at the age of forty-seven.[37]

During the spring of 1771, Woolman canceled an unnamed "distant bargain," a financial arrangement set in the future, with his brother Asher out of reluctance to plan two years ahead. He released his apprentice in October and settled accounts as best he could. Then, on November 4 of that year, his brother Abner died at the relatively young age of forty-seven. Abner, four years younger than he, had apparently been ill much of his life. Whether the debility was tuberculosis or asthma is unclear, but Abner mentions both afflictions in his writings. Three months before his death, he gave John an essay he had written on the West Indies trade, a manuscript copy of which he had already circulated among Burlington Friends; for some unspecified reason, he wanted Quakers in Wilmington, Delaware, to see it too. Nearer to his "departure," as John called it, Abner said he wanted to speak to his brother about a "particular matter." At that time Abner turned over chapters of a spiritual autobiography that he had already shown to a "considerable number" of the active members of Burlington Monthly Meeting and asked John to share it with the local Friends he had missed.[38]

John being John, this "trust" caused him some "exercise of mind," which he resolved by abiding his brother's deathbed requests and writing out copies of both texts, which he sent to the Committee for Sufferings of Philadelphia Yearly Meeting, the normal path for submission for publication. The letter he wrote to accompany the two texts explains the circumstances but contains no comment on the writings or endorsement of their publication. Since John was an overseer of the Quaker press, this was appropriately discreet: if he thought his brother's writings unworthy of publication, he need not have forwarded them at all.[39]

In another note, attached to the papers and copied over in John's hand, Abner touchingly bequeaths the manuscripts to his heirs: "My dear children, the following lines were wrote in tenderness, and the chief part of them in the night when you my dear children were asleep." He had spent, he said, many restless nights during which he felt close to, indeed inspired by, God, and the texts were the written record of revelations that had come to him in the dark.[40]

Abner had begun writing his spiritual autobiography in 1760, about four years after John had commenced his and at the same age as John had been when he started. The manuscript text, which survives in the copy that John transcribed, is not as long, thorough, or sustained, or as inspired or inspiring a piece of spiritual literature, as John's. Still, it is a good example of the genre, reflects Abner's distinctive journey, and sheds light on John and on the brothers' relationship.

Abner quickly summarizes his youthful path from sin to salvation in accordance with the traditions of spiritual autobiography to which John's *Journal* also conforms. For his "sin and folly" he walked mournfully with the grace of the Lord; as an apprentice he was "exposed to vain company" from which God saved him again;

even though he knew better and came to enjoy "peace of mind," carelessness led to folly, "which caused me great sorrow." Had he not heeded the "voice of God," Abner would have perished in the "dark howling wilderness" where his spirit dwelled, but God heard his cries and took pity on him.[41]

After Abner left his "dear father's house," he spent several summers in the New Jersey Pine Barrens on crews constructing sawmills. He often worked "with vain company who were disagreeable to me, which was a trial so deep that I believe I did not mention it to anyone for some years." He married, had children, and then became "so weakly that I could work but little, and had no outward help but what I hired." This incapacity led to financial distress: "The world seemed to frown on me; then I was overwhelmed with troubles." But, Abner continues, the Lord saw him through his flood of hardships and brought him peace of mind in the knowledge that "after the miseries of this life are over we shall enter into everlasting rest."[42]

Abner recalls being "thoughtful" about taxes paid to support the militia for some years before 1758. He remembers feeling quite alone in this, which is odd since we know that John faced the same dilemma in 1754 and started a public ministry on the subject. "My exercise was at times very great," Abner writes, "and I often looked round about and thought no one's state is like mine, neither did I know who to converse with."[43]

But he is adhering to the conventions of Quaker autobiography when he recalls his "exercise" as one experienced alone and resolved by inspiration from the Light within him: "I often was alone endeavoring to have my mind still." True, in the end Abner did have to struggle alone with his conscience to decide how to handle a demand for war taxes, but the motivating force behind his moral crisis surely included the public discussion initiated by his brother John, John Churchman, and others.[44]

Abner faced another trial of the spirit in 1760, when soldiers knocked on his door and asked to buy cider. He declined to sell them anything on the ground of the Quakers' peace testimony. (John might have taken a different approach, agreeing to accept no money for refreshment but then pouring the thirsty soldiers cider out of universal love.) After the soldiers left, their captain asked Abner if he could hire a wagon and horses to take the troops as far as

Cranbury, New Jersey. Abner again declined on religious grounds. The officer asked if Abner could read and showed him a press warrant that authorized him to seize, or "press," wagons and horses for the army's use. "I told him," Abner says in the autobiography, "that I looked upon the life of a man to be precious, and could not consistent with my religious principles do anything to forward them on their march." The captain did not want to anger Abner by insisting on what was within his power, he said, but Abner persevered: he "believed it would not" make him angry, yet he could not consent to the action. At first the captain himself was "warm" (angry), but he slowly calmed down and eventually decided that Abner "differed from all other men that ever he had conversed with, and as from a religious principle I was not easy to help them on their march, it was not easy to him to press my wagon and horses, and so went away on foot without showing any signs of resentment."[45]

Later that same year Abner went for his health to the New Jersey shore, where he had a "fit" of his "old disorder the phthisis which was very afflicting." Phthisis is tuberculosis, but it may have been a general debility of his lungs rather than a specific disease; he later mentions an asthma attack. What fell heaviest on him, though, was not the illness but a feeling that he was "destitute as to divine help." In such a state of body and spirit, Abner recalls viewing the ocean and the shells on the beach in a new light, as evidence of the divine hand in creation and his own "natural" place. He seems to be saying that putting himself in such a universal context depressed him and led him to wallow in a "poor mournful condition" for some time. When he was ready to go home, Abner roused himself enough to visit a woman who lived nearby to give her spiritual comfort, which he thought she greatly appreciated. Feeling that he had done some good by this ministry, Abner shed tears of joy and returned to his wife and children in a much improved state of mind, if not of physical health.[46]

Abner's journal reveals that taverns were moral problems for him, just as they were for John, and Abner recounts a dream about entering a "public house" with an unnamed brother; this came some time after John's challenge in 1763 to the magician's audience at a Mount Holly tavern.

I dreamed that I with one of my brothers went to a public house, and I asking him if he would drink some beer he said no, not at this time. Then I called for a pint of beer, and the woman of the house was displeased, because I called for so little. I told her it was enough for one man. There being a company of men, one of them began to talk to me in a scornful way; then I went and sat near to him, and looking earnestly upon him spake to him of the Lord and the power of Truth coming over him; he spake to me no more, but turned away, upon which I awoke.

If John was the brother, his decline of the beer was true to form. Abner, who is in the moral center of his dream, is not so extreme in his abstemiousness and displays his moral stamina both to the drinking patron and to his brother. Perhaps the dream also contains some hint of sibling rivalry, but in making the risky confrontation in the name of Truth and a concern about the influence of taverns on the community, Abner seizes the moral initiative from his ascetic brother.[47]

Abner's journal shows that he shared John's concerns about Indians, the impoverished, and slaves. He saw the links among the Quakers' vices and social ills. "Now if a true history of the oppressions of the Negroes, together with an account of the costly apparel, household furniture, and high living of many amongst us were published," he writes, "how evidently would it appear that there is a grievous backsliding and degeneracy from that uprightness and simplicity which in time past appeared amongst friends." He had consumed sugar and other goods from the West Indies until he was "repeatedly and credibly informed" that slave labor produced the items. He also abhorred the exorbitant interest and rents charged by "rich men who live in greatness," views he could have read in several of his brother's published pamphlets.[48]

ABNER Woolman's essay on the West Indies trade is dated September 1770, ten months after his brother John had challenged James Pemberton and John Smith on this same subject and sometime after John had had his dream of the fox-cat. Where his brother John's writing focused on the effect of slavery on the souls of Quakers who shared responsibility for oppression, Abner writes about the psychological effects on the slaves. He asks Friends to picture themselves in the slaves' place, growing up ignorant of the Bible, reaching adulthood in bondage for no crime that they have committed, as a result of no contract they have signed, and without any reasonable explanation their masters could give. Imagine, he asks, hearing those who advocated your freedom "often advised not to carry it too far, that the law is such as makes it difficult to set the Negroes free." Imagine knowing when you marry that your children would never experience freedom, watching year after year the master's family exchanging visits with friends whenever they please, having no care provided for you in sickness except what a heartless owner approves, and being separated from spouse and children at the same master's whim. Picture yourself in the last years of your life, seeing your family in a hopeless condition and being powerless to change their circumstances.[49]

Abner also imagines the situation of an elderly male slave who was past his productive years. In his place, with strength waning, and having

> nothing at command to help our selves with, at length, thro[ugh] age and weakness, become unable to labor, and considered by those who have the care of us as a charge to their estates, and feel the warmth of nature very much to abate, yet in cold winter nights are oblige[d] to lie by ourselves, often feel chilly, and thinking on our own unhappy condition, joined with that of our children, desire to sleep but cannot. Were we sincerely to pass through all this, then the case of slaves I believe to many of us would appear very different from what it now doth.

Abner explains that back in the spring of 1767, and continuing for months thereafter, except for brief intervals of respite, he experienced a "sorrowful exercise" on the slaves' behalf. To begin with, his mind was opened (his choice of the passive voice is essential here) to the estates in Pennnsylvania and New Jersey that were "advanced by slaves." He implies a mystical experience, but we may conjecture that John's public, and perhaps private, testimony on slavery may have helped "open" his younger brother's mind. In a prophecy at that time, Abner says, he predicted that the "scales" were about to be "turned" and that "in future those in these two provinces who keep them with a desire of ease [and] profit, in the general would be disappointed and pass through great difficulties which otherwise they might [have] been clear of."[50]

He recalls that toward the end of his exercise, he became settled in his mind that those who ceased to advance themselves by the labor of slaves would please "Providence and add to their happiness even in this life." Again like John's, Abner's prophecy was optimistic. Finally, he addresses Friends on the question of reparations and shares his belief that Burlington Meeting should consider compensating those who had once been slaves of Meeting members.[51]

The Smiths had to be high on Abner's list of offenders, as they were on his brother's. We do not know whether, when Abner circulated his testimony to Friends, he asked John Smith, his brother Samuel, or their sister Elizabeth to read it. It seems clear, given the chronology and the substance of Abner's concerns, that his brother John had deeply influenced him, but perhaps it is truer to say that the brothers affected each other's insights. Abner says that he came to the advocacy of reparations for former slaves before John wrote on the subject, but it is possible that John's earlier anguish about his complicity in the injustice to Thomas Shinn's young slave affected Abner. Since neither brother expressed conscious knowledge of influences beyond their direct relationship with the Light, their development of creative conscience is even less accessible to us than it was to them. And unfortunately no information survives about what Abner read.

Abner attributed many of his moral insights to the experiences of his asthma attacks—gifts, he believed, that smoothed the path from temporary suffering to the eternal bliss of living in the spirit, an opportunity to share in Christ's suffering on the cross: "Under a long continuance of bodily weakness, and my strength gradually wasting, I generally felt a concern on Meeting days, while I was able to walk to the door without outward help, to give my attendance in dry weather." He last attended Meeting for Worship on August 20, 1771, and found it "one of the sweetest . . . that I ever was in."[52]

This is the final entry that Abner made in his journal. John not only copied but completed the story for his brother. He sat with Abner often for the next months, and they shared thoughts about nature and spirit, pain, death, and the afterlife. In a postscript to Abner's journal, John reports that the conversations brought them both peace. During his last five hours on earth Abner resigned himself to his fate and tried to endure the pains of his illness with faith and grace, John writes. He noted his faults and recalled mistakes with repentance but equanimity, confident in the mercy of God. He felt loved and more appreciative of the "beauty of this visible creation."

> He appeared in a quiet state of mind, and was glad to see me, having before expressed a desire of an opportunity with me; and we being left in private, he said, it hath been the [most] humbling time that ever I passed through, and I find nothing to trust in, but in the mercies of the Lord, and I believe the Lord will prepare a place of rest for me. He signified that through Divine Love, his heart had been brought into very great tenderness, and sympathizing love with his fellow creatures.

Abner told John that he desired to live no longer, and he suffered "much bodily pain," greater than any he had experienced before. His speech failed, "under the pangs of death, and at length he did not appear to have much pain; but to outward appearance breathed quiet and easy for half an hour or more, and departed like one going to sleep."[53]

As John mourned his brother, Christmas passed and 1772 began. He read Abner's spiritual autobiography and transcribed it as he was making what were to be the final revisions to his own *Journal*. Woolman faced a double mirror of memory and saw himself reflected in the life he remembered for his own *Journal* and in Abner's death. He was dwelling more in the past and future than ever before. Between what he recalled and what he anticipated, he had little time for the present.

12

Away

1772

"S OME time before" Woolman got to England, he dreamed that he was in its "northern parts."

The spring of the gospel was opened in him, much as in the beginning of Friends such as George Fox and William Dewsbury; and he saw the different states of the people as clear as he had ever seen flowers in a garden; but in his going on, he was suddenly stopt, though he could not see for what end; but looked towards home and thereupon fell into a flood of tears which waked him.

Here again, Woolman was having a premonitory dream, beckoning him to the birthplace of Quakerism in order to fulfill his destiny as a minister in the tradition of its founding generation, a destination from which he might not return. He does not mention the dream in his *Journal* but writes that it was a "religious concern" that prepared him to cross the sea "in order to visit Friends in the northern parts of England." The pure wisdom of the founders had promised a restoration of the primitive church; this was the place to purify again—white clothes, ascetic simplicity, and universal love embodying what God inspired in him.[1]

During March 1772, Woolman reversed the folio in which he had written the pages of his *Journal* and began a dialogue he called *Con-*

versations on the True Harmony of Mankind and How It May Be Promoted. The title is very close to that of *Considerations* on the same subject that he had written two years earlier, but this time he was focused on how true harmony could be "promoted," not "maintained," for he no longer believed that the harmony existed; his people had already lost it and must now promote its return.

This new pamphlet was another prophecy presented as a dialogue, which, like Woolman's earlier parable about the sons of Ham, hewed to a traditional form. Perhaps he intended to consider the prophecy further, even to integrate it into his *Journal* when he returned from England, going through the same process of revision he had used for earlier parts of the manuscript. When he did not return, though, the editors published the *Journal* without integrating the *Conversations.* It was not until 1837 that the essay was published—both as part of the *Journal* and independently.[2]

Woolman's introduction shows that *Conversations* had its origin in his ministry to such Friends as the Smiths, Pembertons, and Logans, with whom "at sundry times" he had felt his "mind opened in true brotherly love, to converse freely and largely with some who were entrusted with plentiful estates, in regard to an application of the profits of them, consistent with pure wisdom." The first of its two dialogues is "the substance of some conversation between a laboring man and a man rich in money," in which the laborer challenges the morality of those who do little or no physical labor, live well, and charge 7 percent interest to their customers, who must work harder "than is agreeable to us" to repay their debts. The rich merchant asks how this practice affects the laborer, since he is not paying the interest himself. The worker explains that he toils for a landowner who cannot pay him a living wage and expects more from him than he once supplied; the interest the landowner pays on his farm's mortgage saps his profits.[3]

Seventeenth-century English usury laws established 6 percent as the maximum interest rate, but in the American colonies the rates varied from 5 percent in Virginia to 8 percent in Massachusetts. Rates fluctuated during the eighteenth century; according to Benjamin Franklin, Pennsylvania's were between 6 and 10 percent. Rates slightly higher than traditional English ones reflected in part a shortage of specie in the colonies, which led to payments in goods and services. Since the value of goods fluctuated more than the value of specie, and the value of labor depended on an assessment of an individual's productivity, setting interest to be paid by barter was always more of an art than a science. The 7 percent that Woolman mentioned may have been the common rate assessed in New Jersey during his lifetime.[4]

According to Woolman's worker, economic pressure led farmers to exhaust the land by producing only cash crops when they might have been increasing the size of their flocks, which after all provided wool for clothing, meat for domestic consumption, and dung to enrich the fields. And more fertile land would result in greater productivity for less work. The cycle begins and ends with the interest charged by the landowner. "The produce of the earth is a gift from our gracious Creator to the inhabitants," the laborer contends, "and to impoverish the earth now to support outward greatness appears to be an injury to the succeeding age."[5]

The rich man thinks that he and his like should be the ones complaining since costs have risen while the rate at which they charge interest has been stable, thus, he implies, resulting in decreased profits. In fact the economy in southeastern Pennsylvania and central New Jersey continued to grow over Woolman's lifetime at a higher rate than in the seventeenth century; there were fluctuations, but the rich grew richer, and although workers also benefited, in relative terms the gap between rich and poor increased. And while American agricultural workers did not face profound poverty, as so much of rural Europe did, it became less and less likely that they would ever own land. On balance, then, each of Woolman's characters has a legitimate perspective, but the modern literature on the economic and social history of colonial America suggests that the worker has the better argument.

If we use Woolman's birth date (1720) as the point of comparison to eighteenth-century England and to the colonies fifty years later, we begin in a society with low population density, low geographic mobility, immediate access to land, widely distributed wealth, and little to no (depending on location) dependency on the intercolonial and international market economies. Over the half century of Woolman's life, population density multiplied, the acreage of the average farm decreased, individual productivity stayed stable, the concentration of wealth grew rapidly and was accompanied by social polarization, migration increased, and the colonies' wealth became concentrated geographically as society became more commercialized. All these changes were part of what Woolman and his worker decried. Men who came of age in 1720 could reasonably expect to have enough land to make a living where they were born and to live as well as their fathers had; thirty years later this was no longer true.[6]

Woolman believed that it was moral decline that caused market growth and the desire for riches. Whether the colonists did in fact abandon the set of values, or *mentalité*, of communalism in order to pursue profits or whether new market opportunities encouraged their individualism is a complex question; it is possible that the traditional ambition for what colonists called competence—to have enough to live on and to help ensure that one's children would enjoy the same living standard—simply fell to changes they were powerless to affect and to economic opportunities their forefathers had lacked. This is not to say that colonists were morally incapable of resisting the allures of the marketplace, but rather that the preceding generations were not necessarily, as Woolman implies, morally superior people.[7]

In the opinion of Woolman's laborer, the rich man suffers from a lack of imagination, an inability to put himself in the workingman's shoes; this moral defect keeps him from living by the Golden Rule. But the rich man is not convinced, believing that if he took the laborer's advice, everyone's living standard would fall and less would be produced, with less trade, lower profits, and decreased availability of staple goods. Anyway, he retorts, he has personally witnessed men who, after a day of hard physical labor, appear cheerful and have ample energy to sing, dance, and carouse. He simply does not accept that the worker's plight is as bleak as the laboring man portrays it.[8]

Woolman's laborer tries another tack. He suggests that it is unseemly for the rich to behave as they do. He recalls the prophet Ezekiel's parable about the cattle that feed on rich pasture and, without regard, trample what they do not eat, that drink their fill at a stream and leave foul mud behind for those who come after them. If, instead, rich men lived "in the Simplicity of the Truth" all would be served.

> Men who live on a supply from the interest of their money, and who do little else but manage it, appear to have but a small share of the labor in carrying on the affairs of a province; and where a member of society doth but a small share of the business thereof, it appears most agreeable to equity and true brotherly love that he should endeavor to live in such sort as may be most easy to them by whose labor he is chiefly supported.[9]

The second conversation is between the same farmworker and a "thrifty landholder." The farmer asks why it is that he must work longer hours to pay for a bushel of grain than he did twenty years earlier. The landlord explains that proportionally fewer people in the colonies are raising crops yet that more grain and flour are being shipped abroad; rising prices for grain in Europe have encouraged the export trade and also affect the cost of grain sold in America. (According to modern economic historians, all these facts are correct.)[10]

To the farmer, much of the business being done in the colonies is unnecessary, "invented to please the pride and vanity of such who wander from pure wisdom." When more grain is harvested with less labor and laborers are still worse off in every way, a less "harmonious" society is the result. If the price of gold is injustice, it is "gold the country had better be without." Society could do very well without currency, Woolman believed. Axes and hoes were worth more than gold in their utility; a man who could tool iron and trade for food contributed more to society than landlords ever did. Farmers, tailors, and blacksmiths were worth more than merchants, however rich the merchants were.

> Gold, where the value fixed thereon is agreed to, appears to be attended with a certain degree of power, and where men get much of this power, their hearts are many times in danger of being lifted up above their brethren, and of being estranged

from that meekness and tender feeling of the state of the poor, which accompanies the faithful followers of Christ.[11]

Gold translates into power, which is misused. This is why "the joints and bands of society are disordered." Love of money and "hearts ensnared with imaginary greatness" spread like a disease from parents to children. To the extent that men have a will to be rich, they work against the interests of "poor honest people." To defend their wealth, powerful men gladly expend the lives of laborers who become soldiers.

The battles of the warrior are not only with confused noise and garments rolled in blood, but commonly contrived in the craft and subtlety of man's wisdom; and if we trust in man, make flesh our arm, and are estranged from that purified state in which the mind relies on God, we are in the way towards an increase of confusion; and this state, even among much gold and great riches, is less settled and quiet than that of a faithful follower of the lowly Jesus, who is contented with those things which our heavenly Father knows that we have need of.[12]

This last observation brings Woolman's argument full circle. Soldiers are society's fodder, poor, landless workers and often out-of-work men who are deluded that their interests coincide with those of the landowners and businessmen who hold their mortgages and sell them goods on credit. The colonies were becoming ever more "disordered," and economic relations were "injuring" posterity. Woolman prophesied that the legacy of market relations would be war, depleted natural resources, and increased suffering for those at the bottom of society. Just as he had seen the French and Indian War as the fruit of slavery, so now—only three years before the American Revolution—he anticipated war as the consequence of greed, impoverishment, and delusion.

Other Quakers from the Middle Atlantic colonies, including those who had fewer scruples, more moral flexibility, and less devotion to the society's peace testimony, took the pacifist position when the Revolution began. Yet the political maelstrom that preceded the

Revolution is undetectable in Woolman's writings. He saw the social and political drift toward greater violence but did not allude to
tensions within the empire that might bring the colonists to war
against their mother country. He seems to have been similarly obliv-
ious to any signs of looming crisis during his months in England.

In the larger picture he drew, politics and the personal pursuit of
wealth came from greed or, at least, from misguided attempts to
leave an inheritance for children. Where there is no ambition to accumulate land, possessions, and money, there will be social justice,
less resentment of taxes raised for legitimate social benefits, and
lower taxes because there are no more wars. Without greed, there is
no slavery and no exploitation of workers; there is domestic peace.
A society inspired by justice emanating from Truth—the Golden
Rule—is a tranquil society that distributes wealth equitably.

Woolman practiced the ministry, and perhaps even applied the
language, of the *Conversations* one last time before he left for England. Not surprisingly, given his past efforts, he practiced it on one
of the Burlington Smiths, this time Elizabeth (1724–72), John and
Samuel's sister, who was four years younger than Woolman. He had
known her since childhood too, and now she simply shows up in his
correspondence as an old friend. Elizabeth was not a business-
woman, an owner of slaves, or personally engaged in the slave trade.
She never married, she lived well from her family's estate, and
she used her money for charity administered through the Society of
Friends. She traveled in her ministry, attending New England Yearly
Meeting in Newport in 1764 with Joyce Benezet, wife of Anthony,
and Sarah Morris of Philadelphia. At her death, an obituary described Elizabeth Smith thus:

> By a steady conformity to the Divine Will, she became emi-
> nently distinguished; being deep in council, sound in judg-
> ment; awful [i.e., dignified in] her manners, refined [in] her
> sentiments, and graceful [in] her deportment . . . She was
> from a child of unusual steadiness and composure of deport-
> ment and character . . . She was of sympathetic heart, much
> given to works of charity. She valued the Scriptures, and tes-
> tified against the fashionable publications of the times.[13]

What prompted Woolman's expression of concern about Elizabeth Smith was the circulation of a traveling certificate in Burlington Monthly Meeting. Late in the winter of 1771–72, Smith solicited the Meeting's endorsement of a planned journey to England; she wanted to accompany Sarah Morris (1703 or 1704–75), who, at the age of sixty-eight, was leaving for England with her niece Deborah Morris (1724–93). Sarah had been recognized by her Meeting as a minister of the gospel and had traveled at least as widely as Woolman had; she too had been at New England Yearly Meeting and gone six times to Maryland.[14]

Custom dictated a "traveling minute," the Meeting's formal endorsement of the bearer's good standing and of the journey as spiritually led. But Woolman had a twinge of conscience—a "concern," a "stop," a "reserve"—about Elizabeth's purity of soul, and he hesitated before he signed her certificate.

> I believe my dear friend the Lord hath weaned thy mind in a great measure from all these things, and when I signed thy certificate, expressing thee to be exemplary, I had regard to the state of thy mind as it appeared to me; but many times since I signed it I felt a desire to open to thee a reserve, which I then and since often felt as to the exemplariness of those things amongst thy furniture which are against the purity of our principles.[15]

But then Elizabeth fell mortally ill; she in fact never made the transatlantic crossing. To Woolman, her sickness was a sign from God: "I believe our afflictions are often permitted by our heavenly Father for our more full and perfect refining." And the failing that Elizabeth needed to "purge" on her deathbed concerned, as he had warned her, her furniture.

> I believe my dear friend, there are lessons for thee and I yet to learn—Friends from the country and in the city are often at thy house, and when they behold amongst thy furniture some things which are not agreeable to the purity of Truth, the minds of some, I believe, at times are in danger of being

diverted from so close an attention to the Light of life as is necessary for us.[16]

Elizabeth did not take Woolman's advice, for on her death the furniture came down to the next generation of Smiths as part of her estate. A twentieth-century descendant notes that her chairs "have only a shell on the back and knees, and, except for their graceful shape, are absolutely without other ornament." Elizabeth died later that year, on October 2, at the age of forty-eight, five days before Woolman and an ocean away from him. Unless Woolman created a nagging doubt, she likely died in good conscience, confident that she had threaded her camel through the needle's eye and lived by Quaker testimonies, including the one on simplicity.[17]

Woolman was inspired to take this hyperdedication to Quaker orthodoxy and uncompromising sense of the link between small moral compromises and grave sins along with his all-encompassing vision of universal love on his ministry to England. He began to separate from family and friends in a fatalistic fashion. Fear of travel was not new to him, and it combined now with his recognition of his own poor health, near-death experience, and enduring weakness, and the dark news of Elizabeth Smith's illness and the deaths of John Smith and his brother Abner. He was certain this would be his last trip.

Woolman acquainted Monthly and Quarterly Meetings of "the religious exercise which attended my mind." In December 1771 his request had been one of those before Meeting for Business in Philadelphia, as Joseph Oxley (1715–75), a Quaker clockmaker from Norwich who had been traveling in the colonies for almost two years, reported in a letter.

Samuel Emlen, at our last monthly meeting at Philadelphia, laid before the meeting a concern he had on his mind to pay a religious visit to Friends in some parts of Great Britain; also another Friend, John Woolman, a wise sensible man having a good gift in the ministry and well approved of, has a concern of the like kind more particularly to Yorkshire. I suppose the latter will hardly leave the continent till the summer.

Woolman presented the same request to General Spring Meeting of Elders and Ministers, all of which "signified their unity by a certificate dated the 24th day of the 3rd month 1772, directed to Friends in Great Britain."[18]

Woolman's formal farewell came in an epistle to members of his Meeting, which he anticipated would be published after he sailed. He sent it in manuscript to Israel Pemberton with a note: "If thou and such in this city, who are careful to look over writings proposed to be printed and to amend what may be imperfect, would employ a little time in correcting that piece, and afterward let me see the proposed alterations, it would be acceptable to me to look over them." Together with Woolman's last draft of his *Journal*, John Pemberton then presented it to the June Meeting for Sufferings, which appointed a subcommittee to "revise it carefully and to treat with a printer for printing it." In July the committee placed an order for two thousand copies, "to send a share to each of the Provinces where there are Meetings of Friends." (New York and New England Friends paid two shillings per dozen. The bill arrived from the printer in September, so the epistle came into circulation at about the same time that Woolman died.)[19]

The epistle was Woolman's last sermon to American Quakers. In it he shared once again his concern for the "pure principle of Light and Life," a phrase that was new to him, which covers the indwelling spirit and the physical manifestation of belief in the way that Friends lived. As professors of the spirit, he reminded them, Quakers had a claim to direct inspiration by the Holy Spirit that burdened them with a responsibility to deliver "pure witness" to gentiles. But many of them had become a "stumbling block" to the conversion of others, deviating "from the purity of our religious principles" instead of demonstrating a "perfect resignation to this Divine Teacher."[20]

Woolman was led to instruct Friends to change their ways. One had to work lovingly but strictly "with offenders," even approaching them as heathens ignorant of Christ's teachings. If disownment—expulsion from the society—was necessary, so be it. To compromise, to tolerate the offenders' unrighteous conduct and defiance of revealed Truth, would mislead the world and betray the mission

God gave the Quakers. The first Friends, despite "many tribulations," had had "fellowship in that which is pure," and they were the standard against which eighteenth-century Quakers had to measure themselves.[21]

This is the path that Woolman had advocated his whole life: self-reform by the guiding Light of pure Truth, leading by example, instructing with pure love, and living by an uncompromising devotion to righteousness. He was delivering the prophecy one more time for the road, and then his American ministry was done.

Woolman still worried about children, those who were poor, who would be spiritually hardened and prone to the vices growing from deprivation, and those who had too much, who were not learning pure wisdom. These spiritually vulnerable children of wealth and of poverty were the responsibility of adults inspired by universal love.

Friends needed to remember the suffering of early Christian martyrs and persecuted Protestants. They needed to recall the travails of those who lived, in the past and the present, without the gift of liberty of conscience. Since Quakers enjoyed the privilege of worshiping freely in the colonies, they bore a "great and weighty trust" to live exemplary lives for the spiritual benefit of their children, the gentiles around them, the church, and themselves: "We stand in a place of outward liberty, under the free exercise of our conscience towards God, not obtained but through great and manifold afflictions of those who lived before us. There is gratitude due from us to our heavenly Father. There is justice due to our posterity." And since Quakers were the standard-bearers of the Christian faith—the chosen people of God—they had to heed the warnings of the prophet Isaiah or fail in their mission.

There was nothing new in any of this; Woolman was repeating, summarizing, concluding his life's work. But he honed the message to a more focused, forceful, and sharper point. It was his clearest articulation of his prophecy and stylistically the most appealing; his prophetic voice had reached its purest pitch.[22]

Friends who continued their "customary way of living" created a barrier to the conversion of "seekers who are wearied with empty forms." But with the Golden Rule as their guide, "waiting on the Lord in humility," Quakers could again become "the light of the world (Mat. 5:14)." A return to peace, quietness, and "harmonious walking" would restore the spirit that had once guided their faith. As "faithful standard-bearers under the prince of peace," Quakers could ensure that "nothing of a defiling nature tending to discord and wars may remain amongst us."[23]

Friends should take an inventory of their ways, asking if they had more than they had an "equitable right" to possess. They needed to recognize that they betrayed the principle of peace to which they testified when they gave just cause for jealousy or fair reason for resentment, and when they lived in contravention of the testimonies they openly endorsed: "Where the wisdom from above is faithfully followed, and therein we are entrusted with outward substance, it is a treasure committed to our care in the nature of an inheritance from him who formed and supports the world."[24]

Those who held land and other wealth in a "selfish spirit" should fear that jealousy would lead to violence against them. Landlords were likely to tempt theft or invite a war of social rebellion. Merchants daily incited to violence those whose labor paid for their silver plate, carriages, mansions, and imported furniture and clothes. If American society was unstable, Quakers bore as much responsibility as other landed and mercantile elites, but were even guiltier because God had chosen them to serve as beacons of light to the world. They daily betrayed that trust, and the prophet warned them about the consequences.

I have seen under humbling exercises that the sins of the fathers are embraced by the children and become their sins, and thus in the days of tribulation, the iniquities of the fathers are visited upon these children who take hold on the unrighteousness of their fathers, and live in that spirit in which those iniquities were committed. To which agreeth that prophecy of Moses concerning rebellious people; they that are left of you shall pine away in their iniquities in your enemies' land, and in the iniquities of their fathers shall they pine away. Levit. 26, 39. And our blessed Lord in beholding the hardness of heart in that generation, and feeling in himself that they lived in the same spirit in which the prophets had been persecuted unto death, signified that the blood of all the prophets shed from the foundation of the world should be required of that generation. From the blood of Abel, to the blood of Zacharias, who perished between the altar and the temple. Verily I say unto you, it shall be required of this generation. Luke 11.51.[25]

Revealingly, Woolman said nothing of slavery, not even mentioning it in his *Conversations* or parting epistle. He was aiming further down the chain of causation, slavery being a consequence of deeper problems within the soul of Quakerism. If he anticipated the day when no one could both be a member of Philadelphia Yearly Meeting and own slaves, which occurred within only two years, he remained nonetheless disconsolate. The epistle prophesied an internal war that would bring suffering and exile to the Friends, and indeed, Quakers who remained neutral or loyal were to suffer both fates during the Revolution.

AFTER finishing the last draft of his *Journal* and the epistle, Woolman settled his accounts; he paid what little he owed and collected what he could from those who owed him for teaching their children and making their clothes. He paid his poor tax and sold four trees from his orchard.

Woolman's daughter and her husband, John Comfort, were settled in their new house, and Mary was pregnant. Sarah Woolman was likewise secure. The orchard, animals, and garden were to feed the whole family. In the last entry in his account book, Woolman put uncollected bills in the hands of his son-in-law, in whose care he left his daughter and wife. If Comfort could collect what customers still owed Woolman, it would provide a small income to supplement what they already had and the produce they could sell. Rather than writing a will, Woolman executed a "Deed of Trust" that transferred his lands to Stephen Comfort, his son-in-law's father, while he was still alive. The elder Comfort was to take responsibility for the estate in his absence and serve as executor in the event of his death.

I the said John Woolman having it in my heart to prepare for a voyage to Great Britain on a religious visit do not see any way in which I may dispose of the lands and buildings which I possess more to my own peace than to commit them to the said Stephen Comfort in trust for my use and for the use of my beloved wife Sarah during the time that we and the survivor of us may live in this world. And that the said Stephen Comfort may convey or devise all the lands which I now possess to his son John or to our daughter Mary or to either of them and to their heirs and assigns forever as he in the fear of the Lord may believe right.

Woolman was being prudent in traditional ways, putting the women under the care of trusted men. The Meeting too would look out for his family.[26]

Woolman also wrote a letter to his daughter and son-in-law, not because he lacked occasion to bid them farewell but to leave them written testimony of his love. With that, he apparently believed that all the loose ends of his life were tied up. ____

> Dear Children:
>
> I feel a tender care for you at this time of parting from you, and under this care, my mind is turned toward the pure Light of Truth, to which if you take diligent heed I trust you will find inward support under all your trials.
>
> My leaving you under the trying circumstances now attending you, is not without close exercise and I feel a living concern, that under these cares of business, and under bodily affliction, your minds may be brought to a humble waiting on Him who is the great preserver of his people. Your loving parent
>
> John Woolman

Pregnancy was the "trying circumstance" that attended Mary and John Comfort. A baby boy was born six weeks after Woolman's departure and named after him; he was the first of their ten children, eight of them boys. Two of the boys died in infancy, and a daughter at age five. Woolman's note suggests that he felt the tug of worldly attachment; he would not be present for the birth of his first grandchild. He could not have forgotten the problems Sarah had faced in her childbearing years, his fears for her in her pregnancies and deliveries, perhaps the grief of stillbirths, and the loss of their infant son. Still in all, his actions displayed his belief that God's call took precedence over his domestic concerns and attachments.[27]

In April, Woolman searched for a suitable ship to sail on. Since he was bound for Yorkshire, a ship headed for Liverpool or Whitehaven would be the best choice, but his old friend and fellow minister Samuel Emlen (1730–99), a veteran transatlantic traveler who made seven round-trip crossings during his lifetime, was sailing to London on the *Mary and Elizabeth*. And Emlen had a reputation among Quakers as a seer. Many theories and superstitions were associated with choosing a ship for passage, and although there is no telling which of these, if any, Woolman put stock in, the fact that the ship's names were those of his mother and daughter and that it had been chosen by a seer could have been reassuring.

Quakers believed that Emlen had awe-inspiring insight into people's characters and past experiences; some thought he was so accurate in his revelations that they were afraid to be in his presence lest he detect their secret sins. The stories were legion, all of them about his inspired public discovery of information unknown to any mortal but the sinner. In one account he delivered a revelation that applied to none of those in the room, which led Friends to assume that he had missed the mark this time. When someone went to close a door that was ajar, he found a young man weeping behind it, the sinner for whom the message was intended. Recollections of such events became oral traditions among Friends that lasted for generations and supported the faith's mystical core.[28]

There were also several other Quakers who would be Woolman's shipmates, for example, the twenty-year-old John Bispham (1752–1812), one of several men by that name who belonged to Mount Holly Meeting. He may even have been one of the Bisphams whom Woolman had taught in his school; he was now apprenticed to a merchant in Philadelphia; his trip was for business and to visit relatives. John Till-Adams (1748–86) was an English physician returning home from a yearlong mission to American Quakers. James Reynolds, who some speculate was a relative by marriage of Bispham's, was also apparently connected to the group.[29]

And there was Sarah Logan (1744–97), traveling with her maid.

She was from London and had eloped with William Logan (son of William and a grandnephew of James) of Philadelphia in 1770, when he was a medical student at Edinburgh, where they married without the knowledge of either family. William and Sarah had settled in Philadelphia, where he practiced surgery, but he had died in January at the age of twenty-five, and Sarah was going home to live with her parents, having left her infant son with the Logans.[30]

The *Mary and Elizabeth*, a 180-ton ship that was both fast and stable, was jointly owned by a trio of Quakers, the London merchants Daniel Mildred and John Roberts, and John Head (1723–92), one of Philadelphia's richest men. The captain was James Sparks, not a Quaker but an Anglican vestryman at Philadelphia's Christ Church, an experienced seaman who had made many Atlantic crossings, in whose capable hands the Quakers on board had a chance of arriving in time for Yearly Meeting the first week of June. (The same ship, with the same captain, leaving on exactly the same day the previous year with Woolman's cousin William Hunt on board, had not made it in time.)[31]

Woolman had help selecting and packing stores of food, drink, and medication for his personal use on board. According to Emlen in a letter to his wife, "Margaret Haines* I suppose was kindly careful for him and he is much better provided with necessaries than thou may perhaps expect." He may have taken the mattress that he had made for his aborted West Indies trip, or perhaps he stuffed and sewed a new one. There was the question of where in the ship he would bunk; his age and status suggested the cabin, but his ascetic nature drew him to steerage—belowdecks, in the hold with the sailors—when he saw the cabin's luxurious woodwork and accommodations.

I told the owner that on the outside of that part of the ship where the cabin was I observed sundry sorts of carved work

---

*Margaret Wistar Haines (1729–93) was married to Woolman's cousin Reuben (1728–93). (Their mothers were sisters.) She was born in Germantown, and both she and her husband were elders of Market Street Meeting in Philadelphia. They died caring for the sick during the yellow fever epidemic of 1793. Reuben was a brewer and a successful businessman; he was reputed to have been Woolman's financial adviser (whatever that might mean). Woolman always stayed with them in Philadelphia.

and imagery, and that in the cabin I observed some superfluity of workmanship of several sorts, and that [on a reasonable computation] according to the way of men's reckoning, the sum of money to be paid for a passage in that apartment hath some relation to the expense in furnishing the room to please the minds of such who give way to a conformity to this world, and that in this case, as in other cases, the moneys received from the passengers are calculated to answer every expense relating to their passage, and amongst the rest, the expense of these superfluities; and that in this case I felt a scruple with regard to paying my money to defray such expenses.[32]

Benjamin Franklin sailed in steerage on his first round trip to London, as did most passengers who had to count their pennies. To this Woolman added moral concerns, not wishing to be "entangled in the spirit of oppression" that the cabin furnishings represented. The "exercise" of Woolman's soul was "such that I could not find peace in joying [enjoying] in anything which I saw was against that wisdom which is pure." The decision and the logic behind it were pure Woolman.[33]

Woolman took leave of his family one last, tearful time, and also parted with friends in Mount Holly and "several of my beloved friends" in Philadelphia, "who appeared to be concerned for me on account of the unpleasant situation of that part of the vessel where I was likely to lodge." He found these concerns unsettling, especially the ones about the increased risks of disease and seasickness. But, he recorded later, he was grateful that his mind "was kept low," by which he meant that he could rest content in the spiritual leading of God, "and friends, having expressed their desire that I might have a place more convenient than the steerage, did not urge but appeared disposed to leave me to the Lord."[34]

Woolman stayed two nights in Philadelphia while the ship's crew made ready to sail. He attended Darby Meeting one last time and then boarded the ship.* It left the dock in Philadelphia and

---

*The Quaker botanist John Bartram (1699–1777) attended Darby Meeting, even though Friends had disowned him for publicly doubting the divinity of Christ. His son, the nature artist and writer William Bartram (1739–1823), was also a member of Darby Meeting.

sailed downriver the short distance to Chester, where it took on supplies and where Samuel Emlen, Sarah Logan, and her maid boarded.
The ship left the shore on May 1, 1772. "And as I sat down alone
on a seat on the deck," Woolman wrote, "I felt a satisfactory evidence [in my mind] that my proceedings were not in my own will
but under the power of the cross of Christ." This time Woolman was
confident that he followed God.[35]

On the morning of May 2, off New Castle, Delaware, and still in
sight of land, Emlen wrote to his wife.

> We are in much harmony among ourselves, mutual kindness
> prevails and I am hopeful that we in the cabin especially shall
> continue in those dispositions during our confinement to-
> gether. John Woolman is as free and open as I at any time re-
> member him. He has been several times in my stateroom and
> inclines to make it a receptacle for some of his matters which
> are not proper to be in the steerage loose.

The next day, now out on the high sea, Emlen mentioned Woolman
again in a letter.

> John Woolman just now tells me that he is pretty well, his
> mind feels easy, and that he is quite contented with his lodg-
> ing. He was just now in my stateroom in which most of his
> clothes and sea store are. It is a receptacle for them, and I
> think far more proper than the steerage, he having access
> thither frequent, or when he inclines. He is much more free
> and conversable than some expected and expressed himself
> glad in having me so near him.[36]

Woolman had never done much writing when he was away from
home, but the long days on board gave him time not only for many
conversations and for silent contemplation but for keeping a sea
journal and perhaps drafting five essays that he would finish over
the summer. Countless passengers and literate sailors filled part of
their days with diaries, generally writing more when nothing was
happening—just the rhythmic rolling and creaking of the ship, the

barks of officers, and the profane grumbles of sailors aloft and be-lowdecks.

Six days after they lost sight of land, Woolman made the first en-try in his journal. This one turned out differently from his spiritual *Journal.* He made more frequent entries in it and wrote soon after the events occurred, sometimes on the same day. He took no time for extensive revision or for retrospection. The sea journal was idio-syncratic, since he had never read another traveler's journal and was not bound by any known traditions and forms. He imposed no co-herence, plot, or character development on the entries. He wrote as thoughts and experiences came to him, though surely with reflec-tion and an audience in mind.

Woolman was grateful that God had thus far—one week into the journey—"preserved" him from the seasickness other passengers were enduring. He was not without "afflictions," but his were spiri-tual rather than physical. The captain and the other passengers dis-played "an openness" that apparently surprised and pleased him, and his decision to berth with the sailors gave him more time for contemplation, he reported, since he could retire to his quarters without giving offense, and this happily resulted in "quietness of mind."[37]

Woolman frequently visited Emlen's cabin, ate, and passed time. He preferred to sit on a wooden box rather than a bench or chair, and there he read, wrote, sewed, and prayed. Perhaps he repaired clothes for the seamen and his fellow passengers. He had the tools of his trade and could work peacefully. He was friendly, even outgo-ing, surprising some of the passengers who did not know him. Wool-man may even have surprised himself. "He kept, I think, much within his usual restrictions on board," Emlen writes, "though not so confined as to be unwilling to partake of some parts of our stores."[38]

But it was belowdecks that Woolman experienced his spiritual "afflictions," for it was there that he had "sundry opportunities of seeing, hearing, and feeling with respect to the life and spirit of many poor sailors." He felt "an inward exercise of soul" about their ignorance of God, and he had "from a motion of love sundry times taken opportunities with one alone and in a free conversation labored to turn their minds toward the fear of the Lord." Woolman had found a new ministry in the hold.[39]

Five apprenticed boys, two of whom had been raised among Quakers, for example, were the focus of Woolman's solicitude. One of them, a Friend by birth—"birthright"—was a great-nephew of James Nayler, a celebrated and controversial early Quaker. Imagine the shock for Woolman, a mystic who lived by spiritual signs, to be following God's call back to the origins of Quakerism and to meet another James Nayler along the way. What a blessing to have such a confirmation that he was on the right path! Yet a great sadness came over Woolman when he interpreted the two boys' lives in steerage as symbolic of Quakerism's decline: "I often feel a tenderness of heart towards these poor lads and at times look at them as though they were my children according to the flesh." He already had written about the recklessness of routinely sending ships across the ocean with boys such as these at risk, exploiting their labor and perhaps their lives to fulfill greedy earthly ambitions: "Oh, that all may take heed and beware of covetousness! Oh, that all may learn of Christ who is meek and low of heart! Then in faithfully following him, he will teach us to be content with food and raiment without respect to the customs or honors of this world."[40]

In sympathy for the sailors, and in criticism of the Quaker shipowners, Woolman described the sailors' close quarters. There, in steerage on the *Mary and Elizabeth*, was the whole chain of greed, oppression, and violence he had written about for decades. During rough weather, and especially at night, when the hold was dark even with the lamps lit, sailors were suddenly called above deck for work; when they returned, physically exhausted, they dropped their wet clothes in heaps and stumbled to their bunks for rest. Arguments and fights broke out regularly when they later quickly grabbed garments that may or may not have been theirs. Woolman, his sleep interrupted time and again, heard the tempers flare, breathed the dampness, smelled the sweat, witnessed the bloodshed. He did not blame the sailors, but rather those who exploited them: "Great reformation in the world is wanting! And the necessity of it amongst these who do business in great waters hath at this time been abundantly opened before me."[41]

Storms at sea made bad conditions worse, and one encountered by the *Mary and Elizabeth* kept Woolman confined for seventeen hours, which he spent in Emlen's cabin. He took advantage of the frequent invitations to share the better accommodations, he explained to himself, because "the poor, wet, toiling seamen had need of all the room in the crowded steerage." The ship, battened down and lying to rather than actually sailing, tossed through a day that looked like night. Woolman says that he experienced little fear during the "tempest" since he was "preserved in a good degree of resignation," confident that his journey was in God's hands. From his "tender frame of mind," Woolman writes, he tried to reassure his fellow passengers that God "sometimes through adversities intends our refinement." The storm was for their own good.[42]

At one point in the middle of the night Woolman went on deck to witness the storm. The waves looked like fire that gave off no light. A sailor at the helm reported a corposant (from the Latin *corpus sanctum*, or holy body) at the head of the mast. This was Saint Elmo's fire, an electrical discharge off the point of the mast that is named for the patron saint of sailors, who see it as an auspicious sign, another sign. The captain ordered a carpenter with an ax to remain on deck in case it became necessary to demast the boat to keep it afloat. But "soon after this the vehemency of the wind abated, and before morning they again put the ship under sail." Woolman never performed miracles, as it was claimed George Fox and James Nayler had done, but here he thought he came close to witnessing one.[43]

The half dozen Quakers on board regularly held Meeting for Worship in Emlen's cabin. Eventually some of the sailors attended the services. "Most of the seamen were present," Woolman writes of one First Day Meeting. "This meeting to me was a strengthening time." Yet although he thought that "sailing is of some use in the world," this was not a career for young Friends.

A pious father whose mind is exercised for the everlasting welfare of his child may not with a peaceful mind place him out to an employment amongst a people whose common course of life is manifestly corrupt and profane. So great is the present defect amongst seafaring men in regard to piety and virtue, and through an abundant traffic and many ships of war, so many people are employed on the sea, that this subject of placing lads to the employment appears very weighty.[44]

Seamen's language disturbed Woolman. His parents had taught him the power of silence. Frivolous speech was carnal, and the profanity in steerage scandalized him. The hold was a Babel of voices, a charnel of verbal chaos, the very antithesis of pious silence. If anywhere on earth was a saintly Quaker's hell, it was here, where the only peace came in sleep, where the only sounds were profane, and where the quiet voice of God was drowned out by oaths and blasphemy.

Woolman had sympathy for the sailors' plight—"a sympathizing tenderness toward poor children" who ended up in this life—and he found them open to his ministry.

> I have sometimes had weighty conversation with the sailors in the steerage, who were mostly respectful to me, and more and more so the longer I was with them . . . They mostly appeared to take kindly what I said to them, but their minds have appeared to be so deeply impressed with that almost universal depravity amongst sailors that the poor creatures, in their answers to me on this subject, have revived in my remembrance that of the degenerate Jews a little before the captivity, as repeated by Jeremiah the prophet, "There is no hope" [Jer. 18:12].

The two qualifiers—"mostly"—and another identification with an Old Testament prophet, who was resigned to his people's fate: Woolman once again would have to accept that he accomplished the prophetic task by delivering God's message and that he could not be too concerned with how the seamen received it.[45]

The sailors told Woolman about their lives at sea. He learned about the slave trade from their perspective and about the dangers, oppression, and tragedies they endured. The depravity Woolman witnessed in steerage was the responsibility of wealthy men in and outside his religion, he knew, but fellow Quakers should know better, had a greater responsibility, and thus bore more of the blame.

> When I remember that saying of the Most High through his prophet, "This people have I formed for myself: they shall show forth my praise" [Is. 43:21], and think of placing children amongst them to learn the practice of sailing joined with a pious education, as to me, my condition hath been like that mentioned by the prophet, "There is no answer from God" [Mic. 3:7].

There he was, in the same situation as the prophet Isaiah, reminding Quakers that they were the chosen people of God, with all the gifts and responsibilities that entailed. They were not following the path that God intended for them. But Woolman was resigned to continue his ministry, "humbled under the power of divine love," to listen and learn more about the plight of the poor seamen, and to "labor in his love for the spreading of pure universal righteousness in the earth."[46]

By the fourth week of the voyage Woolman thought he was weakening. "My appetite failing, the trial hath been the heavier," he writes in the entry for May 24. He continues with biblical citations that addressed his condition and were from the prophets with whom he so closely identified. In the fog and becalmed, he hears the lessons of clarity and resignation: "In an entire subjection of our wills the Lord graciously opens a way for his people, where all their wants are bounded by his wisdom; and here we experience the substance of what Moses *the prophet* figured out in the water of separation as a purification from sin."[47]

With so much time and under such conditions, Woolman dwelled understandably on death. When he could see no end to the sea journey, he thought about meeting God when he died, for, as the prophet explained, "no man can see God and live." Woolman continued, as he had throughout his adulthood, to prepare for a new life: "Blessed are the pure in heart, for they shall see God."[48]

He recalled the limitations of nature and the truth that the "natural mind is active about the things of this life." It was "natural activity" that accounted for the business practices he abhorred: "As long as this natural will remains unsubjected, so long there remains an obstruction against the clearness of divine light operating in us." Universal love was the key to escape, the lesson taught by the prophets of the Old Testament and by Christ and his apostles in the New Testament. If he had known more about world religions, Woolman would have realized that when Quakers hear God in silence reinforced by the revealed Word, they share in the experience of Muslims who find their faith by reciting the Qur'an, Jews who hear God when chanting the Torah, and medieval Catholics who heard the divine in sacred music. The mystical experience that transcended Woolman's faith came home with him to England; it was the baggage that he brought on the ship.[49]

May 31 was First Day, and "near all" of the thirty people on board joined Woolman in Meeting for Worship, where "the Lord in mercy favored us with the extendings of his love." On June 2 the seamen found bottom at seventy fathoms. The morning was pleasant with a fair wind. Woolman's spirits lifted. The roosters remaining among the fowl taken on board for food crowed for the first time since leaving the Delaware River, and the passengers saw land for the first time in a month. On June 4 a pilot appeared to lead them from Dover to London. Samuel Emlen, Sarah Logan, and her maid disembarked there to travel the seventy-two miles to London by land, but Woolman "felt easy in staying in the ship."[50]

It was a small thing, the decisions each took about how to travel the last short leg of the journey, but it reflects the differences among them. Emlen, a seer, minister, and revered man of God among Quakers, chose a coach as he had paid for a cabin on the *Mary and Elizabeth*. The overland route would be quicker, and he wanted to reach London in time for the beginning of Yearly Meeting. Woolman rejected passage on a vehicle that sped across the countryside pulled by horses that were driven hard. He chose purity over compromise, over comfort, convenience, and a worldly attention to conventions dictated by time. He might be late, but he would not be guilty; Emlen silently (at least to us) rejected Woolman's higher moral road, quite possibly without looking back guiltily.

On June 7, a clear morning, the ship's company waited for the tide to carry them up the Thames and into port. It being a First Day, they had their last shipboard Meeting for Worship. They watched the bustle of ships, which only reminded Woolman of the moral problems associated with trade. The seafaring life was "so opposite to that of a pious education, so full of corruption and extreme alienation from God, so full of examples the most dangerous to *young people* that in looking toward a young generation I feel a care for them."[51]

In a note at the end of his sea journal dated June 13, 1772, Woolman indicates that he is passing the pages written at sea to Sophia Hume (1702–74). This Englishwoman was a great-granddaughter of Mary Fisher, one of the first two Quakers to arrive in Massachusetts in 1656. Fisher had moved to South Carolina with her second husband, and Sophia had been born there, married Robert Hume of Charleston in 1721, and been widowed in 1737.

Although her mother had been a Quaker, like her grandmother, her father was an Anglican. It was not until 1741, at about the time that she moved to London, that Sophia joined the Quakers. Woolman probably first met her in 1747, when she was on a religious visit to the colonies and wrote a pamphlet advocating the simplicity of a Quaker lifestyle, *An Exhortation to the Inhabitants of the Province of South Carolina* (1748). Woolman and John Smith were two of the overseers who approved its publication. While Hume was in Philadelphia, she had lived in Israel Pemberton's home; she returned to London on the same ship as James Pemberton. Woolman now asked only that "if she hath a mind to revise [the pages] and place them in better order, I am free to it; but I desire she may not show them to anyone, but with a very weighty consideration." After his death Sophia Hume did indeed send the manuscript back to Philadelphia, apparently with Samuel Emlen, without having changed a word.[52]

13

Home

1772

J OHN Pemberton (1727–95), brother of the merchant James, had known Woolman all his life and often heard his testimony on the chain of connections that bound spirit to earth. He knew of Woolman's inability to sit in a soft chair, walk on a plush carpet, sleep in a filigreed bed, eat a sumptuous meal, drink a fine wine, or even dine abstemiously with a cup, plate, or fork that would morally compromise him. With his friend's asceticism in mind, Pemberton wrote a letter of introduction soliciting appropriate accommodation for Woolman in England, explaining that he was

> a good minister, a sensible man, and though he may appear singular, yet from a close knowledge of him he will be found to be a man of a sweet, clean spirit and preserved from harsh censure of those who do not see and conform as he does. It will be safest for Friends with you to leave him much to his own feelings, and to walk and steer in that path which proves most easy to him, without using much arguments or persuasion. He will do nothing knowingly against the Truth, and has had long experience in the Truth. He is much beloved and respected among us, and I doubt not will on close acquaintance be so to the truly religious with you.[1]

When Woolman left the ship, he set foot in a country that had the same problems he lamented in America, but to a greater degree. The English were capitalist, materialist, and market-oriented—no difference there. English Quakers too. But English society was less egalitarian and more hierarchical, and wealth was distributed less equitably than in the colonies. In England success was more closely linked to one's inherited privileges, yet acquisitiveness and opportunism were respected values; charity was administered locally and even more grudgingly than in Anglo-America.[2]

In England, blood sports were ubiquitous, children were routinely beaten at home and in school, and dueling was common among men of wealth and standing. Woolman was to discover that the English ate and drank liberally and that the swearing that scandalized him on board ship was not confined to sailors or, for that matter, to men. The poor still rioted when there were shortfalls in the grain harvests and the price of bread rose, and this happened often. About 20 percent of babies died, and a third of children did not survive to the age of five, victims of fevers and gastroenteric disorders; poor children were of course most vulnerable, and both epidemic diseases and the vast consumption of inexpensive distilled spirits—the gin craze—took a disproportionate toll among the impoverished. A family of five could live without debt or charity on forty pounds annually, but about half the families in England had incomes of less than fifteen pounds. Woolman's passage from America cost more than most English families earned in a year.[3]

Woolman docked in a city where women convicted of murdering their husbands were still occasionally burned at the stake. A London judge ruled that a man had the right to beat his wife with a stick as long as the weapon was no thicker than his thumb: larger men, bigger sticks, more brutalized wives. Textile factories were only just beginning to provide opportunities for women to get paid jobs. As in America, schools were segregated by gender; there were no children of color with either group, and paupers remained illiterate. (There had been Africans living in London since the mid-sixteenth century, before the founding of England's colonies in North America, and by the 1770s 2 or 3 percent of London's population was black—about fifteen thousand souls. Most of them were slaves, and many of the rest were among the city's most abject poor.)[4]

Land values doubled in England during the century after 1690, and this only contributed to a widening gap between rich and poor. Rents rose accordingly, making tenants worse off than those in the colonies whose plight Woolman had written about. Landowners had a chokehold on politics as well as on society, translating their economic power into control of the state. Servants, tenants, and other laborers generally worked from dawn to dusk, but employment was seasonal and affected by economic downturns. There were more professional criminals in London than in the countryside or in American cities, an underground network of perpetual paupers, vagrants, beggars, and thieves. Violence and disorder were closer to the surface and more frequently displayed than in Boston, New York, Philadelphia, or Charleston. A servant convicted of stealing from his master in England was subject to hanging; stealing sheep was a capital offense, as was forgery. The large majority of those executed in England during the eighteenth century had been found guilty of theft, although not of any violent act. But crime rose nonetheless; the harsh penal code had no greater effect than the workhouses had on poverty. Neither capital punishment nor the poor laws addressed the economic roots of unemployment and criminal behavior.[5]

Turnpikes had increased the speed of travel dramatically in Great Britain. It once took six days to reach London from Newcastle by coach; now it was half that time. London to Edinburgh overland was about sixty hours; it had been ten and a half days at the beginning of the century. The opportunity for speedier journeys created a perceived need for them, so teamsters drove horses harder than in America and had a reputation as the cruelest handlers in Europe. Speeding coaches jostled the passengers more violently than ever, even though the seats now had springs and were upholstered. Woolman of course disapproved of both the brutality and the opulence.[6]

Epidemics of smallpox, typhus, and typhoid fever ravaged England regularly. The worst plagues were capable of wiping out a decade of population growth in a few months; even the least deadly spread fear and grief across the land. People were not so inclined as they once had been to view disease as divine retribution, fate, or, at least, an expression of God's will. Cures were becoming the provenance of Enlightenment science and of a more rational, secular worldview. Woolman of course rejected both the modern worldview and modern medical practice, believing himself in the hands of God.[7]

A high proportion of the English, more than in the Middle Colonies and New England, never entered a church between their baptism and funeral. Whether Anglican or Dissenter, faith was prudent, practical, and undemanding. People were less passionate about religion than had been the case a century earlier, and toleration was good for commerce, which contributed to its triumph. Although Dissenters remained more conservative, they too had loosened up considerably. The number of Quakers declined from thirty-eight thousand at the beginning of the century to twenty thousand at the end. By 1800 there would be only twice as many Quakers as Jews, where English Friends had once outnumbered Catholics during the seventeenth century. To Woolman, it would appear that English Quakers were declining in spirituality as well. As their worldly success increased, their religious practice became less rigorous.[8]

Woolman disembarked on June 8 and "went straight from the water side" to London Yearly Meeting, which met at Devonshire House, the site of the great mansion by that name on Bishopsgate Street. Always seen as something of a monstrosity, the house had been built around 1570 and was "the most prominent object on the landscape" in the early seventeenth century. Through a succession of courtly owners—the De Vere and Cavendish families and the earl of Oxford—it passed in the mid-seventeenth century to the Right Honourable Christian Countess Dowager of Devonshire, from whom it took its name. Rooms were rented out to a church of Anabaptists, to Presbyterians, and to Quakers beginning in 1654; in the Great Fire of 1666, when a large portion of the city burned, the Quakers' rooms were damaged, resulting in some movement and reconstruction within the existing structure. The Quakers took a short-term lease in 1667 on "the lobby, the great parlour, and dining room lying next the said lobby, with all the cellars lying under the said lobby, and half of the arched vault or cellar lying before the garden under the said great dining room and parlour, and the three chambers lying over the said lobby and dining room, and over the three said chambers one large garret and the evidence room." They took a long-term lease on the same rooms in 1678, at which time they cleared the grounds of old buildings and constructed a substantial meetinghouse. Extensive renovations were made in 1741, in 1762 a gallery and stairs were added, and in 1766 the Quakers purchased the building and grounds. (They continued to add and remodel into the twentieth century, when they sold the property and moved to the current location at Friends House on Euston Road. The building on Bishopsgate Street no longer stands.)[9]

Woolman arrived about thirty minutes into the morning Meeting of ministers and elders, unanticipated and without introduction— typical American transgressions of English etiquette. He still smelled of the ship, had not taken time to bathe or clean his clothes, and wore his distinctive undyed, now soiled, garments, which were a novelty to English Quakers as they had been to Americans. Not surprisingly he made a bad impression.

The late entry may have embarrassed Woolman, who thought of promptness as a sign of respect for others and did not abide rudeness. Tardiness called attention to the latecomer, which made him seem proud, and in the case of Meeting, it disrupted business or, worse yet, broke silence inappropriately. Had he come from Dover in a public carriage with Emlen and Logan, he would have been on time that morning.

Tradition has it that when Woolman presented his travel certificates from Burlington Quarterly Meeting and Philadelphia Yearly Meeting, English Friends received them as coldly as they welcomed its bearer. In one story, a Friend suggested that Woolman should consider his mission accomplished and feel free to return home immediately, that they did not need another American itinerant proclaiming his personal vision of Truth. As the story goes, the insult reduced Woolman to tears, and he sat silently weeping while awaiting inspiration. He then rose calmly from the silence and explained that he could not return home, as the Friend had scoffed, until he had completed God's work, nor could he travel without the endorsement of London Friends. Since he was unwilling to burden Friends while he waited for a consensus supporting his ministry, he proposed working as a tailor so that he could remain in London without cost to anyone. Woolman sat again, and silence ensued.

This time it was others who were perplexed. Perhaps they had misjudged the man; possibly he was more than he appeared. From the quiet, Woolman eventually stood and spoke again. This time he preached from the heart, moving some of his audience, if not to tears, at least to remorse. "When he closed, the Friend who had advised against his further service rose up and humbly confessed his error, and avowed his full unity with the stranger. All doubt was removed; there was a general expression of unity and sympathy, and John Woolman, owned by his brethren, passed on to his work."[10]

Another version of the story attributes the suggestion about returning home to Woolman himself. In this telling, his humble manner won Friends over when he declined to be a burden until he could find an appropriate ship on which to sail. Yet a third account simply recalls that "when John Woolman landed in England many Friends were much straightened with his appearance and were ready to conclude such a man could not be of service amongst them. But he having opportunity to exercise his gift, it made way for him to pass, and so he got along." Although differing in a significant detail, all three stories report essentially the same negative reaction.[11]

Woolman reports nothing in the *Journal* of an awkward start but instead recalls experiencing an "enlarged" heart and a union "in true love to the faithful laborers now gathered from the several parts of this Yearly Meeting." Others had more to say about him. Dr. John Fothergill, a wealthy patron of botany and art, found Woolman "solid and weighty in his remarks. I wish he could be cured of some singularities. But his real worth outweighs the trust."* Elihu Robinson (1734–1809), a meteorologist from Eaglesfield, Cumberland, who

---

*Biographers have disagreed passionately about this last word, some of them reading it as "trash," "husk," or "them." But Fothergill clearly wrote "trust" in the next line directly under the disputed word. The first four letters are identical: *trus*. The last is either a *t* or an *h*. What Fothergill apparently meant was that despite Woolman's eccentricities, he was even wiser ("solid and weighty") than the reputation that preceded him. It was a compliment. One biographer (Whitney, *John Woolman*, 395–96) has said, perhaps on authority of oral tradition, that the initial insult to Woolman in London, and the subsequent apology, were Fothergill's, but there is no documentary evidence to support this.

witnessed Woolman's arrival at London Yearly Meeting, perceived that "the singularity of his appearance might in some Meetings draw the attention of the youth and even cause a change of countenance in some. Yet the simplicity, solidity and clearness of many of his remarks made all these vanish as mists at the sun's rising." Samuel Emlen believed that Woolman's meekness and simplicity found acceptance among English Friends but that "his singularity in white garb gets sometimes into his way with those who do not know him worthy." Another Friend later recalled, "John Woolman had some singularities . . . yet I believe that he had been building on a solid foundation."[12]

When John Pemberton heard about the hostile reception from a correspondent, he replied:

> If our dear friend J.W. is singular and walks in a manner no doubt in a cross to nature, yet how many are there whose demeanor, etc. is opposite to the simplicity of the gospel, and perhaps his appearance may excite thoughts in some such, though not immediately known to others, yet may prove profitable, and as I believe our dear Friend is mercifully preserved from a censorious spirit, so I wish that a disposition of harshly judging him may be watched and guarded against, he being a man of integrity of heart, though perhaps he may at times misapprehend and take less liberty than Truth might allow. I love him and desire his preservation.[13]

To be "in a cross to nature"—at odds with material existence—ran against the grain of Enlightenment sensibilities that celebrated nature as a source of wisdom and truth and against Christian notions of the goodness of God's creation. The merchants John Smith and James Pemberton had known that; to them, "nature" was good and "unnatural" bad, and Woolman had flipped the earthly wisdom of their day. But they had believed that Woolman had "integrity of heart"; what he said he believed in his heart to be true. They also knew that Woolman loved them, that he was a better man than they were, and that he did not so much judge as instruct them about what he believed to be God's will. They also thought that he sometimes misapprehended God's will and his eccentricities got in the way of his prophecy, but on balance they valued him, knew he meant well, and believed he was often a source of prophetic insight and therefore warranted being taken seriously.

Yearly Meeting lasted from June 8 to 15. There were seven business sessions for men and four more for ministers and elders. Women had two Meetings for Business. In addition, a series of Meetings for Worship were held at a number of different locations. About his participation in one Meeting of ministers and elders, it was said that Woolman

> made several beautiful remarks . . . and though the singularity of his appearance might in some meetings draw the attention of the youth and even cause a change of countenance in some, yet the simplicity, solidity and clearness of many of his remarks made all these vanish as mists at the rising sun. He made several beautiful remarks with respect to the benefit of true silence, and how incense ascended on the opening of the seventh seal, and there was silence in heaven for the space of half an hour, etc.

In the women's Meeting, which men attended only by invitation, Woolman testified to the power of divine love to "cleanse all filthiness of flesh and spirit, which must in degree be witnessed before we could experience an union with the Divine Nature, for God did not unite with anything contrary to His Nature."[14]

As John Pemberton had recommended, Woolman stayed at the home of John Townsend (1725–1801), a pewterer, while in London. Townsend's first trip to America came after Woolman's death; during it he mentions "visiting the widow Woolman." While on this journey, he was reprimanded in explicit reference to Woolman's teachings for wearing a red spotted handkerchief. He was also known for making "Guinea basins," bowls from which slaves ate, and he made the same item for the army and navy. When challenged on this practice, he was said to have replied that soldiers, sailors, and slaves had to eat too. One of his apprentices refused to make the bowls. From this summary of what we know about Townsend, it is unclear why John Pemberton chose him as Woolman's host, but it worked out.[15]

In London, Woolman could see other Friends whom he had known in New Jersey, both English visitors and American Quakers. Later Townsend recalled that Woolman's "company and self-denying example were truly profitable" for both him and his family. Woolman told him "divers times" that since he had not had smallpox, he was reluctant to visit the homes of other Friends in London, "but if he was spared to return again to this city he believed he should have liberty to visit them." He felt obliged to focus on his mission to the northern counties and not allow sociability to be the death of him before he even reached his destination. According to Townsend, Woolman "frequently said he was resigned to the will of Providence. He was not afraid of the disorder, and if he caught it in going to meetings and in the way of his duty he should have no cause to reflect upon himself."[16]

During the last two days of Yearly Meeting, Woolman wrote letters to his family. He encouraged them to correspond with him as little as possible. A postscript to one letter committed it to the hands of a mutual friend, asking him to deliver the note the next time he was in the company of the person to whom it was addressed. "I have sent no letter by post in England," he explained, "and if thou feels a concern to write to me and art easy to wait an opportunity of conveyance some other way than post or flying coaches, I believe it would be most acceptable. J. W. [By] Flying coaches, I mean those coaches which run so fast as oft to oppress the horses."

To his wife he wrote, "My heart hath been often melted into contrition since I left thee, under a sense of divine goodness being extended for my help and preparing in me a subjection to His will. I have been comforted in the company of some sincere hearted Friends." And he shared with her "the tender concern which I have many times felt for thee, and for Mary and for John . . . I may not easily express. I have often remembered you with tears, and my desires have been that the Lord, who hath been my helper through many adversities, may be a father to you, and that in His love, you may be guided safely along." Woolman also wrote to his nephew John, son of his deceased brother Abner, recalling the "deep trials of thy father and his inward care for you." Woolman felt a particular responsibility for the spiritual growth of his namesake, and he wanted the boy to know of his father's "inward life to which his mind, whilst among us, was often gathered."[17]

Sunday, June 14, was the last day of Yearly Meeting and very hot; Woolman attended Meeting for Worship at Devonshire House, and

> in a lively testimony, observing divine love was yet able to cleanse from all filthiness of flesh and spirit, which must in degree be witnessed before we could experience an union with the divine nature, for God did not unite with any contrary to his nature—Christ with Belial, nor the temple of God with idols, desiring all might endeavour after that purity of heart so necessarily connected with our happiness.[18]

To Woolman's certain satisfaction, the Yearly Meeting's summary epistle addressed slavery as one of its concerns.

> The practice of holding negroes in oppressive and unnatural bondage, hath been so successfully discouraged, by Friends in some of the colonies, as to be considerably lessened. We cannot but approve of these salutary endeavours, and earnestly entreat they may be continued, that, through the favour of divine providence, a traffic so unmerciful and unjust in its nature, to a part of our own species made equally with ourselves for immortality may come to be considered by all in its proper light; and be utterly abolished, as a reproach to the Christian profession.

While Woolman would have been grateful for this epistle's implied endorsement of his mission, he would also have been disappointed by its authors' self-satisfied lack of urgency and the very brief notice that slavery got, two sentences buried in four printed pages. English Friends seemed to be saying that slavery was a distinctively American problem and to be endorsing American Quakers' continued attention to ending it. On balance, the endorsement of abolition was good, and the best that English Friends would give; they did not

personally own slaves, and they were unable to see their own implication as merchants and consumers in the slave trafficking from
which they profited.[19]

Woolman walked out of London, where he had been for a week.
Someone probably drew him a map and gave him a list of names and
addresses of potential hosts. At least that was the common practice
for other American Quakers who traveled through England at that
time. Some of the visitors had guides; Woolman did not. But he
had met people at Yearly Meeting, and a dozen or more Friends he had
met during their American journeys lived along the path he took.
He walked to five Quarterly Meetings between June 15 and July 1. He
writes in his *Journal* about those first two weeks on the road: "15th
day 6th mo. Left London and went to a Quarterly Meeting in Hertford. 1st day 7th mo. Have been at Quarterly Meetings at Sherrington, at Northampton, at Banbury and at Shipton, and had sundry
meetings between." That is all he writes.[20]

Woolman also carried a crude calendar he had made. It consists
of two lists of numbers written in the margins of the small hand-
made notebook he carried; although it may be obscure to us, its
shorthand kept him from getting lost in time. If he was going to
keep to a schedule that got him to a Meeting for Worship on the
right day of the week, he had to keep track.

7.16	1–5
1.17	2–6
2.18	3–7
3.19	4–1

The first column lists days of the week and days of the month. In
September, as in the first column, the sixteenth was Seventh Day
(Saturday), the seventeenth First Day (Sunday), and so on. In the
second column, for some reason (maybe he was already ill), he reversed week and month: October 1 was on a Fifth Day (Thursday),
et cetera.[21]

In all, he spent 122 days in England, but mentions only 14 of
them in his journal, 8 of them successive Sundays from July 26 to
September 13. He names a few people but has little or nothing to

The places covered in John Woolman's English ministry, June–October 1772

say about them and tells us no more about the towns and cities he visited, the paths and roads he traveled, the meetinghouses he worshiped in, or the homes that extended him hospitality. He gives no account of the weather, food, wildlife, or terrain, whether he walked uphill or down in mud or dust; we do not know from him when he was parched by the sun or drenched by rain.

Daniel Mildred, one of the owners of the *Mary and Elizabeth*, wrote to John Pemberton shortly after Yearly Meeting: "John Woolman is gone northward. His peculiar habit may render him disagreeable to some few, but there is that, I think, which attends his words, both in testimony and private converse, which will make its way wherever he goes." When Woolman walked from London north to Hertford on June 16, he told a correspondent that he was "middling well." The minutes of Hertford Quarterly Meeting note that "John Woolmer" was one of three Americans whose "company and labour of love was likewise greatly to our comfort and satisfaction." Woolman's cousin William Hunt (1733–72) was one of the other Americans. (Hunt's mother was Woolman's aunt; after his father died, he was raised in Virginia by a paternal relative. He moved to Cane Creek, North Carolina, in 1752 and married there the following year; he and his wife lived in Guilford, North Carolina, where they had eight children. Hunt traveled even more in his ministry than Woolman; he was reputed to have preached in all the meetinghouses in America.) After the two men parted company in Herefordshire, Hunt wrote to Uriah Woolman about his brother.

> We parted with dear cousin John two days since. He was then as well as usual. He has great and acceptable service here. The singularity of his appearance is not only strange but very exercising to many valuable Friends, who have had several opportunities of conference with him. Some are still dissatisfied; others are willing to leave it. The purity of his ministry gains universal approbation. I hope he stands on that foundation which will bear him through all. He is now gone towards Yorkshire.[22]

In the small town of Baldock, on June 19, Woolman described himself as "near as well as when I left London." By the time he

reached Sherrington on June 24, he had a cold. When he left Northampton for Banbury on June 25, he appeared weak. On June 30,
Samuel Emlen "saw a Friend just now who was yesterday at meeting with John Woolman at Banbury in Oxfordshire. [I] believe he is
pretty well, though not strong in bodily might. He is apprehensive
of taking the small pox and lives abstemiously to a great degree, I
fear to the hurt of weakening of his health at times unnecessarily."
He arrived at Shipston, a small town west of Banbury, on July 1 feeling poorly and with a "very troublesome cough." Nonetheless,
Woolman persisted to Warwick, Coventry, and Birmingham, about
all of which he wrote nothing, at each stop attending Meetings and
sharing what he believed to be Truth. He was still coughing at the
end of the first week of July.[23]

Woolman continued to read and to write while on the road. He
had access to a recent edition of William Penn's *Select Works*, from
which he cited a passage in the French Roman Catholic philosopher
Pierre Charron's *Les Trois Vérités* in translation (1601). It is about covetousness and accumulation of wealth. The imagery is bold, the
observations mundane. The desire for riches is "gangrene in our
souls"; covetousness is the "vile and base passion of vulgar fools."
What greater folly can there be, Charron asks rhetorically, than to
"adore that which nature itself hath put under our feet, and hidden
in the bowels of the earth as unworthy to be seen?" Nothing could
be more miserable than to "bind the living to the dead . . . to tie the
spirit unto the excrement and scum of the earth."[24]

On July 17, Woolman had reached Birmingham, where, according to a Friend, "he appeared some time and to much satisfaction,
principally cautioning Friends against being too much engaged in
worldly affairs, which was not only a sensible hurt to themselves
but to their children." Woolman greatly impressed William Forster
(1747–1824) of Tottenham, a schoolmaster and surveyor, who wrote
that "his steady uniform deportment, his meekness and unaffected
humility, his solidity, no less in conversation than in his ministry,
which is instructing and edifying, creates much esteem and well
corresponds with his appearance." A week later Woolman was forty
miles farther on, in Nottingham, where he attended a large Meeting
of about 130 people in the morning; in the afternoon there was another Meeting in a Friend's home, and "curiosity brought more than

the house (which was not small) could hold." On July 28, nine miles away at Oxton, there was another Meeting in a private home, and "the house was near full, though few Friends." This last comment reveals that in such a small village the curiosity was not confined to Quakers. Afterward Deborah Morris and her aunt Sarah "prevailed upon" Woolman to ride with them to Mansfield in their private coach, suggesting that he was ill and trusted their hired coachman to treat his horses gently. The two women traveled for Sarah's public ministry until the fall of 1773.[25]

Two days later Deborah and Sarah Morris met up again with Woolman at Chesterfield, fourteen miles distant, to which Woolman had continued on foot. There they all attended a weekday Meeting, where another Friend spoke in prayer. Deborah recorded in her diary:

> J. Woolman spoke most of the rest of the time. He was deep in his gift, and but few there could understand him. Poor aunt sat under her exercise, I thought. If he had stood up after her he would have been of more service. If she should return there again I should not wonder. Her omission was not will-ful . . . It was a good Meeting on the whole.

Whether it was Woolman's accent, his delivery, or the content of his message that eluded Friends is not clear from this journal entry, but it is clear that Morris and her aunt believed that their friend spoke too long and thoughtlessly to the exclusion of at least one other minister who was moved to speak.[26]

Woolman was lonely among all the strangers and friends. On July 31 he wrote to his wife, "Though I feel in a good degree resigned in being absent from you, my heart is often tenderly affected toward you, and even to weeping this morning, while I am about to write." He had no clear insight to the future: "I see but a little way at a time." He was losing ground, crossing space, and unsure about his next step. He was spiritually fulfilled but emotionally drained and physically exhausted.[27]

Woolman was in nearby Sheffield the next day, having "been at sundry Meetings last week." When he spoke at the afternoon Meeting on August 2, First Day, it was so crowded that "many went away and stood out of doors." According to Deborah Morris, "John was very large and lively, but too deep for the greatest part. Aunt much favoured in prayer, and after her John stood up again and spoke more affectingly to the youth. Wherever we go there is such thronging; there is not time but when in bed for retirement." Now it seems that the reason some could not comprehend Woolman's meaning was that they found him "too deep," over their heads, delivering a message of linkage—perhaps from familial love to slavery—that not all could follow.[28]

Tabatha Hoyland (1750–1809) of Sheffield, in a letter to Sarah Tuke of York, described the Meeting attended by Woolman and Sarah Morris as

> exceedingly crowded, part through curiosity to see John's particular dress, and part I hope from a better motive, whom I apprehend went away well satisfied with what they heard from the man whose uncouth appearance will be likely to prejudice many. But he is certainly a very deep minister that searches things quite to the bottom, greatly exercised in a life of self-denial and humility

Hoyland understood perfectly well the chain of connections that linked Woolman's ministry.

> [The] will of the creature must be subdued . . . to wean many from the things which outwardly adorn the body, and likewise other luxuries and delicacys. Too much prevailing amongst those in exalted stations as to this world's enjoyments, besides the testimony he apprehends it a duty to bear against the iniquitous trading in Negroes that so deeply affected his mind as to make his tears both as meat and drink for many days.[29]

Another person at the Meeting that day described Woolman's appearance in detail, and showed how fascinated people were with his garb.

> John Woolman, a publick friend from America . . . was remarkable for the singularity of his dress. His shoes were of uncurried leather, tied with leather strings, his stockings of

white yarn, his coat, waistcoat, and breeches of a strong kind of cloth undyed, the natural colour of the wool, the buttons of wood with brass shanks; his shirt of cotton unbleached, about 14d. per yard, fastened at the neck with three large buttons of the same stuff, without either cravat or handkerchief about his neck; his hat a very good one was white, his countenance grave, sensible and expressive; in conversation rather reserved (except with a few individuals) being at all times more ready to hear than to offer the sacrifice of fools.

This same unidentified witness was just as interested in Woolman's character. Anyone who assumed he was "whimsical" because of his "odd appearance" would be mistaken, the writer explains; he was a man of "great understanding and had good natural abilities," a "mild and benevolent" disposition, an unaffected simplicity, and the total respect of those who knew him: "he said the cause why he appeared so, was that he believe[d] it to be his duty to bear a testimony not in words only, but to be a sign to the people, to testify against the pride and extravagancy of those days, which greatly abounded with superfluities." Woolman also "avoided the company of the rich and great," visiting the homes of poor Friends in Sheffield, the "honest simplicity" of whom gave him great pleasure. "His diet was plain, chiefly consisting of bread, milk, or butter, and he was truly a valuable, good man, a friend and well wisher to mankind universally." Perhaps the poor were more impressed by Woolman than were wealthy Quakers, which may account, at least in part, for the range of reactions to him and his message. He made some people uncomfortable, put others at ease, but was a striking presence to all who saw and heard him.[30]

From Sheffield, Woolman walked another eighteen miles to High Flatts Monthly Meeting, arriving on August 5. Here another anonymous Friend was impressed too. He found him "a man of very deep experience in the things of God" and was fascinated by Woolman's account of the spiritual inspiration that led him to eliminate "all superfluity in meat, drink, and apparel, being a pattern of remarkable plainness, humility, and self denial." The white hat, as usual, was striking, as was the lack of adornment around his neck.

The "coarse raw linen shirt" and the "breeches of white coarse woolen cloth with wool buttons" were unique, and the "uncured leather" of Woolman's shoes, with leather laces rather than buckles, completed the costume, "so that he was all white."[31]

Deborah Morris also described that day:

> Fourth day fifth [August] we went to their meeting which was large for a country meeting and quiet. Here we again met John Woolman, who had a fine time, and aunt also, although she was short. We dined at Edward Dickenson's, close by the meeting house. After dinner John and aunt had a seasonable and uniting time with the young folks and a few others. It was a solemn parting time indeed. He then went to Haddonfield, and we to Hollingsthorp . . . We had bad roads, but beautiful prospects.

The phrase "fine time" referred to Woolman's speaking in Meeting and was a compliment to the quality of his message; Sarah was "short," meaning she spoke only briefly. According to Deborah, her frail aunt rallied spirit and body for these Meetings, on several occasions speaking for an hour and a half. Clearly, the Meetings could go on for hours when the American ministers were there, for at least several hours when both Sarah and John spoke, and sometimes John spoke more than once; and on Sunday they were attending morning and afternoon Meetings and then gathering again in the evenings at someone's home. In this Meeting, from Deborah's description of it as "quiet," the two American ministers may have been the only ones who rose from the silence to give messages. Deborah also found it worthy of comment on those occasions (as at Gildersome on August 13) when "there was not a sleeper among them"; by way of contrast, the Meeting at Fairfield on August 24 consisted of "a poor, sleepy, thoughtless company."[32]

Throughout the summer Woolman drank nothing stronger than herbal tea sometimes sweetened with a little honey, other Friends reported. He declined sugar, Asian tea, and "foreign liquors," which could have meant rum, Madeira, or claret. He would not use silver spoons or forks, of course, and continued to ask for a replacement when provided with a silver cup. He also "chose to walk." All of these habits displayed a "striking pattern of temperance and humility" to those who saw him for the first time.

The number and the detail of the descriptions of John Woolman in England are, if anything, more striking than the descriptions themselves. We have precious few accounts of Woolman during his half century in America, but for his last four months we have many. He was a novelty in England, while American Friends, who knew Woolman their whole lives, had evidently acclimated themselves to his charms and eccentricities over time. It was not as great a shock to see Woolman in odd clothes as it was to meet Woolman in them. Even attired less conspicuously, Woolman would have been a remarkable figure, as surviving testimony to the nature and effects of his ministry shows.

None of the numerous descriptions of Woolman during his English journey described him as bearded. Three years after his death William Forster wrote to a young woman to compliment her on the likeness of her father that she had captured in wax: "a long white beard adorns his face which is very expressive and not unlike John Woolman's." Perhaps Forster meant only that Woolman had an "expressive" face like that of the subject of the wax bust and not that he had a long white beard. It would be odd, no matter how commonplace long beards were in Woolman's lifetime, if no one mentioned it, since that would have made the total effect of his whiteness even more stunning.[33]

Mid-August was a spiritually fallow time for Woolman, a "time of inward poverty," of "painful labour" that he tried to wade through patiently. He found England expensive, and he noted that the wages of working people were too low for them to live comfortably. Rye, wheat, and oatmeal were dear; rents collected weekly were high; wood was scarce and expensive. He exclaimed in his *Journal*: "Oh, may the wealthy consider the poor!" The worldliness of English Quakers saddened him; their participation in the slave trade defied the Golden Rule; their trafficking in "superfluities" betrayed the spirit of the sect's founders. Driving horses to death in the mad rush of commerce was another sin, contravening the peace testimony as it did.[34]

Sophia Hume found Woolman convincing on the subject of simplicity but recognized she was in a minority. When Quakers met at Yearly Meeting, she wrote, their zeal was kindled, but then they returned "to the practice of minding our own things, worldly things and not the things of another." In that context they received Woolman politely, tolerantly, even affectionately, but they did not expect him to have any long-term effect on their personal behavior. "My love is to every member who loves the Lord Jesus Christ in sincerity. I have great unity with John Woolman; though perhaps will hear few besides has, though they commend and say, if he has this faith to himself, they can be quite easy with him; but desire to be excused if he is proposed as an example."[35]

William Forster shared another description of Woolman with an American correspondent in a letter of August 16: "The remarkable appearance of your countryman John Woolman . . . attracts the notice of many. His steady uniform deportment, his meekness and unaffected humility, his solidity, no less in conversation than in his ministry, which is instructing and edifying, creates much esteem and well corresponds with his appearance." These comments were part of comparisons between public ministers from America and England. "I think your ministers in general far exceed ours though we are favoured with several eminent ones," Forster wrote. He included Sarah Morris and Sophia Hume in his list of most admired Quaker ministers. Others mentioned Samuel Emlen in the same company.[36]

In late August, Woolman was at Preston Patrick, in Cumbria, Westmoreland, where he dreamed of his mother. (The editorial committee deleted the passage from the *Journal*.) He also was moved to write about his near-fatal illness two years previously. Why now; why here? All he says is "It being now so long since I passed through this dispensation and the matter remaining fresh and livingly on my mind, I believe it safest for me to write it." This was the "safest" time to write about his illness because death might be at hand, which is not necessarily a premonition but the philosophy he lived by; death was "livingly" his traveling companion.[37]

———

WOOLMAN continued through late August to work on six essays, some or all of which he may have drafted while at sea. One essay, *On Loving Our Neighbours as Ourselves*, expresses his expansive vision of universal love, extended to all of humanity and the "animal creation" as well. Paralleling the spiritual logic shared by Jainists, Buddhists, and Hindus, which he did not know, Woolman suggests that intemperate acts committed against any creature disorder the "affairs of society" and estrange us from the "pure sympathizing spirit." Disparities of wealth too are evidence of a disordered world. We must act with integrity, limited only by the "strength of mind and body" with which God has endowed us. Those who have received "larger gifts"—of intellect, constitution, or wealth—have a greater responsibility for right use of our resources. There is no "right end" for which a wrong means is justifiable. Never forget that "the wisdom of this world is foolishness with God," he writes, straight from St. Paul's letter to the Corinthians, "for what seems to be God's foolishness is wiser than human wisdom, and what seems to be God's weakness is stronger than human strength."[38]

The second essay was entitled *On the Slave Trade*. He had little new to say but bared it emotionally. This short essay, like the one before it, is among his most eloquent work, and it focuses especially on a comparison between the childhood of a slave and that of his fellow Quakers. Slaves growing up amid violence, impoverishment, ignorance, and cruelty matured with mayhem in their hearts and embraced vengeance as their principal ambition. This was a total contradiction to divine love.

> There is a love which stands in nature; and a parent beholding his child in misery, has a feeling of the affliction, but in Divine Love, the heart is enlarged towards mankind universally, and prepared to sympathize with strangers, though in the lowest stations in life. Of this the prophet appears to have had a feeling, when he said, "have we not all one father? Has not one God created us? Why then do we deal treacherously every man with his brother in profaning the covenant of our fathers?"[39]

During this time in England, Woolman had access to the works of Humphrey Smith (1624–63), one of the founding generation of Quakers who was first imprisoned for preaching in 1655 and a number of times thereafter in Exeter, Dorchester, and Winchester, finally dying in jail. An essay that Woolman drew on from the martyr's writings was titled *To All Parents of Children upon the Face of the Whole Earth*. Refrain from provoking anger in children, Smith had advised, and try never to display your own in their presence. Spare violence against children, and protect them from witnessing the violent acts of others. Misguided discipline pulls children from natural inclinations, which are their gifts: "Let the children come to me, and do not stop them, because the kingdom of heaven belongs to such as these" (Matthew 19:14). Spirituality is manifest in children, whose natural simplicity, innocence, and meekness should be the models for all of us.[40]

These instructions on child rearing are consistent with Woolman's past ruminations on the subtle links between parental love and enslavement, and he naturally enough found authority in the Old Testament prophets for this vision of humanity and implicitly rejected, as Quakers generally did, the message of Proverbs 13:24: "He that spares the rod hates his son." Hosea 10:13 warned that people would reap what they had plowed and sown: "You planted evil and reaped its harvest. You have eaten the fruit produced by your lies." And the violence of slavery was, after all, a family enterprise, Woolman wrote: plowed by mercantile families, planted by farmers and their kin, harvested by families of slaves, and consumed by all society. He continued to draw on the admonitory prophets, having incorporated their frustration and prediction of heavenly reprisal into his once-gentle ministry.

The third essay, *On Trading in Superfluities*, was based on what Woolman had witnessed both on shipboard and in England, though it covers ground he had already turned fourteen years earlier with *Serious Considerations on Trade*. "While Friends were kept truly humble," Woolman explains again, "and walked according to the purity of our principles, the Divine Witness in many hearts was reached; but, when a worldly spirit got entrance, there came in luxuries and superfluities, and spread by little and little, even among the foremost rank in society, and from there others took liberty in that way more abundantly." By small steps, from linen handkerchiefs, to silk scarves, to silver teapots, Quakers had sold their souls; they had abandoned their testimonies on sloth and greed and had sacrificed other people's blood, which was on their hands just as surely as if they had wielded the whips that scarified the backs of slaves.[41]

The fourth essay, *On a Sailor's Life*, reflected the shipboard inspiration of the hold and especially the two young sailors who had been raised as Quakers. A mistake Woolman had made in his journal entry for May 28 suggests how moved he may have been by the experience, as he wrote "1752," missing the year by two decades. This was the period when he and Sarah may have suffered multiple prenatal losses. The young men he connected to were about the same age as his infant son would have been had he lived, and they apparently jarred melancholy memories that connected Woolman's public ministry with his private life, the one he didn't write about in his *Journal*.

In the trade to Africa for slaves, and in the management of ships going on these voyages, many of our lads and young men have a considerable part of their education.

Now, what pious father beholding his son placed in one of these ships, to learn the practice of a mariner, could forbear mourning over him?

The corruption of life at sea was the fruit of too much travel for insufficient cause, too much trade for unnecessary goods, greed, vanity, and the slave trade.[42]

Quakers needed to return to the principles of George Fox, John Gratton, and Gilbert Latey, and Woolman quoted all of them in this essay. Latey (1626–1705) was born in Cornwall, apprenticed to a tailor, and worked at his trade in Plymouth until 1648, when he set up shop in The Strand, London, and became a popular tailor among the aristocracy. After his conversion to Quakerism, which was one of the first in London, he had doubts about supplying his customers with lace and other fancy adornments, and for a time his trade declined. In 1660 he wrote *To All You Taylors and Brokers, Who Lyes in*

testHS

Wickedness, and to All You Tradesmen of What Trade, Employment, or Office Soever, which prophesied an imminent judgment day when all the secrets in men's hearts would be revealed, and the "servants of sin" among them would receive their comeuppance.

It is unclear when Woolman first became aware of Latey, but now he wrote about him. Latey too lived an ascetic life that set him off from others of his faith and the larger society: "Through the powerful operations of the Spirit of Christ in his Soul, [he] was brought to that depth of self-denial that he could not join with that proud Spirit in other people, which inclined them to want vanities and superfluities." If Woolman had mentioned Latey earlier, we could construe him as a model; coming this late, the reference demonstrates only inspiration for one of Woolman's last essays.[43]

John Gratton (1641–1712) lived in Derbyshire and traveled extensively in the Midlands. He was jailed for five and a half years (1680–86) for professing Quakerism; Friends published his *Journal* in 1720. Woolman believed that Gratton, like Latey and Fox, was the sort of Quaker who seldom appeared anymore. According to Gratton's *Journal*, had he not met a Quaker when he was a boy, he might have continued down his wayward path and would not have discovered the Truth subsequently revealed to him. Woolman believed that in order for the Quakers to escape the snares they had caught themselves in, they would have to adopt Gratton's self-abnegation and focus on the indwelling presence of God.[44]

Woolman's next essay, *On Silent Worship*, addresses the silence that separates the worshiper from material existence and connects to the spirit within. Lamenting the younger generation's distraction from the quiet voice of God, Woolman acknowledged that the true Quaker way was not easy and could be dangerous: "Within the last four hundred years, many pious people have been deeply exercised in soul on account of the superstition which prevailed amongst the professed followers of Christ, and in support of their testimony against oppressive idolatry, some in several ages have finished their course in the flames." Still, he believed that "through the faithfulness of the martyrs, the understandings of many have been opened, and the minds of people, from age to age, been more and more prepared for a real spiritual worship." That the experience of such worship was in decline did not leave Woolman despondent but wary. He warned that only a return to the primitive church of the apostles, and its recovered state in the first years of the Quaker faith, would resolve the dilemmas faced by the next generation.[45]

One editor hypothesized that Woolman wrote *Concerning the Ministry*, the last of his essays, during the days in late August when he stopped in Westmoreland, where he "rested a few days in body and mind with our Friend Jane Crosfield [1712 or 1713–84], who was once in America." (She was there in 1760 and 1761, riding from Meeting to Meeting on horseback.) Jane and George (1706–84) Crosfield lived at Low Park in Preston Richard and attended Preston Patrick Meeting. Woolman was by now in extremely poor physical condition, weaker even than when he arrived in London, and certainly less strong than when he had left home.[46]

At the Crosfields' he also wrote the last entry in his own hand in his *Journal*; all that follows are the copy of a letter and an account of a dream that he dictated when he had become too weak to write. But before that came his advice to those who "shared the station of a minister of Christ." In retrospect, and he was now looking back on his English ministry, Woolman believed that he had prepared well for the task. During the first days in London,

> my heart was like a vessel that wanted vent; and for several weeks at first, when my mouth was opened in Meetings, it often felt like the raising of a gate in a water course, where a weight of water lay upon it; and in these labours there appeared a fresh visitation of love to many, especially the youth. But some time after this, I felt empty and poor, and yet felt a necessity to appoint Meetings.[47]

Woolman had, at that point of spiritual fallowness, to "abide in the pure life of Truth, and in all my labours to watch diligently against the motions of self in my own mind." He needed to let go of the message that he had brought with him across the ocean and wait for the "fresh instructions of Christ." The barrier, or "stop," that he still felt in late August suggested to him that God now dictated silence, patience, quiet waiting, and trust. He must not rise in Meeting just to make "noise." He wrote: "Christ knows when the fruit-bearing branches themselves have need of purging." Did he consider himself fruit, branch, or tree? What would it mean for Christ to prune him?

> The natural man loves eloquence, and many love to hear eloquent orations: and if there is not a careful attention to the gift men who have once laboured in the pure gospel ministry, growing weary of suffering, and ashamed of appearing weak, may kindle a fire, compass themselves about with sparks, and walk in the light—not of Christ who is under suffering—but of that fire which they, going from the gift, have kindled.

Having switched metaphors, Woolman believed that his light had dimmed. Whether it would rekindle or if his candle was spent, he had to accept God's will without his ego intruding. He knew from experience that discerning the difference between ego and inspiration was the prophet's most difficult task. Ministers who came after him should not expect an easier one.[48]

He dragged himself the six miles from Kendal to Greyrigg on August 30 and to Countersett, in Yorkshire, on September 6; there he spoke at a "large Meeting House," which was "very full, and through the opening of pure love it was a strengthening time to me, and I believe to many more." He left Leyburn on September 13 and that day walked the nine miles to Richmond, where he heard that his cousin William Hunt had died in Newcastle of smallpox. This news led him to reflect on the meaning of Hunt's life.

> He appeared in public testimony when he was a youth. His ministry was in the pure love and life of Truth and his conduct in general agreeable thereto. He traveled much in the work of the Gospel in America, and I remember to have heard [him] say in public testimony that his concern was in that visit to be devoted to the service of Christ so fully that he might not spend one minute in pleasing himself, which words joined with his example, was a means of stirring up the pure mind in me.[49]

The news of Hunt's death reached Deborah Morris when she and her aunt were in Scarborough, both ill with colds.

Aunt had a poor night, and rose late. She was poorly, and I doubt[ed] whether to go to meeting or not. However, we went, and therein she was more favoured than usual. Though much spent, she went again in the afternoon . . . We returned to our lodgings, and there I heard the sorrowful account of the death of our dear worthy friend, William Hunt, of the small pox, and that he had been buried on the 11th instant. This filled our hearts with sorrow, which we concealed as well as we could from Aunt, until the next morning.[50]

The villages Woolman passed through shared dirt roads, a vile stench, and general filthiness, he writes in the *Journal.* The countryside contributed to his feeling "weakly," he thought, and caused him "distress both in body and mind with that which is impure." Dye coursing through the mud, runoff from a practice he deemed unnecessary, was a metaphor for his mood after hearing about Hunt's death, for his own physical weakness, and perhaps, at this low point, for his entire overland journey.

Here I have felt a longing in my mind that people might come into cleanness of spirit, cleanness of person, cleanness about their houses and garments. Some who are great carry delicacy to a great height themselves, and yet the real cleanliness is not generally promoted. Dyes being invented partly to please the eye and partly to hide dirt, I have felt in this weak state, traveling in dirtiness and affected with unwholesome scents, a strong desire that the nature of dyeing cloth to hide dirt may be more fully considered.

Nor was Woolman pleased to witness the slaughter of animals in the public markets of the big towns, where "from their blood, etc., arises that which mixes in the air." He was breathing the "opposite to the clear pure country air," and he thought that "the minds of people are in some degree hindered from the pure operation of the Holy spirit, where they breathe a great deal in it."[51]

WOOLMAN contracted smallpox at about the same time that Hunt died of the disease. An incubation period of ten to fourteen days suggests that he was probably exposed in the neighborhood of Countersett. The disease is communicated by contact, but since it can live outside a human host for years, Woolman might have been infected from a blanket or from airborne particles that he inhaled.

14

How to End

1772

WOOLMAN wrote from Carlton Miniott, in Yorkshire, on September 16, "to the children of Stephen Comfort," one of whom was his son-in-law. He wanted the nine of them to know that he was

> so well as to continue traveling, though but slowly. Yesterday, as I was walking over a plain on my way to this place, I felt a degree of divine love attend my mind, and therein an openness toward the children of Stephen Comfort, of which I believed I should endeavor to inform them. My mind was opened to behold the happiness, the safety and beauty of a life devoted to follow[ing] the heavenly shepherd; and a care that the enticements of vain young people may not ensnare any of you.

Call it a premonition or a prophecy, but Woolman was accustomed to abiding by it. "I cannot form a concern," he explains, "but when a concern comes, I endeavor to be obedient." He was obeying by delivering a message across the ocean from God. Although his voice was that of Woolman's own adolescent experience, the prophecies were out of his control. He would not "form a concern" of his own volition, but he was a messenger communicating to the Comforts a warning that may have been intended for one or all of them.[1]

The next day Woolman walked the few miles from Carlton Miniott to Thirsk, where "many of the townspeople coming in, the house was much crowded, amongst whom my heart was enlarged and the gospel love flowed forth toward them." Woolman reached Thornton, eleven miles northeast of York, two days later. Deborah Morris and her aunt had been there three weeks earlier: "It was on the side of a high hill, overlooking a beautiful fruitful valley. There are but twelve Friends in this town, and the only public Friend belonging to the meeting, George Dawson, is aged 82 years." ("Public Friend" is another term for a sanctioned minister, who took his message to others outside his home Meeting.) On Sunday, September 20, Woolman was in Hewby, nine miles due west of Thornton and nine miles north of York, where he attended Meeting for Worship and ate dinner; on Monday he walked to York, entering the walled city in the company of seventeen-year-old Henry Tuke (1755–1814), whose father, William (1732–1822), had sent him out to watch for Woolman on the main road. Henry, who later became an accomplished Quaker writer, remembered his walk with Woolman for the rest of his life. After he died, Henry's own son eventually wrote down the story as Henry had told it countless times:

> That truly lowly and self-denying disciple of Jesus, John Woolman, came to York in the course of his religious labours, in the year 1772. He traveled entirely on foot, and my father, then in his eighteenth year was sent to be his guide and companion from his last stopping place into the city. I have frequently heard him speak of the indescribable sweetness of this walk, and of the satisfaction which he felt in the remembrance of it. Friends traveling in the ministry at that time usually resorted to my grandfather's house; but J. Woolman chose the hospitality of a Friend who lived a little out of the city in the "clean country."[2]

According to his host, Woolman was sick when he arrived, "having been poorly in health for some time before, [and] apprehended the like feverish disorder he usually had at that season of the year was coming upon him." Woolman said he could not tolerate the urban din where the Tukes lived in York's business district. He wanted—apparently required—a more tranquil setting and cleaner air.³

Residents of and visitors to eighteenth-century English towns complained of the noise and stench. Barrelmakers, tinsmiths, ironmongers, and blacksmiths hammered; butchers plied their trade in the open; sellers hawked their wares; and taverns were raucous affairs. The streets were sluices for sewage, with human waste that was dumped from windows and tossed out doors. The runoff from dyers, tanners, soapmakers, and tallow chandlers was noxious. Towns and cities had dung piles, scavengers, and scrapers; residents and tradesmen were responsible for cleaning the streets in front of their properties, and sewers were an eighteenth-century improvement but inadequate to carry the load and break the centuries-long habits of town dwellers. There were regulations against wandering pigs, but the frequency of fines shows that this and other problems were still rampant, albeit addressed, and sanitation was, at least, improving.⁴

Sarah and Deborah Morris arrived later the same day as Woolman and accepted the hospitality of the Tukes that he had declined: "Second-day, 21st, set off of York, our kind friend, J. Dickason, went with us as far as market-Weighton . . . where we dined. He then left us, the other Friends seeing us safely to York, where William [Tuke] and his kind wife received us like parents." By the time the Morrises arrived, the Tukes had already moved Woolman to the home of Thomas Priestman (1736–1812), a tanner on Marygate Lane, away from the town's clamor. Priestman himself was a bit eccentric, resisting novelties and innovations such as umbrellas all his life; a son of his was married to one of the Tukes' daughters, a connection on which they imposed. Had either of the families known the nature of Woolman's illness, they would not so lightly have moved him. There were small children in the Priestmans' home, who were vulnerable apparently because they had been neither inoculated nor exposed. Of his guest, Priestman wrote:

> His appearance was singular, apprehending it his duty to wear undyed clothes, and in his diet was very abstemious, eating no sugar nor anything that came thro' the hands of the Negro slaves, he having suffer'd abundance on this account

which his writings will set forth. He was a man of deep judgment on natural things, and a very upright heavenly minded man. His dwelling seems very near the Fountain.[5]

According to York's early-nineteenth-century historian, "no place near the city could be more calculated for the exercise of serious contemplation" than the environs of St. Mary's Abbey, which is where the Priestmans lived. (The building is still there, with a marker as the death place of Woolman.) The walled abbey ruins were once the site of a Roman temple and of a church destroyed by accidental fire in 1137 and rebuilt between 1270 and 1292, only to be demolished during the church lootings of Henry VIII's reign.[6]

Here Woolman was, about two hundred miles from London, three thousand miles from home, in a city that was about two thousand years old. Had he been well enough, he would have appreciated the antiquity, the beauty, and the peaceful setting in which he spent his last days. Instead he languished in agony, eventually becoming mute and blind, with no cognizance of the world outside the window, bathed in the sunlight that now pained his eyes. But that was a week off. There was still time to venture out of doors, and he used it to attend York Quarterly Meeting.

On Tuesday, before participating in Quarterly Meeting of ministers and elders that evening, Woolman wrote a letter to John Wilson (1748–1801), with whom he had boarded at Kendal several weeks before. It was at Kendal that Woolman had observed the dye running in the roadside ditch and written about it in his *Journal*, and Wilson was a shearman-dyer, a man who sheared sheep and dyed wool.

When I followed the trade of a tailor, I had a feeling of that which pleased the proud mind in people; and growing uneasy, was strengthened to leave off that which was superfluous in my trade.

When I was at your house, I believe I had a sense of the pride of people being gratified in some of the business thou followest, and I feel a concern in pure love to endeavor to inform thee of it.[7]

The next day Woolman wrote to his cousins Reuben and Margaret Haines in Philadelphia. He reported that he was at York Quarterly Meeting and "so well in health as to continue traveling. I appoint a few meetings, but not so fast as I did some time ago. I feel quiet in my mind, believing it is the Lord's will that I should for a time be in this part of the world." In closing, he noted that he had left his bedding and other possessions on the ship that had brought him to England, with instructions to return them to the Haineses when it docked in Philadelphia.[8]

He was at Quarterly Meeting that Wednesday, participating in his last public Meeting for Worship that morning, and his last Meeting for Business the next day. At one session, he contributed a reference to Matthew 15:13: "Every plant that's not of my Heavenly Father's planting shall be plucked up by the roots." William Tuke later wrote that "he appeared in the ministry at our Quarterly Meeting greatly to the comfort and satisfaction of Friends, the spring of the Gospel flowing through him with great purity and sweetness." His last public testimony, on Thursday, September 24, was against the slave trade. Woolman asked that Friends keep the poor slaves in mind and "remonstrate their hardships and sufferings to those in authority." It was Tuke's opinion that this testament "made a deep impression on many minds."[9]

The prophet was too weak to attend the concluding Meeting for Worship that same afternoon. The memorial from York Friends written six months later recalled that Woolman "was enabled to attend all the sittings of that meeting except the last . . . The Spring of the Gospel Ministry often flowed through him with great purity and sweetness as a refreshing stream to the weary travelers towards the city of God."[10]

The Morrises were still in York on Wednesday and Thursday: "Fourth-day, 23d, went to meeting at nine o'clock in the morning, in which John Woolman and others had service; it was held for worship." Deborah makes no comment about Woolman's health. According to her, he also attended Women's Meeting on Thursday:

Fifth-day, 24th, I staid at home, from the meeting for business. Women friends came home rejoicing, that Aunt was set at liberty therein, to her comfort, and John Woolman likewise, who visited their meeting. This set her at liberty, and she concluded to leave the city. York is a large city; in its regular streets and buildings it exceeds Hull, although Hull is a good town. The steeple houses exceed any in England, we are told, though I saw them not.

The two women left York on Friday morning, the day before Woolman's symptoms clarified. On Saturday, September 26, according to Tuke, "some spots appeared upon his face like the smallpox . . . and the next day it appeared beyond a doubt that this was his disorder."[11]

The usual course of smallpox begins with a fever that abates after a day or two. By the fourth day the fever rises again and the first sores appear in the mouth, throat, and nasal passages. Within twenty-four hours sores break out on the skin, often concentrating on the soles of the feet, palms, forearms, face, neck, and back. Saturday, then, was about Woolman's fourth day, meaning he would have another ten to sixteen days of suffering ahead.[12]

Now Woolman had the disease he had so long feared and strived so hard to avoid. As he well knew, and had often preached and written, there was no hiding from death's hand, no choosing the time, place, or nature of one's last illness. If he feared the pain and suffering more than he did the end, he had good reason. The disease ran its course in its own time. Not everyone died, and he still hoped to be among the majority who lived, but the symptoms would be excruciating in any event. Moreover, his immune system had been undermined by the rigors of traveling on foot and by whatever accounted for the bulbous growth on his nose; the weakness he had suffered for years had worsened under the stress of his Atlantic voyage and his exposure to the elements on land. It didn't look good to the Tukes, the Priestmans, and the others who were caring for him, but for his sake they tried to maintain a positive mien. In his own opinion, he had been rescued from the brink of death twice, and he tried to remain hopeful that God would come to his aid again.

The very next day, with the dread diagnosis clear, Woolman wrote to John Eliot (1734–1813), in London, whose hospitality he had declined because of a recent outbreak of smallpox in his house, with instructions for disposition of the sea journal he had left with Sophia Hume, the journal he had kept since arriving in England, and four of the six short essays he had composed since he left home. All were to go to John Pemberton, who would submit them for publication to the Committee for Sufferings, which he clerked. Woolman wanted the fifth essay, *On Silent Worship*, sent to London Yearly Meeting to be considered for publication in England. Tuke thought Woolman's behavior remarkable; he was arranging for the disposition of his papers "with the same ease and composure as if going [on] a journey."[13]

Priestman, Tuke, and their wives—Esther Tuke (1727–94) and Sarah Priestman (1736–96), who were carrying the load of the nursing along with the Tukes' sixteen-year-old daughter, Sally (1756–90)—now wanted to call in a physician, but Woolman declined, explaining that "he had not liberty in his mind so to do, standing wholly resigned to His will who gave him life, and whose power he had witnessed to heal him in sickness before, when he seemed nigh unto death." If he was to die this time, he was "perfectly resigned, having no will either to live or die" (echoing St. Paul). An apothecary, who was a Quaker, stopped by unbidden, and Woolman agreed that "if anything should be proposed as to medicine that did not come through defiled channels or oppressive hands, he should be willing to consider and take it so far as he found freedom." He did ask for his countryman John Bispham, who had crossed on the same ship; we do not know where in England Bispham was, but he arrived in time to sit with Woolman for his last two days.[14]

On Monday, Woolman dictated to Priestman an entry for his *Journal*:

9th month, 28, '72. Being now at the house of my friend Thomas Priestman in the city of York, so weak in body that I know not how my sickness may end, I am concerned to leave in writing a case the remembrance whereof hath often affected me. An honest-hearted Friend in America, who departed this life a little less than a year ago, some months before his departure, he told me in substance as follows.

Woolman then recounted the Friend's story: It was a "dream or night vision" of "a great pond of blood from which a fog rose up. Some distance from him he saw this fog spread round about and great numbers of people walking backwards and forward in it, the garments of whom had a tincture of blood in [th]em." The Friend in question may have been his cousin Peter Harvey (1721–71), who had died in New Jersey the previous year, and with whom Woolman had sat during his last illness.[15]

Woolman's interpretation, which he had given this Friend and now wanted to record, was that the pool of blood represented the "hard-hearted" men who participated in the slave trade: slavers, merchants, sailors, traffickers, travelers, and customers who benefited financially from the commerce that slavery produced. He thought that the fog "represented the gain arising on merchandise or traffic which many were taking hold of and, at the same time, knew that the gain was the gain of oppression." The envisioned souls wore garments dyed in blood and wandered in a fog—spiritual or mental, perhaps, but certainly moral. They were lost, blinded or at least hindered by defective insight into the trauma that they caused and the evidence they wore. They knew, but they did not acknowledge their sin.[16]

The dreamer had considered this interpretation. If the dream was a message from God, what did it mean? He sent for Woolman again, asking for a private conversation.

> He then told me some matters in particular in regard to the gain of oppression, which he felt not easy to leave the world without opening to me. All this time he appeared calm and quiet, and the family coming in by his consent, death in about one hour appeared evidently upon him, and I believe in about five hours from my going in he quietly breathed his last; and as I believe he left no memorandum in writing of that dream or vision of the night, at this time I believe it seasonable for me to do it.

The entry in the *Journal* manuscript is signed "John Woolman" in a shaky hand. Consistent with its practice, the editorial committee left it out of the first edition.[17]

On Monday, Woolman noticed that the fever left him light-headed, affecting the clarity of his thinking. He elicited promises from those nursing him that "if his understanding should be more affected to have nothing given him that those about him knew he had a testimony against." As he spoke, his attendants began to record his proclamations. Woolman was "greatly afflicted," according to Tuke, "but bore it with the utmost meekness, patience, resignation and Christian fortitude frequently uttering many comfortable and instructive expressions, some of which were minuted down or remembered." Those around him felt blessed to witness such saintly comportment.

> O Lord my God! The amazing horrors of darkness were gathered around me, and covered me all over, and I saw no way to go forth. I felt the depth and extent of the misery of my fellow creatures, separated from the divine harmony; and it was heavier than I could bear, and I was crushed down under it. I lifted up my hand, and I stretched out my arm, but there was none to help me; I looked round about, and was amazed in the depths of misery. O Lord! I remember that thou art omnipotent; that I had called thee Father, and I felt that I loved thee; and I was made quiet in thy will, and I waited for deliverance from thee; thou had pity upon me when no man could help me; I saw that meekness under suffering was showed unto us in the most affecting example of thy son, and thou was teaching me to follow Him; and I said, thy will, O Father, be done.

It is a prayer that comes from fear, compassion, humility, and faith. Ultimately it is a prayer of resignation that asks for nothing but declaims the dying man's state between a flawed world and infinite grace. The eloquence is moving, and the spiritual core is pure Woolman. He was staring death in the face, and although he blinked, he did not blanch.[18]

On Tuesday, September 29, Woolman made plans for his funeral. He was concerned that too much would be spent on it. The Friends around him reassured him that they would bear the costs, but he would not accept this gift. He instructed them to sell all the clothes he had brought on the trip and spend no more than the proceeds to bury him. He also vetoed an oak coffin, reasoning that it was a wood better used for other purposes than just to rot in the ground.

> An ash coffin made plain without any manner of superfluities, the corpse to be wrapped in cheap flannel, the expense of which I leave my wearing clothes to defray, as also the digging of the grave; and I desire that W T [William Tuke] may take my clothes after my decease, and apply them accordingly.
>
> [signed] John Woolman, York, 29th of 9th month, 1772.[19]

By September 30 the number and severity of the pustules had given those who nursed Woolman less reason to hope for his recovery. That morning he declared that he had not slept the previous night and thought the disease "making its progress; but my mind is mercifully preserved in stillness and peace." Later he observed that "he was sensible the pains of death must be hard to bear, but if he escaped them now, he must some time pass through them, and did not know he could be better prepared, but had no will in it." He wanted to be sure that Friends would not misunderstand his conferral with the apothecaries who had visited him. "Nature needed support during the time permitted to struggle with the disorder," he believed—that is, he thought it permissible to use medications that would ease the body's decline, but nothing that would interfere in the process or dull his mental faculties. He needed to be aware of his journey out of this world, lucid, prayerful, and cognizant of anything that God might communicate to him in his last hours.[20]

Woolman was never left alone in his room. One Friend or another sat with paper and pen handy to preserve his words. He lay serenely for long periods, then punctuated the silence with declamations that those in attendance believed were inspired.

> My soul is poured out unto thee like water, and my bones are out of joint. I saw a vision, in which I beheld the great confu-

sion of those that depart from thee. I saw their horror and great distress. I was made sensible of their misery, then was I greatly distressed; I looked unto thee; thou wast underneath and supported me. I likewise saw the great calamity that is coming upon this disobedient nation.

At points Woolman appears to have been in a dialogue with God: "O my Father, my Father! How comfortable are thou to my soul in this trying season!" At other times he communicated clearly to the people with him. They encouraged Woolman to eat, but it was difficult and perhaps unnecessary: "My child, I cannot tell what to say to it; I seem nearly arrived where my soul shall have rest from all its troubles." To Sally Tuke, who brought him a drink, he said, "My child! Thou seemest very kind to me a poor creature; the Lord will reward thee for it." This was a prophecy she was sure to record, for his every word was laden with potential revelation.[21]

Woolman also dictated revelations intended for his *Journal*, but eventually he brought the task to a close: "I believe the Lord will now excuse me from exercises of this kind, and I see now no work but one, which is to be the last wrought by me in this world." All he had to do now was die: "The Messenger will come that will release me from all these troubles, but it must be in the Lord's Time, which I am waiting for." Did he expect an angel, a "messenger" to deliver him from natural torment to spiritual bliss?

> I have labored to do whatever was required according to the ability received, in the remembrance of which I have peace; and though the disorder is strong at times and would come over my mind like a whirlwind, yet it has hitherto been kept steady and centered in Everlasting Love, and if that is mercifully continued, I [neither] ask nor desire more.[22]

Woolman also reported the dream he had before he left Mount Holly—long before the journey, he said—in which he pictured himself in northern England reanimating Quakerism with a prophetic gift that he shared with the first Friends. He was founding the faith anew. In the dream, his mission had come to a sad, abrupt end, a prophecy that his death in York would fulfill. He realized now that he had known all along, or at least should have known if he had understood the message, that he would die there. "My draught seemed strongest to the North," he recalled, "and I mentioned in my own Monthly Meeting that attending the Quarterly Meeting at York, and being there, looked like home to me." And it was the last home of Woolman's corporeal self, where his remains still reside.[23]

On Thursday night, October 1, the medication that Friends were giving Woolman to settle his stomach no longer helped. In frustration, his nurse declaimed in distress, "What shall I do now?" Woolman replied with "great composure, 'rejoice evermore, and in everything give thanks;' but added a little after, 'this is sometimes hard to come at.'" Then he was quiet until the following morning, when he uttered a prayer of supplication for spiritual, never physical, relief.

O Lord! It was thy power that enabled me to forsake sin in my youth, and I have felt thy bruises since for disobedience, but as I bowed under them, thou healed me; and though I have gone through many trials and sore afflictions, thou hast been with me, continuing a father and a friend. I feel thy power now, and beg that in the approaching trying moments, thou wilt keep my heart steadfast unto thee.[24]

During the night on Saturday, "about eight hours before his departure," according to William Tuke, "the fever (which had not been immoderate) left him, and Nature sunk under its load." In other words, although the fever had passed, Woolman's "nature"—his body—was too compromised to recover. When he gave Sally Tuke, who was attending him, directions about wrapping his corpse, she began to weep. He encouraged her not to cry or to mourn him: "I sorrow not, though I have had some painful conflicts; but now they seem over, and matters all settled; and I look at the face of my dear Redeemer, for sweet is his voice and his countenance comely."[25]

On Sunday, October 4, an apothecary whose treatment Woolman had conditionally accepted was considering bleeding or purging him, and Woolman heard the conversation about this. He was content, he said, to rest with God's will and to put his fate in Christ's hands, but "if thou canst not be easy without trying to assist Nature in order to lengthen out my life, I submit." Perhaps he thought there was still hope, and possibly he wanted to live more than he knew, more than he said. He mentioned Job and identified with the "tedious days and wearisome Nights" he had endured. Woolman gave Job's despair a selfless twist, though, lamenting the time and money spent on "vanity and superfluities, while thousands and tens of thousands want the necessaries of life."[26]

Shortly thereafter, Woolman's throat seized up and he could no longer speak. By now he was also blind but wrote nonetheless when he had something to say: "I believe my being here is in the wisdom of Christ; I know not as to life or death." At 6:15 a.m. Woolman fell into what appeared to those around him "an easy sleep, which continued about half an hour; when seeming to awake, he breathed a few times with a little more difficulty, and so expired without sigh, groan, or struggle."[27]

The funeral on October 9 was in the larger of York's two meetinghouses, the one that was used for Quarterly Meeting. Even the apothecary who was not a Quaker attended and later told Esther Tuke that he "could scarce forbear giving testimony concerning him to the audience, but forebore knowing it would be an intrusion upon us." She added that "indeed, a Methodist preacher did, in a few words at the graveside, with which divers of us were well satisfied, tho' not prudent to tell him so." Other details of the Meeting and burial have not survived.[28]

The gravedigger and carpenter who made the ash coffin for Woolman preferred cash to the odd, worn clothes of a smallpox victim, though the gravedigger did accept Woolman's shoes in addition to money. The cash economy that Woolman prophesied against had followed him to the grave. Friends sent the garments back to America. The by-now-famous hat, suit, and shirt went back to Woolman's wife, apparently from John Bispham to Samuel Emlen, who made the delivery, but first precautions had to be taken: "They have been hung in the air a considerable time lest they should retain the infection, and are intended to be sent in a box with some leather from Thomas Priestman," the last apparently a gift from the tanner to Woolman's widow.[29]

About six months after Woolman's burial, when Friends in York gathered again for Quarterly Meeting, they wrote a collective remembrance. In their short time with him, Woolman had made a powerful impression. They recalled "many" of his "weighty expressions" but printed only one. They knew that London Yearly Meeting planned to publish a collection of Woolman's *Remarks on Sundry Subjects*, and saw no purpose to printing those, but they did want to share words spoken in his last trial. Woolman struggled at the end with the "amazing horrors of darkness" that gathered around him. Friends witnessed his physical pain. They recounted his deliverance from the "depths of misery" and the peace he achieved through meek acceptance of God's will. They found his death a model of the process through which all believers must pass.[30]

The York Friends recalled Woolman as "a man endued with a large natural capacity" for the Lord's work. This of course is not the language that Woolman used to describe himself. He found little that was "natural" about his spiritual capacities and struggled lifelong against his nature. Friends saw him as a man who dwelled in "awful fear and watchfulness," always on the alert for any slippage from the divinely determined path. Woolman would take solace from this insight to the qualities that he shared with the prophet Ezekiel.[31]

"He was careful in his public appearances," the York Quakers explained, "to feel the putting forth of the divine hand so that the spring of the gospel ministry often flowed through him with great purity and sweetness as a refreshing stream to the weary travelers towards the city of God." There are echoes of Revelation in such bucolic language—a spring, a stream, pure water flowing through a peaceful resting place for those weary from their earthly travels. This was Woolman's goal, the final resting place to which he had aspired since childhood.[32]

York Friends remembered Woolman as "skillful in dividing the Word." They found him successful in sorting his words from the Lord's and delivering only the revelation entrusted to him. They accepted Woolman's prophecy and considered him uniquely blessed. They believed that he labored under the "guidance of divine wisdom, which rendered his whole conversation uniformly edifying." They recalled his testimonies against slavery and in behalf of animals and understood that they were linked, as they were also with his denunciation of consumption beyond basic human needs. They felt his pain over the suffering inflicted on fellow beings and sensed that "his life has been often a life of mourning." Friends perceived Woolman's overwhelming sadness for the state of the world and also the hope that he tried to instill in them. Finally, they heard Woolman when he cautioned against compromise. They understood that his prophecy was directed specifically to good people. Woolman taught that following their consciences was insufficient. He warned against "contenting themselves with acting up to the standard of Truth manifested to them." The prophecy aspired to a higher standard of purity than what earthly wisdom endorsed.[33]

Burlington Friends also wrote a memorial to Woolman, which recounted his life and the influence of his parents. They recalled him as the model of a loving husband and father, as a minister who prophesied against slavery and in behalf of the poor. They too understood Woolman's indictment of them.

> He was desirous to have his own mind and the minds of others redeemed from the pleasures and immoderate profits of this world and to fix them on those joys which fade not away; his principal care being after a life of purity, endeavouring to avoid not only the grosser pollutions, but those also which, appearing in a more refined dress, are not sufficiently guarded against by some well-disposed people. In the latter part of his life he was remarkable for the plainness and simplicity of his dress, and as much as possible avoided the use of plate, costly furniture and feasting, thereby endeavouring to become an example of temperance and self-denial, which he believed himself called unto; and he was favoured with peace therein, although it carried the appearance of great austerity in the view of some.[34]

In other words, Woolman was a good man but extreme. Friends admired him for running a school and for other evidence of his loving concern for children. The Burlington Quakers, who had known Woolman all their lives, believed that "his ministry was sound, very deep and penetrating, sometimes pointing out the dangerous situation which indulgence and custom lead into, frequently exhorting others, especially the youth, not to be discouraged at the difficulties which occur, but to press after purity." They endorsed his judgment as "sound and clear" and found him "very useful in treating those who had done amiss; he visited such in a private way in that plainness which truth dictates, showing great tenderness and Christian forbearance." He was effective in promoting reform, where others were more likely to provoke anger among those they eldered. They found some signed reflections of Woolman's written in the minutes of a Meeting for ministers and elders about five years before his death, and they granted him the last words of their memorial:

> As looking over the minutes made by persons who have put off this body hath sometimes revived in me a thought how ages pass away, so this list may probably revive a like thought in some when I and the rest of the persons above named are centered in another state of being. The Lord who was the guide of my youth hath in tender mercies helped me hitherto; He hath healed my wounds; He hath helped me out of grievous entanglements; He remains to be the strength of my life; to whom I desire to devote myself in time and in eternity.
>
> John Woolman[35]

Epilogue: A New Beginning

JOHN Woolman was not the first Quaker abolitionist, any more than he was the last American prophet, but he was an effective spokesman for the cause and one of a group of leading reformers who shared his dedication to restoring the Society of Friends to its founding precepts. His was an unambiguously moral opposition to slavery derived from spiritual experience and religious tradition. Shortly after Woolman began advocating his abolitionism publicly, what became a movement headed down two tracks; one was the spiritual line that Woolman articulated prophetically. The Enlightenment and the American revolutionary environment also inspired abolitionism focused on political and legal rights, and they helped create an environment receptive to Woolman's antislavery prophecy. After Woolman's death, the two strands entwined in secular antislavery societies and political lobbying by Quakers among many others. Each line had a historical lineage and an effect, but neither convinced society to eradicate slavery during the eighteenth century or the first half of the nineteenth century.

In the year Woolman died there were still 731 slaves in his home county of Burlington, 3,313 in all New Jersey, and the numbers were increasing. Slaves constituted 6.2 percent of New Jersey's population in 1790. The census of 1800 reflects declining numbers, but 5.8 percent of New Jerseyans were still slaves. There were 18 left in

New Jersey in 1860, when the Civil War began. It was a slow process of emancipation, torturously slow for the enslaved. As Woolman well knew, slavery was not a uniquely southern curse.[1]

Woolman was ahead of the secular wave of antislavery reformers, but it was not far behind him. Close on his heels, Benjamin Franklin was developing a merchant capitalist indictment of slavery on the grounds of its inefficiency compared with free labor systems. The impulse was not humanitarian, and the initial articulations were not abolitionist (Franklin continued to own slaves), but the implications of his critique were the seedbed of an evolving antislavery stance. Two years after Woolman traveled to the South for the first time and drafted *Some Considerations on the Keeping of Negroes*, the French philosopher Charles Montesquieu published an attack on slavery in his *Spirit of the Laws* (1748). One year before the second part of Woolman's *Considerations* appeared, Adam Smith condemned slavery in his *Theory of Moral Sentiments* (1759). In Massachusetts, James Otis's *The Rights of the British Colonies Asserted and Proved* (1764) also contains an attack on slavery that drew on the same Enlightenment vein, equating the rights of white colonists with the rights of their slaves. As Anglo-American politics heated up, debates over slavery and freedom became commonplace in colonial circles. Arthur Lee's "Address on Slavery," the only antislavery essay published by a southerner during the revolutionary era, appeared in the *Virginia Gazette* in 1767. Lee's "Address" lacked Woolman's humanitarianism, inasmuch as he advocated ridding Virginia of the institution by selling slaves to the West Indies. The Congregational minister Samuel Hopkins brought an antislavery message that was more like Woolman's to his Newport, Rhode Island, church in the 1770s, as did other New England ministers and politicians after him in sermons and speeches inspired by the Enlightenment, the revolutionary movement, economic ambitions, and the Bible.[2]

A week after Woolman left London, Lord Mansfield handed down his decision in the now-famous *Somerset* case, which freed a slave named James Somerset, who had arrived in England from Massachusetts with his master in 1769. He had escaped and been recaptured in 1771. Granville Sharp (1735–1813), an antislavery activist, argued the case for Somerset's freedom before the Court of

King's Bench. The ruling invigorated English abolitionists, although it applied only to one person in a particular set of circumstances and was not, as is often believed, a de facto manumission of English slaves. Woolman was in England at this key moment, but we do not know if he heard about the case, the judgment, or Sharp.[3]

Anthony Benezet had read and published an extract of one of Sharp's antislavery pamphlets and wrote him a letter that arrived on June 22, 1772; in it he encouraged Sharp to introduce himself to Benjamin Franklin because the three of them shared abolitionist views. In Sharp's reply on August 21, he reported the decision in Somerset's case and said that he had taken Benezet's advice and initiated a meeting with Franklin. He also said that he was working on a pamphlet that framed the abolitionist argument in biblical terms. On November 8, 1772, Benezet replied: "As thou mentions thy thoughts on the inconsistency of the Gospel with Slavery I herewith send thee two tracts wrote on that head sometime past by a truly pious man (John Woolman) now on a religious visit in some parts of Great Britain." By that time Woolman had been dead for a month, but the news had not yet reached Benezet.[4]

The Harvard University commencement debate in 1773, the year after Woolman's death, was on abolition. In that same year the Philadelphia physician Benjamin Rush published *An Address to the Inhabitants of the British Settlements in America upon Slave-keeping*, and the clergymen Ezra Stiles and Samuel Hopkins sent a circular to New England churches arguing for abolition of the slave trade. *Poems on Various Subjects* by the slave Phillis Wheatley (1753?–84), which she published in London during 1773, called attention to the cause. Even before it became mandatory in 1776 for all Quakers living under the authority of Philadelphia Yearly Meeting to release their slaves, the process of divesting had spread to small numbers of American masters affiliated with other faiths.[5]

Massachusetts, Connecticut, and Rhode Island banned the slave trade in 1774, as did Virginia and North Carolina in the South. Pennsylvanians legislated a high tariff on imported slaves, and the Second Continental Congress outlawed the slave trade in all the colonies. With such monumental reforms, many believed that abolishing the slave trade was an intermediary step toward eliminating slavery from the mainland English colonies, but the final leap was longer than reformers anticipated and was not taken quickly or everywhere.[6]

During the spring of 1775 a group of leading Philadelphians established the Society for the Relief of Free Negroes Unlawfully Held in Bondage, which became after the Revolution the first corporate group dedicated to abolition. A wealthy Quaker merchant from Philadelphia named Joshua Fisher decided in 1776, at the age of sixty-nine, to free his slaves and to trace all those he had previously owned in order to purchase their freedom. And there were many more promising signs that Quakers and others had heard the call.[7]

African Americans were active in this process, running away, rebelling, and fighting against their former masters in the Revolution. Uprisings led politicians to fear social revolution in the South; fear spurred reform motivated by self-interest rather than simply the logic of revolutionary rhetoric or the moral implications of Christianity. Many rich merchants and other masters in the northern colonies acted in behalf of their perceived self-interest by divesting themselves of slaves. There was a slave regiment in the British army, and one out of every four able-bodied male slaves in Rhode Island fought on the patriot side after they were guaranteed freedom for their contributions to the war effort.[8]

We cannot know how many slaves escaped to the British during the Revolution, but estimates range through the tens of thousands. About two-thirds of those who thus seized their freedom died of disease, and most of the survivors went to Nova Scotia after the war; some left Canada for Sierra Leone, on the coast of West Africa, during the 1790s. The rest fished the rough seas and farmed the hardscrabble soil in a colder climate with a shorter growing season than they were accustomed to in the colonies they had left. Those who gained their freedom and stayed behind in the new United States gravitated north, many of them to cities—especially Baltimore, Philadelphia, and New York. Most, however, remained slaves, living after the Revolution much as they had before, if not in worse conditions precipitated by their masters' debts, economic dislocation caused by the war, and the cotton economy that brought an even harsher work environment to plantation agriculture. As the eighteenth century ended, the lot of slaves was worse than ever, and their numbers were growing.[9]

The Pennsylvania Abolition Act of 1780 was the first adopted by a legislative body anywhere in the world. This was a law of monumental significance, but not an entirely altruistic one. Born of fear and grudging support, in addition to more humanitarian motives, the act was slow to take effect and thus gradual, accommodating the state's masters rather than those held in bondage. The bill freed no slaves but recognized the freedom of future children born to enslaved women. It obliged the children of slaves to serve as indentured servants until the age of twenty-eight, a year less than what Woolman regretted imposing as an estate executor on the slave youth James. It abolished Pennsylvania's slave code, which punished blacks more harshly than whites for the same crimes and established barriers to social integration. It freed slaves brought into the colony within six months of arrival, exempting the slaves of politicians from out of state and ambassadors from foreign nations. Four other northern states passed gradual abolition laws by 1804, and none of them dictated such lengthy service.[10]

Quakers were not very effective on the national scene in the immediate aftermath of the Revolution. Partly this was because their pacifism or outright loyalism lost them credibility. Partly, as well, their withdrawal from Pennsylvania politics in the 1750s was an enduring aspect of the quietism that drew them ever more inward. Their liberalism on racial issues was also out of the political mainstream in the increasingly conservative postwar environment. When more than five hundred Quakers from Pennsylvania, New Jersey, and Delaware petitioned the Continental Congress in 1783 to prohibit reopening the slave trade, Congress ignored them. Friends were more effective at the local level, laboring for enforcement of Pennsylvania's Abolition Act and assisting newly freed African Americans who lived in abject poverty.[11]

When abolitionists looked back from the nineteenth century to John Woolman as a founding father of their movement, it was from a bunker in an ongoing battle they were not winning. The gains of the late eighteenth century were frozen in place and undermined by racism and social conflict in the North. In the South, slavery was more entrenched, and southern voices speaking against slavery had long since gone mute. It took another war, America's bloodiest, to end slavery, and the Civil War did not begin to address the social issues that divided races and classes, which had been Woolman's focus for wholesale reform.

When reformers looked back to Woolman from the twentieth century, it was with no clearer sense that his goals had been universally realized. He still spoke to the spirit that enlightened peace activists, war tax resisters, and those seeking social change that would bring justice for women, immigrants, minorities, and other workers across the globe. His pamphlets and *Journal* still spoke to enduring injustices in a gentle, calming voice that advocated love over stridency, humility against claims for the moral high ground, and nonviolence rather than ecoterrorism or guerrilla war.

Also during the twentieth century, the prophetic tradition reached from Reinhold Niebuhr to Martin Luther King, Jr., and other leaders of the civil rights movement. King found Jeremiah during his youthful experience as a Baptist, but he appreciated the Old Testament prophet through Niebuhr's shared pessimism about human nature. Social liberalism on racial issues in mid-twentieth century America derived from a critique of liberal theology and a rejection of political liberals' optimism and blindness on race. It is no coincidence that there was a revival of interest in Woolman and his writings during the years of the civil rights movement and amid protests against the Vietnam War. When civil rights leaders such as King and Bayard Rustin reached back to the prophetic tradition, they tapped into the same spiritual vein that had inspired Woolman. Rustin shared the Quaker saint's resignation and hope. An interviewer asked him late in his life, when he had shifted his energies to the cause of gay and lesbian rights, whether he was hopeful for the human race and whether he expected prejudice to be overcome; he answered:

> I have learned a very significant lesson from the Jewish prophets. If one really follows the commandments of these prophets, the question of hopeful or non-hopeful may become secondary or unimportant, because these prophets

taught that God does not require us to achieve any of the good tasks that humanity must pursue. What God requires of us is that we not stop trying.[12]

Woolman took the same lesson from the prophets and reminded himself frequently that God did not want him to judge others or to argue his message but to work for what is right and good. The Enlightenment and its liberal offshoots are all about reasonable compromise, about negotiation for betterment with a realistic eye to what is possible in this flawed world. Woolman and others more influenced by the prophetic tradition are disinclined to negotiate Truth or accept halfway measures. They remain fixed on delivering the message without dilution. Woolman was not a liberal in our modern understandings of the word; he was a radical spirit, as are the inheritors of his social legacy. The rhetoric of radical reformers shares with Woolman and the prophets before him a sense of mission; they communicate by exhorting a frightened, self-indulgent, or otherwise reluctant audience. They deliver a mandate that embodies its own justification. The radical's appeal is not to reason or what is reasonable and is to that extent not an inheritance of the Enlightenment. Prophetic Truth is absolute, and the radical reminds his audience of principles that it already knows, fundamentals that are honored rhetorically more often than lived.

The prophet warns of imminent danger, often demands either an ascetic approach that he embodies, as in the case of Woolman or Gandhi, or an aspiration that he fails to achieve, as with Martin Luther King, Jr. Passion is a defining characteristic of prophets, and their messages often divide as much as heal. Woolman was distinctive among American reformers for the calming effect of his rhetoric. He eschewed a heroic role, sometimes to the point of hiding himself behind others assumed to be speaking in their own voices.

The prophet submerges the self beneath his role as messenger. Woolman's feverish dream about the death of "John Woolman" is an event oft replicated in the history of prophecy. Coming long after his conversion experience, the symbolic death of Woolman's identity signaled acceptance of a less egocentric role as God's messenger. The dream highlights a transition from social integration to isolation from those around him; it marks a spot on the path toward martyrdom, as the prophet seeks an end that coincides with the demise of his mission. Prophets do not retire; they ascend, more often with a thunderclap than quietly from a retiring old age.[13]

Woolman's *Journal* reflects an eighteenth-century turn of mind, even though it was not an Enlightenment one. He lived in an age that was more polarized than the medieval past; during the eighteenth century, traditions were beleaguered, putting some on the defensive while others rallied to attack a weakened enemy of secularizing forces. Greater independence carried with it deeper introspection and harsher self-analysis. Some, just as Woolman, displayed an exaggerated sense of morality while others defended libertinism with little concern about victims; philosophers and merchants endorsed the operations of free markets with little or no compunction about the disadvantaged. There was a tendency, also exhibited by Woolman and throughout the Bible, to resolve the increasing complexity of the modernizing world through binaries, to reduce options to absolutes and to seize one side while predicting doom should the other triumph. Apocalypse loomed in politics, in religion, and within individuals.[14]

Self-definition took on a negative tone for many people at the same time that the past surrendered limits on self-praise. Those who formed counteridentities in response to the liberalizing forces around them tended toward the gloomy, which was certainly true of Woolman. His *Journal* was a dissent from the optimism of a forward-looking age. The simultaneously heightened ambition for purity was not Woolman's alone. The quest for both an ideal community and a perfectly realized self, which permeates the *Journal*, was widely pursued. Woolman, like others, was equally capable of dwelling on difference and similarity, sharing unbounded hope and despair, and loathing the same self that he celebrated as a vessel of God. That was Woolman, his times, and his *Journal*. It is the extremes, not the complexities, that provide the man's measure.

WOOLMAN'S influence only grew after his death, reaching its peak among antebellum abolitionists, for whom he became an iconic figure. After the Civil War he was rediscovered as a social reformer and pacifist. New editions of his *Journal* in 1871, 1903, 1909, 1922, 1948, and 1971 kept his major writings in print and found them new audiences. Numerous excerpts, often annotated with thoughtful meditations on their meaning, continue to appear in pamphlet form; these number in the dozens. Abridged devotional editions of the *Journal* have an enduring audience as well. Quakers and other mystically inclined Christians have never lost contact with Woolman's *Journal*. Social reformers remain in touch with his legacy. As a literary figure Woolman has risen and fallen to the rhythms of fashion that affect the posthumous reputations of all authors.

Memorials to Woolman in stained glass filter light into churches and chapels across the country. Grace Cathedral, a magnificent Episcopal church in San Francisco and a historic site of humanitarian endeavors, includes Woolman in one of nine panes dedicated to Christian reform. Marguerite Gaudin designed the panels; Henry Lee Willet of Philadelphia, one of the country's leading artists working in medieval glass, created them, and their installation was in 1966, two years after the cathedral's consecration. The thematically related windows also commemorate the Old Testament prophets Amos and Jeremiah, St. James the Just, St. Bernard, the apostle Paul, and the English antislavery reformer William Wilberforce (1759–1833). The legend that connects the images prays, "Help employ our freedom in the maintenance of justice among men and nations."

Woolman sits astride a horse in his Grace Cathedral window. The prophet has white hair and is clean-shaven; he lifts his head and right hand, and his eyes gaze heavenward to accept inspiration. He wears, as Woolman never did in his life, a black cape, a liturgical purple jacket, blue knee-length trousers, white stockings, and blue shoes with gold buckles. He holds a book, apparently the *Journal*, in his extended left hand. The line formed through his torso from hand to hand suggests that the book is an inspired work of literature and that Woolman is the conduit for the revelations it contains.

A Woolman window at Plymouth Congregational Church in Minneapolis also commemorates the *Journal*. It was commissioned in 1955; its design dates from 1958, and the installation came shortly thereafter. Henry Lee Willet created the design from themes and symbolism selected by the church's pastor, a lifelong admirer of

Woolman. The Woolman windows are the second in a projected series of glass images dedicated to "the Devotional Classics." (The first is to St. Paul's letter to the Ephesians, which universalizes the New Testament message as a proclamation of God's connection with all peoples.) The entire installation dedicated to Woolman is significantly larger and more elaborate than the same church's windows memorializing the New England Congregationalist figures William Brewster, John Robinson, William Bradford, Thomas Hooker, John Winthrop, and Jonathan Edwards.

In Plymouth Congregational's windows, as in the later one in Grace Cathedral, Woolman appears in liturgical purple. Here he wears a purple coat and hat, a white cravat and matching white ruffled shirt, red sleeves, green trousers, an orange vest, white stockings, and brass-buckled shoes. His left hand points aloft, and his right hand gestures down to a black man, clearly a slave, working on his hands and knees. Above Woolman, to his left, are bread and a knife; above him to the right are a red cup and a matching gold and red pitcher. The central pane below this image shows Woolman again, this time riding a horse in the company of another figure. Paired windows feature a basket, flowers, and a red coat with gold buttons. Yet another image of Woolman shows him seated with a man and woman whose heads are bowed and eyes are downcast in apparent shame. One pane depicts a trumpet; another shows a bird and nestlings. At the bottom of the series is a male slave dressed in ragged pants standing with his head bowed near a table with quill, paper, and ink. A white man points at the slave and table. Woolman is seated with his back to the man but with his head turned to look at him.

A red lantern and open shackles appear at the top in the third array of Woolman panels at Plymouth. In the center, Woolman sits cross-legged sewing an orange coat. Nearby stand a barrel and a large vessel, perhaps of wine; there are cheese, bread, and containers on the shelves and a red basket with bread. The legend is "Mount Holly." There is also a small Indian figure, Woolman writing, and a ship at sea. Two quotations from the *Journal* are displayed on the windows. "I was made thankful to God that I might have a quick and lively feeling" addresses Woolman's mystical experience;

the other recalls his role as a social reformer: "of the afflictions of my fellow creatures whose situation in life is difficult."

All these windows recall scenes from Woolman's *Journal*. The master instructs Woolman to write the bill of sale for a slave; the trumpet recognizes Woolman's role as a prophet; the shamed couple are slaveowners; the coat recalls his tailoring trade, as does the imagined shop, which also shows the simple products he sold; the bread suggests his life as a farmer and provider; the horse and companion commemorate his traveling ministry. Woolman is once again dressed inappropriately and shown riding when he should be walking. It makes no sense, though, to dispute such details in these stained glass windows in magnificent churches such as Grace and Plymouth. There is no color, scene, or artful approach that could diminish the irony of such a portrayal of Woolman. The idea behind the windows is to celebrate and inspire, and the intended audience is not Quaker, ascetic, or only the mystically inclined.

In the Prayer Chapel at Boston University's School of Theology eight stained glass windows are dedicated to Walter G. Muelder, who served as dean from 1945 to 1972. Those memorialized in the windows are celebrated mystics: St. John of Damascus (ca. 674–749), St. Bernard of Clairvaux (1091–1153), St. Catherine of Siena (1347–80), St. Teresa of Avila (1515–82), St. John of the Cross (1542–91), and William Law (1686–1761). The seventh pane recalls a collective that included Meister Eckhart (ca. 1260–1327), Gerhard Groote (1340–84), and Thomas à Kempis (1379–1471), all of whom were associated with the Friends of God, a secret order dedicated to maintaining the discipline of the church during turbulent times. From the Friends of God emerged another movement, the Brethren of the Common Life, which focused on the spirit within and thus bears a relationship (in the minds of those who created the windows) to Quakers and to Woolman, who is remembered in the eighth and final window. As one of only two Protestants in the series, the only American, and the most modern figure of the ten, Woolman occupies a place of honor that links the mystical thread to those who study in the School of Theology and pray in the chapel.

The Woolman window features a flash of light, centered on a shield, above which a sword stands as a cross. A shaft of light shatters a slave's chain. A black man and a white man kneel together in silent prayer. A basket of bread and a sheaf of wheat complete the presentation and are intended to symbolize Quakers' traditions of piety and fruitful service. The sword is an awkward symbol of Woolman's mystical Christianity, and Quakers do not traditionally kneel, but sit prayerfully. Yet the window captures the relationship between Inner Light and social reform to which Woolman dedicated his life.

Quaker schools named for Woolman dot the American landscape. All are inspired by his social activism, humanitarianism, and dedication to the education of children. The John Woolman Memorial in Mount Holly, New Jersey, receives a steady trickle of pilgrims. Many of the visitors are Quakers, some are schoolchildren, but others who know him as a mystic, literary figure, and social activist come too. The John Woolman House is the memorial's central feature. It may be the one he had built for his daughter the year before he died; if so, Mary and her husband, John Comfort, expanded it during the next decade and sold it in 1783 or 1786—a commemorative stone placed by the new owners contradicts the date on the deed—before moving to a larger house in Pennsylvania.

The house conforms loosely (in an eighteenth-century fashion) to the specifications that Woolman commissioned. It is about twenty-seven feet by seventeen feet, give or take a yard; it is two stories with a brick exterior; it has the paved cellar he called for and the number and location of windows he specified. The stairs are in the opposite corner from Woolman's design, and other deviations reflect different tastes or ad hoc decisions made on the ground.[15]

The memorial sits on land where Woolman's orchard once grew. Admirers purchased another house, which they moved several blocks and reconstructed on the property in 1924 in the understanding that it was his. The Memorial Association's directors now live in that home. The houses are the principal physical connections between the site and the man it memorializes. There are also two rocking chairs, one in the house and another in the Burlington County Historical Society, that oral traditions associate with Woolman. The Windsor rocker at the historical society is plain, but not austere, with stylized turnings on the legs and armposts. The headrest has a decorative swirl carved on each rounded end. The "Woolman chair" at the memorial is plainer. Both are eighteenth-century chairs, but neither was a rocker during Woolman's lifetime. It was subsequent owners who modified them for greater comfort and in conformance with a popular style. They valued the chairs for their association with Woolman and kept alive the oral tradition of his ownership, but his descendants did not inherit his asceticism; he would not have rocked.

The Brainerd Street schoolhouse, where one tradition maintains that Woolman taught beginning in 1759, entertains tours, principally of schoolchildren. Surrounding buildings dwarf the tiny twenty-by-thirty-foot brick structure, but it weathers the ages well. The roof lines are not original, and the fireplace (without its stove) was remodeled at some point; the ceiling and contents are also revisions. Still, it is more than the shell of the original school, an instructive example of what it once was, and is cared for lovingly by the Colonial Dames of New Jersey.

The tradition that Woolman taught in the schoolhouse may be accurate, but it is just as likely that he taught in his shop, his home, or the old Quaker meetinghouse. There is no direct evidence to support any of these hypotheses. Woolman walked from home to his tailor shop on Mill Street; the meetinghouse was behind it, and the school in the next block. In the 1930s, when the tailor shop was still standing, WPA investigators reached the conclusion that the "little meetinghouse" and the Quaker school were the same building. Their reasoning hinged on local tradition and on the proximity of the shop and the structure on Meetinghouse Alley. On the other hand, a contradictory local tradition and the list of Quaker and non-Quaker subscribers who bought a stove for the Brainerd Street schoolhouse in 1759, the first year that we think Woolman taught, are also intriguing.[16]

The Three Tuns Tavern, where Woolman may have confronted the magician and his audience, still stands, but it is now the Mill Street Hotel, a smoky, run-down bar with devoted customers, who are apparently content with only one brand of beer on tap in regular and "lite" versions. The Three Tuns dates to 1726. Woolman's former master sold the tavern in 1748, one year after selling his shop to Woolman. Mount Holly had two other inns during the mid-eighteenth century, the Cross Keys and the Black Horse Tavern, so it could have been in one of them that the magician performed. Other Woolman sites in his hometown are locations where structures once stood.

The memorials to Woolman in York, England, are even simpler and in keeping with his gentle modesty. The house where he died is still in use. There is a historical plaque beside the entry: "John Woolman American Quaker and Anti-Slavery Pioneer Died Here Oct. 1772." That is more than he would have wanted. The print used for his name is larger than the rest of the lettering; he would have opposed a commemorative notice and would wonder whether the four spikes that fasten the sign to the brick wall have created a weakness in the structure. Woolman would have recommended a better use for the brass, maybe a plainer knocker than the lion that now adorns the door, and would have found the raised rim around the perimeter of the plaque an unnecessary embellishment. The neighborhood is no longer a suburb, but the lane runs up to the stone wall that encloses the ruins of St. Mary's Abbey. The Ouse River and the park that includes the abbey still provide a peaceful oasis that invites contemplation.

The room where Woolman died apparently became something of a pilgrimage site in the early nineteenth century, but it was a "lumber and apple room" by the 1840s, and the house's interior had been remodeled by then. This of course did not deter pilgrims who thought they could connect with Woolman there. A "large arm chair" that was reputed to be where he died passed into the hands of the superintendent of the local Friends school.[17]

Woolman's grave is on the opposite shore inside York's ancient walls. It remains undisturbed in the old Quaker burial ground, which dates to 1659 and was closed to interments in 1855. Fifty years after Woolman's burial, there were still no gravestones or tombs, "plain mounds of earth being its only marks of a cemetery," York's historian wrote, and "the ground is completely covered with thick grass." Markers date to the late nineteenth century and are memorials dedicated by Victorian ancestors of the deceased whose families were no longer Quaker. One remembers a man who died in "about" 1725. Woolman's marked a spot that is "near" his grave. The actual location of plots is open to speculation.[18]

NEAR THIS STONE
REST THE REMAINS OF
JOHN WOOLMAN
OF MOUNT HOLLY
NEW JERSEY NORTH AMERICA
WHO DIED AT YORK
7TH OF 10TH MONTH 1772
AGED 51 YEARS

The essential John Woolman, the meaningful core, was elusive in life; the man barely lived inside his skin. He has not gotten easier to find. He largely succeeded in detaching himself from material objects—things as well as people and himself—before he died. His trail was faint and got fainter. A wisp of inspiration, a glimmer of insight, a glimpse of the divine, and then he was gone. We are not even sure where his house was; his childhood home and the meetinghouse and school he attended as a child have disappeared without traces. Where they once stood, the New Jersey Turnpike parallels Interstate 295 as they pass the village of Rancocas. The river view that his family and fellow settlers shared is obliterated, as is the hill where the second incarnation of the Woolman homestead sat. The highways and an industrial park have taken their spots.

The location of Woolman's tailor shop in Mount Holly is a parking lot adjacent to a warehouse. The site of the old meetinghouse is also paved. Devonshire House, where Woolman attended London Yearly Meeting, was torn down, and the York meetinghouse where he attended his last Meeting for Worship is also gone. The cemetery where Friends buried his body is not where he resides. We find him instead in the quiet places, the small things, and the words that he wrote and what contemporaries wrote about him. To a lesser extent he is reflected in what he read and how others since his death have contemplated his life's meaning.

We find Woolman in such artifacts as a scrap of paper about three by four inches. Its heavy stock is creased down the middle and grimy from his handling. It was in his wallet when he died. Someone had the presence, and ill grace, to remove it before his personal belongings were shipped off to his widow. Woolman had taken it in and out of his pocket, folded and unfolded it, sweat on it, and read the words that faded with use over time. We cannot know how long he carried it. The words are not his, but are a summary in miniature of how he tried to live and what he believed. It is a passage from the Apostle Paul's Epistle to the Romans (Romans 6:13): "Neither yield you your members as instruments of unrighteousness and sin, but yield yourselves unto God as those that are alive from His deed and your members as instruments of righteousness unto God." Do not allow sin to rule over your mortal body, thereby enslaving you to your "natural self," as one modern translation puts it. Do not surrender any part of yourself to sin. Instead, give yourself to God, as one of those "who have been brought from death to life." Dedicate your "whole being" to God to be used for righteous purposes. "Sin must not be your master; for you do not live under law but under God's grace."

That was Woolman's map to help keep him on course. It could also be his epitaph. It provides a fleeting glimpse of his beautiful soul.

A Note on Sources

Phillips P. Moulton's edition of Woolman's *Journal* is an exemplary model of documentary editing. Not only are Moulton's transcriptions reliable, but his careful research in extant drafts is a signal contribution to our understanding of the text's provenance. The Introduction and appendices explain the relationship of the drafts to one another, and the notes detail deviations in the first published edition, what the editorial committee changed and excised from Woolman's intended text. The drafts are in the Historical Society of Pennsylvania; Friends Historical Library at Swarthmore College; the Friends Historical Library, Dublin; and the Quaker Collection at Haverford College Library.

There are drafts of pamphlets, epistles, and letters at Haverford, Swarthmore, the Historical Society of Pennsylvania, Rutgers University, and Friends House Library in London. Woolman's brother Abner's manuscript journal is at Haverford in the records of the Committee for Sufferings of Philadelphia Yearly Meeting; the parable of the sons of Ham is also at Haverford. Henry J. Cadbury, ed., *John Woolman in England, 1772: A Documentary Supplement* (London, 1971) is an extremely helpful guide to manuscripts related to Woolman's journey to England, quirky but a godsend for anyone interested in the subject. Swarthmore has microfilm of eighteenth-century records of Philadelphia Yearly Meeting and its committees, and Burlington Monthly and Quarterly Meetings, which are also useful. The Woolman Memorial, Burlington County Historical Society, and the New Jersey State Library have limited Woolman materials, but some official records—deeds, wills and estate papers, and marriage certificates—bearing on Woolman and his family. Amelia Mott Gummere's 1922 edition of the *Journal* and essays is the most comprehensive collection of Woolman's published writings and also contains editions of some manuscript material that still is in private hands. Gummere's Introduction and John Greenleaf Whittier's Introduction to the 1871 edition of the *Journal* are also valuable, as is the manuscript "Dictionary of Quaker Biography" available at Friends House Library and Haverford.

Gummere's Introduction and Janet Whitney's *John Woolman* (Boston, 1942) are the most comprehensive biographical treatments. Both made mistakes, which are largely corrected by Cadbury and Moulton; Whitney's book was sometimes more inspired than informed by research, but in fairness, her analysis did benefit from the influence of oral traditions that may be true but simply undocumented. Rufus Jones's writings on Quakerism, mysticism, and Woolman within theological and historical contexts are invaluable. The works by William C. Braithwaite, Roger Bruns, James Darsey, David Brion Davis, Thomas E. Drake, J. William Frost, Carla Gerona, Abraham J. Heschel, William James, Susan Juster, Emma Jones Lapsansky and Anne A. Verplanck, Rebecca Larson, Barry Levy, Jack Marietta, Bernard McGinn, Gary Nash, Lee Eric Schmidt, Jean Soderlund, Ann Taves, Frederick B. Tolles, and Evelyn Underhill, all of which are referred to in the notes, are essential to establishing the meaningful contexts for appreciating Woolman. Classic works on dreams and dreaming, but especially those of Carl Jung, have been extremely useful, as has recent work on the eighteenth-century history of dreaming, especially that of Carla Gerona and Mechal Sobel. The work on seventeenth-century Quakerism, mysticism, the Reformation, the Dissenting tradition, quietism, the English Revolution, and the Enlightenment is too vast to note, even in passing.

Among recent work specifically on Woolman, David Sox's compact treatment, *John Woolman, 1720–1772: Quintessential Quaker* (York, 1999), and the collection of essays edited by Mike Heller, *The Tendering Presence: Essays on John Woolman* (Wallingford, Pa., 2003), are particularly useful.

Notes

Abbreviations Used in the Notes
AHR   *American Historical Review*
FHL   Friends Historical Library, Swarthmore College
HCL   Haverford College Library
HSP   Historical Society of Pennsylvania
JAH   *Journal of American History*
JER   *Journal of the Early Republic*
WMQ   *William and Mary Quarterly*

Prologue: How to Begin?

1. Psalm 143. I quote here and throughout from the New Revised Standard Version of the Bible. Woolman's humanitarian sensibilities are those identified by Thomas Haskell, "The Quaker Ethic and the Antislavery International," Parts 1 and 2, in Thomas Bender, ed,, *The Antislavery Debate: Capitalism and Abolitionism as a Problem in Historical Interpretation* (Berkeley, 1992), 107–60.
2. Phillips P. Moulton, ed., Introduction, *The Journal and Major Essays of John Woolman* (New York, 1971); Henry J. Cadbury, *John Woolman in England* (London, 1971); Edwin H. Cady, *John Woolman* (New York, 1966).
3. Thomas E. Drake, *Quakers and Slavery in America* (New Haven, 1950), 188–89; John G. Whittier, Introduction, *The Journal of John Woolman* (Boston, 1871); John Woolman, *A Word of Remembrance and Caution to the Rich* (London, 1897), 2.
4. Charles A. Beard and Mary R. Beard, *Rise of American Civilization* (New York, 1930), 161; Moulton, ed., Introduction, *Journal.*
5. Charles W. Eliot, ed., *John Woolman's Journal* (New York, 1909; 1939), 168; Moulton, ed., Introduction, *Journal.*
6. Several titles give a flavor of the claims that are made on Woolman: David Sox, *John Woolman: Quintessential Quaker* (York, U.K., 1999); Frederic J. Masback, *The Economics of Evil: A Study of John Woolman's Thought* (Philadelphia, n.d.); Ann

Sharpless, *John Woolman: Pioneer in Labor Reform* (Philadelphia, 1920); Moulton, ed., Introduction, *Journal;* Cady, *John Woolman.*

7. Ira Berlin, *Many Thousands Gone: The First Two Centuries of Slavery in North America* (Cambridge, Mass., 1998), Table 1, "Slave Population of Mainland North America, 1680–1810," 369–71.
8. Ibid.; P. J. Marshall, *The Making and Unmaking of Empires: Britain, India, and America c. 1750–1783* (Oxford, U.K., 2005), 25, 32; David Richardson, "The British Empire and the Atlantic Slave Trade, 1660–1807," in P. J. Marshall, ed., *Oxford History of the British Empire,* vol. 2, *The Eighteenth Century* (Oxford, U.K., 1998), 442; Philip Morgan, "The Black Experience in the British Empire, 1680–1810," in Marshall, ed., *Oxford History,* vol. 2, 466.
9. Jean Soderlund, *Quakers and Slavery: A Divided Spirit* (Princeton, 1985), 8–10 and passim; Gary B. Nash, "Slaves and Slave-owners in Colonial Philadelphia," *WMQ,* 3d ser., 30 (1973): 223–56. Adam Hochschild, *Bury the Chains: Prophets and Rebels in the Fight to Free an Empire's Slaves* (New York, 2005); Sydney V. James, *A People Among Peoples: Quaker Benevolence in Eighteenth-Century America* (Cambridge, Mass., 1963); David Brion Davis, *The Problem of Slavery,* 2 vols. (Ithaca, N.Y., 1966, 1975).
10. Bender, ed., *Antislavery Debate;* T. H. Breen, *The Marketplace of Revolution* (New York, 2004); Seth Rockman, "The Unfree Origins of American Capitalism," in Cathy Matson, ed., *The Economy of Early America* (University Park, Pa., 2006), 335–61.
11. Haskell, "The Quaker Ethic," in Bender, ed., *Antislavery Debate,* 111. In England before 1750, Richard Baxter (Presbyterian), Thomas Tryon (Boehmenist), and Morgan Godwyn (Anglican) and, in America, Samuel Sewall (Congregationalist) were non-Quakers who opposed slavery. Davis, *Problem of Slavery in Western Culture,* 338–48; Richard Francis, *Judge Sewall's Apology: The Salem Witch Trials and the Forming of an American Conscience* (New York, 2005), chapter 11.
12. William James, *Varieties of Religious Experience* (London, 1902; New York: Library of America, 1987), lectures 11–15, 239–341; Wayne Proudfoot, *Religious Experience* (Berkeley, 1985); J. Samuel Preus, *Explaining Religion* (New Haven, 1989); Ann Taves, *Fits, Trances, and Visions: Experiencing Religion and Explaining Experience from Wesley to James* (Princeton, 1999); Eric Leigh Schmidt, *Hearing Things: Religion, Illusion, and the American Enlightenment* (Cambridge, Mass., 2000). Evelyn Underhill, *Mysticism: The Nature and Development of Spiritual Consciousness* (1910; 1919; Oxford, U.K., 1993), chapter 4.
13. James, *Varieties,* 249, 245.
14. Natalie Davis, *Women on the Margins: Three Seventeenth-Century Lives* (Cambridge, Mass., 1995), 63–139.
15. Amelia Mott Gummere, *The Journal and Essays of John Woolman* (New York, 1922), ix.

1. Revelations, 1720–28

1. Woolman, *Journal,* 23.
2. John Bunyan, *Grace Abounding to the Chief of Sinners* (London, 1666); Augustine of Hippo, *The Confessions* (397–401; New York, 1998); Benjamin Franklin, *The Autobiography* (1818; New Haven, 1964).

3. John L. Nickalls, ed., *Journal of George Fox* (London, 1952, 1975), 1; John Churchman, *An Account of the Gospel Labours, and Christian Experiences of a Faithful Minister of Christ* (Philadelphia, 1779), 2; Daniel B. Shea, ed., "Some Account of the Fore Part of the Life of Elizabeth Ashbridge," in William L. Andrews, ed., *Journeys in New Worlds: Early American Women's Narratives* (Madison, Wis., 1990), 147; Woolman, *Journal*, 23, and manuscript draft, FHL.

4. Susan Clair Imbarrato, *Declarations of Independency in Eighteenth-Century American Autobiography* (Knoxville, Tenn., 1998).

5. Jonathan Edwards, "Personal Narrative," in George S. Claghorn, ed., *Works of Jonathan Edwards*, vol. 16, *Letters and Personal Writings* (New Haven, 1998), 791; Augustine, *Confessions*, trans. William Watts (Cambridge, Mass., 1912), Book 2, 75.

6. Edwards, "Personal Narrative," 790–91.

7. Ibid., 794–95.

8. Teresa of Avila, *The Interior Castle*, trans. Mirabai Starr (New York, 2003), 29; Lynn Staley, ed., *The Book of Margery Kempe* (New York, 2001), 3; Jill Ker Conway, *When Memory Speaks: Reflections on Autobiography* (New York, 1998).

9. Mary Hagger, *Extracts from the Memoranda of Mary Hagger, Ashford, Kent* (Philadelphia, 1843), 432; Thomas Story, *The Life of Thomas Story* (Newcastle upon Tyne, U.K., 1747), 1; Howard H. Brinton, *Quaker Journals: Varieties of Religious Experience Among Friends* (Philadelphia, 1972), chapter 2.

10. William C. Braithwaite, *The Beginnings of Quakerism to 1660* (London, 1912; Cambridge, U.K., 1955); Christopher Hill, *The World Turned Upside Down. Radical Ideas During the English Revolution* (London, 1972); Rosemary Moore, *The Light in Their Consciences: The Early Quakers in Britain, 1646–1666* (University Park, Pa., 2000); Diarmaid MacCulloch, *The Reformation: A History* (New York, 2004).

11. Rufus M. Jones, *George Fox: Seeker and Friend* (New York, 1930); Jones, *Spiritual Reformers in the Sixteenth and Seventeenth Centuries* (New York, 1914); Rachel Hadley King, *George Fox and the Light Within, 1650–1660* (Philadelphia, 1940); Geoffrey F. Nuttall, *The Holy Spirit in Puritan Faith and Experience* (London, 1946; Chicago, 1992).

12. Barry Reay, *The Quakers and the English Revolution* (New York, 1985), 11.

13. Jones, *Spiritual Reformers*, Conclusion.

14. Richard Bailey, *New Light on George Fox and Early Quakerism: The Making and Unmaking of a God* (San Francisco, 1992); Henry J. Cadbury, ed., *George Fox's "Book of Miracles"* (Philadelphia, 2000); Leo Damrosch, *The Sorrows of the Quaker Jesus: James Nayler and the Puritan Crackdown on the Free Spirit* (Cambridge, Mass., 1996).

15. Moore, *The Light in Their Consciences*, 92.

16. Reay, *Quakers and the English Revolution*, chapter 4.

17. G. Fox, *Instructions for Right-Spelling, and Plain Directions for Reading and Writing True English* (London, 1694; Philadelphia, 1702), 10; Robert Barclay, *An Apology for the True Christian Divinity* (London, 1678), 67–68.

18. Fox, *Instructions for Right-Spelling*, 12.

19. Barclay, *Apology*, 217; Reay, *The Quakers and the English Revolution*, 8–9 and passim; Moore, *The Light in Their Consciences*, chapter 2.

20. Barry Levy, *Quakers and the American Family* (New York, 1988).

21. David Hackett Fischer, *Albion's Seed: Four British Folkways in America* (New York, 1989), 419–23.
22. William Wills, manuscript journal, in George DeCou, *Burlington: A Provincial Capital* (Burlington, N.J., 1945), 27–29; Dr. Daniel Wills to William Biddle, London, 1679, in DeCou, *Burlington*, 29.
23. John Pomfret, *Colonial New Jersey: A History* (Princeton, 1973); Pomfret, *The Province of East New Jersey, 1609–1702* (Princeton, 1962).
24. Herbert C. Kraft, *The Lenape: Archaeology, History, and Ethnography* (Newark, N.J., 1986), 5. Kraft points out that the story may be of modern creation and that it greatly underestimates how long Indians lived along the Delaware River.
25. Ibid., chapters 1–4.
26. Peter O. Wacker and Paul G. E. Clemens, *Land Use in Early New Jersey: A Historical Geography* (Newark, N.J., 1995).
27. Peter Kalm, *Travels in North America*, 2 vols., trans. and ed. Adolph B. Benson (1770; New York, 1937; 1964), vol. 1, 76–77.
28. Wacker and Clemens, *Land Use*, chapters 1–7.
29. The family history and genealogy here and below are from Janet Whitney, *John Woolman: American Quaker* (Boston, 1942); Gummere, *Journal*, "Biographical Sketch," 1–150.
30. Gummere, *Journal*, 3; Whitney, *John Woolman*, chapter 2.
31. Gummere, *Journal*, 4–5; Whitney, *John Woolman*, chapters 2 and 3.
32. Gummere, *Journal*, 8–9; Whitney, *John Woolman*, chapters 22 and 23 and 450.
33. J. William Frost, *The Quaker Family in Colonial America: A Portrait of the Society of Friends* (New York, 1973), chapter 5.
34. John Locke, *Some Thoughts Concerning Education* (London, 1693, 1695; Indianapolis, 1996), 11–16.
35. Fox, *Instructions for Right-Spelling*, 10, 49, 58, 59, 62.
36. [William Penn,] *Some Fruits of Solitude, in Reflections and Maxims Relating to the Conduct of Human Life*, 2nd ed. (London, 1693), Preface and passim.
37. Elizabeth Jacob, *An Epistle in True Love Containing a Farewell Exhortation to Friends Families* (1712; Boston, 1757), 2, 10, 11.
38. Richard Bauman, *Let Your Words Be Few: Symbolism of Speaking and Silence Among Seventeenth-Century Quakers* (Cambridge, U.K., 1983).
39. Frost, *Quaker Family*, 35–39.
40. Woolman, *Journal*, 23.
41. Ibid.
42. Ibid.
43. Ibid., 23–24; Bauman, *Let Your Words Be Few*.
44. Bauman, *Let Your Words Be Few*.

2. Transition, 1729–30

1. *Pennsylvania Gazette*, May 13, 1731.
2. Jon Coleman, *Vicious: Wolves and Men in America* (New Haven, 2004).
3. N. Scott Momaday, *The Ancient Child* (New York, 1989); Matt Cartmill, *A View to a Death in the Morning: Hunting and Nature Through History* (Cambridge, Mass., 1993); Daniel J. Gelo, "The Bear," in Angus K. Gillespie and Jay Mechling,

eds., *American Wildlife in Symbol and Story* (Knoxville, Tenn., 1987); Calvin Martin, "Time and the American Indian," in *The American Indian and the Problem of History* (New York, 1987).

4. *Pennsylvania Gazette*, December 9, 1729; December 18, 1735.
5. Ibid., August 12, 1736; October 21, 1736; June 8, 1738; June 15, 1738.
6. Ibid., March 20, 1740; July 3, 1740; January 11, 1744; March 1, 1744; February 5, 1744–45.
7. Ibid., March 7, 1731–32; Elizabeth A. Fenn, *Pox Americana: The Great Smallpox Epidemic of 1775–82* (New York, 2001).
8. *Pennsylvania Gazette*, October 15, 1730.
9. Jon Butler, "Magic, Astrology, and the Early American Religious Heritage, 1600–1760," *American Historical Review*, 84 (1979): 333–34; Fischer, *Albion's Seed*, 528.
10. *Pennsylvania Gazette*, October 15, 1730.
11. Keith Thomas, *Religion and the Decline of Magic* (New York, 1971); Herbert Leventhal, *In the Shadow of the Enlightenment: Occultism and Renaissance Science in Eighteenth-Century America* (New York, 1976); David Hall, *Worlds of Wonder, Days of Judgment: Popular Religious Belief in Early New England* (New York, 1989); D. Michael Quinn, *Early Mormonism and the Magic World View* (Salt Lake City, 1999).
12. *Pennsylvania Gazette*, October 15, 1730.
13. Ibid.
14. Ibid.
15. Ibid.
16. Ibid.
17. On the persistence of folk belief, see Leventhal, *In the Shadow of the Enlightenment*, and Thomas, *Religion and the Decline of Magic*.
18. Woolman, *Journal*, 23–24.
19. William Cave, *Primitive Christianity: or, the Religion of the Ancient Christians in the First Ages of the Gospel* (London, 1686), unpaginated Preface.
20. Brinton, *Quaker Journals*, 6, 9; John Gratton, *A Journal of the Life of That Ancient Servant of Christ, John Gratton* (London, 1720, 1779), 3; John Hunt's Journal, FHL; William Penn, *Select Works of William Penn, to Which Is Prefixed a Journal of His Life* (London, 1771), 478; Joseph Pike, *Some Account of the Life of Joseph Pike* (Philadelphia, 1838), 357.
21. Augustine, *The Confessions* (397; New York, 1912; 2001), Book 2, 36.
22. Woolman, *Journal*, 24.
23. Carl Jung, *Dreams*, trans. R.F.C. Hull (New York, 1974); James A. Hall, *Jungian Dream Interpretation: A Handbook of Theory and Practice* (Toronto, 1983); Jack H. Wallis, *Jung and the Quaker Way* (London, 1988); Anthony Stevens, *Private Myths: Dreams and Dreaming* (Cambridge, Mass., 1995), 3, 4, 10, 62, 67, 114, 129, 147–49, 155, 177, 180, 187, 190–91, 204, 267, 292, 301; Kelly Bulkeley, *An Introduction to the Psychology of Dreaming* (Westport, Conn., 1997); Howard H. Brinton, "Dreams of the Quaker Journalists," in Brinton, ed., *Byways of Quaker History* (Wallingford, Pa., 1944), 209–31.
24. Carla Gerona, *The Power of Dreams in Transatlantic Quaker Culture* (Charlottesville, Va., 2004).
25. Brinton, "Dreams of the Quaker Journalists," 213, 219, 230–31.

26. Books of dream interpretations read in eighteenth-century Anglo-America include Artimedorus, *The Interpretation of Dreams, Digested into Five Books* (London, 1710); [Anonymous,] *The Complete Fortune Teller* [n.p., n.d., 179?]; Erra Pater, *The Book of Knowledge: Treating of the Wisdom of the Ancients* (Hartford, Conn., 1793); *The Universal Interpreter of Dreams and Visions* (Baltimore, 1795); [Anonymous,] *The Universal Dream Book, or Interpreter of all Manner of Dreams* (Philadelphia, 1829).
27. John 2:16.
28. Jacob Behme [Boehme or Jakob Böhme], *Considerations upon Esaiah Stiefel His Little Book of The Threefold Life of Man and of His New Birth*, trans. John Sparrow (London, 1661).
29. Ibid., 1–7.
30. Ibid., 23.
31. Roger Bastide, "Dreams and Culture," in *Dream Dynamics: Scientific Proceedings* (New York, 1971), 38–45; Bastide, "The Sociology of the Dream," in Gustave E. Van Grunebaum and Roger Sallois, eds., *The Dream and Human Societies* (Berkeley, 1966), 199–211.
32. Woolman, *Journal*, 24–25; John Bunyan, *The Pilgrim's Progress* (London, 1678); Bunyan, *Grace Abounding* (London, 1666).
33. Woolman, *Journal*, 24–25; James Turner, *Reckoning with the Beast: Animals, Pain, and Humanity in the Victorian Mind* (Baltimore, 1980).
34. Woolman, *Journal*, 24–25.
35. Genesis 1:26.
36. Woolman, *Journal*, 25.
37. Margaret N. Abruzzo, "Polemical Pain: Slavery, Suffering, and Sympathy in Eighteenth- and Nineteenth-Century Moral Debate," Ph.D. diss., University of Notre Dame, 2005.
38. Woolman, *Journal*, 25.

3. Sinner and Saints, 1731–35

1. John Foxe, *Book of Martyrs* (1563; London, 1686); ed. John Cumming (London, 1875), 17, 23–25.
2. Ibid., 23–24.
3. Ibid., 26.
4. Cave, *Primitive Christianity*.
5. William Sewel, *The History of the Rise, Increase, and Progress of the Christian People Called Quakers*, 2 vols. (London, 1722, 1795, 1800; Amsterdam, 1766; Burlington, 1774; Philadelphia, 1811, 1823, 1856), vol. 1, xi, 118, 248; William C. Braithwaite, *The Second Period of Quakerism* (Cambridge, U.K., 1955), chapters 2, 3, and 4.
6. Sewel, *History*, vol. 2, 3, 102, 179, 182, 221, 274–75.
7. Sewel also reports a case of brutal torture in New Amsterdam (later New York) in 1659, in vol. 1, 287–90; Rufus M. Jones, *The Quakers in the American Colonies* (London, 1911).
8. Ibid., vol. 1, 252.
9. Ibid., vol. 1, 253.
10. Ibid., vol. 1, 251.
11. Ibid., vol. 1, 256.

12. Ibid., vol. 1, 286.
13. Carla Gardina Pestana, *Quakers and Baptists in Colonial Massachusetts* (Cambridge, U.K., 1991).
14. Woolman, *Journal*, 24.
15. Ibid., 25.
16. Ibid.; Mechal Sobel, *Teach Me Dreams* (Princeton, 2000), n. 47, 269–70, identifies a pattern of three consecutive references to mothers—the tree, the bird, and Woolman's biological mother—in the *Journal*.
17. Ibid.
18. Locke, *Some Thoughts Concerning Education*, 38, 51, 54.
19. Woolman, *Journal*, 25.
20. Ibid., 25–26.
21. Whitney, *John Woolman*, and Gummere, *Journal*, describe Woolman and the two eldest Smith boys as fast friends and believe that Woolman was intimate with all five of the Smith children. Gummere, who was a direct descendant of the Smiths, was working with oral tradition; it is unclear what Whitney's sources were, but they were probably oral traditions as well.
22. Abner Woolman, Religious Memoir, HCL, Special Collections, Philadelphia Yearly Meeting, Committee for Sufferings, Miscellaneous Papers, 1772, carton B5.1.
23. John Smith, "John Smith's Memorandum Book" (1738–45) and diaries 1745–52, 11 vols., Library Company of Philadelphia manuscript collection, housed in HSP, yi 2 7417 F.10; Whitney, *John Woolman*, chapter 6
24. Edwin Wolf, *The Library of James Logan of Philadelphia, 1674–1751* (Philadelphia, 1974).
25. Smith, memorandum book and diaries.
26. Ibid.
27. Miguel de Cervantes, *Don Quixote*, trans. Edith Grossman (Madrid, 1605–15; London, 1612–16; New York, 2003), Introduction by Harold Bloom, xxi–xxxv.
28. John Milton, *Paradise Lost* (London, 1667; Cutchogue, New York, 1976).
29. John Smith, Memorandum Book, 9 mo. 1741, HSP.
30. Woolman, *Journal*, 25. Brinton, *Quaker Journals*, chapters 3 and 4.

4. Young Man Wool, 1736–43

1. Brinton, *Quaker Journals*, chapter 3.
2. Woolman, *Journal*, 26, 27; Churchman, *An Account of the Gospel Labours*, 5; *Friends' Miscellany*, 10 (Philadelphia, 1837), 9–10.
3. Woolman, *Journal*, 28.
4. Brinton, *Quaker Journals*, chapter 4; James, *Varieties*, 86–87, 116, 121–22, 127, 136, 151–54; Jung, *Dreams*, 155, 270.
5. Woolman, *Journal*, 29; Margaret E. Stewart, "John Woolman's 'Kindness Beyond Expression': Collective Identity vs. Individualism and White Supremacy," *Early American Literature*, 26 (1991), 263.
6. Woolman, *Journal*, 28.
7. Stewart, "John Woolman's 'Kindness Beyond Expression,'" 260.
8. Woolman, *Journal*, 28.

9. Ibid., 27–28.
10. Thomas à Kempis, *The Imitation of Christ* (1420–27; New York, 1998), Book 3, chapter 31, 124; Book 2, chapter 7, 55–56.
11. Anthony Benezet to Samuel Fothergill, October 17, 1757, in George Brookes, *Friend Anthony Benezet* (Philadelphia, 1937), 223. Benezet refers directly to the new edition of Everard's sermons and includes a copy with his letter.
12. John Everard, *Some Gospel Treasures* (London, 1653; Germantown, Pa., 1757), iii, iv, vii, viii, ix, 3, 25, 27, 31, 33, 35.
13. I thank Father Robert E. Sullivan for the insights of this paragraph. Barclay, *Apology*, 167.
14. Woolman, *Journal*, 118.
15. Ibid., 29.
16. Ibid., 29–30.
17. Ibid., 30.
18. More obviously, Franklin and Woolman were vastly different from each other, as are their autobiographies. See Leonard W. Labaree, ed., Introduction, *The Autobiography of Benjamin Franklin* (New Haven, 1964), 3–4.
19. Woolman, *Journal*, 30.
20. Ibid., 31; James, *A People Among Peoples*, chapter 2; Lynn Hunt, *Inventing Human Rights: A History* (New York, 2007).
21. Everard, *Some Gospel Treasures*, 33.
22. Thomas Hamm, *The Quakers in America* (New York, 2003), 29–31; Frost, *The Quaker Family*; James, *A People Among Peoples*; Soderlund, *Quakers and Slavery*; Arthur J. Mekeel, *The Quakers and the American Revolution* (York, U.K., 1996); Jack Marietta, *The Reformation of American Quakerism, 1748–1783* (Philadelphia, 1984).
23. Henry F. May, *The Enlightenment in America* (New York, 1976), xiv.
24. J. William Frost, "John Woolman and the Enlightenment," in Mike Heller, ed., *The Tendering Presence: Essays on John Woolman* (Wallingford, Pa., 2003), 167–89. This paragraph draws on Frost's insights in this essay and an exchange of correspondence.
25. Ibid.; Alexander Arscott, *Some Considerations Relating to the Present State of the Christian Religion* (Philadelphia, 1731).
26. Haskell, "The Quaker Ethic and the Antislavery International," Parts 1 and 2, in Bender, ed., *Antislavery Debate*, 107–60.
27. Woolman, *Journal*, 31.
28. Ibid.
29. Ibid.
30. Burlington Monthly Meeting, June 1, 1743, Minutes 1737–56, MR-Ph 60, FHL.
31. Woolman, *Journal*, 32–33.
32. Ibid., 33.
33. Manuscript, FHL.
34. Woolman, *Journal*, 33.
35. Soderlund, *Quakers and Slavery*, 4, 13.
36. James, *A People Among Peoples*, 104–105; J. William Frost, "George Fox's Ambiguous Antislavery Legacy," in Michael Mullet, ed., *New Light on George Fox, 1624–1691* (York, U.K., 1991), 69–88.

37. Drake, *Quakers and Slavery*, 5–7.
38. Soderlund, *Quakers and Slavery*, 3; J. William Frost, ed., *The Quaker Origins of Antislavery* (Norwood, Pa., 1980).
39. James, *A People Among Peoples*, 105–106.
40. Richard Baxter, *Chapters from a Christian Directory* (London, 1673); Morgan Godwyn, *The Negro's and Indians Advocate* (London, 1680); Godwyn, *The Revival* (London, 1682); Godwyn, *Trade Preferr'd Before Religion, and Christ Made to Give Place to Mammon* (London, 1685); Thomas Tryon, *Friendly Advice to the Gentlemen-Planters of the East and West Indies* (London, 1684).
41. Germantown Friends' Protest Against Slavery (1688), Roger Bruns, ed., *Am I Not a Man and a Brother: The Antislavery Crusade of Revolutionary America, 1688–1788* (New York, 1977), 3–5; Drake, *Quakers and Slavery*, 13.
42. Drake, *Quakers and Slavery*, 14–15; Bruns, ed., *Am I Not a Man and a Brother*, 5–8.
43. James, *A People Among Peoples*, 128–29; Soderlund, *Quakers and Slavery*, 18–19; Kenneth L. Carroll, "William Southeby, Early Quaker Antislavery Writer," *Pennsylvania Magazine of History and Biography*, 89 (1965): 416–27; Thomas E. Drake, "Cadwalader Morgan: Antislavery Quaker of the Welsh Tract," *Friends Intelligencer*, 98 (1941): 575–76; "Cadwalader Morgan's Paper on Slavery, Submitted to Philadelphia Yearly Meeting in 1696," *Friends Intelligencer*, 105 (1948), 576.
44. Robert Pile [or Piles or Pyle], "Paper About Negroes," 1698; reprinted in Bruns, ed., *Am I Not a Man and a Brother*, 9–10; Drake, *Quakers and Slavery*, 21.
45. Richard Hill, Jr., to James Dickenson, London, June 11, 1698, in Frost, "George Fox's Ambiguous Anti-slavery Legacy," 81–82.
46. Samuel Sewall, *The Selling of Joseph a Memorial* (Boston, 1700); Bruns, ed., *Am I Not a Man and a Brother*, 10–14.
47. Drake, *Quakers and Slavery*, 26–27.
48. Ibid.
49. John Hepburn, *The American Defence of the Christian Golden Rule, or an Essay to Prove the Unlawfulness of Making Slaves of Men. By Him Who Loves the Freedom of the Souls and Bodies of All Men* (n.p., 1715); Bruns, ed., *Am I Not a Man and a Brother*, 16–31.
50. Drake, *Quakers and Slavery*, 27.
51. Ibid., 40–41.
52. Ralph Sandiford, *A Brief Examination of the Practice of the Times* (Philadelphia, 1729); Bruns, ed., *Am I Not a Man and a Brother*, 31–38; Drake, *Quakers and Slavery*, 41, 50, 62–66; James, *A People Among Peoples*, 128–29.
53. Elihu Coleman, "A Testimony Against That Anti-Christian Practice of Making Slaves of Men" (1733); *Friends' Review*, 5 (1851): 84–85, 102–104; Bruns, ed., *Am I Not a Man and a Brother*, 39–45.
54. Davis, *The Problem of Slavery in Western Culture*, 144–48; Drake, *Quakers and Slavery*, n. 5, 4; Darien Protest (1739), in Allen D. Chandler, ed., *The Colonial Records of the State of Georgia* (Atlanta, 1905), reprinted in Bruns, ed., *Am I Not a Man and a Brother*, 64–65.
55. Hugh Bryan, "Public Retraction of Antislavery Statements" (1742), in South Carolina Commons House of Assembly, *Commons House Journal*, March 1742, no. 17, part 2, 285–87; Bruns, ed., *Am I Not a Man and a Brother*, 66–68.

56. Benjamin Lay, *All Slave-keepers That Keep the Innocents in Bondage: Apostates* (Philadelphia, 1737), excerpted in Bruns, ed., *Am I Not a Man and a Brother*, 46–64.
57. John Smith, Diary 1746–47, 11 mo. [January] 8, 1746/7, HSP.
58. Woolman, *Journal*, 29, 31–32.
59. Ibid., 32.
60. Ibid.

5. Charity, 1743–53

1. Burlington Monthly Meeting, Minutes 1737–56, MR-Ph 60, FHL. The first mention of Woolman in the minutes is in 1742, when the Meeting appointed him and his father, along with others, as representatives to Quarterly Meeting.
2. Woolman, *Journal*, 34.
3. Ibid.
4. Ibid., 34–35.
5. *Pennsylvania Journal*, July 7, 1757; May 3, 1759; November 10, 1763. This is just a selection; there are many more advertisements of this sort in the *Journal* and some in the *Pennsylvania Gazette*.
6. Woolman, *Journal*, 35.
7. Ibid.; manuscript draft, FHL.
8. Manuscript draft, FHL.
9. Woolman, *Journal*, 35; manuscript draft, FHL.
10. Woolman, *Journal*, 35–36.
11. Ibid., 36.
12. J. Hector St. John de Crèvecoeur, *Letters from an American Farmer* (1782; New York, 1963, 1981), 198.
13. Kalm, *Travels*, vol. 1, 48; James T. Lemon, *Best Poor Man's Country: Early Southeastern Pennsylvania* (Baltimore, 1972).
14. Lemon, *Best Poor Man's Country*.
15. Woolman, *Journal*, 36.
16. Ibid., 37; manuscript draft, FHL.
17. Woolman, *Journal*, 38.
18. This paragraph draws heavily on the analysis of Frost, "John Woolman and the Enlightenment," especially 181–83; John Woolman, *Some Considerations on the Keeping of Negroes* (Philadelphia, 1754), in Moulton, ed., *Journal and Major Essays*, 198–209.
19. Woolman, *Some Considerations*, 198.
20. Thomas Paine, *Common Sense and Related Writings*, ed. Thomas P. Slaughter (New York, 2001), 73; Thomas Jefferson to James Madison, September 6, 1789, in Merrill D. Peterson, ed., *Thomas Jefferson: Writings* (New York, 1984), 959.
21. Woolman, *Some Considerations*, 198.
22. Tryon, *Friendly Advice to the Gentlemen-Planters*, 129.
23. Shaftesbury, *Characteristicks*, 3 vols. (London, 1711; 4 vols., 1758), vol. 3, 222; Isabel Rivers, *Reason, Grace, and Sentiment: A Study of the Language of Religion and Ethics in England, 1660–1780*, vol. 2, *Shaftesbury to Hume* (Cambridge, U.K., 2000), chapter 2, esp. 122–24.

24. Kempis, *The Imitation of Christ*, book 3, chapter 54, 163.

25. Ibid., book 3, chapters 54–55, 161–67.

26. Woolman, *Some Considerations*, 198.

27. Ibid., 198–99.

28. Ibid.

29. Ibid., 199.

30. Locke, *Some Thoughts Concerning Education*, 81; Jeremy Waldron, *God, Locke, and Equality: Christian Foundations in Locke's Political Thought* (Cambridge, U.K., 2002).

31. Woolman, *Some Considerations*, 199, 200. Insertion mine. Woolman's suggestions for deleting conciliatory language in a second edition is in a letter of September 2, 1762, to Israel Pemberton, in Pemberton Papers, box 15, no. 112, HSP.

32. James, *A People Among Peoples*, 32.

33. Ibid., chapter 6.

34. Ibid.

35. Ibid.

36. Ibid.

37. Marietta, *Reformation*, chapter 1; Soderlund, *Quakers and Slavery*; James, *A People Among Peoples*.

38. Marietta, *Reformation*; Soderlund, *Quakers and Slavery*; James, *A People Among Peoples*.

39. Woolman, *Some Considerations*, 199.

40. Woolman, *Journal*, 39.

41. Ibid.

42. Ibid., 39–40.

43. Sobel, *Teach Me Dreams*, 65 and 268, n. 34, speculates that Woolman and his family had a longer and closer relationship with Maria.

44. Woolman, *Journal*, 40–42.

45. Ibid., 43.

46. Ibid., 44; manuscript draft, FHL.

47. Woolman, *Journal*, 44–45.

48. Ibid., 45.

49. Gummere, *Journal of John Woolman*, 330.

50. Woolman, book of executorship and smaller account book, John Woolman, Woolman Papers, HSP. There has been confusion about a reference in Woolman's book of executorship to indentures he wrote "binding Aquilla and Gamiliel to trades." These were the third and fourth sons, the seventh and eighth of Shinn's nine children, not his slaves. Josiah H. Shinn, *The History of the Shinn Family in Europe and America* (Chicago, 1903); John Woolman, larger account book, Woolman Papers, HSP, loose leaf in front of book; Woolman, *Journal*, 152.

51. Woolman, *Journal*, 152.

52. Ibid., 153.

53. Ibid.

54. Moulton, ed., *Journal*, 268, 270.

55. Burlington Monthly Meeting, Minutes 1737–56, MR-Ph 60, FHL.

56. John Churchman, quoted in Marietta, *Reformation*, 35.
57. James, *A People Among Peoples*, 32.
58. Ibid., chapter 6.

6. Nightmares, 1754–55

1. Woolman, *Journal*, 46–47.
2. Manuscript draft, Woolman Papers, HSP.
3. Marietta, *Reformation*, chapters 6 and 7; James, *A People Among Peoples*, chapter 10; Richard Ryerson, "The Quaker Elite in the Pennsylvania Assembly," in Bruce C. Daniels, ed., *Power and Status: Officeholding in Colonial America* (Middletown, Conn., 1986), 106–35; Alan Tully, *William Penn's Legacy; Politics and Social Structure in Provincial Pennsylvania, 1726–1755* (Baltimore, 1977).
4. Richard Bauman, *For the Reputation of Truth: Politics, Religion, and Conflict among the Pennsylvania Quakers, 1750–1800* (Baltimore, 1971), 25–27; Matthew C. Ward, *Breaking the Backcountry: The Seven Years' War in Virginia and Pennsylvania, 1754–1765* (Pittsburgh, 2003).
5. Woolman, *Journal*, 46.
6. Ibid.
7. Ibid., 47.
8. Whitney, *John Woolman*, n. 5, 194, first attributed the epistle to Woolman, a view that has been subsequently ratified by Drake, *Quakers and Slavery*, n. 21, 56, and James, *A People Among Peoples*, 137.
9. Waldron, *God, Locke, and Equality*, 12; John Dunn, *The Political Thought of John Locke: An Historical Account of the Argument of the "Two Treatises of Government"* (Cambridge, U.K., 1969), 99.
10. John Locke, *Two Treatises of Government*, ed. Peter Laslett (New York, 1963, 1966), vol. 2, 345.
11. Ibid., vol. 2, 350.
12. Ibid., vol. 2, 324–26, 412–13, 425–30.
13. James, *A People Among Peoples*, 128 and chapters 8 and 9; Marietta, *Reformation*.
14. *An Epistle of Caution and Advice, Concerning the Buying and Keeping of Slaves* (Philadelphia, 1754), 3–4, Quaker Collection, HCL.
15. Ibid., 7.
16. Woolman, *Some Considerations*, 208. Sobel interprets the red streams in the dream as references to slavery; *Teach Me Dreams*, 68–69.
17. Barclay, *Apology*, 85.
18. Bauman, *For Reputation of Truth*; Ward, *Breaking the Backcountry*.
19. Churchman, *An Account of the Gospel Labours*, 175–76.
20. Woolman, *Some Considerations*, 209.
21. John Woolman to John Ely and his wife, May 9, 1754, Special Collections, 851, box 19, HCL.
22. Ibid.
23. Ibid.
24. Woolman, *Journal*, 47.
25. Ibid.

26. Ibid., 50.

27. Ibid., 50–51.

28. Ibid., 51.

29. Margaret E. Hirst, *The Quakers in Peace and War: An Account of Their Peace Principles and Practice* (New York, 1923); Peter Brock, *Pacifism in Europe to 1914* (Princeton, 1972); Marietta, *Reformation*, chapter 8.

30. Woolman, *Journal*, 75.

31. *Chambers Biographical Dictionary*, rev. ed. (London, 1986), 705, 763.

32. Ibid., 1443–44.

33. Woolman, *Journal*, 75–76.

34. Ibid. Malcolm Lambert, *Medieval Heresy: Popular Movements from the Gregorian Reform to the Reformation* (London, 1977; 2002).

35. Woolman, *Journal*, 47–50; manuscript in Woolman Papers, HSP.

36. Woolman, *Journal*, 50; Woolman Papers, HSP.

7. Taxed, 1756–57

1. Hirst, *Quakers in Peace and War*; Marietta, *Reformation*.

2. John Woolman, 1756, "Supposed to have been written by John Woolman. Paraphrase of early biblical history of origin of Negro race," Special Collections 851, HCL. The parable is in Woolman's hand, but the archivist was mistaken in characterizing the manuscript as biblical history. David M. Goldenberg, *The Curse of Ham: Race and Slavery in Early Judaism, Christianity, and Islam* (Princeton, 2003); Christopher Hill, *The English Bible and the Seventeenth-Century Revolution* (New York, 1993), 29, 118, 398.

3. This last sentence reveals the significance of choosing Nimrod, distinguished as a hunter in the Bible, for the name of the parable's monarch. The symbolism of the name reflects Woolman's equation of hunting with violence and hunters with cruelty toward animals and men. Farmers, by comparison, were in his eyes more peaceful and humane.

4. Caroline Robbins, *The Eighteenth-Century Commonwealthman: Studies in the Transmission, Development and Circumstance of English Liberal Thought from the Restoration of Charles II Until the War with the Thirteen Colonies* (Cambridge, Mass., 1959); J.G.A. Pocock, *The Ancient Constitution and the Feudal Law: English Historical Thought in the Seventeenth Century* (Cambridge, U.K., 1957); Bernard Bailyn, *The Ideological Origins of the American Revolution* (Cambridge, Mass., 1967); J.C.D. Clark, *The Language of Liberty 1660–1832: Political Discourse and Social Dynamics in the Anglo-American World* (Cambridge, U.K., 1994).

5. Woolman, "Paraphrase"; Lawrence Friedman, *Gregarious Saints: Self and Community in American Abolitionism* (New York, 1982).

6. Marietta, *Reformation*, chapters 7 and 8.

7. Joshua Evans, journal, transcribed and edited by George Churchman in 1804, *Friends' Miscellany*, 10 (Philadelphia, 1837), 17–21.

8. Woolman, *Journal*, 89.

9. Ibid., 88.

10. Benezet to "A Schoolmaster," ca. 1752, in George S. Brookes, *Friend Anthony Benezet* (Philadelphia, 1937), 210–11; Benezet to John Smith, July 1, 1760, in

Brookes, 241; Benezet to Thomas Secker, [n.d.], in Brookes, 273; Benezet to George Dillwyn, July 5, 1773, in Brookes, 304.

11. Jones, *Later Periods of Quakerism*, vol. 1, 32–56; Schmidt, *Hearing Things*.
12. Jeanne Marie Bouvier de La Motte Guyon, *The Worship of God, in Spirit and Truth: or, A Short and Easy Method of Prayer* (Philadelphia, 1789), 2, 54, 56, 90.
13. François Fénelon, *Dissertation on Pure Love* (London, 1735), v–viii, 2–5, 14–16.
14. Woolman, *Journal*, 51–52.
15. Benezet to Susanna Pyrleus and her husband [1751], in Brookes, *Friend Anthony Benezet*, 207.
16. Woolman, *Journal*, 53.
17. Arthur O. Lovejoy, *The Great Chain of Being: A Study of the History of an Idea* (Cambridge, Mass., 1936); E.M.W. Tillyard, *The Elizabethan World Picture* (New York, 1959); Woolman, *Journal*, 54.
18. Woolman, *Journal*, 54–55.
19. Gummere, *Journal*, 32–33.
20. Ibid., 33, 44–45.
21. Woolman, *Journal*, 56–57.
22. Ibid., 58.
23. Ibid., 59.
24. Ibid., 60.
25. Ibid., 63.
26. Ibid.
27. Ibid., 59.
28. Ibid., 72.
29. Ibid., 70.
30. Ibid., 73.
31. Gummere, *Journal*, 55.
32. James, *A People Among Peoples*, 152, 1–3.
33. Gail McKnight Beckman, ed., *The Statutes at Large of Pennsylvania in the Time of William Penn, 1680–1700* (New York, 1976), 1, 78; A. Leon Higginbotham, Jr., *In the Matter of Color: Race & the American Legal Process: The Colonial Period* (New York, 1978), chapter 7; Edward R. Turner, *The Negro in Pennsylvania* (Washington, D.C., 1911).
34. Higginbotham, *In the Matter of Color*, chapter 7.
35. Drake, *Quakers and Slavery*, 22.
36. Higginbotham, *In the Matter of Color*, chapter 7.
37. Drake, *Quakers and Slavery*, 26–29, 39.

8. *Pure Wisdom, 1758–59*

1. Woolman, *Journal*, 89.
2. Esther Greenleaf Murer, compiler, *Quaker Bible Index: An Index to Scripture References in the Works of Fox, Barclay, Penn, Woolman and Others* (Philadelphia, 2002), 456–57, 501–10; Jay Fliegelman, *Prodigals and Pilgrims* (Cambridge, U.K., 1982).
3. Hillel Schwartz, *The French Prophets: The History of a Millenarian Group in Eighteenth-Century England* (Berkeley, 1980).

4. Clarke Garrett, *Spirit Possession and Popular Religion: From the Camisards to the Shakers* (Baltimore, 1987), 2–3, 10–11, 13–14, 20, 37, 47, 51, 56, and 142.
5. Bernard McGinn, *The Foundations of Mysticism: Origins to the Fifth Century*, vol. 1, *The Presence of God: A History of Western Christian Mysticism* (New York, 1991), xi–xx.
6. Ibid., 3–8.
7. Denys Turner, *The Darkness of God: Negativity in Christian Mysticism* (Cambridge, U.K., 1995); McGinn, *The Presence of God*, 6 vols. (New York, 1991–2005).
8. Leigh Eric Schmidt, "The Making of Modern 'Mysticism,'" *Journal of the American Academy of Religion*, 71 (2003): 273–302; Phyllis Mack, "In a Female Voice: Preaching and Politics in Eighteenth-Century British Quakerism," in Beverly Mayne Kienzle and Pamela S. Walker, eds., *Women Preachers and Prophets Through Two Millennia of Christianity* (Berkeley, 1998), 248–63.
9. Frank Manuel, *The Eighteenth Century Confronts the Gods* (Cambridge, Mass., 1959); Susan Juster, *Doomsayers: Anglo-American Prophecy in the Age of Revolution* (Philadelphia, 2003), 3, 12, 14–15, 17–19, 37–41; James Darsey, *The Prophetic Tradition and Radical Rhetoric in America* (New York, 1997); David S. Reynolds, *John Brown, Abolitionist: The Man Who Killed Slavery, Sparked the Civil War, and Seeded Civil Rights* (New York, 2005).
10. Jeremiah 7:5; Jeremiah 22:4; Isaiah 32:16–18; Jeremiah 3:12; Isaiah 35:1; Isaiah 54:1–17.
11. Isaiah 2:4.
12. Habakkuk 2:20.
13. Isaiah 21:3–4.
14. Jeremiah 6:10.
15. Jeremiah 20:7.
16. Jeremiah 6:16, 9:24.
17. Woolman, *Considerations on Pure Wisdom and Human Policy* (Philadelphia, 1758), published in *Serious Considerations on Various Subjects of Importance* (London, 1773), in Gummere, *Journal*, 382, 384. No copy of the 1758 edition is known to survive; Gummere reprinted the 1773 London edition.
18. Matthew 5:11–12; Gummere, *Journal*, 384.
19. Gummere, *Journal*, 384.
20. Ibid., 385.
21. Ibid., 386.
22. Ibid., 387.
23. Ibid.
24. Ibid., 389.
25. Ibid., 390, 392.
26. Ibid., 394.
27. John Woolman, manuscript journal, HSP.
28. Gummere, *Journal*, 397.
29. Ibid.
30. Ibid., 398.
31. Ibid., 399.
32. Ibid., 399–400.
33. Woolman, *Journal*, 102.

34. Ibid., 103.
35. Ibid., 105; manuscript draft, FHL.
36. Woolman, *Journal*, 95.
37. Ibid., 101–102.
38. Ibid.
39. John Woolman, notes handwritten on blank fourth page of printed epistle, Woolman Manuscripts, FHL.
40. Ibid.
41. Ibid; John Woolman, letter, n.p., n.d., no recipient named, *Friends Miscellany*, 1 (Philadelphia, 1831), 8–9.
42. Woolman, letter, 8–9.
43. Ibid.
44. Draft of Epistle from Philadelphia Yearly Meeting to Quarterly and Monthly Meetings, 1759, in miscellaneous papers of Philadelphia Yearly Meeting, FHL.
45. Ibid.
46. Articles of the New Jersey Association for Helping the Indians, April 16, 1757, Special Collections, 975B, HCL.
47. Ibid.
48. Ibid.
49. Samuel Smith, *The History of the Colony of Nova Caesaria, or New Jersey* (Philadelphia, 1765), 467, 482–84.
50. Mircea Eliade, *The Sacred and the Profane: The Nature of Religion* (translation from the German, New York, 1959), 25, 29.

9. Words, 1760–63

1. Woolman, manuscript draft of journal, 267, FHL.
2. Small account book, Woolman Papers, HSP.
3. Ibid.
4. Sally A. Queen, *Textiles for Colonial Clothing: A Workbook of Swatches and Information* (Arlington, Va., 2000).
5. Woolman, account book, 1743–46 [*sic*], Woolman Papers, HSP. The coat for John Kaighin's servant and the trousers for Cupid were in 1747.
6. Woolman, ledger, 1752–67, Woolman Papers, HSP. The transactions with Negro Sam were in 1754 and 1757. Negro Baccus chopped wood in 1759.
7. Linda Baumgarten, *What Clothes Reveal: The Language of Clothing in Colonial and Federal America* (Williamsburg, 2002), 148–49 and passim; account book, 1743–46, Woolman Papers, HSP.
8. Merideth Wright, *Everyday Dress of Rural America, 1783–1800: With Instructions and Patterns* (New York, 1992), 90–93.
9. Woolman, *Journal*, 106.
10. Ibid., 107.
11. Woolman to Jane Crosfield, December 12, 1760, Misc. Mss., FHL.
12. Woolman to Sarah Woolman, May 18, 1760, Woolman Papers, HSP.
13. Woolman to Sarah Woolman, June 14 and 23, 1760, Woolman Papers, HSP.
14. Habakkuk 3:16; Woolman, *Journal*, 107–109.

15. Sidney V. James, *Colonial Rhode Island: A History* (New York, 1975); Winthrop D. Jordan, "The Influence of the West Indies on the Origins of New England Slavery," *WMQ*, 3d ser., 18 (1961): 343–50; Davis, *Problem of Slavery in Western Culture*, 144–48; William B. Weeden, *Early Rhode Island* (New York, 1910), chapter 8.
16. Woolman, *Journal*, 109–10.
17. Ibid., 110–11.
18. Mercy Redman, journal, 1760, FHL.
19. Woolman, *Journal*, 111–12.
20. Ibid., 112.
21. Ibid., 112–13.
22. Ibid., 114.
23. Ibid., 114–15.
24. Ibid., 115; manuscript journal, HSP.
25. Woolman, *Journal*, 119.
26. Ibid.
27. Ibid.
28. Ibid., 120.
29. Ibid.
30. Ibid., 121
31. Ibid., 121–22.
32. Tristram Stuart, *The Bloodless Revolution: A Cultural History of Vegetarianism from 1600 to Modern Times* (New York, 2006).
33. Revelation 1:14; 3:2–5, 18.
34. Woolman, manuscript ledger, HSP.
35. Woolman, *Journal*, 117.
36. Woolman to Israel Pemberton, November 17, 1761, Pemberton Papers, HSP.
37. Woolman, *Journal*, 117; Woolman to Israel Pemberton, February 9, 1762, Pemberton Papers, HSP.
38. *Considerations on Keeping Negroes: Recommended to the Professors of Christianity of Every Denomination*, Part Second (Philadelphia, 1762), in Moulton, ed., *Journal*, 211.
39. Ibid., 212.
40. Ibid.
41. Ibid., 213–14; Jeremiah 1:8 and 26:2; Ezekiel 2:6–7.
42. Moulton, ed., *Journal*, 219, 221.
43. Ibid., 221–22.
44. Ibid., 224–27.
45. Ibid., 227.
46. Ibid., 231.
47. William Monter, *Judging the French Reformation: Heresy Trials by Sixteenth-Century Parlements* (Cambridge, U.K., 1999), 95–101.
48. [John Foxe,] *The Book of Martyrs, with an Account of the Acts and Monuments of Church and State*, 2 vols. (London, 1702), vol. 2, 401–11. For the African experiences, Woolman drew on John Lockman, ed., *The Travels of the Jesuits in Various Parts of the World* (London, 1743), and Joseph Randall, *System of Geography* (London, 1744).

49. Moulton, ed., *Journal*, 232–33.
50. Ibid., 235–37.
51. Ibid., 237.
52. Woolman, *Journal*, 122–23; Gregory Evans Dowd, *War Under Heaven: Pontiac, the Indian Nations, and the British Empire* (Baltimore, 2002).
53. Woolman, *Journal*, 123.
54. Ibid.
55. Ibid., 123–24.
56. Ibid., 124.
57. Ibid., 124–25.
58. Ibid., 124.
59. Woolman to Sarah Woolman, June 8, 1763; William Lightfoot to Sarah Woolman, June 13, 1763, Woolman Papers, HSP.
60. Woolman, *Journal*, 137.
61. Woolman to Sarah Woolman, June 8, 1763, Woolman Papers, HSP.
62. Woolman, *Journal*, 125–26.
63. Ibid., 126.
64. Ibid.
65. Ibid., 127–28.
66. Ibid., 128–29.
67. Ibid., 129.
68. Ibid., 130.
69. Ibid., 130–32.
70. Ibid., 132.
71. Ibid.
72. Ibid.
73. Ibid., 133.
74. Ibid. On Papunhank's conversion, see George Henry Loskiel, *History of the Mission of the United Brethren Among the Indians of North America* (London, 1794). On Papunhank's tragic later life, see Dowd, *War Under Heaven*, 194–96.
75. Woolman, *Journal*, 133–34.
76. Ibid., 134–36.
77. Ibid., 136.
78. John Woolman to Israel Pemberton, June 27, 1763, Friends House Library, London; John Pemberton to Israel Pemberton, Jr., 7 mo., 2, 1763, Pemberton Papers, vol. 16, 109, HSP.
79. Woolman, *Journal*, 138.
80. Ibid., 138–39.

10. Travels, 1764–69

1. James, *Varieties*, 15–16.
2. Ibid., 243–44, 252–53.
3. Ibid., 11–15.
4. Ibid., 317–18.
5. Ibid., 324, 334–35.
6. Woolman's dream of a peace mission, Alexander Library, Rutgers University. The dream is published in Moulton, ed., *Journal*, Appendix E.

7. Ibid.

8. Ibid.

9. Ibid.

10. Moulton, ed., *Journal*, 238. Albert O. Hirschman, *The Passions and the Interests: Political Arguments for Capitalism Before Its Triumph* (Princeton, 1977) discusses ways in which Enlightenment thinkers on both sides of the Atlantic theorized a benign capitalism very different from what Woolman envisioned.

11. Moulton, ed., *Journal*, 239.

12. Ibid., 255, 259–60.

13. Ibid., 266.

14. Ibid., 267.

15. Woolman, manuscript *A Plea for the Poor*; Gummere, *Journal*, 401–402.

16. Moulton, ed., *Journal*, 263; Benezet to Samuel Fothergill, November 27, 1758, in Brookes, *Friend Anthony Benezet*, 232.

17. *The Friend*, 4 (1831); Brookes, *Friend Anthony Benezet*, 29–59.

18. Woolman, ledger, 1752–67, Woolman Papers, HSP; bill to Asher Woolman in Gummere, *Journal*, 102.

19. Woolman, ledger, 1752–67, Woolman Papers, HSP.

20. Woolman, ledger, 1769–95, Woolman Papers, HSP.

21. Ibid.

22. John Woolman, *A First Book for Children* (Philadelphia, 1774[?]), Friends House Library, London; photocopy in FHL.

23. Ibid; Anthony Benezet, *A First Book for Children* (Philadelphia, 1778).

24. Woolman, *First Book*.

25. Ibid.

26. Jacob, *An Epistle in True Love*.

27. Ibid.

28. John Griffith, *Some Brief Remarks on Sundry Subjects* (London, 1764; Dublin, 1765).

29. Ibid.

30. Woolman, *Journal*, 139–40.

31. Ibid.

32. Ibid., 142.

33. Ibid., 142–43.

34. Ibid., 145.

35. Ibid., 146.

36. Ibid., 147.

37. Ibid., 148.

38. Ibid., 150.

39. Ibid., 149–50; manuscript journal, HSP.

40. Woolman, *Journal*, 150.

41. Ibid., 151.

42. Ibid.

43. Ibid.

44. Ibid., 151–152.

45. Ibid., 152.

11. Growth, 1769–72

1. Woolman, *Journal*, 155.
2. Woolman to [?], October 22, 1769; Woolman to J. C., May 10, 1769, Woolman Papers, HSP; Woolman, *Journal*, 155.
3. Woolman, *Journal*, 155–56; Woolman to John Pemberton, November 11, 1769; Woolman to Israel Pemberton, November 17, 1769, Pemberton Papers, vol. 21, 85 and 87, HSP; Woolman, account book, Woolman Papers, HSP.
4. Woolman, *Journal*, 155–57.
5. Ibid., 156–57. Gummere, *Journal*, n. 1, 284, identifies John Smith and James Pemberton as the ship's owners.
6. Woolman, *Journal*, 158.
7. Ibid.
8. Ibid.
9. Ibid., 159.
10. Ibid., 159–60.
11. Ibid.; Whitney, *John Woolman*, 358–59; Gummere, *Journal*, 111; Woolman, account book, Woolman Papers, HSP; Whittier edition of Woolman's *Journal*, 213.
12. Woolman, *Journal*, 159–60; Whitney, *John Woolman*, 359–60; Gummere, *Journal*, 111–12; Woolman, account book, Woolman Papers, HSP.
13. Aaron Smith, utterance of John Woolman, January 13, 1770, attached to inserted leaves, journal of Woolman's English trip, FHL.
14. Woolman, *Journal*, 160.
15. Ibid.
16. Ibid., 185–86.
17. Ibid., 186.
18. Ibid.
19. Ibid.
20. Ibid.
21. Ibid., 186–87. Whitney, *John Woolman*, 362, identifies the owner of the silver vessel as John Smith; Gummere, *Journal*, 114; John Smith, "Account of my wrought silver plate," January 1764, Smith manuscripts, vol. 6, 1762–65, HSP.
22. John Woolman, statement of use of silver vessels, January 20, 1770, Woolman manuscripts, FHL.
23. Woolman, *Journal*, 161–62.
24. Ibid., 162; Breen, *The Marketplace of Revolution*.
25. Woolman, "Considerations on the True Harmony of Mankind and how it is to be maintained," Woolman manuscripts, FHL; *Considerations on the True Harmony of Mankind and How It Is to Be Maintained* (Philadelphia, 1770); Gummere, *Journal*, 438–41; Daniel J. Boorstin, *The Lost World of Thomas Jefferson* (Chicago, 1948); Staloff, *Hamilton, Adams, Jefferson*.
26. Gummere, *Journal*, 441–42; Benjamin Franklin, *The Autobiography*, ed. Leonard W. Labaree et al. (New Haven, 1964), 126.
27. Gummere, *Journal*, 442.
28. Ibid., 440–41.
29. Ibid., 442–45.
30. Ibid., 444–46.
31. Ibid., 446–47.

32. Ibid., 449.
33. Ibid., 450–51.
34. Ibid., 451–52.
35. Ibid., 452–54.
36. Ibid., 456–57.
37. Ibid., 42, 536.
38. John Woolman to Meeting for Sufferings, Philadelphia Yearly Meeting, 1772, Quaker Collection, HCL.
39. Ibid.
40. Abner Woolman to his children, n.d., copied over in John Woolman's hand, Meeting for Sufferings records, Philadelphia Yearly Meeting, HCL.
41. Abner Woolman to active members of Burlington Monthly Meeting, September 1770, Meeting for Sufferings records, Philadelphia Yearly Meeting, HCL.
42. Ibid.
43. Ibid.
44. Abner Woolman, spiritual autobiography, Meeting for Sufferings records, Philadelphia Yearly Meeting, Haverford College, chapter 1. Abner's journal is not paginated but is divided into short chapters.
45. Ibid., chapters 3 and 5.
46. Ibid., chapter 9.
47. Ibid.
48. Ibid., chapter 6.
49. Ibid.
50. Ibid., chapter 7.
51. Ibid., chapter 12.
52. Ibid., chapter 42.
53. Ibid., last three pages of manuscript.

12. Away, 1772

1. Woolman, *Journal*, Appendix H, 304; Gummere, *Journal*, 314; Cadbury, *John Woolman in England*, 37.
2. Gummere, *Journal*, 459.
3. Ibid., 460–61.
4. There are no studies of changes in colonial interest rates over time. It is apparently true that interest rates were higher in the American colonies than in England; John J. McCusker and Russell R. Menard, *The Economy of British America, 1607–1789* (Chapel Hill, N.C., 1985), n. 10, 59–60, and n. 18, 69; Stanley Homer and Richard Sylla, *A History of Interest Rates*, 3d ed. (New Brunswick, N.J., 1991), 275.
5. Gummere, *Journal*, 462.
6. McCusker and Menard, *Economy of British America*; James T. Lemon, *Best Poor Man's Country: Early Southeastern Pennsylvania* (Baltimore, 1972, 2002); Kenneth Lockridge, "Social Change and the Meaning of the American Revolution," *Journal of Social History*, 6 (1973): 403–39.
7. James Henretta, "Families and Farms: Mentalité in Pre-Industrial America," *WMQ*, 3d ser., 35 (1978): 3–32; Daniel Vickers, "Competency and Competition: Economic Culture in Early America," *WMQ*, 3d ser., 47 (1990): 3–29.

8. Gummere, *Journal*, 463–64.
9. Ibid., 465–66.
10. Ibid., 466–67; McCusker and Menard, *Economy of British America*.
11. Gummere, *Journal*, 468–69.
12. Ibid., 470–73.
13. Ibid., 528–29.
14. Cadbury, *John Woolman in England*, 10–12; Gummere, *Journal*, 562.
15. Gummere, *Journal*, 120–21; Woolman to Elizabeth Smith, April 28, 1772, Woolman Papers, HSP.
16. Gummene, *Journal*, 120–21; Woolman to Elizabeth Smith, April 28, 1772.
17. Gummere, *Journal*, n. 1, 121. Gummere was the descendant who inherited the travel certificate, the letter, and some of Elizabeth Smith's furniture.
18. Cadbury, *John Woolman in England*, 29.
19. Woolman to Israel Pemberton, April 1772, Pemberton Papers, vol. 23, 117, HSP; Woolman, *Journal*, 299.
20. Gummere, *Journal*, 475–76.
21. Ibid., 477.
22. Ibid., 482–83.
23. Ibid., 485–86.
24. Ibid., 486.
25. Ibid., 486–87.
26. New Jersey State Archives, Liber Y, 543; copy in Woolman Papers, HSP and in Gummere, *Journal*, 604.
27. Woolman "for John Comfort," Woolman Papers, HSP.
28. Gummere, *Journal*, 122–23, 515–16; Cadbury, *John Woolman in England*, 13–16; "Dictionary of Quaker Biography" (henceforth DQB), Friends House Library, London.
29. DQB; Cadbury, *John Woolman in England*, 13–15.
30. Cadbury, *John Woolman in England*, 13–15.
31. Ibid., 10–12, 14–16.
32. Woolman, *Journal*, 164.
33. Ibid., 165.
34. Ibid.
35. Ibid.
36. Emlen correspondence in Cadbury, *John Woolman in England*, 16–17; and in Cadbury, ed., "Sailing to England with John Woolman," *Quaker History*, 55 (1966): 88–103; the originals are in Letters of Samuel Emlen during his Religious Mission to Europe with those of his wife and other Correspondents (1772–91), HSP.
37. Samuel Emlen to Sarah Emlen (wife), May 2, 1772, Letters of Samuel Emlen, HSP; Cadbury, *John Woolman in England*, 16, 17.
38. Samuel Emlen to Sarah Emlen, May 3 and June 6, 1772, HSP; Cadbury, *John Woolman in England*, 17.
39. Woolman, *Journal*, 166.
40. Ibid., 167.
41. Ibid., 167–68.
42. Ibid., 168–69.
43. Ibid., 169.

44. Ibid., 169–70.
45. Ibid.
46. Ibid., 171–72.
47. Ibid., 175.
48. Ibid., 176.
49. Ibid., 177.
50. Ibid., 178–79.
51. Ibid., 179–80.
52. Ibid., 180; Gummere, *Journal*, 589–90.

13. Home, 1772

1. John Pemberton to Joseph Row, April 28, 1772, Cadbury, *John Woolman in England*, 52.
2. Roy Porter, *English Society in the Eighteenth Century* (London, 1982, 1991), 2, 3; Linda Colley, *Britons: Forging the Nation, 1707–1837* (New Haven, 1992); J.C.D. Clark, *English Society 1660–1832*, 2d ed. (Cambridge, U.K., 2000).
3. Porter, *English Society in the Eighteenth Century*, 11–15.
4. Ibid., 36; Steven M. Wise, *Though the Heavens May Fall: The Landmark Trial That Led to the End of Human Slavery* (Cambridge, Mass., 2005), 8.
5. Porter, *English Society in the Eighteenth Century*, 56, 95.
6. Ibid., 174, 178.
7. Ibid., 192, 228.
8. Ibid., 202, 284.
9. William Beck and T. Frederick Ball, *The London Friends' Meetings* (London, 1869), 167–69; [Anonymous] *Devonshire House* (London, 1920).
10. Walt Whitman recounts the story told him by William J. Allinson, in Whitman, ed., *Journal of John Woolman*, note, 257–59.
11. The account by Rebecca Jones, who was not there herself but repeated what others recalled, appeared in *Friends Review*, 18 (April 29, 1865): 554, was reprinted several times in the nineteenth century, and was printed again in Cadbury, *John Woolman in England*, 45–46.
12. Cadbury, *John Woolman in England*, 47–48; Gummere, *Journal*, 130; John Fothergill to Samuel Fothergill, London, June 9, 1772, portfolio 22/126, Friends House Library.
13. Cadbury, ed., *John Woolman in England*, 53; manuscript vol., 163–64, Friends House Library.
14. John Townsend to [Sarah] Woolman, November 9, 1772; Cadbury, *John Woolman*, 50; Gummere, *Journal*, 149–50.
15. Gummere, *Journal*, 149–50; DQB.
16. Gummere, *Journal*, 149–50.
17. Woolman to Sarah Woolman, June 13, 1772, manuscript A, HSP; Woolman to John Woolman, Jr., June 14, 1772, HCL; Gummere, *Journal*, 130–31.
18. Elihu Robinson, diary, Friends House Library; DQB; Gummere, *Journal*, 129; Cadbury, *John Woolman in London*, 71.
19. Epistle, 1772, *Yearly Meeting of Friends Held in London* (London, 1858), vol. 2, Friends House Library.
20. Woolman, *Journal*, 181.

21. Cadbury, *John Woolman in England*, 84–85, first translated the calendar.
22. Woolman, *Journal*, 183; Daniel Mildred to John Pemberton, July 1, 1772, Pemberton Letters, HSP; Woolman to Reuben and Margaret Haines, June 14, 1772, *Friends Miscellany*, 1 (1831): 9; John Pemberton to Joseph Row, October 16, 1772, Pemberton Papers, HSP; John Fothergill, letter, Friends House Library; Elihu Robinson, manuscript diary, Friends House Library; Gummere, *Journal of John Woolman*, 128–29, 131; William Hunt to Uriah Woolman, June 21[?], 1772, *Friends Review*, 4 (1851): 434; Gummere, *Journal*, 132; Cadbury, *John Woolman in England*, 77, 81; Minute of Hertford Quarterly Meeting, June 6, 1772, *Journal of the Friends Historical Society*, 36 (1939): 58.
23. Samuel Emlen to his wife, June 30, 1772, HSP; John Woolman to John Townsend, June 19, 1772, Spriggs manuscript 66, Friends House Library; Cadbury, *John Woolman in England*, 17.
24. William Penn, *Select Works* (London, 1771), 85.
25. William Forster to William Birkbeck, Jr., July [?], 1772; Forster to Rebecca Haydock, July 16, 1772, manuscripts vol. 77, Friends House Library; Deborah Morris, journal, July 28, 1772; Cadbury, *John Woolman in England*, 88–89, 91.
26. Deborah Morris, journal, July 30, 1772; Cadbury, *John Woolman in England*, 92.
27. John Woolman to Sarah Woolman, July 31, 1772, Woolman Papers, HSP.
28. Deborah Morris, journal, August 1, 1772; Cadbury, *John Woolman in England*, 58, 88, 93, 94.
29. Tabatha Hoyland to Sarah Tuke, August 9, 1772, *Friends Journal*, 10 (1964): 81.
30. Mary Andrews, manuscript book of extracts, Friends House Library; Cadbury, *John Woolman in England*, 95–96.
31. Cadbury, *John Woolman in England*, 96–97.
32. Deborah Morris, journal, *The Friend* [Philadelphia], 36 (1862): 149.
33. Cadbury, *John Woolman in England*, 96; Cadbury, "Did Woolman Wear a Beard?" *Quaker History*, 20 (1923): 96.
34. Woolman, *Journal*, 182–83.
35. Sophia Hume to [?], July 7, 1772, *The Friend*, 35 (1862), 194; Woolman, *Journal*, 183; Woolman to Rachel Wilson, July 30, 1772, *Journal of the Friends Historical Society*, 22 (1925): 18.
36. Cadbury, *John Woolman in England*, 89.
37. Woolman, *Journal*, 184–85, 187.
38. Gummere, *Journal*, 489, 492; Corinthians 1:25.
39. Gummere, *Journal*, 499.
40. Humphrey Smith, *A Collection of the Several Writings and Testimonies of That Suffering Servant of God, and Patient Follower of the Lamb, Humphr[e]y Smith, Who Dyed a Prisoner for the Testimony of Jesus, in Winchester Common-Goal the 4th day of the 3d Month, in the Year 1663* (London, 1683), 123–34.
41. Gummere, *Journal*, 503–504.
42. Ibid., 505; John Woolman, manuscript draft of sea journal, Friends House Library, manuscript vol. 150/27.
43. Gilbert Latey, *To All You Taylors and Brokers, Who Lyes in Wickedness, and to All You Tradesmen of What Trade, Employment, or Office Soever* (London, 1660).
44. John Gratton, *A Journal of the Life of That Ancient Servant of Christ, John Gratton* (London, 1720), 2, 3, 4, 18, 21, 44; Gummere, *Journal*, 506.

45. Gummere, *Journal*, 508–10.
46. Woolman, *Journal*, 188.
47. Gummere, *Journal*, 314.
48. Ibid., 314–15.
49. Woolman, *Journal*, 188, n. 17.
50. Deborah Morris, journal.
51. Woolman, *Journal*, 190; Emily Cockayne, *Hubbub: Filth, Noise, and Stench in England, 1600–1770* (New Haven, 2007).

14. How to End, 1772

1. *Friends' Miscellany*, 1 (1831): 11; Gummere, *Journal*, 137; Cadbury, *John Woolman in England*, 109.
2. Gummere, *Journal*, 313, n. 1; Cadbury, *John Woolman in England*, 119; Deborah Morris, journal; Samuel Tuke to Henry Tuke Mennell, 1851, Friends House Library, manuscripts 13/14.
3. Woolman, *Journal*, Appendix H, 301.
4. Cockayne, *Hubbub*.
5. Deborah Morris, journal; DQB; [Thomas Priestman?,] account of John Woolman's death, HCL; Woolman, *Journal*, Appendix H, 301; Cadbury, *John Woolman in England*, 116; quoted in *Journal of John Woolman*, New Century ed, (New York, 1900), 299.
6. William Hargrove, *History and Description of the Ancient City of York*, 2 vols. (York, 1818), vol. 2, 583, 601; vol. 1, 17, 18, 129; Nathaniel Spencer, *The Complete English Traveller* (London, 1771), 510–14.
7. Gummere, *Journal*, 141.
8. HSP; Cadbury, *John Woolman in England*, 111.
9. Comly, *Miscellany*, 8 (1836), 230; Cadbury, *John Woolman in England*, 116.
10. Gummere, *Journal*, 326–27.
11. Deborah Morris, journal; Gummere, *Journal*, 318.
12. Fenn, *Pox Americana*, chapter 1.
13. Woolman to John Eliot, September 27, 1772; Cadbury, *John Woolman in England*, 111; Gummere, *Journal*, 319.
14. Gummere, *Journal*, 319.
15. Woolman, *Journal*, 191.
16. Ibid.
17. Ibid., 191–92; Gummere, *Journal*, 321–22.
18. Gummere, *Journal*, 318–20.
19. Ibid., 325.
20. Ibid., 320.
21. Ibid., 320–21.
22. Ibid., 321.
23. Ibid., 322.
24. Ibid., 322–23.
25. Ibid., 323.
26. Ibid., 323–24.
27. Ibid., 324.

28. Cadbury, *John Woolman in England*, 120; Gummere, *Journal*, 147.
29. Gummere, *Journal*, 325; Cadbury, *John Woolman in England*, 120–21.
30. Gummere, *Journal*, 327.
31. Ibid.
32. Ibid.
33. Ibid., 327–28.
34. Ibid., 329–31.
35. Ibid., 331–32.

Epilogue: A New Beginning

1. Burlington County Historical Society; U.S. Bureau of the Census, *Historical Statistics of the United States, Colonial Times to 1970*, 2 vols. (Washington, D.C., 1975).
2. David Waldstreicher, "Capitalism, Slavery, and Benjamin Franklin's American Revolution," in Matson, ed., *The Economy of Early America*, 189; Gary B. Nash, *The Unknown American Revolution: The Unruly Birth of Democracy and the Struggle to Create America* (New York, 2005), 62–65.
3. Wise, *Though the Heavens May Fall*; Nash, *The Unknown American Revolution*, 114–24, 137; Christopher Leslie Brown, *Moral Capital: Foundations of British Abolitionism* (Chapel Hill, N.C., 2006).
4. Brookes, *Friend Anthony Benezet*, 86–91 and passim.
5. Nash, *The Unknown American Revolution*, 151–66.
6. Ibid.
7. Ibid.
8. Ibid.
9. Simon Schama, *Rough Crossings: Britain, the Slaves and the American Revolution* (London, 2005).
10. Nash, *The Unknown American Revolution*, 320–39.
11. Ibid., 411.
12. Devon W. Carbado and Donald Weise, eds., *Time on Two Crosses: The Collected Writings of Bayard Rustin* (San Francisco, 2003), 289, from a 1987 interview; David L. Chappell, *A Stone of Hope: Prophetic Religion and the Death of Jim Crow* (Chapel Hill, N.C., 2004), chapters 3, 4, and 5.
13. Darsey, *The Prophetic Tradition*, chapters 1 and 2; Heschel, *The Prophets*, chapter 1.
14. Michael Zuckerman, "The Fabrication of Identity in Early America," in Zuckerman, *Almost Chosen People: Oblique Biographies in the American Grain* (Berkeley, 1993).
15. Photocopy of manuscript list of specifications in Woolman house.
16. Historic American Buildings Survey, U.S. Department of the Interior, National Park Service, Branch of Plans and Design, 1937, WPA official project No. 165-22-6999; survey No. NJ457; Henry Shinn, *The History of Mount Holly* (1957; Pemberton, N.J., 1996), 26.
17. Cadbury, *John Woolman in England*, 124–36.
18. Hargrove, *History and Description of the Ancient City of York*, vol. 2, 153, 159–61, 168; David M. Butler, *The Quaker Meeting Houses of Britain* (London, 1999), vol. 2, 715, 717.

Acknowledgments

The inspiration to study Woolman came from a lecture I prepared on the origins of abolitionism for an undergraduate course on the American Revolution in the spring of 1985. When I consulted the essential books by David Brion Davis, Gary Nash, and Jean Soderlund, I became both intrigued by Woolman and curious about what had made him tick. So I owe those three historians a debt of gratitude for pointing out the path, although I have no reason to believe that Davis or Nash would approve of where it led me. During my earliest ruminations on the subject I had an enlightening conversation over lunch with Jean Soderlund. I recall bothering her again about the subject when I made my second attempt to work on Woolman, and again she received me patiently and helpfully. In July and August 1985 I was in London to do research on Quaker connections to a fugitive slave "riot" and used the occasion to begin nosing around in Woolman manuscripts. At that point I was hooked and bewildered.

I picked up Woolman's *Journal* again in 1990, when I finished my second book, and in 1995 and 2001 under similar circumstances. The problem I encountered each time was coming to terms with his dreams. I could not gain access to an inner life that he did not explain. The meaning of a dream that was "instructive" to him as a child did not speak to me. That was not the only problem, but it was formidable; there was also the question of how to approach a spiritual autobiography for biographical purposes.

In retrospect, I see that I initially believed Woolman's *Journal* was the key to understanding him. I now consider it the lock for which I needed keys. The Old Testament (especially the prophets), writings in the ancient mystical tradition of Christianity (especially Thomas à Kempis and Jacob Boehme), martyrologies (especially those by William Cave, John Foxe, and William Sewel), the writings of the founding generation of Quakers, and the Quaker spiritual autobiographies that preceded Woolman's opened Woolman's *Journal* for me.

Working on two books based principally on the analysis of autobiographical texts of different sorts—William Bartram's imaginative reconstruction of his travels and Lewis and Clark's personally revealing journals—also helped me address both obstacles. Reading in Quaker literature of the seventeenth and eighteenth centuries also helped, as did more reading in the Bible, theology, and modern writings on mysticism, prophets and prophecy, and dream analysis. And with help along the way from experts who know these literatures better than I ever will, I achieved a new comfort level with what Woolman lived, read, and wrote.

So this project had a long gestation, but there was no rushing it. Twenty years is a long time to live with a biographical subject, but I consider the time well spent. It certainly contributed to my personal and professional growth.

I am grateful for the help of David Kuzma at Rutgers University's Alexander Library, Christopher Densmore at Swarthmore, Diana Franzusoff Peterson at Haverford, Kerry McLaughlin and R. A. Friedman at the Historical Society of Pennsylvania, Michael Lampen and Benjamin Privitt at Grace Cathedral, Ralph Henn at Plymouth Congregational Church, James Green and Philip Lapsansky at the Library Company of Philadelphia, and Margaret Frame at the Burlington County Historical Society. At the Friends House Library in London, Josef Keith, Jennifer Milligan, and Heather Rowland all were helpful. In York I was contentedly on my own.

Jack and Carol Walz, the directors of the Woolman Memorial, were kind beyond reason and shared their intimate knowledge of the house and grounds. Jack served as my guide to Mount Holly and regional landmarks that I would never have seen without his help. Far from least, they invited me to spend the night alone in the house with its gentle ghosts, which were so quiet as to escape my perception. Maureen O'Connor Leach of the Colonial Dames of New Jersey was similarly gracious with her time and knowledge, opened the Brainerd Street schoolhouse for me, and gave me a tour of Peachfield, the Burr estate nearby. Judy Gauntt, a direct descendant of Woolman's, also kindly accompanied us on the tour and has since shared photos and other valuable information about her ancestors. Judith Burr helped via e-mail to put me in touch with all these wonderful people.

At Hill and Wang, Elisabeth Sifton's confidence in the project was inspiring. It has been a joy to work with her, and I treasure the sparks caused by the editorial interplay. Nobody knows the business better, and I am blessed to have the opportunity to work with her again on my next project. She is an inspired editor with an intensity of commitment to her craft that is simply awesome. I can't overstate how much better this book is for her work. Also at Hill and Wang, Charles Battle, Debra Helfand, Thomas LeBien, Jonathan Lippincott, Lisa Silverman, and Stephen Weil all contributed to the process, for which I am very grateful.

Colleagues and students at the University of Notre Dame have been kind, patient, and helpful. Experts on theology, religious practice, philosophy, the Reformation, and the Enlightenment can be found there, including brilliant intellectual historians, so the institution's strengths happily matched the gaping holes in my knowledge. Lauren Phelan was an exemplary research assistant through two years, a toddler, a pregnancy, and her daughter's infancy; obviously, I am both grateful and mightily impressed. Anna Moscatiello was very helpful in the last stages of fact-checking and proofreading. Brad Gregory, Sandra Gustafson, George Marsden, and Robert Sullivan have shared their expertise generously and tolerated my ignorance patiently. Gail Bederman, Jon Coleman, and John McGreevy have heard less about

Woolman over the years, but each has been a supportive friend and colleague. Gail, John, and Bob have also been extremely kind through thick and thin, and there have been some thick times over the past few years. I thank them all deeply and appreciate their enduring friendship and support.

Members and attenders of South Bend Friends Meeting read early drafts of a number of chapters and discussed them with me. Brad Laird, Monica Tetzlaff, Doug and Marjorie Kinsey, John Kindley, Martha Turner, Chris Morrissey, JaVaughn Fernanders, Matthew Bell, and Bob and Madylyn Godsey all shared their Light generously. Brad, Doug, Marjorie, Chris, and Ernie Bean also participated in a conference about Woolman at Notre Dame, which was very kind and much appreciated.

Scholars more expert on its subject than I graciously agreed to read the manuscript, advised me on revisions, and took part in the Woolman conference at South Bend. I thank Richard L. Bushman, Susan Juster, and Michael Zuckerman for reading the manuscript and then taking a couple of days out of their busy lives to join Margaret Abruzzo, Brad Gregory, Matthew Grow, Sandra Gustafson, George Marsden, Erin Miller, Christopher Osborne, Matthew Salafia, Bryan Smith, Father Robert Sullivan, and me for the conference in early May 2006.

Graduate students with whom I have worked at Notre Dame have been similarly generous with their time and support. Erin Miller (and Eoghan), Christopher Osborne, Matthew Salafia, and Bryan Smith are fine historians and good friends. Matthew Grow and Margaret Abruzzo share some research interests, which has also been beneficial to me. All of them, except Eoghan, read the manuscript and participated in the Woolman conference, for which I am grateful.

The University of Notre Dame was an ideal place to work on this project, and its resources, support, intellects, and environment made the book possible. Mark Roche and Gregory Sterling, the dean and senior associate dean, respectively, of the College of Arts and Letters, are strong supporters of committed teaching and engaged scholarship. Nathan Hatch, provost and colleague, who left for warmer climes and the presidency of Wake Forest University, and his successor, Thomas Burish, were both kind and extremely supportive.

Louis Masur, my longtime friend and collaborator, read the manuscript, parts of it more than once. Knowing as I do just how far this project is from his personal and academic interests, I am all the more appreciative for his wise counsel. My longer-time friend and collaborator, who is also my wife, was there for me again. My debts to Dennee and Lou are more personal than professional, and they have seen me through a lot during the past decade. The dedications of my last book and this one say what I feel, but cannot possibly reflect what is in my heart.

Finally, there are my children, Jasmine and Moses, in alphabetical order. I adore them both. They are the thin and thick of it all and the joys of my life.

Index

Page numbers in *italics* refer to illustrations.

piracy, 30
Plainfield, New Jersey, 120, 331
plants, 31–32, 129
Platonists, 100
pleurisy, 290–95
Plymouth, Massachusetts, 76
Plymouth Congregational Church,
    Minneapolis, 391–93
politics, 156–57, 198, 205, 318–19; slave
    laws and, 199–201
Polo, Marco, 16
Pontiac, Chief, 250, 267
Pontiac's War, 250–51, 260
population growth, 315–16
potage, 38 and *n*
potatoes, 34
prayer, 186, 294, 374
predestination, 25, 76
Preparative Meeting, 27
Presbyterians, 129, 144
press, Quaker, 159, 165, 209, 213, 271,
    300, 306
Price, Sterling, 5
Priestman, Sarah, 372
Priestman, Thomas, 368–69, 371, 372,
    378
primers, school, 273–74
prophets and prophecy, 195, 202–210,
    233, 388–89; dreams and, 152–59,
    202–203, 266–69, 290–91, 389–90;
    Indian, 260; Old Testament, 179,
    203, 205–208, 245–46; personal
    burden of mystical experience,
    207–208; violence and, 205;
    Woolman and, 187, 202–210, 233,
    245–46, 259, 264–69, 279, 290–300,
    313, 323, 366, 377, 389–90
Protestants, 15, 21, 22, 71, 203;
    dissident, 21–23, 72, 139, 161
Proverbs, 67
Providence, Rhode Island, 234
Providence Meeting, 283
Puritans, 17, 21, 26, 28, 91, 107, 139;
    beliefs and theology, 26, 37;
    charity, 140; origin of, 21; Quakers
    persecuted by, 71–78, 140;
    spiritual biographies, 17–18, 19

Pyle, Robert, 109, 115
Pyrleus, Susanna, 188

Quaker Act (1662), 72
Quakers, 11; administrative levels,
    26–27 and *n*; aesthetic of
    simplicity, 37–39, 43–46, 275, 321;
    backsliding and degeneracy
    among modern Quakers, 275–77,
    309, 332; beliefs and theology, 21,
    22–26, 37–46, 89, 98, 100, 111,
    162, 185; charity, 98, 101, 107,
    139–42, 198; childhood stages of
    spiritual development, 57–68;
    child rearing, 37–39, 78–79, 138,
    212–13, 275, 276, 359; dreams,
    60–61; early, 20–29, 105;
    education, 37, 39–42, 142, 212–13,
    271–76; in England, 20–28, 71–73,
    139, 150, 280, 313, 322, 339,
    341–65, 366–79; family structure,
    29, 160; fear of, 23; French and
    Indian War and, 154–57, 165–68,
    176, 178–84, 223, 225–26, 250;
    Indians and, 141, 142, 223–27;
    landownership, 29; language,
    44–46; martyrs, 70, 73–78, 79, 174;
    migration to America, 27–29;
    mysticism and prophecy, 202–210;
    New Jersey settlement of, 29–46,
    80; origin of, 21–22, 105; pacifism,
    24, 163, 178, 182–84, 215, 318;
    persecution of, 23–24, 28, 71–78,
    112, 140, 323; politics, 156–57,
    198, 205; population, 28–29; post-
    Woolman, 383–91; press, 159, 165,
    209, 213, 271, 300, 306; quietism,
    44–45, 98–99, 185–87; radicalism
    of, 24; reform, 150–51, 157, 160,
    185; as slaveowners, 87, 103–117,
    132, 141, 160, 187, 220, 244,
    279–85, 325, 385; South/North
    comparison, 280; spiritual
    autobiography model, 14–20, 58,
    89, 306–312; teachers and school
    books, 271–75; terminology, 22;

Various Subjects of Importance, 214; ship ministry of, 331–37; as shopkeeper, 96–97, 103–104, 123–25, 215; sibling relationships, 142–43, 305–312; on silver vessel use, 297–300, 355–56; sins and moral failures of, 66–68, 77–79, 90, 103–104, 119, 285, 287, 292–93; smallpox infection, 365, 367, 371–78; *Some Considerations on the Keeping of Negroes*, 6, 132–39, 142, 146, 158, 165, 209, 213, 227, 243–44, 384; spiritual development and influences, 11–12, 14–15, 57–68, 69–77, 89–101, 113, 117–19, 123, 174–75; stages of spiritual development, 57–68; in steerage, 328–39, 332–36; sun worm dream, 59–66; as a tailor, 125–26, 189, 190, 191, 192, 193, 215, 228–31, 237–40, 272, 342, 395; temperament of, 4, 10, 42, 264, 293, 354, 380; on trade and commerce, 190, 213–17, 287–89, 300–303, 324, 359–60; traveling ministries of, 120–21, *121*, 126–31, 144–45, 170–71, 187–89, 194–96, 202, 208, 219, 231–37, 243, 250–62, 279–84, 286, 289; undyed clothing and, 237–39, 241–43, 284, 293, 301, 342, 344, 353–56, 364, 369; vegetarianism and, 240–41; walking ministries of, 279–84; on war and slavery, 159, 165–68, 173; war tax resistance, 173–75, 178–84, 202–203, 307; on wealth, 100–101, 209–217, 221, 223, 269–71, 277–78, 297–304, 314–19, 323, 324, 351, 358; wife and children of, 10, 125, 145–47, 168–71, 187–88, 289, 292, 305, 325–27, 329, 346, 352, 360, 366; *A Word of Remembrance and Caution to the Rich*, 269–71; writing style,

14–15, 138–39, 169–70, 176, 214, 221–22; see also *Journal* (Woolman)
Woolman, John (grandfather of JW), 35–37
Woolman, John (nephew of JW), 346–47
Woolman, Jonah, 37
Woolman, Patience, 37
Woolman, Rachel, 37
Woolman, Samuel, 37, 44, 57, 62, 65, 66, 69, 78–79, 81–82, 96; death of, 145–46, 147
Woolman, Sarah (sister of JW), 37
Woolman, Sarah (wife of JW), 145, 146–47, 168, 170, 187–88, 232, 233, 252, 253, 261, 289, 290, 325, 326, 329, 346, 352, 360; death of, 305
Woolman, Uriah, 37, 194 and *n*
Woolman, William (grandfather of JW), 37, 168
Woolman, William (son of JW), 168–71, 327, 360
Woolman farm, Northampton, New Jersey, 35–37, 94–96
Wyalusing, Pennsylvania, 250, 253, 258–61
Wycliffe, John, 11, 174
Wyoming, 257, 261

Yearly Meeting, 27, 61, 120, 141, 176, 198, 219, 221, 244, 277, 287, 348, 357; on slavery, 107–17, 159, 163, 201; see also *specific locations*
yellow fever, 328*n*
York, duke of, 30
York, England, 367–79; Woolman memorials, 396–97
York, Quarterly Meeting, 369, 370, 377, 378, 379, 397
Yorkshire, England, 327